Calculations

CHEMISTRY

Jim Clark

WITHDRAWN

Longman

Edinburgh Gate
Harlow, Essex

Pearson Education Limited
Edinburgh Gate
Harlow
Essex
CM20 2JE

ISBN 0 582 41127 0

First published 2000
Second impression 2001
Printed in Singapore (B & JO)

The Publisher's policy is to use paper manufactured from sustainable forests.

CONTENTS

CONTENTS

Formulae, Equations and Oxidation States

It may seem perhaps surprising to begin a book on A level chemistry calculations with a chapter on formulae and equations, but a very high proportion of the problems you will come across will need an equation for a reaction. You may be asked to work this out for yourself, but even if it is given in the question, you need to be able to interpret it properly. If you learnt to be comfortable about writing equations at GCSE, then feel grateful. If not, take your time working through this chapter. There is no short cut – it just takes patience and practice. By the end of the chapter you will be able to write and understand equations for some very complicated reactions indeed.

Formulae

Working out formulae for ionic compounds

> If you are already competent at writing formulae, you could reasonably skip this next bit. Do, however, try the problems at the end of it to make sure that you are not being over-confident.

You can't write equations until you can write formulae. People tend to remember the formulae for common covalent substances like water or carbon dioxide or methane, and will rarely need to work them out. That is not true of ionic compounds. You need to know the symbols and charges of the common ions and how to combine them into a formula.

The need for equal numbers of "pluses" and "minuses"

Ions are atoms or groups of atoms which carry electrical charges, either positive or negative. Compounds are electrically neutral. In an ionic compound there must therefore be the right number of each sort of ion so that the total positive charge is exactly the same as the total negative charge. Obviously, then, if you are going to work out a formula, you need to know the charges on the ions.

> **The logic behind this:** Any element in group 2 has two outer electrons which it will lose to form a 2+ ion. Any element in group 6 has six outer electrons, and it gains two electrons to give a noble gas structure. This leads to a 2− ion. A similar argument applies in the other groups shown.

Cases where you can work out the number of charges on an ion

Element in Periodic Table group	Charge on ion
1	+1
2	+2
3	+3
6	−2
7	−1

Cases where the name tells you

A name like lead(II) oxide tells you that the charge on the lead (a metal) is +**2**. Iron(III) chloride contains a **3+** iron ion. Copper(II) sulphate contains a Cu^{2+} ion. Notice that **all metals form positive ions**.

Ions that need to be learnt

Positive ions:	zinc	Zn^{2+}
	silver	Ag^+
	hydrogen	H^+
	ammonium	NH_4^+
Negative ions:	nitrate	NO_3^-
	hydroxide	OH^-
	hydrogencarbonate	HCO_3^-
	carbonate	CO_3^{2-}
	sulphate	SO_4^{2-}

You will come across other ions during the course, but these are the important ones for now. The ions in this list are the tricky ones – be sure to learn both their formulae and the number of charges.

Confusing endings!

Do not confuse ions like sulph**ate** with sulph**ide**. A name like sodium sulph**ide** means that it contains sodium and sulphur **only**. Once you have an "**ate**" ending, it means that there is something else there as well – often, but not always, oxygen. (There are also "**ite**" endings, although these are a bit old-fashioned, and there is a more modern way of naming such compounds. These also have oxygen as well as the other element, but not as much as if it were an "**ate**" ending. For example, sodium sulph**ate** is Na_2SO_4 whereas sodium sulph**ite** is Na_2SO_3. By contrast, sodium sulph**ide** is Na_2S.)

> ➤ The more modern way of naming sodium sulphite is described on page 17.

Magnesium nit**rate** means it contains magnesium and nitrogen **and oxygen** – $Mg(NO_3)_2$. Magnesium nit**ride** contains **only** magnesium and nitrogen – Mg_3N_2.

Calcium carbon**ate** contains calcium, carbon **and oxygen** – $CaCO_3$. Calcium carb**ide** contains **only** calcium and carbon – CaC_2 (not a formula that you could easily work out).

Working out the formula of an ionic compound

Example 1

To find the formula for sodium oxide

Sodium is in group 1, so the ion is Na^+.

Oxygen is in group 6, so the ion is O^{2-}.

To have equal numbers of positive and negative charges, you would need 2 sodium ions for each 1 oxide ion.

The formula is therefore **Na_2O**.

Example 2

To find the formula for barium nitrate

Barium is in group 2, so the ion is Ba^{2+}.

Nitrate ions are NO_3^- (you will have learnt this) .

> ➤ This is barium nit**rate**, not barium nit**ride**. You must notice the endings – they matter!

To have equal numbers of positive and negative charges, you would need 2 nitrate ions for each barium ion.

The formula is **$Ba(NO_3)_2$**.

Notice the brackets around the nitrate group. **Brackets must be written if you have more than one of these complex ions** (ions containing more than one type of atom). In any other situation, they are unnecessary.

Example 3

➤ Notice the "ate" ending again.

To find the formula for iron(III) sulphate

Iron(III) tells you that the ion is Fe^{3+}.

Sulphate ions are SO_4^{2-} (you will have learnt this).

To have equal numbers of positive and negative charges, you would need 2 iron(III) ions for every 3 sulphate ions – to give 6+ and 6− in total.

The formula is $\mathbf{Fe_2(SO_4)_3}$.

Why aren't ion charges shown in formulae?

Actually, they can be shown. For example, the formula for sodium chloride is NaCl. It is sometimes written Na^+Cl^- if you are trying to make a particular point, but for most purposes the charges are omitted. In an ionic compound, the charges are there – whether you write them or not.

Problem • 1

Work out the formulae of the following compounds.

lead(II) oxide, sodium bromide, magnesium sulphate, zinc chloride, potassium carbonate, ammonium sulphide, calcium nitrate, iron(III) hydroxide, iron(II) sulphate, copper(II) carbonate, aluminium sulphate, calcium hydroxide, cobalt(II) chloride, calcium oxide, silver nitrate, iron(III) fluoride, ammonium nitrate, rubidium iodide, sodium sulphate, chromium(III) oxide.

Equations

Writing equations

➤ If this all seems very trivial to you, skip over it to the next set of problems and check that you are not being over-confident.

What all the numbers mean

When you write equations it is important to be able to count up how many of each sort of atom you have got. In particular you must understand the difference between big numbers written in front of formulae, such as the **2** in 2HCl, and the smaller, subscripted (written slightly lower on the line) numbers such as the **4** in CH_4.

Some examples

Na	1 atom of sodium
2Na	2 separate atoms of sodium
N	1 atom of nitrogen
N_2	2 atoms of nitrogen joined to make a molecule
$3N_2$	3 separate nitrogen molecules, each containing 2 atoms joined together – i.e. 6 atoms of nitrogen altogether
H_2O	1 molecule of water, containing 2 hydrogen atoms joined to 1 oxygen atom
$5H_2O$	5 separate molecules of water, containing a total of 10 atoms of hydrogen and 5 atoms of oxygen
H_2SO_4	1 molecule of sulphuric acid, containing 2 atoms of hydrogen, 1 atom of sulphur and 4 atoms of oxygen

3

Summary

- The small subscripted numbers inside a formula only refer to the atom immediately in front of them, e.g. the **4** in H_2SO_4 only refers to the oxygen and not to the sulphur as well. The only exception to this is if you put brackets around something. For example, in the formula $Ca(OH)_2$, the **2** applies to both the oxygen and the hydrogen.

- A big number in front of a formula multiplies up the whole of that formula. For example, $5CH_4$ means **5** lots of CH_4 – in other words, 5 carbon atoms and 20 hydrogen atoms.

> *When you are writing equations, you must not alter any formula by adding or changing any small number which is an essential part of that formula. You may, however, write any number you wish in front of a formula.*

Balancing equations

This is the term given to adjusting the numbers written in equations so that you end up with the same number of atoms as you started with. The aim is to make sure that the number of each type of atom is the same on both the left hand and right hand sides of the equation.

It is largely a matter of common sense, but it does help to approach the problem systematically.

- Work across the equation from left to right checking one element after another, **except** if an element appears in several places in the equation. Leave it until the end – often, you will find that it has sorted itself out.

- If you have a group of atoms (like a sulphate group, for example) which is unchanged from one side of the equation to the other, there is no reason why you can't just count that up as a whole group, rather than counting individual sulphurs and oxygens. It saves time.

- Check everything at the end to make sure you have not changed something that you have already counted.

Examples make this process much clearer than words.

Example 4

> This is the reaction between zinc metal and hydrochloric acid. The zinc slowly dissolves to give a colourless solution of zinc chloride. Bubbles of hydrogen will be seen.

Balance the equation:

$$Zn + HCl \rightarrow ZnCl_2 + H_2$$

Work from left to right. Count the zinc atoms: 1 on each side – so no problem.

Count the hydrogen atoms: 1 on the left, 2 on the right. If you end up with 2 you must have started with 2. The only way of achieving this is to have $2HCl$. (You **must not** change the formula to H_2Cl – there is no such substance.)

$$Zn + 2HCl \rightarrow ZnCl_2 + H_2$$

Count the chlorines: 2 on each side. No problem. Quick final check of everything: looks good. This is the final version.

Example 5

> ➤ Mixing colourless solutions of silver nitrate and calcium chloride produces white solid silver chloride. The calcium nitrate stays in solution.

Balance the equation:

$$AgNO_3 + CaCl_2 \rightarrow Ca(NO_3)_2 + AgCl$$

Work from left to right. Count the silver atoms: 1 on each side.

The nitrate group is intact as it goes from left to right, so save time by counting it as a whole rather than splitting it into individual elements. There is 1 NO_3 group on the left, 2 on the right. This needs correcting:

$$2AgNO_3 + CaCl_2 \rightarrow Ca(NO_3)_2 + AgCl$$

Now check the calcium: 1 on each side.

Now the chlorine: 2 on the left, but only 1 on the right. You need 2AgCl:

$$2AgNO_3 + CaCl_2 \rightarrow Ca(NO_3)_2 + 2AgCl$$

Finally, check everything again. It's all OK – but it might not have been. You actually changed the numbers of silver atoms on the left hand side after you checked them at the beginning. It so happens that the problem corrected itself when you put the 2 in front of the AgCl on the right – but that won't always happen.

Example 6

> ➤ This is what happens if you heat lead(II) nitrate crystals. They split up to give solid lead(II) oxide, and a mixture of nitrogen dioxide and oxygen gases. NO_2 is a brown poisonous gas.

Balance the equation:

$$Pb(NO_3)_2 \rightarrow PbO + NO_2 + O_2$$

Work from left to right. Count the lead atoms. No problem.

Leave the oxygen until the end, because it appears in many places on the right hand side.

Count the nitrogens: 2 on the left, only 1 on the right. Correct it:

$$Pb(NO_3)_2 \rightarrow PbO + 2NO_2 + O_2$$

Now count the oxygens: there are 6 on the left, but 7 on the right $(1 + 4 + 2)$. There isn't an immediately obvious solution, but there is an easy way around it. It usually applies to cases where you have oxygen (O_2) or hydrogen (H_2) on one side of the equation.

Whatever you do to the oxygen (O_2) will not affect anything else – you won't upset elements you have already balanced. Essentially, you need to lose an oxygen atom from the right hand side to bring the total down to 6. Suppose you only had half an oxygen molecule:

$$Pb(NO_3)_2 \rightarrow PbO + 2NO_2 + \tfrac{1}{2}O_2$$

You might reasonably argue that you can't have half an oxygen molecule, but to get rid of this problem you only have to double everything:

$$2Pb(NO_3)_2 \rightarrow 2PbO + 4NO_2 + O_2$$

In fact, it is not totally wrong to leave halves in equations – just a bit unusual. In some of the cases that you will meet later, you will have to write equations with halves in them, and leave them there.

5

Problem . 2

Balance the following equations:

(a) $Ca + H_2O \rightarrow Ca(OH)_2 + H_2$

(b) $Al + Cr_2O_3 \rightarrow Al_2O_3 + Cr$

(c) $Fe_2O_3 + CO \rightarrow Fe + CO_2$

(d) $CH_4 + O_2 \rightarrow CO_2 + H_2O$

(e) $C_8H_{18} + O_2 \rightarrow CO_2 + H_2O$

(f) $NaHCO_3 + H_2SO_4 \rightarrow Na_2SO_4 + CO_2 + H_2O$

Problem . 3

Rewrite the following equations as balanced symbol equations:

(a) sodium carbonate + hydrochloric acid (HCl)
    $\rightarrow$ sodium chloride + carbon dioxide + water

(b) sodium hydroxide + sulphuric acid (H_2SO_4)
    $\rightarrow$ sodium sulphate + water

(c) sodium + water $\rightarrow$ sodium hydroxide + hydrogen (H_2)

(d) sodium + chlorine (Cl_2) $\rightarrow$ sodium chloride

(e) iron(III) oxide + nitric acid (HNO_3) $\rightarrow$ iron(III) nitrate + water

Ionic equations

Ionic equations look worrying to start with, but once you understand how to read them and to put them together they are often easier to use than the full equations we have looked at up until now. In some cases that you will meet later, they are the only sensible way of constructing an equation.

Understanding ionic interactions in solution

Imagine what is going on in a solution of sodium chloride. It contains sodium ions, Na^+, chloride ions, Cl^-, and water molecules – all moving around at random. Some of the water molecules are free; others are attached to the ions present.

Now imagine what happens if various ions hit each other.

If ions with the same charge come close, they will repel each other and just bounce away.

What happens if sodium ions meet chloride ions? It is tempting to say that they will stick together to form sodium chloride – but that would be wrong! If ions stick together, then they aren't in solution any more, and you would start to see solid being formed. If you have some sodium chloride solution, that simply is not happening (provided the solution isn't saturated).

So what does happen when sodium ions meet chloride ions? They are certainly attracted, but the attraction is not strong enough to persuade them to shed their cloak of water molecules and form permanent attractions between the ions. You have a promiscuous situation where ions will come together for an instant, but almost immediately lose interest and form a new, equally temporary attachment to some other ion. This rather casual interaction is a feature of any soluble ionic compound in solution in water.

Ionic equations for precipitation reactions

If you mix certain liquids together, a solid is formed. This solid is called a **precipitate**. Reactions producing precipitates are called **precipitation reactions**.

Suppose you mixed together a solution of sodium chloride and a solution of silver nitrate.

The sodium chloride solution contains	$Na^+_{(aq)}$	$Cl^-_{(aq)}$
The silver nitrate solution contains	$Ag^+_{(aq)}$	$NO_3^-_{(aq)}$

(The "(aq)" is called a "state symbol". It stands for "aqueous" which means "in solution in water".)

What happens when the various ions meet?

■ If ions with like charges meet, they will simply repel each other.

■ If ions of opposite charges meet, what happens depends on how strongly they are attracted.

As we have just been describing, in any solution of a soluble salt, ions of opposite charges are meeting all the time. However, their attractions are not enough to hold them together, so they wander off to associate with other ions. In this case, this is what will happen if silver meets nitrate, sodium meets chloride, or sodium meets nitrate – all of these combinations are soluble salts.

If silver ions meet chloride ions the attractions are so strong that they stick together, forming an increasing mass of ions that is soon seen as a white precipitate of silver chloride. This sort of thing happens whenever ions from an insoluble compound meet.

The ionic equation

All that has happened in the reaction is that silver ions have clumped together with chloride ions to produce a precipitate of silver chloride:

$$Ag^+_{(aq)} + Cl^-_{(aq)} \rightarrow AgCl_{(s)}$$

State symbols

(s)	solid
(l)	liquid
(g)	gas
(aq)	in aqueous solution (solution in water)

State symbols should always be given in ionic equations.

The spectator ions

The sodium ions and nitrate ions take no part in this reaction – they simply "swim around watching" as the silver and chloride ions get together. Ions like these are called **spectator ions**. It means that the reaction would be just the same whichever chloride was being used. If the chloride was magnesium chloride or zinc chloride or iron(II) chloride or whatever, the same white precipitate would be formed because the magnesium, zinc, iron(II), (etc.) ions are just spectator ions.

The only minor difference in appearance would be in a case like copper(II) chloride where, because the copper(II) ion is blue, the white precipitate would come out of a blue solution instead of a colourless one.

➤ Because the same white precipitate is formed when silver nitrate solution is added to a solution of any chloride, this reaction is used **to test for a chloride**. A solution of a suspected chloride is acidified with dilute nitric acid. This destroys any other ions which might also give white precipitates with silver ions. If a white precipitate is formed, then the unknown substance was indeed a chloride.

How to write ionic equations for precipitation reactions

Ionic equations are much easier to write than the full equation.

■ Decide what the precipitate is, and write down its formula on the right hand side of the equation with "(s)" written after it.

■ On the left hand side of the equation write down the symbols for the ions which have clumped together to produce the precipitate. Write the symbol "(aq)" after each of them.

Example 7

> ➤ The addition of barium chloride solution to unknown solutions is used to **test for sulphates**. The unknown solution is acidified with dilute hydrochloric acid, and then barium chloride solution is added. A white precipitate means that sulphate ions were present in the unknown solution.

Mixing barium chloride solution with magnesium sulphate solution produces a white precipitate. The only combination of ions present which produces an insoluble salt is barium meeting sulphate to give insoluble barium sulphate. (You may have come across this at GCSE. If not, it doesn't matter in the least.)

Write the formula of the precipitate on the right hand side of the equation with "(s)" after it:

$$\rightarrow BaSO_{4(s)}$$

Decide what ions clumped together to produce it and write them on the left hand side with "(aq)" after them:

$$Ba^{2+}_{(aq)} + SO_4^{2-}_{(aq)} \rightarrow BaSO_{4(s)}$$

And that's it!

How to read an ionic equation

The last equation would be read like this: "Barium ions (from any soluble barium compound in solution) mixed with sulphate ions (from any soluble sulphate in solution) will give a precipitate of barium sulphate."

This one equation covers a multitude of different mixtures. All of the following (and lots more) could be represented by the same simple ionic equation:

$$BaCl_2 + H_2SO_4 \rightarrow BaSO_4 + 2HCl$$
$$Ba(NO_3)_2 + CuSO_4 \rightarrow BaSO_4 + Cu(NO_3)_2$$
$$BaCl_2 + Na_2SO_4 \rightarrow BaSO_4 + 2NaCl$$
$$Ba(NO_3)_2 + K_2SO_4 \rightarrow BaSO_4 + 2KNO_3$$

In all of these cases, the only change taking place is the clumping together of the barium ions and sulphate ions to give a precipitate. Everything else remains swimming around in the solution as spectator ions. The ionic equation gives you the simple uncluttered truth – and saves you from having to work out lots of formulae into the bargain.

Problem • 4

Write ionic equations for the following precipitation reactions:

(a) mixing solutions of silver nitrate and potassium bromide, giving a cream precipitate of silver bromide

(b) mixing solutions of calcium nitrate and sodium carbonate, giving a white precipitate of calcium carbonate

(c) mixing solutions of magnesium sulphate and sodium hydroxide, giving a white precipitate of magnesium hydroxide.

Ionic equations for some familiar GCSE reactions

Ionic equations for reactions between acids and metals

If you drop magnesium into dilute sulphuric acid, it reacts to give off hydrogen. The reaction gives out a lot of heat and the magnesium eventually all disappears if the acid is in excess:

$$Mg + H_2SO_4 \rightarrow MgSO_4 + H_2$$

It would look exactly the same if you dropped magnesium into dilute hydrochloric acid:

$$Mg + 2HCl \rightarrow MgCl_2 + H_2$$

If you rewrite these as ionic equations, the reason that they look the same becomes obvious. This section explains how you can take a full equation apart to unearth the ionic equation hiding underneath.

Rewrite the equation showing everything ionic as ions

How do you know what is ionic? As a rough and ready guide,

A metal (or ammonium) compound or an acid in solution . . .	ionic
Anything else . . .	not ionic

> ➤ Some metal compounds are actually covalent, but this guide works in almost all the cases that you are likely to come across with writing ionic equations.

Applying to this reaction:

$$Mg + H_2SO_4 \rightarrow MgSO_4 + H_2$$

■ Magnesium is not a metal **compound**, so is not ionic. Write as Mg.

■ Sulphuric acid is an acid in solution. It is ionic. Write down the ions present.

■ Magnesium sulphate is a metal compound, so it is ionic. Write down its ions as well.

■ Hydrogen gas does not fall into either possible class of ionic compounds, so leave it alone.

$$Mg_{(s)} + 2H^+_{(aq)} + SO_4^{2-}_{(aq)} \rightarrow Mg^{2+}_{(aq)} + SO_4^{2-}_{(aq)} + H_{2(g)}$$

If you look at this carefully, the sulphate ions haven't changed in any way. They are swimming around in the solution before the addition of the magnesium and are still there afterwards. These are spectator ions and are not included in the ionic equation:

$$Mg_{(s)} + 2H^+_{(aq)} \rightarrow Mg^{2+}_{(aq)} + H_{2(g)}$$

Repeating this process with the **hydrochloric acid** gives:

$$Mg_{(s)} + 2H^+_{(aq)} + 2Cl^-_{(aq)} \rightarrow Mg^{2+}_{(aq)} + 2Cl^-_{(aq)} + H_{2(g)}$$

This time the chloride ions are spectator ions and if these are removed from the ionic equation, you end up with exactly the same equation as before:

$$Mg_{(s)} + 2H^+_{(aq)} \rightarrow Mg^{2+}_{(aq)} + H_{2(g)}$$

What this equation is saying is that if you add magnesium to any source of hydrogen ions in solution (i.e. any acid) you will get the same reaction. This is a useful generalisation which the full equations obscure.

Ionic equations for reactions between acids and metal hydroxides

Here are three apparently completely different reactions:

1. $HNO_3 + LiOH \rightarrow LiNO_3 + H_2O$

2. $HCl + NaOH \rightarrow NaCl + H_2O$

3. $H_2SO_4 + 2KOH \rightarrow K_2SO_4 + 2H_2O$

In these reactions, everything is ionic – that is, either a metal compound or an acid in solution – apart from the water. If you rewrite these as ionic equations:

1. $H^+_{(aq)} + NO_3^-{}_{(aq)} + Li^+_{(aq)} + OH^-_{(aq)} \rightarrow Li^+_{(aq)} + NO_3^-{}_{(aq)} + H_2O_{(l)}$

Taking the spectator ions out leaves:

$H^+_{(aq)} + OH^-_{(aq)} \rightarrow H_2O_{(l)}$

2. $H^+_{(aq)} + Cl^-_{(aq)} + Na^+_{(aq)} + OH^-_{(aq)} \rightarrow Na^+_{(aq)} + Cl^-_{(aq)} + H_2O_{(l)}$

Taking the spectator ions out leaves:

$H^+_{(aq)} + OH^-_{(aq)} \rightarrow H_2O_{(l)}$

3. $2H^+_{(aq)} + SO_4^{2-}{}_{(aq)} + 2K^+_{(aq)} + 2OH^-_{(aq)} \rightarrow 2K^+_{(aq)} + SO_4^{2-}{}_{(aq)} + 2H_2O_{(l)}$

Taking the spectator ions out leaves:

$2H^+_{(aq)} + 2OH^-_{(aq)} \rightarrow 2H_2O_{(l)}$

That would simplify (by dividing by 2) to the same as before:

$H^+_{(aq)} + OH^-_{(aq)} \rightarrow H_2O_{(l)}$

All of these are just reactions between a hydrogen ion from an acid and a hydroxide ion from a metal hydroxide to make a molecule of water.

Ionic equations for reactions between acids and metal carbonates

At GCSE you may have come across the test for metal carbonates by adding a dilute acid to the solid (most carbonates are insoluble in water). All carbonates give off carbon dioxide under these circumstances. Some typical reactions might be:

$CaCO_3 + 2HCl \rightarrow CaCl_2 + CO_2 + H_2O$

$MgCO_3 + 2HNO_3 \rightarrow Mg(NO_3)_2 + CO_2 + H_2O$

$Na_2CO_3 + H_2SO_4 \rightarrow Na_2SO_4 + CO_2 + H_2O$

It probably will not surprise you to discover that if you dig out the ionic equations in each case, they turn out to be the same. Convince yourself by doing it. You should find in every case that you get:

$CO_3^{2-}{}_{(s)} + 2H^+_{(aq)} \rightarrow CO_{2(g)} + H_2O_{(l)}$

What this ionic equation says is that if you add any old acid (a source of hydrogen ions) to any old carbonate, you will get carbon dioxide and water. This is a useful generalisation which only the ionic equation can show.

➤ You might be worried that the metal ions in each case start as "(s)" and end up in solution as "(aq)". In these examples, this counts as being unchanged, and so the metal ions can be counted as spectators.

Summary

Extracting ionic equations from full ones is a bothersome process. It is much easier to learn these two common equations:

$$H^+_{(aq)} + OH^-_{(aq)} \rightarrow H_2O_{(l)}$$
$$CO_3{}^{2-}_{(s)} + 2H^+_{(aq)} \rightarrow CO_{2(g)} + H_2O_{(l)}$$

Ionic equations for redox reactions (see below) are derived in a quite different way.

Problem . 5

Write the following reactions as ionic equations (they are examples of all the types of ionic equation you have met):

(a) the reaction between iron and copper(II) sulphate solution to give iron(II) sulphate solution and copper
(b) the reaction between calcium chloride solution and sodium hydroxide solution to give a precipitate of calcium hydroxide
(c) the reaction between strontium hydroxide and dilute hydrochloric acid to give strontium chloride solution and water
(d) the reaction between citric acid solution and solid sodium carbonate which gives off carbon dioxide. (Don't know the formula for citric acid? Do you need to know it?)

Redox reactions and oxidation states

Oxidation and reduction

Oxidation is most easily thought of as **adding oxygen**.

Reduction is most easily thought of as **removing oxygen**.

A **redox reaction** is one in which both **red**uction and **ox**idation are occurring.

For example, magnesium powder heated with copper(II) oxide produces copper and magnesium oxide:

$$Mg + CuO \rightarrow MgO + Cu$$

The magnesium is being oxidised to magnesium oxide; the copper(II) oxide is being reduced to copper.

If you rewrite this as an **ionic** equation, you find (with some surprise) that the oxide ions are actually spectator ions – and so the oxygen is irrelevant.

$$Mg_{(s)} + Cu^{2+}{}_{(s)} \rightarrow Mg^{2+}{}_{(s)} + Cu_{(s)}$$

Underlying the change is a transfer of electrons from the magnesium to the copper(II) ions.

The definitions of oxidation and reduction are widened to:

➤ Remember: OIL RIG

Oxidation Is Loss of electrons; Reduction Is Gain of electrons.

The reaction can be looked at from the point of view of each of the reactants. The magnesium loses electrons to form magnesium ions (an oxidation):

$$Mg_{(s)} \rightarrow Mg^{2+}{}_{(s)} + 2e^-$$

The copper(II) ions gain electrons to form copper metal (a reduction):

$$Cu^{2+}{}_{(s)} + 2e^- \rightarrow Cu_{(s)}$$

Because the magnesium reduces the copper(II) ions, the magnesium is described as a **reducing agent**. The copper(II) ions oxidise the magnesium and so copper(II) ions are the **oxidising agent** in this reaction.

The equations we have just written are described as **half equations** (sometimes as electron half equations; sometimes as ionic half equations – as long as the phrase includes "half equations", it means the same thing).

Using half equations to work out ionic equations

Example 8

Chlorine gas oxidises iodide ions in solution to iodine, and in the process is reduced itself to chloride ions. Write the ionic equation for the reaction.

All you need to do is to write the two half equations, and then combine them.

Working out the half equations

Chlorine gas is Cl_2; chloride ions are Cl^-. Write those down on each side of the equation:

$$Cl_2 \rightarrow Cl^-$$

Now balance the atoms:

$$Cl_2 \rightarrow 2Cl^-$$

Finally, the charges need to be balanced by adding electrons where necessary. In this case, you need two on the left hand side:

$$Cl_2 + 2e^- \rightarrow 2Cl^-$$

Repeating this process (first balancing the atoms and then the charges) for the other half equation involving the iodine gives you:

$$2I^- \rightarrow I_2 + 2e^-$$

These two equations can now literally be added together:

$$Cl_2 + 2e^- \rightarrow 2Cl^-$$
$$\underline{2I^- \rightarrow I_2 + 2e^-}$$
$$Cl_2 + 2I^- \rightarrow 2Cl^- + I_2$$

Because there are two electrons on both sides, they cancel out, and we are left with the ionic equation.

> ➤ So that things don't get too cluttered, state symbols will not be written for the rest of this section. Technically they should be there, but they are often omitted when constructing equations for redox reactions. The process needs a bit of concentration, and worrying about state symbols gets in the way.

Rules for constructing half equations

You are only allowed to write certain things into half equations:

- The substance you start from and what it is oxidised or reduced to. You have to **know** this (or be told it in the question).

- Hydrogen ions, H^+ (unless the solution is alkaline, in which case these are replaced by hydroxide ions, OH^-).

- Water.

- Electrons.

➤ Writing half equations for reactions in alkaline solution is much trickier than in acid or neutral solution. Luckily, you are much less likely to meet this problem at A level.

Example 9

An acidic solution of hydrogen peroxide, H_2O_2, oxidises iron(II) ions to iron(III) ions. The hydrogen peroxide is reduced to water. (You have to know this, or be told it.) Write the ionic equation for the reaction.

Starting with hydrogen peroxide:

Known facts : $\qquad H_2O_2 \rightarrow H_2O$

Balance the oxygens : $\quad H_2O_2 \rightarrow 2H_2O$

There aren't enough hydrogens on the left hand side. Add two hydrogen ions:

$$2H^+ + H_2O_2 \rightarrow 2H_2O$$

The atoms balance, but not the charges. There are 2 positive charges on the left, but zero charge on the right. Add two electrons to the left:

$$2H^+ + H_2O_2 + 2e^- \rightarrow 2H_2O$$

Now for the iron. This is much easier.

Known facts: $\qquad Fe^{2+} \rightarrow Fe^{3+}$

Everything is OK except the charges. Add an electron to supply a negative charge to the right, and cut 3+ down to 2+:

$$Fe^{2+} \rightarrow Fe^{3+} + e^-$$

This leaves

$$2H^+ + H_2O_2 + 2e^- \rightarrow 2H_2O$$
$$Fe^{2+} \rightarrow Fe^{3+} + e^-$$

➤ You must not start writing hydrogen molecules, H_2, into half equations unless you know that they are actually involved. If you need extra hydrogens, you must use H^+ (unless you have an alkaline solution – in which case you may need either OH^- or H_2O as the source of hydrogen).

Warning!
You can't just add these equations together – the electrons will not cancel out because there aren't the same number in both equations. To supply the 2 electrons that the first equation needs, the second equation would have to happen twice:

$$2H^+ + H_2O_2 + 2e^- \rightarrow 2H_2O$$
$$2x \qquad (Fe^{2+} \rightarrow Fe^{3+} + e^-)$$
$$\overline{2H^+ + H_2O_2 + 2Fe^{2+} \rightarrow 2H_2O + 2Fe^{3+}}$$

➤ When you have worked out your final equation, check that **everything balances** – both atoms and charges. It is very easy to make careless slips, particularly when adding the two half equations together if you have to do any multiplying at the same time.

Example 10

Potassium manganate(VII) – once called potassium permanganate – is an important oxidising agent. Its solution is purple and contains MnO_4^- ions. When it is used as an oxidising agent in acidic solution, it is reduced to a colourless solution containing Mn^{2+} ions. It oxidises iron(II) ions to iron(III) ions.

Known facts : $MnO_4^- \rightarrow Mn^{2+}$

Balance the oxygens. The only thing you are allowed to write into a half equation to do this is water:

$$MnO_4^- \rightarrow Mn^{2+} + 4H_2O$$

Write in hydrogen ions to balance the hydrogens:

$$MnO_4^- + 8H^+ \rightarrow Mn^{2+} + 4H_2O$$

Finally balance the charges (currently a net 7+ on the left, 2+ on the right):

$$MnO_4^- + 8H^+ + 5e^- \rightarrow Mn^{2+} + 4H_2O$$

The half equation for the iron is exactly the same as before. Before combining the equations, we have to make sure that the right number of electrons are being transferred.

> ➤ **Don't worry** if this seems a long-winded process. It is! Even with practice, it is going to take you a couple of minutes to work out one of these equations. Trying to do it any other way will take longer, though!

$$MnO_4^- + 8H^+ + 5e^- \rightarrow Mn^{2+} + 4H_2O$$
$$5x \quad \underline{(Fe^{2+} \rightarrow Fe^{3+} + e^-)}$$
$$MnO_4^- + 8H^+ + 5Fe^{2+} \rightarrow Mn^{2+} + 4H_2O + 5Fe^{3+}$$

Problem · 6

Write half equations for the following changes. Remember that all you are allowed to write apart from the given substances are water, hydrogen ions and electrons.

(a) H_2O_2 to O_2
(b) SO_3^{2-} to SO_4^{2-}
(c) CH_3CH_2OH to CH_3COOH
(d) $Cr_2O_7^{2-}$ to Cr^{3+}

Problem · 7

Combine 6(c) and (d) to give the ionic equation for the reaction between CH_3CH_2OH and $Cr_2O_7^{2-}$ in acidic solution.

Oxidation states (or oxidation numbers)

Oxidation state is a really useful number which is quite difficult to define in any neat way. An uncombined element is given an oxidation state of zero. If it is oxidised it is then given a positive oxidation state; if it is reduced, it then has a negative oxidation state. The actual number tells you how much it has been oxidised or reduced.

For example, uncombined chromium has an oxidation state of 0. If it is oxidised to Cr^{2+} by losing two electrons it now has an oxidation state of +2. If it loses a further electron to form Cr^{3+}, it moves up an oxidation state to become +3. It looks at the moment, then, as if oxidation state is simply the charge on the ion. This is true as long as you have simple ions – a positive oxidation state tells you how many electrons have been removed to make that ion.

However, you can oxidise Cr^{3+} ions still further to give you an ion with the formula CrO_4^{2-}. This ion is covalently bound. The half equation for this change is:

$$Cr^{3+} + 8OH^- \rightarrow CrO_4^{2-} + 4H_2O + 3e^-$$

Another three electrons have been lost by the chromium and so the oxidation state is now +6. This does not mean to say that the CrO_4^{2-} ion contains Cr^{6+}. The energy needed to create such an ion would be prohibitive. Provided you remember that you don't have to form simple ions. . .

> *A positive oxidation state of an element in a compound tells you how many electrons have been lost by the element in forming that compound. A negative oxidation state tells you how many electrons have been gained by the element in forming that compound.*

Working out oxidation states

> ➤ Elements which have giant structures include metals and carbon (as diamond or graphite). In a giant structure, huge but variable numbers of atoms are all held by strong forces throughout the whole structure.
>
> In a substance such as O_2, a small fixed number of atoms are joined strongly into a molecule, with only weak attractions between one molecule and its neighbours.

> ➤ **Electronegativity** is a measure of the ability of an atom to attract a bonding pair of electrons towards itself. Fluorine is the most electronegative element, and oxygen the next most electronegative.

You need to learn and apply a few simple **rules**:

1. The oxidation state of an uncombined element is always zero. This applies whether the element consists of a giant structure or molecules, and whether the molecules are O_2, P_4, S_8 or whatever.

2. The sum of the oxidation states of all the atoms or ions in a neutral compound is zero.

3. The sum of the oxidation states of all the atoms in an ion is equal to the charge on the ion.

4. The more electronegative element in a substance is given a negative oxidation state. The less electronegative element is given a positive oxidation state.

5. Some elements, when forming compounds, almost always have the same oxidation states:

Group 1 metals:	always +1
Group 2 metals:	always +2
Oxygen:	usually −2 (except in peroxides and F_2O)
Hydrogen:	usually +1 (except in metal hydrides)
Fluorine:	always −1
Chlorine:	usually −1 (except in compounds with O or F)

Notes

The exceptions look a bit daunting, but there is a simple reason for each – it prevents a conflict with one of the earlier rules.

For example, sodium hydride is NaH. It contains Na^+ ions and H^- ions. The oxidation state of the sodium is +1, and sodium hydride is a neutral compound. If you add up all the oxidation states the answer must come to zero (**rule 2**). The hydrogen must therefore have an oxidation state of −1 ($+1 - 1 = 0$). This is also the charge on the H^- ion, and so obeys **rule 3**.

In oxygen's case, sodium peroxide is Na_2O_2. The two sodiums each have an oxidation state of $+1$. The compound is neutral so the sum of all the oxidation states is zero. If the oxidation state of oxygen is some unknown (x):

$$2(+1) + 2x = 0$$

That gives a value for the oxidation state of -1.

When it combines with fluorine, oxygen is not the most electronegative element – and so in this case it has an oxidation state of $+2$.

Example 11

To find the oxidation state of Mn in MnO_2

➤ **Remember:** Oxygen has an oxidation state of -2.

MnO_2 is a neutral compound. If manganese has an oxidation state of x:

$$x + 2(-2) = 0$$

This solves to give an oxidation state of $+4$. (Note: the $+$ sign with the 4 is **essential**.)

Example 12

To find the oxidation state of Mn in MnO_4^-

This time we have an ion with a charge of -1:

$$x + 4(-2) = -1$$

The oxidation state is now $+7$.

Example 13

To find the oxidation state of Mn in $Mn(H_2O)_6^{2+}$

➤ A **complex ion** contains a central ion (in this case manganese) which has a number of other things covalently bonded to it.

There is a short cut you can use on complex ions of this kind. Water is a neutral molecule, and so the sum of the oxidation states is zero. Essentially, therefore, you can ignore it in doing the sum. It would be exactly the same as having just Mn^{2+}. The oxidation state is the charge on the ion: $+2$.

Example 14

To find the oxidation state of Cu in H_2CuCl_4

Hydrogen has an oxidation state of $+1$, chlorine of -1 (neither exception applies here):

$$2(+1) + x + 4(-1) = 0$$

Solving this for x gives an oxidation state of $+2$.

Problem • 8

Work out the oxidation state of the named elements:

(a) nitrogen in NH_3, NO_2, KNO_3, NO_2^-, N_2H_4
(b) sulphur in H_2S, SO_2, SO_3^{2-}, H_2SO_4
(c) vanadium in V_2O_5, $V(H_2O)_6^{3+}$, VO^{2+}, VO_2^+
(d) cobalt in $CoCl_2$, $CoCl_4^{2-}$, $Co(NH_3)_6^{3+}$

Using oxidation states in naming compounds

➤ **Work out** the oxidation states of manganese in these two compounds, and confirm that they are $+7$ and $+6$ respectively.

You will have come across names like copper(II) oxide. The (II) is the oxidation state of the copper ($+2$).

Potassium manganate(VII) is $KMnO_4$, and the manganese has an oxidation state of $+7$. A related compound has the formula K_2MnO_4. Here the oxidation state of the manganese is $+6$, so this compound is potassium manganate(VI).

> ➤ Even sodium sulphate(VI) is not the full name! It should be called sodium tetraoxosulphate(VI) – in other words, the oxygens should also be identified in the name.

Na_2SO_4 should properly be called sodium sulphate(VI) rather than just sodium sulphate, because the oxidation state of the sulphur is +6. On this basis, Na_2SO_3 – usually called sodium sulphite – ought to be called sodium sulphate(IV), because the oxidation state is now +4. To avoid confusion (particularly in the early stages of learning chemistry), these compounds are often called by their old names.

Using oxidation states to recognise oxidation and reduction

This is easily the most important use of oxidation states.

> *An increase in oxidation state is oxidation; a decrease is reduction.*

Example 15

> ➤ **Work out** the oxidation states of everything in these equations. Don't just read the answers.

Which of the following are redox reactions? Where redox is occurring, what is being oxidised and what reduced?

1. $Cl_2 + 2KBr \rightarrow 2KCl + Br_2$

2. $MnO_2 + 4HCl \rightarrow MnCl_2 + Cl_2 + 2H_2O$

3. $2CrO_4^{2-} + 2H^+ \rightarrow Cr_2O_7^{2-} + H_2O$

In equation 1, the chlorine goes from 0 to −1 (a reduction). The bromine goes from −1 to 0 (an oxidation). The potassium is unchanged.

In equation 2, the manganese goes from +4 to +2 (a reduction). Some of the chlorine goes from −1 to 0 (an oxidation). Everything else is unchanged.

In equation 3, the chromiums are +6 before and after, and nothing else has changed either – the oxygen is still −2, the hydrogen +1. This is not a redox reaction.

Using oxidation states to work out reacting proportions

In any reaction, an oxidation state gain by one participant has to be offset by an equal oxidation state loss in another participant. This gives an alternative way of working out equations.

For example, MnO_4^- ions are reduced to Mn^{2+} ions when they oxidise Fe^{2+} ions to Fe^{3+} ions. The manganese has gone from oxidation state +7 to +2, a fall of 5 oxidation states. The iron has only gained 1 in oxidation state. There must therefore be five Fe^{2+} ions reacting for every one MnO_4^- ion. You can make a start on the equation:

> ➤ **Complete** this equation and then compare it with the one built up from half equations on page 14.

$$MnO_4^- + 5Fe^{2+} + \ldots \quad \rightarrow Mn^{2+} + 5Fe^{3+} + \ldots$$

You would then have to make sensible guesses about the rest. You are more likely to be asked to work out this sort of equation using half equations.

End of chapter check list

Can you do the following things?

- Balance simple equations, converting word equations into symbols where necessary.
- Write ionic equations for simple precipitation reactions, reactions of acids, and redox reactions, given necessary information about the reaction.
- Understand and use half equations in building ionic equations, and in explaining redox behaviour.
- Define redox behaviour in terms of oxygen and electron transfer.
- Work out and use oxidation states to determine whether redox has occurred in a reaction.

Revision problems

Answers are provided for these problems, but no worked solutions.

Problem • 9

Write equations (full or ionic as you feel appropriate) for the following reactions:

(a) burning magnesium in oxygen to give magnesium oxide
(b) reacting lithium with water to give lithium hydroxide and hydrogen
(c) burning C_5H_{12} in oxygen to give carbon dioxide and water
(d) reacting calcium with dilute hydrochloric acid (HCl) to give calcium chloride and hydrogen
(e) reacting magnesium carbonate with dilute sulphuric acid (H_2SO_4) to give magnesium sulphate, carbon dioxide and water
(f) reacting sodium carbonate solution with magnesium chloride solution to give a precipitate of magnesium carbonate
(g) reacting silver nitrate solution with potassium iodide solution to give a precipitate of silver iodide
(h) reacting chromium(III) sulphate solution with sodium hydroxide solution to give a precipitate of chromium(III) hydroxide
(i) oxidising iron(II) to iron(III) ions using a solution containing $Cr_2O_7{}^{2-}$ ions, acidified with dilute sulphuric acid; the chromium ends up as Cr^{3+} ions
(j) oxidising $SO_3{}^{2-}$ ions to $SO_4{}^{2-}$ ions using a solution containing $MnO_4{}^-$ ions, acidified with dilute sulphuric acid; the manganese ends up as manganese(II) ions.

> **Hint:** Treat the sulphuric acid simply as a source of H^+ in parts (i) and (j).

Problem • 10

Which of the following reactions involve redox? In each case where redox occurs, state what has been oxidised and what reduced.

(a) $NaOH + HCl \rightarrow NaCl + H_2O$ (b) $2FeCl_2 + Cl_2 \rightarrow 2FeCl_3$
(c) $2Na + H_2 \rightarrow 2NaH$ (d) $Fe + 2H^+ \rightarrow Fe^{2+} + H_2$
(e) $ZnO + 2HCl \rightarrow ZnCl_2 + H_2O$ (f) $Zn + CuCl_2 \rightarrow ZnCl_2 + Cu$
(g) $3MnO_2 + 6OH^- + ClO_3{}^- \rightarrow 3MnO_4{}^{2-} + 3H_2O + Cl^-$

2 Basic Calculations Involving Formulae and Equations

If you did chemistry as a single subject at GCSE and achieved a good grade, quite a lot of this chapter will probably be familiar to you. If not, no specific knowledge of chemistry is assumed, but you will need to be reasonably confident at **reading** equations. So that we can concentrate on one skill at a time, you will not be expected to **write** any chemical equations in the problems you are asked to do.

You don't need any high level maths skills either, but it will make life easier for you if you can rearrange easy mathematical equations and do simple proportion sums (If 50 bars of chocolate cost £27, what do 3 cost?) If you find either of those things hard, don't worry about it. There are ways around the difficulty.

Relative atomic mass

Atoms are amazingly small. In order to get a gram of hydrogen, you would need to count out 602,204,500,000,000,000,000,000 atoms (to the nearest 100,000,000,000,000,000).

It would be silly to measure the masses of atoms in conventional mass units like grams. Instead, their masses are compared with the mass of an atom of the carbon-12 isotope, taken as a standard. We call this the "carbon-12 scale".

On this scale one atom of the carbon-12 isotope weighs **exactly** 12 units.

> **Isotopes** are atoms of the same element but with different masses. They contain the same numbers of protons and electrons, but the number of neutrons varies from one isotope to another.

An atom of the commonest isotope of magnesium weighs twice as much as this and is therefore said to have a **relative isotopic mass** of 24.

An atom of the commonest isotope of hydrogen weighs only one twelfth that of the carbon-12 isotope, and so has a **relative isotopic mass** of 1.

The basic unit on this scale is therefore 1/12 of the mass of a ^{12}C atom. Everything else is measured relative to that.

The **relative atomic mass (RAM) of an element** (as opposed to one of its isotopes) is given the symbol A_r and is defined by:

> *The RAM is the weighted average of the masses of the isotopes relative to 1/12 of the mass of a carbon-12 atom.*

What is a "weighted average"? Finding the RAM of chlorine

In any sample of chlorine, some atoms have a relative mass of 35; others a relative mass of 37. A simple average of 35 and 37 is, of course, 36 – but this is not the relative atomic mass of chlorine. The problem is that there aren't equal numbers of ^{35}Cl and ^{37}Cl atoms.

A typical sample of chlorine has:

^{35}Cl   75%

^{37}Cl   25%

If you had 100 typical atoms of chlorine, 75 would be ^{35}Cl, and 25 would be ^{37}Cl.

The total mass of the 100 atoms would be $(75 \times 35) + (25 \times 37)$

$= 3550$

The average mass of 1 atom would be $3550 \div 100$

$= 35.5$

The weighted average is closer to 35 than to 37, because there are more ^{35}Cl atoms than ^{37}Cl atoms. A weighted average allows for the unequal proportions.

We have just calculated the relative atomic mass (RAM) of chlorine as 35.5.

"Weighing" atoms – the mass spectrometer

Atoms have masses in the range of about 10^{-24} to 10^{-22} grams, and you can't weigh them in any conventional sense. You can, however, get around the problem.

Suppose you were throwing three balls around a field on a very windy day. The three balls all have the same diameter so they each present the same profile to the wind, but their masses are distinctly different – say, a foam rubber ball, a tennis ball and a cricket ball. If you threw them all at exactly the same speed, they would all end up in different places – the lightest ball being deflected most by the wind (see Figure 2.1).

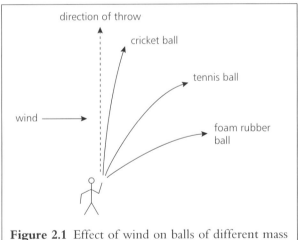

Figure 2.1 Effect of wind on balls of different mass

Atoms can be deflected in a similar way by magnetic fields – provided the atom is first turned into an ion. Electrically charged particles are affected by a magnetic field although electrically neutral ones are not.

An outline of how the mass spectrometer works

Stage 1: Ionisation

The atom is ionised by knocking one or more electrons off to give a positive ion. This is true even for substances which, in a test tube, would form negative ions (chlorine, for example) or never form ions at all (argon, for example). Mass spectrometers always work with positive ions.

➤ **Note:** This is only intended to be a brief outline to show how a mass spectrometer produces its results. For full details, refer to a standard text book.

Stage 2: Acceleration

The ions are accelerated so that they all have the same kinetic energy.

Stage 3: Deflection

Different ions are deflected by the magnetic field by different amounts. The amount of deflection depends on:

■ The mass of the ion. Lighter ions are deflected more than heavier ones.

■ The charge on the ion. Ions with 2 (or more) positive charges are deflected more than ones with only 1 positive charge.

These two factors can be combined, such that the amount of deflection depends on the **mass/charge ratio.** Mass/charge ratio is given the symbol m/z (or sometimes m/e).

What this means is that an ion with a mass of 12 and a charge of 1+ ($m/z = 12$) will be deflected by exactly the same amount as an ion with a mass of 24 and a charge of 2+ ($m/z = 12$).

> ➤ **Hint:** When you have to interpret mass spectra at A level, you can almost always assume that the charge on the ions is 1+, so that an m/z value of 28 means a relative isotopic mass of 28. If there were 2+ ions, the spectrum would have major lines at, say, 28, 29 and 30, and then much, much smaller lines at 14, 14.5 and 15. Unless all your lines have accompanying lines at half the value, you can assume that $z = 1$.

Stage 4: Detection

Only the ions which have exactly the right m/z ratio will pass all the way through the machine to be detected electrically. As well as recognising their presence, the detector also gives a measure of the number of ions arriving.

If you vary the magnetic field, you can bring ions of different m/z ratios in turn on to the detector to produce a current which is proportional to the number of ions arriving. The mass of each ion being detected is related to the size of the magnetic field used to bring it on to the detector. The machine can be calibrated to record the current (which is a measure of the number of ions) against m/z directly. The mass is measured on the ^{12}C scale.

Interpreting mass spectra for elements

Mass spectra are used to find relative atomic masses. You will remember:

> *Relative atomic mass is the weighted average of the masses of the isotopes relative to 1/12 of the mass of a ^{12}C atom.*

The output from a mass spectrometer is usually simplified and stylised into a "stick diagram". The stick diagram for lithium shows that there are two types of ions present – one with a mass/charge ratio of 6, and the other with a mass/charge ratio of 7. Assuming that these are both 1+ ions, the relative isotopic masses are 6 and 7, respectively.

The height of the peaks gives a measure of the numbers of each type of ion. The highest peak (the most abundant ion) is often given a height of 100 units. In the diagram shown in Figure 2.2, the peak at $m/z = 6$ has a height of 8.0 units, while that at $m/z = 7$ has a height of 100.

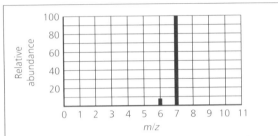

Figure 2.2 Stick diagram showing relative abundance of ions plotted against mass/charge ratio for lithium

Example 1   Calculating the relative atomic mass of lithium

The isotopes are in the ratio of 8 atoms of ^{6}Li to every 100 atoms of ^{7}Li.

The total mass of 108 atoms would be $(8 \times 6) + (100 \times 7)$
$= 748$
The average mass of 1 atom (the RAM) $= 748 \div 108$
$= 6.9$

Example 2   Calculating the relative atomic mass of germanium

The actual values are listed below and plotted in Figure 2.3.

m/z	Relative abundance
70	56.4
72	75.1
73	21.4
74	100
76	21.1

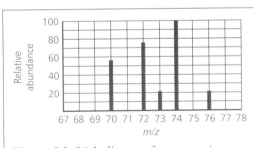

Figure 2.3 Stick diagram for germanium

You can think of the relative abundance as being a count of the number of atoms of each different isotope.

Total number of atoms $= 56.4 + 75.1 + 21.4 + 100 + 21.1$
$= 274$
Total mass of 274 atoms
$= (56.4 \times 70) + (75.1 \times 72) + (21.4 \times 73) + (100 \times 74) + (21.1 \times 76)$
$= 19921$
The average mass of 1 atom (the RAM) $= 19921 \div 274$
$= 72.7$

Example 3

Calculating the relative atomic mass of magnesium

The figures might be given to you differently – for example as percentages. The isotopes of magnesium and their percentage abundances are:

^{24}Mg   78.6%
^{25}Mg   10.1%
^{26}Mg   11.3%

This time, all you need to do is to assume that you have 100 typical atoms.

The total mass would be $= (78.6 \times 24) + (10.1 \times 25) + (11.3 \times 26)$
$= 2432.7$
The RAM would be $2432.7 \div 100$
$= 24.3$ (to 3 significant figures (sig figs) –
don't give any more)

> **Be careful** how many significant figures you quote answers to. You should never quote to more significant figures than your least accurate input number. In this case, the 24, 25 and 26 can be taken as totally precise, because they are mass numbers. The percentages are only quoted to 3 sig figs, and so your answer must not exceed that. If in doubt, you will usually be OK if you give answers to 3 sig figs.

The mass spectrum for chlorine, Cl_2

Chlorine has two isotopes, ^{35}Cl and ^{37}Cl, in the approximate ratio of 3 atoms of ^{35}Cl to 1 atom of ^{37}Cl. You might suppose that the mass spectrum would just consist of two lines at m/z 35 and 37, with the 35 line three times higher than the 37 line. You would be wrong!

The problem here is that chlorine consists of molecules, not individual atoms. When chlorine is passed into the ionisation chamber, an electron is knocked off the molecule to give a **molecular ion**, Cl_2^+. Some of these ions will fall apart to give a chlorine atom and a Cl^+ ion. The term for this is **fragmentation**:

$Cl_2^+ \rightarrow Cl + Cl^+$

If the Cl atom formed is not then ionised by collision with an electron, it simply gets lost in the machine – neither accelerated nor deflected. The Cl^+ ions will pass through the machine and will give lines at 35 and 37, depending on the isotope, with the $m/z = 35$ line 3 times taller than the 37 line. This is what you would expect. The problem is that you will also record lines for the unfragmented Cl_2^+ ions.

There are three different possible masses for a Cl_2^+ ion depending on what combination of ^{35}Cl and ^{37}Cl atoms it contains. The masses could be:

$35 + 35 = 70$
$35 + 37 = 72$
$37 + 37 = 74$

So in addition to the lines at 35 and 37, there will also be lines at 70, 72 and 74. If you are competent at maths, you could work out that these lines will have a height ratio of 9:6:1 respectively. (If you aren't good at maths, it's not important!)

What you can't do is make any predictions about the relative heights of the lines at 35/37 compared with those at 70/72/74. That depends on what proportion of the molecular ions break up into fragments.

> **Beyond A level:** We have been taking values of relative isotopic masses as being the same as the mass number. This is not a bad approximation, but it is not quite true. The mass of an isotope is not just the sum of the protons and neutrons (which, in any case, do not weigh *exactly* 1 unit on the ^{12}C scale). Surprisingly the mass of most atoms is less than the sum of the actual masses of the protons and neutrons added together – never mind the electrons. If you are interested to find out more, you might like to do some research on **binding energy** – but it is not needed for A level.

Problem • 1

Calculate the relative atomic mass of silicon, given:

Relative isotopic mass	Relative abundance
28	100
29	5.10
30	3.36

Problem • 2

Calculate the relative atomic mass of gallium given the percentage abundances: ^{69}Ga 60.2%, ^{71}Ga 39.8%.

Problem • 3

Bromine has two isotopes, ^{79}Br and ^{81}Br. At what values of m/z would you expect to find lines in the mass spectrum of bromine, Br_2? (Assume that only 1+ ions are formed.)

Relative formula mass

Relative formula mass tells you the relative mass (on the ^{12}C scale) of the substance whose formula you have written. **Relative formula mass (RFM)** is sometimes called **relative molecular mass (RMM)**. Avoid this term, because it can only properly be applied to substances which are actually molecules – in other words, to covalent substances. You should not use it for things like magnesium oxide or sodium chloride which are ionic. RFM covers **everything**. Relative formula mass is given the symbol M_r.

Working out some relative formula masses

Example 4

> You will **never** have to remember RAMs. They will always be given to you in an exam.

To find the RFM of magnesium carbonate, $MgCO_3$

Relative atomic masses: $C = 12; O = 16; Mg = 24$

All you have to do is to add up the relative atomic masses to give you the relative formula mass of the whole compound.

$$RFM = 24 + 12 + (3 \times 16)$$
$$= 84$$

Examples 5 and 6

> Most people have no difficulty with RFM sums until they get to an example involving water of crystallisation (the $5H_2O$ in this example). $5H_2O$ means 5 molecules of water – so to get the total mass of this, work out the RFM of water (18) and then multiply it by 5. It is dangerous to do the hydrogens and oxygens separately. The common mistake is to work out 10 hydrogens (quite correctly!), but then only count 1 oxygen rather than the proper 5.

To find the RFM of calcium hydroxide, $Ca(OH)_2$

Relative atomic masses: $H = 1; O = 16; Ca = 40$

$$RFM = 40 + (16 + 1) \times 2$$
$$= 74$$

To find the RFM of copper(II) sulphate crystals, $CuSO_4.5H_2O$

Relative atomic masses: $H = 1; O = 16; S = 32; Cu = 64$

$$RFM = 64 + 32 + (4 \times 16) + 5 \times [(2 \times 1) + 16]$$
$$= 250$$

Problem . 4

Calculate the relative formula masses of the following compounds:

(a) CO_2
(b) $(NH_4)_2SO_4$
(c) $Na_2CO_3.10H_2O$

(Relative atomic masses: H = 1; C = 12; N = 14; O = 16; Na = 23; S = 32)

Using RFMs to find percentage compositions

Example 7

To find the percentage of copper in copper(II) oxide, CuO

Relative atomic masses: O = 16; Cu = 64

$$RFM \text{ of } CuO = 64 + 16$$
$$= 80$$

Of this, 64 is copper.

$$\text{Percentage of copper} = \frac{64}{80} \times 100$$
$$= 80\%$$

Example 8

To find the percentage of nitrogen in ammonium nitrate, NH_4NO_3

Relative atomic masses: H = 1; N = 14; O = 16

$$RFM \text{ of } NH_4NO_3 = 14 + (4 \times 1) + 14 + (3 \times 16)$$
$$= 80$$

Of this, (2×14) is nitrogen.

$$\text{Percentage of nitrogen} = \frac{(2 \times 14)}{80} \times 100$$
$$= 35\%$$

Problem . 5

Find the percentage of the named substance in each of the following examples:

(a) carbon in propane, C_3H_8
(b) water in magnesium sulphate crystals, $MgSO_4.7H_2O$

(Relative atomic masses: H = 1; C = 12; O = 16; Mg = 24; S = 32)

The mole

In chemistry, the mole is a measure of **amount of substance**. You can use such expressions as:

■ a mole of copper(II) sulphate crystals, $CuSO_4.5H_2O$

■ a mole of oxygen gas, O_2

■ 0.1 mole of zinc oxide, ZnO

■ 3 moles of magnesium, Mg.

A mole is a particular mass of that substance. You find the mass of 1 mole of a substance in the following way:

> *Work out the relative formula mass, and attach the units "grams".*

Working out the masses

Example 9   1 mole of iron(II) sulphate crystals, $FeSO_4.7H_2O$

Relative atomic masses: $H = 1$; $O = 16$; $S = 32$; $Fe = 56$

RFM of crystals $= 56 + 32 + (4 \times 16) + 7 \times [(2 \times 1) + 16]$
$$= 278$$

1 mole of iron(II) sulphate crystals weighs 278 g.

Example 10   1 molez of oxygen gas, O_2

Relative atomic mass: $O = 16$

RFM of oxygen, $O_2 = 2 \times 16$
$$= 32$$

1 mole of oxygen, O_2, weighs 32 g.

The importance of quoting the formula

Whenever you talk about a mole of something, you **must** quote its formula, otherwise there is the risk of confusion, which you must avoid.

For example, if you talk about 1 mole of oxygen, this could mean:

■ 1 mole of oxygen atoms, O, weighing 16 g or

■ 1 mole of oxygen molecules, O_2, weighing 32 g.

Or if you were talking about 1 mole of copper(II) sulphate, this could mean:

■ 1 mole of anhydrous copper(II) sulphate, $CuSO_4$ (160 g) or

■ 1 mole of copper(II) sulphate crystals, $CuSO_4.5H_2O$ (250 g).

The abbreviation for mole

The abbreviation for mole is **mol.**

Simple calculations with moles

You need to be able to carry out interconversions like the following:

(a) What is the mass of 0.2 mol of calcium carbonate, $CaCO_3$?

(b) How many moles is 54 g of water, H_2O?

There are two different approaches you could use depending on your confidence with numbers. It doesn't matter in the least which you choose, as long as you get the answer right.

If you are confident with numbers

(a) 1 mol of $CaCO_3$ weighs 100 g. (Assume you have just worked that out.)
Therefore, 0.2 mol weighs 0.2×100 g $= 20$ g

(b) 1 mol of H_2O weighs 18 g. (Assume you have just worked that out.)
54 g is 3 times 18 g, and so is 3 moles.

If you aren't confident with numbers

There is a simple formula that you can learn:

$$\textit{Number of moles} = \frac{\textit{mass (g)}}{\textit{mass of 1 mole (g)}}$$

You can rearrange this to find whatever you need to find. For example:

Mass (g) = number of moles × mass of 1 mole (g)

$$\text{Mass of 1 mole (g)} = \frac{\text{mass (g)}}{\text{number of moles}}$$

If rearranging this expression causes you problems, you can learn a simple triangular arrangement which does the whole thing for you (see Figure 2.4).

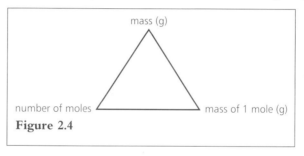

Figure 2.4

Look at this carefully and make sure that you understand how the three expressions given above derive from it.

Using the formulae to do the sums

Example 11

What is the mass of 0.2 mol of calcium carbonate, $CaCO_3$?

1 mol of $CaCO_3$ weighs 100 g. (Assume you have just worked that out.)

Mass (g) = number of moles × mass of 1 mole (g)
$= 0.2 \times 100$ g
$= 20$ g

Example 12

How many moles is 54 g of water, H_2O?

1 mol of H_2O weighs 18 g. (Assume you have just worked that out.)

$$\text{Number of moles} = \frac{\text{mass (g)}}{\text{mass of 1 mole (g)}}$$

$$= \frac{54}{18}$$

$$= 3 \text{ mol}$$

Relative atomic masses: H = 1; O = 16; Na = 23; Cl = 35.5; Ca = 40; Cu = 64

Problem • 6

What is the mass of 4 mol of sodium chloride, NaCl?

Problem • 7

How many moles is 37 g of calcium hydroxide, $Ca(OH)_2$?

Problem • 8

How many moles is 1 kg (1000 g) of calcium, Ca?

Problem • 9

What is the mass of 0.125 mol of copper(II) oxide, CuO?

Problem • 10

0.1 mol of a substance weighs 4 g. What is the weight of 1 mole?

Problem • 11

0.004 mol of a substance weighs 1 g. What is the relative formula mass of the compound?

What is special about moles?

You have seen how to work out the mass of a mole of a particular substance, and you know how to do some simple sums with moles – but what is the point of them?

The Avogadro Constant, *L*

Carbon-12 has a relative atomic mass of 12, magnesium a relative atomic mass of 24. In other words, magnesium atoms are twice as heavy as carbon atoms.

Suppose you had **1 mole** of ^{12}C. It would weigh 12 g, and contain a huge number of carbon atoms – in fact, 6.022×10^{23} carbon atoms (to 4 significant figures). Scientific notation doesn't really do this justice. The number is actually:

602 200 000 000 000 000 000 000

This number of atoms in 12 g of ^{12}C is called the Avogadro Number or Avogadro Constant. The Avogadro Constant has units of mol^{-1} (read as "per mole").

If you had the same number of magnesium atoms, each of which is twice as heavy, they would obviously weigh twice as much – in other words, 24 g.

But 24 g is the mass of **1 mole** of Mg. 1 mole of Mg contains the same number of atoms as 1 mole of C.

Defining the mole

A mole of substance is the amount of that substance that contains the same number of stated elementary units as there are atoms in 12 g of ^{12}C.

The off-putting thing about this definition is the term **stated elementary units.** It is easier to see what it means with some examples. The following all contain the same number (the Avogadro Constant) of the **stated elementary units:**

■ 16 g (1 mole) of oxygen **atoms**, O.

■ 32 g (1 mole) of oxygen **molecules**, O_2. (This, of course, contains twice as many oxygen atoms, O.)

■ 18 g (1 mole) of water **molecules**, H_2O.

■ 58.5 g (1 mole) of sodium chloride **formula units**, NaCl. (You can't call this a molecule because sodium chloride is ionic.)

■ 24 g (1 mole) of magnesium **ions**, Mg^{2+}.

Taking a final, really complicated example, 1 mole (250 g) of copper(II) sulphate crystals, $CuSO_4.5H_2O$, contains the Avogadro Number of formula units, $CuSO_4.5H_2O$.

But you could break this down into its individual components. So, 250 g of copper(II) sulphate crystals contains

6.022×10^{23} lots of $CuSO_4.5H_2O$ units

Or you could think of it as containing:

6.022×10^{23} copper(II) ions, Cu^{2+},

and 6.022×10^{23} sulphate ions, SO_4^{2-},

and $5 \times (6.022 \times 10^{23})$ water molecules, H_2O.

And you could go further and break down the individual sulphate ions and water molecules into their individual atoms and count them as well if you wanted to.

An important lesson from all this

Whenever you talk about a mole of something you **must** quote the formula of the substance – otherwise you will not know what elementary unit you are talking about.

Some examples using the Avogadro Constant

In all the following examples, we will take the Avogadro Constant to be 6×10^{23} mol^{-1} to make the sums look a bit less unfriendly.

Example 13

How many water molecules, H_2O, are there in 9 g of water?
($H = 1; O = 16$)

1 mol of water, H_2O, weighs 18 g and contains 6×10^{23} water molecules. 9 g is 0.5 mol and so contains $0.5 \times 6 \times 10^{23}$ molecules $= 3 \times 10^{23}$ molecules.

Example 14

How many atoms are there in 11 g of propane, C_3H_8?
($H = 1; C = 12$)

This is a sneaky question, because it isn't asking about propane molecules, C_3H_8, but the total number of atoms. You must read the question very carefully in this sort of problem.

1 mol of propane, C_3H_8, weighs 44 g and contains 6×10^{23} propane molecules. 11 g is 0.25 mol of propane and so contains $0.25 \times 6 \times 10^{23}$ propane molecules $= 1.5 \times 10^{23}$ propane molecules

Each propane molecule contains 11 atoms (3 carbons and 8 hydrogens).

Therefore the total number of atoms $= 11 \times 1.5 \times 10^{23}$
$$= 1.65 \times 10^{24}$$

Example 15

What mass of magnesium contains the same number of magnesium atoms, Mg, as there are molecules of CO_2 in 1000 g of carbon dioxide?
($C = 12; O = 16; Mg = 24$)

In this case, you don't actually need to work out how many molecules or atoms there are. You simply have to remember that if you have equal numbers of moles, you have equal numbers of the stated particles.

1 mol of CO_2 weighs 44 g.

Therefore, 1000 g of CO_2 is $\dfrac{1000}{44}$ mol $= 22.73$ mol

To have the same number of atoms of magnesium as molecules of CO_2, you would need to have the same number of moles.

The mass of magnesium with this number of atoms $= 22.73 \times 24$ g
$$= 546 \text{ g}$$

Problem • 12

In all of these problems take the Avogadro Constant to be $6 \times 10^{23} \text{mol}^{-1}$.

How many water molecules, H_2O, are there in 1 drop of water? Assume 1 drop of water is 0.05 cm^3, and that the density of water is 1 g cm^{-3}.
($H = 1; O = 16$)

Problem • 13

Sea water contains about 30 g of ionic sodium chloride, Na^+Cl^-, in every 1000 cm^3 of water. What volume of sea water contains 10^{20} ion pairs, Na^+Cl^-? ($Na = 23; Cl = 35.5$)

Problem • 14

Which of the following contains the greatest number of stated particles?

A   molecules of hydrogen in 1 g of hydrogen gas, H_2
B   atoms of helium in 1 g of helium gas, He
C   atoms of beryllium in 1 g of beryllium, Be

($H = 1$, $He = 4$, $Be = 9$)

Using moles to find formulae

Interpreting symbols in terms of moles

Assume that you know the formula for something like copper(II) oxide, for example. The formula is CuO.

When you are doing sums, it is often useful to interpret a symbol as meaning more than just "an atom of copper" or "an atom of oxygen". For calculation purposes we take the symbol Cu to mean **1 mole of copper atoms.**

In other words, "Cu" means "64 g of copper". "O" means "16 g of oxygen". (RAMs: $O = 16, Cu = 64$) So in copper(II) oxide, the copper and oxygen are combined in the ratio of 64 g of copper to 16 g of oxygen.

In a formula like H_2O, you can read this as meaning that 2 moles of hydrogen atoms are combined with 1 mole of oxygen atoms. In other words, 2 g of hydrogen are combined with 16 g of oxygen. (RAM: $H = 1$)

Example 16

Working out the formula for magnesium oxide

Suppose you did an experiment to find out how much magnesium and oxygen reacted together to form magnesium oxide. Suppose 2.4 g of magnesium combined with 1.6 g of oxygen. You can use these figures to find the formula of magnesium oxide. ($O = 16; Mg = 24$)

> ➤ **Remember:** Number of moles is mass in grams divided by the mass of 1 mole in grams.

	Mg	O
Combining masses	2.4 g	1.6 g
Number of moles of atoms	2.4/24	1.6/16
	= 0.1	= 0.1
Ratio of moles	1 :	1
Simplest formula:	MgO	

This simplest formula is called the **empirical formula.** The empirical formula just tells you the **ratio** of the various atoms. It isn't possible without more information to work out the "true" or "molecular" formula which could be Mg_2O_2, Mg_3O_3, etc. For ionic substances, the formula quoted is **always** the empirical formula.

Example 17

A compound contained 4.6 g Na, 2.8 g N, 9.6 g O. Find the empirical formula. ($N = 14; O = 16; Na = 23$)

	Na	N	O
Combining masses	4.6 g	2.8 g	9.6 g
Number of moles of atoms	4.6/23	2.8/14	9.6/16
	= 0.2	= 0.2	= 0.6
Ratio of moles	1 :	1 :	3
Simplest (empirical) formula:	$NaNO_3$		

31

Example 18

Find the empirical formula of a compound containing 85.7% C, 14.3% H by mass. (H = 1; C = 12)

Often, figures for the compound are given as percentages by mass, as here. This isn't a problem! Those percentage figures apply to any amount of substance you choose – so choose 100 g. In which case, the percentages convert simply into masses: 85.7% of 100 g is 85.7 g.

> **Hint:** Usually the ratio will be fairly obvious, but if you can't spot it at once, divide everything by the smallest number and see if that helps.
> e.g. Ratio of moles:
>   1.4 : 1.4 : 2.1
> Divide everything by 1.4, giving the ratio
>   1 : 1 : 1.5
> That would simplify to 2:2:3

	C	H
Given percentages	85.7%	14.3%
Combining masses in 100 g	85.7 g	14.3 g
Number of moles of atoms	85.7/12	14.3/1
	= 7.14	= 14.3
Ratio of moles	1 :	2
Simplest (empirical) formula:	CH_2	

Converting empirical formulae into molecular formulae

In the example we have just looked at, CH_2 can't possibly be the real molecular formula of the hydrocarbon – the carbon would have spare unbonded electrons. The true (molecular) formula would have to be some multiple of CH_2, like C_2H_4 or C_3H_6 or whatever – as long as the ratio is still 1 carbon to 2 hydrogens.

You could find the molecular formula if you knew the relative formula mass of the compound (or the mass of 1 mole – which is just the RFM expressed in grams).

In the previous example, suppose you knew that the RFM was 56.

CH_2 has a relative formula mass of 14. (H = 1, C = 12)

How many multiples of that do you have to take in order to get a total of 56?

$\frac{56}{14} = 4$ and so you need 4 lots of CH_2 – in other words, C_4H_8.

A short cut method of finding molecular formulae

If you are given percentage composition figures and a relative formula mass (or the mass of 1 mole) and are just asked to find the molecular formula, you can go straight to it without having to work out the empirical formula first.

A compound contained the following percentages by mass: 52.2% C, 13.0% H, 34.8% O. 1 mole of it weighed 46 g. Find the molecular formula of the compound. (H = 1, C = 12, O = 16)

> **Note:** If having two different methods of solving the same problem confuses you, stick to the route via the empirical formula. It will take a bit longer, but you have got to know how to do it that way in case they ask you for both empirical formula and molecular formula.

Find the mass of each element in the compound.

Carbon: 52.2% of 46 g = 24.01 g
Hydrogen: 13.0% of 46 g = 5.98 g
Oxygen: 34.8% of 46 g = 16.01 g

That is 2 moles of carbon atoms, 6 moles of hydrogen atoms and 1 mole of oxygen atoms (to a very close approximation).

The molecular formula is therefore C_2H_6O.

Problem • 15

1.24 g of phosphorus was burnt completely in oxygen to give 2.84 g of phosphorus oxide. Find (a) the empirical formula of the oxide, and (b) the molecular formula of the oxide, given that 1 mole of the oxide weighs 284 g. (O = 16, P = 31)

Problem • 16

An organic compound contained 66.7% C, 11.1% H, 22.2% O by mass. Its relative formula mass was 72. Find (a) the empirical formula of the compound, and (b) the molecular formula of the compound. (H = 1, C = 12, O = 16)

Problem • 17

➤ **Hint:** This is a much trickier sum. Use the information to calculate the weights of calcium and iodine in the original solution. Think about percentage composition sums.

A student took 2 exactly equal volumes of calcium iodide solution. To one, she added an excess of silver nitrate solution which precipitated all the iodine out as 9.40 g of silver iodide, AgI. To the second volume, she added an excess of sodium carbonate solution which precipitated all the calcium out as 2.00 g of calcium carbonate, $CaCO_3$. Confirm that the formula of calcium iodide is CaI_2. (C = 12; O = 16; Ca = 40; Ag = 108; I = 127)

Calculations from equations

If you write a formula for a substance in a calculation, it is often convenient to take that formula as meaning **1 mole of that substance.** This enables you to attach a mass to it and therefore to work things out from it.

Example 19

What mass of calcium oxide could be obtained by heating 25 g of limestone, $CaCO_3$? (C = 12; O = 16; Ca = 40)

$$CaCO_3 \rightarrow CaO + CO_2$$

Interpret the equation in terms of moles

1 mol $CaCO_3$ produces 1 mol CaO (and 1 mol CO_2)

Substitute masses where relevant

100 g (1 mol) $CaCO_3$ produces 56 g (1 mol) CaO

(Notice that we have not calculated the mass of carbon dioxide. We haven't been asked about it, and so working it out is just a waste of time – and potentially confusing.)

➤ **Maths not very good?**
Put an extra step in if it helps:
100 g $CaCO_3$ gives 56 g of calcium oxide.
1 g of $CaCO_3$ gives 56/100 g of CaO = 0.56 g
25 g of $CaCO_3$ gives 25 × 0.56 g of CaO = 14 g

Do the simple proportion sum

If 100 g of calcium carbonate gives 56 g of calcium oxide

25 g of calcium carbonate gives $\frac{25}{100} \times 56$ g of calcium oxide

= 14 g of calcium oxide

Example 20

In the blast furnace, haematite, Fe_2O_3, is converted to iron:

$$Fe_2O_3 + 3CO \rightarrow 2Fe + 3CO_2$$

What mass of iron can be obtained from 16 tonnes of iron oxide?
($O = 16$; $Fe = 56$)

Interpret the equation in terms of moles:

1 mol Fe_2O_3 gives 2 mol Fe

(You can ignore the other substances because they aren't relevant to the question.)

Substitute masses where relevant:

160 g (1 mol) Fe_2O_3 gives 112 g (2 mol) Fe

Now a problem appears to arise. The question is asking about tonnes and not grams. You could work out how many grams there are in a tonne and then do hard sums with large numbers. However, it is much easier to think a bit, and realise that the ratio is always going to be the same between the iron oxide and the iron, whatever the units – so that

if   160 g Fe_2O_3 gives 112 g Fe

then   160 kg Fe_2O_3 gives 112 kg Fe

or   160 tonnes Fe_2O_3 gives 112 tonnes Fe

or whatever units!

> ➤ **Hint:** If you need another step, use it. Work out what 1 tonne would give by dividing by 160. Then multiply that answer by 16 to find out what 16 tonnes would give.

Do the simple proportion sum:

160 tonnes Fe_2O_3 gives 112 tonnes Fe

16 tonnes Fe_2O_3 gives $\dfrac{16}{160} \times 112$ tonnes Fe

$= 11.2$ tonnes Fe

Example 21

You can carry this same process through several equations if necessary. For example nitric acid is manufactured from nitrogen by converting it into ammonia and then oxidising the ammonia. The equations are:

$$N_2 + 3H_2 \rightarrow 2NH_3$$

$$4NH_3 + 5O_2 \rightarrow 4NO + 6H_2O$$

$$2NO + O_2 \rightarrow 2NO_2$$

$$2H_2O + 4NO_2 + O_2 \rightarrow 4HNO_3$$

What mass of nitric acid can be produced from 1 tonne of nitrogen gas?
($H = 1$, $N = 14$, $O = 16$)

Interpret the equation in terms of moles:

1 mol N_2 gives 2 mol NH_3

4 mol NH_3 gives 4 mol NO

2 mol NO gives 2 mol NO_2

4 mol NO_2 gives 4 mol HNO_3

Trace it through. 1 mol N_2 gives 2 mol NH_3 which gives the same number of moles of NO (2 mol), which gives the same number of moles of NO_2 (still 2 mol), which in turn gives the same number of moles of HNO_3 (again 2 mol).

So overall:

1 mol N_2 gives 2 mol HNO_3

Substitute masses where relevant:

28 g N_2 gives 2×63 g HNO_3

so   28 tonnes N_2 gives 2×63 tonnes HNO_3

Do the simple proportion sum:

If   28 tonnes N_2 gives 2×63 tonnes HNO_3

1 tonne N_2 gives $\dfrac{2 \times 63}{28}$ tonnes HNO_3

$= 4.5$ tonnes HNO_3

> ➤ In practice, you probably wont write anything down except this last line. Everything else is done in your head. On the other hand, if you feel happier writing it all down, do so.

Problem • 18

Titanium is manufactured by heating titanium(IV) chloride with sodium

$TiCl_4 + 4Na \rightarrow Ti + 4NaCl$

What mass of sodium is required to produce 1 tonne of titanium?
(Na = 23; Ti = 48)

Problem • 19

2.67 g of aluminium chloride was dissolved in water and an excess of silver nitrate solution was added to give a precipitate of silver chloride:

$AlCl_{3(aq)} + 3AgNO_{3(aq)} \rightarrow Al(NO_3)_{3(aq)} + 3AgCl_{(s)}$

What mass of silver chloride precipitate would be formed?
(Al = 27; Cl = 35.5; Ag = 108)

Problem • 20

Calcium hydroxide is manufactured by heating calcium carbonate strongly to produce calcium oxide, and then adding a controlled amount of water to produce calcium hydroxide:

$CaCO_3 \rightarrow CaO + CO_2$

$CaO + H_2O \rightarrow Ca(OH)_2$

(a) What mass of water would you need to add to the calcium oxide produced from 1 tonne of calcium carbonate?
(b) What mass of calcium hydroxide would you ultimately produce from 1 tonne of calcium carbonate? (H = 1; C = 12; O = 16; Ca = 40)

Percentage yield calculations

In the last set of calculations we have been assuming that when the reactions are carried out, nothing is wasted, and that things happen exactly as the equation says. In the real world, that is far from the truth.

35

Particularly in organic chemistry, there are often side reactions which waste some of the starting material, and you usually end up with a mixture from which you have to extract what you want – often in a number of stages. At each of these stages, product tends to get lost. In many organic preparations, if you end up with 50% of the theoretical yield, you are doing well!

In the examples which follow, do not be put off by unfamiliar chemistry. Provided you have the equation and some relative atomic masses, it doesn't matter how complicated the chemistry looks.

Example 22

In an experiment to produce a sample of hex-1-ene, 10.2 g of hexan-1-ol was heated with an excess of phosphoric(V) acid. (The phosphoric(V) acid simply acts as a dehydrating agent, removing water from the hexan-1-ol.)

$$CH_3CH_2CH_2CH_2CH_2CH_2OH \rightarrow CH_3CH_2CH_2CH_2CH=CH_2 + H_2O$$

hexan-1-ol   hex-1-ene

After purification of the hex-1-ene, 5.04 g was produced. Calculate the percentage yield. (H = 1; C = 12; O = 16)

There are always two stages to this sort of problem:

■ Work out what you would get if the yield was 100%.

■ Use this figure to calculate the actual percentage yield.

From the equation:

       1 mol hexan-1-ol gives 1 mol hex-1-ene

       102 g hexan-1-ol gives 84 g hex-1-ene

So   10.2 g hexan-1-ol gives $\dfrac{10.2}{102} \times 84\,g = 8.40\,g$

Since only 5.04 g of hex-1-ene was produced, the percentage yield is

$$\frac{5.04}{8.40} \times 100\% = 60.0\%$$

Example 23

More realistically, if you are dealing with organic liquids, you are more likely to measure volumes rather than masses. In this case, you would have the added step of converting volumes into masses using density values.

A sample of 1-bromobutane was made by treating 8.0 cm³ of butan-1-ol with an excess of sodium bromide and concentrated sulphuric acid. After purification, 3.7 cm³ of 1-bromobutane had been produced. Calculate the percentage yield. (H = 1; C = 12; O = 16; Br = 80. Densities: butan-1-ol: 0.810 g cm⁻³; 1-bromobutane: 1.28 g cm⁻³)

$$C_4H_9OH + NaBr + H_2SO_4 \rightarrow C_4H_9Br + NaHSO_4 + H_2O$$

butan-1-ol   1-bromobutane

First change all the volumes into masses using the density values, so that you bring all the information into a familiar format:

     Mass of butan-1-ol   = 8.0 × 0.810 g = 6.48 g
     Mass of 1-bromobutane = 3.7 × 1.28 g = 4.736 g

> ➤ **Don't panic!** It doesn't matter if the chemistry looks unfamiliar. It doesn't make the calculation any more difficult.

> ➤ **Hint:** Density is measured in g cm⁻³ (grams per cm³). In the butan-1-ol case, if the density is 0.810 g cm⁻³, it means that every cm³ weighs 0.810 g. 8 cm³ weighs 8 times as much as 1 cm³.
>
> Alternatively, you can use the fact that density = mass/volume, and rearrange that expression to give
>
>   mass = volume × density

From the equation:

> 1 mol butan-1-ol gives 1 mol 1-bromobutane
> 74 g butan-1-ol gives 137 g 1-bromobutane

So   6.48 g gives $\dfrac{6.48}{74} \times 137\,g = 12.0\,g$

Since only 4.736 g of 1-bromobutane was produced, the percentage yield is

$$\frac{4.736}{12.0} \times 100\% = 39\%$$

> ➤ **Hint:** Work out what 1 g would give by dividing by 74. 6.48 g then gives 6.48 times as much as that.

> ➤ You can't quote this answer to more than 2 significant figures because the original volumes are only given to 2 sig figs.

Example 24

Often, it isn't clear from the instructions for a practical preparation which of the starting substances is/are in excess. This matters because the potential yield is going to be determined by the starting material not in excess.

This example includes all the complications that you can think of! The chances of meeting a question like this in a written paper are remote. You might however come across something similar as a part of a practical exercise. Once again, do not be put off by the nasty looking chemistry.

This question involves the preparation of a sample of the drug "antifebrin" (N-phenylethanamide) by the reaction between ethanoic anhydride and phenylamine:

$$(CH_3CO)_2O \ + \ C_6H_5NH_2 \ \rightarrow \ CH_3CONHC_6H_5 \ + \ CH_3COOH$$

ethanoic anhydride   phenylamine   N-phenylethanamide   ethanoic acid

$4.0\,cm^3$ of phenylamine was treated with $6.0\,cm^3$ of ethanoic anhydride under suitable conditions, and the solid product (N-phenylethanamide) was purified. 4.15 g was produced. Calculate the percentage yield. (H = 1; C = 12; N = 14; O = 16. Densities: ethanoic anhydride $1.08\,g\,cm^{-3}$; phenylamine $1.02\,g\,cm^{-3}$.)

The first thing you need to do is to work out how many moles of each of the starting materials there are in the mixture, so that you know which you have the least of. You must not assume that because you have a smaller volume of phenylamine that there are necessarily fewer moles of this – although in this case, it does turn out that there are.

To work out the number of moles you need masses, not volumes. Use the density values to do the conversion.

> Mass of ethanoic anhydride = $6.0 \times 1.08\,g = 6.48\,g$
> Mass of phenylamine = $4.0 \times 1.02\,g = 4.08\,g$

Now to work out the number of moles:

$$\text{Number of moles of ethanoic anhydride} = \frac{6.48}{102} = 0.0635$$

$$\text{Number of moles of phenylamine} = \frac{4.08}{93} = 0.0439$$

> ➤ See the **Hint** on density in example 23 if you aren't happy about this conversion.

> ➤ Number of moles is mass in grams divided by the mass of 1 mole in grams.

> ➤ **Hint:** 102 is the RFM of ethanoic anhydride. 93 is the RFM of phenylamine.

Because the reaction is 1:1, there is obviously an excess of ethanoic anhydride. The amount of product will be limited by the amount of phenylamine.

> We are actually doing this one slightly differently from the last two examples. Because we have already worked out the number of moles of phenylamine, we can go directly to the number of moles of product from the equation. This can be converted to a mass using the relationship

mass = number of moles × mass of 1 mole.

That's all the tedious bit done – now we're back to normal. The equation shows that:

1 mole of phenylamine gives 1 mole of N-phenylethanamide

So 0.0439 mol phenylamine gives 0.0439 mol N-phenylethanamide
$$= 0.0439 \times 135\,g = 5.93\,g$$

Because only 4.15 g was produced, the percentage yield is

$$\frac{4.15}{5.93} \times 100\% = 70\%$$

Problem • 21

A student had to produce some magnesium sulphate crystals, $MgSO_4.7H_2O$. He reacted 1.20 g of magnesium with a slight excess of sulphuric acid to give magnesium sulphate solution, and then evaporated off about three-quarters of the liquid, before leaving it to crystallise. He separated the crystals from the remaining liquid, dried them and weighed them. 9.84 g of crystals had been produced. Calculate the percentage yield.

Making the solution: $\quad Mg + H_2SO_4 \rightarrow MgSO_4 + H_2$
Crystallising the solution: $\quad MgSO_4 + 7H_2O \rightarrow MgSO_4.7H_2O$

(H = 1; O = 16; Mg = 24; S = 32)

Problem • 22

A teacher demonstrated the formation of silicon tetrachloride, $SiCl_4$, by passing dry chlorine over 1.0 g of heated silicon powder until all the silicon had reacted. She collected the liquid chloride produced and then purified it by distillation. At the end of the preparation she had 3.5 cm³ of silicon tetrachloride. Calculate her percentage yield.

$$Si_{(s)} + 2Cl_{2(g)} \rightarrow SiCl_{4(l)}$$

(Si = 28; Cl = 35.5. Density of $SiCl_{4(l)}$ = 1.48 g cm^{-3})

End of chapter checklist

Can you do the following things?

■ Define relative atomic mass.

■ Use the output from a mass spectrometer to calculate the relative atomic mass of a monatomic element (e.g. Ar or Mg, but not H_2 or Cl_2 or S_8).

■ Calculate relative formula mass and use it to find percentage composition.

■ Define the mole and understand the importance of the Avogadro Number.

■ Convert from moles to mass and vice versa.

■ Calculate empirical and molecular formulae.

■ Perform calculations from equations involving masses.

■ Calculate percentage yields from experimental data.

Revision problems

Numerical answers are provided for these problems, but no worked solutions.

Problem • 23

(a) Define **relative atomic mass.**
(b) Calculate the relative atomic masses of copper and sulphur from the percentage abundances of their isotopes. What is the relative formula mass of copper(II) sulphide, CuS?

^{63}Cu 69.1%; ^{65}Cu 30.9%
^{32}S 95.0%; ^{33}S 0.76%; ^{34}S 4.22%; ^{36}S 0.020%

Problem • 24

Calculate the relative atomic masses of titanium and chlorine from the relative abundances of their isotopes found from a mass spectrometer. What is the relative formula mass of titanium(IV) chloride, TiCl$_4$?

^{46}Ti 10.8; ^{47}Ti 9.89; ^{48}Ti 100; ^{49}Ti 7.45; ^{50}Ti 7.18
^{35}Cl 100; ^{37}Cl 32.5

Problem • 25

Calculate the relative formula masses of the following compounds:

(a) CaCO$_3$
(b) Cr$_2$(SO$_4$)$_3$
(c) (NH$_4$)$_2$SO$_4$.FeSO$_4$.6H$_2$O

(H = 1; N = 14; C = 12; O = 16; S = 32; Ca = 40; Cr = 52; Fe = 56)

Problem • 26

Which of the following substances (all used as nitrogen fertilisers) contains the greatest percentage by mass of nitrogen? What is that percentage?

(a) urea, CO(NH$_2$)$_2$
(b) potassium nitrate, KNO$_3$
(c) ammonium nitrate, NH$_4$NO$_3$
(d) ammonium sulphate, (NH$_4$)$_2$SO$_4$

(H = 1; C = 12; N = 14; O = 16; S = 32; K = 39)

Problem • 27

Work out the mass of:

(a) 1 mole of lead(II) nitrate, Pb(NO$_3$)$_2$
(b) 4.30 moles of methane, CH$_4$
(c) 0.24 moles of sodium carbonate crystals, Na$_2$CO$_3$.10H$_2$O

(H = 1; C = 12; N = 14; O = 16; Na = 23; Pb = 207)

Problem • 28

How many moles are represented by:

(a) 50 g of copper(II) sulphate crystals, CuSO$_4$.5H$_2$O
(b) 1 tonne of iron, Fe (1 tonne is 1000 kg)
(c) 0.032 g of sulphur dioxide, SO$_2$?

(H = 1; O = 16; S = 32; Fe = 56; Cu = 64)

Problem . 29

(a) How many sugar molecules, $C_{12}H_{22}O_{11}$ are there in a 1 kg bag of sugar?
(b) How many carbon atoms are there in a 50 kg sack of coke? (Assume that coke is pure carbon.)
(c) A cylinder of bottled gas contains 47 kg of propane, C_3H_8. How many propane molecules does it contain?

(H = 1; C = 12; O = 16. The Avogadro Constant, $L = 6.0 \times 10^{23}$ mol^{-1}.)

Problem . 30

Assume a beach is made of identical grains of sand – each a cube of side 1 mm. Assume also that these are packed tidily with no wasted space. What volume of sand (measured in cubic metres) would contain the same number of grains as there are molecules in 1 drop (0.05 cm^3) of water? (You might also like to work out how big a beach that would be, making reasonable assumptions about the depth of sand and the distance between low water and the base of the cliffs. The answer is mind blowing!)

(H = 1; O = 16. The Avogadro Constant, $L = 6.0 \times 10^{23}$ mol^{-1}. The density of water is 1 g cm^{-3}.)

Problem . 31

Find the empirical formulae of the following compounds which contained:

(a) 5.85 g K; 2.10 g N; 4.80 g O
(b) 3.22 g Na; 4.48 g S; 3.36 g O
(c) 22.0% C; 4.6% H; 73.4% Br (by mass)

(H = 1; C = 12; N = 14; O = 16; Na = 23; S = 32; K = 39; Br = 80)

Problem . 32

A hydrocarbon contained 82.76% C and 17.24% H by mass. 1 mole of the hydrocarbon weighed 58 g. Find the molecular formula of the hydrocarbon.

Problem . 33

If the mineral pyrite, FeS_2, is heated strongly in air, iron(III) oxide and sulphur dioxide are produced. What mass of

(a) iron(III) oxide, and
(b) sulphur dioxide could be made by heating 1 tonne of an ore which contained 50% by mass of pyrite?

$4FeS_2 + 11O_2 \rightarrow 2Fe_2O_3 + 8SO_2$

(O = 16; S = 32; Fe = 56)

Problem . 34

A student prepared some deep ruby crystals of "chrome alum" by treating a solution of potassium dichromate(VI) in dilute sulphuric acid with an excess of ethanol, and then crystallising the solution formed. What is the maximum mass of chrome alum crystals that could be made from 2.94 g of potassium dichromate(VI)?

$K_2Cr_2O_7 + 4H_2SO_4 + 3CH_3CH_2OH$
potassium dichromate (VI)

$\rightarrow K_2SO_4 + Cr_2(SO_4)_3 + 7H_2O + 3CH_3CHO$

$K_2SO_4 + Cr_2(SO_4)_3 + 24H_2O \rightarrow K_2SO_4.Cr_2(SO_4)_3.24H_2O$
"chrome alum"

(H = 1; O = 16; S = 32; K = 39; Cr = 52)

➤ Don't be put off by these horrible equations. You do not have to work them out! This is a trivial sum – the most difficult thing is adding up the RFM of chrome alum.

Problem • 35

A student was asked to find the relative atomic mass of an element X. Crystals of the chloride of X were known to have the formula $XCl_2.6H_2O$. The student dissolved 2.03 g of the crystals in water, and then added an excess of silver nitrate solution to the solution formed. A white precipitate of silver chloride was formed, which was filtered, dried and weighed. 2.87 g were formed.

$$Ag^+_{(aq)} + Cl^-_{(aq)} \rightarrow AgCl_{(s)}$$

Calculate:

(a) the number of moles of silver chloride formed
(b) the number of moles of X chloride in the solution (you may assume that all the chlorine in X chloride is in solution as $Cl^-_{(aq)}$ ions)
(c) the mass of 1 mole of $XCl_2.6H_2O$
(d) the relative atomic mass of X.

($H = 1$; $O = 16$; $Cl = 35.5$; $Ag = 108$)

Problem • 36

In an experiment to produce a sample of aspirin, 10 g of 2-hydroxybenzoic acid was treated under suitable conditions with 7.5 cm^3 of ethanoyl chloride (an excess). After purification 11 g of aspirin were formed. Calculate the percentage yield.

$$CH_3COCl + HOC_6H_4COOH \rightarrow CH_3COOC_6H_4COOH + HCl$$
$$\text{2-hydroxybenzoic acid} \text{aspirin}$$

($H = 1$; $C = 12$; $O = 16$)

Problem • 37

34.2 g of sucrose (sugar: $C_{12}H_{22}O_{11}$) was dissolved in water, yeast was added, and the mixture was left in a warm place for several days. When bubbling stopped, the mixture was carefully distilled to collect the ethanol (alcohol: CH_3CH_2OH) formed. 18.7 cm^3 of ethanol was collected. Assuming the ethanol was collected pure (untrue, but it makes the calculation easier!), calculate the percentage yield.

$$C_{12}H_{22}O_{11} + H_2O \rightarrow 4CH_3CH_2OH + 4CO_2$$

($H = 1$; $C = 12$; $O = 16$. Density of ethanol $= 0.789$ g cm^{-3}.)

Basic Calculations Involving Gases

This chapter builds on Chapters 1 and 2, but needs no greater knowledge of chemistry or skill at maths.

Avogadro's Law

In Chapter 2 we were looking at calculations involving the masses of substances taking part in reactions, but with gases it is often more convenient to measure the volume rather than the mass. Avogadro's Law underpins gas volume calculations.

> *Equal volumes of gases at the same temperature and pressure contain equal numbers of molecules.*

This means that if you have $100 \, cm^3$ of hydrogen at some temperature and pressure it contains exactly the same number of molecules as there are in $100 \, cm^3$ of carbon dioxide or any other gas under those conditions – irrespective of the size of the molecules.

A note on units of volume

Volumes (of gases or liquids) are measured in:

■ cubic centimetres (cm^3)

■ cubic decimetres (dm^3)

■ litres (L)

> *1 litre = 1 dm^3 = 1000 cm^3*

If you want to talk about $1000 \, cm^3$, the cubic decimetre is the preferred unit rather than the litre, but it doesn't actually matter.

Example 1

Methane (natural gas) burns in air according to the equation:

$$CH_{4(g)} + 2O_{2(g)} \rightarrow CO_{2(g)} + 2H_2O_{(l)}$$

The equation says that you need twice as many molecules of oxygen as you do of methane. According to Avogadro's Law, this means that you will need twice the volume of oxygen as the volume of methane.

So, if you have to burn 1 litre ($1 \, dm^3$) of methane, you will need 2 litres ($2 \, dm^3$) of oxygen.

Similarly, for every molecule of methane you burn, you will get a molecule of carbon dioxide formed. Therefore every litre of methane will give 1 litre of carbon dioxide, because 1 litre of methane and 1 litre of CO_2 contain the same number of molecules.

Care!

Avogadro's Law only applies to gases. If the water is formed as a liquid, you can say nothing whatsoever about the volume of water produced. However, if it is formed as steam, then you could say that every litre of methane will produce 2 litres of steam.

> **Avogadro's Law allows equations involving gases to be interpreted directly in terms of volumes.**

Example 2

Carbon monoxide burns in oxygen to give carbon dioxide:

$$2CO_{(g)} + O_{2(g)} \rightarrow 2CO_{2(g)}$$

If you burned 1 litre of carbon monoxide, you would only need half of that volume of oxygen (0.5 litres) because you only need half as many molecules.

Because the number of molecules of carbon dioxide produced is the same as the number of molecules of carbon monoxide burnt, the volume of CO_2 produced will be 1 litre.

> ➤ People sometimes worry if the total volume at the end isn't the same as the total volume at the beginning. It is bound to be different if the number of molecules changes. In this case, 2 molecules are formed from 3 original molecules. According to Avogadro's Law they are bound to take up a different volume.

Example 3

What volume of air is needed to burn completely $100\,cm^3$ of propane?

$$C_3H_{8(g)} + 5O_{2(g)} \rightarrow 3CO_{2(g)} + 4H_2O_{(l)}$$

You need 5 times as many molecules of oxygen as you do of propane, and so you need 5 times the volume.

The volume of oxygen needed is therefore $500\,cm^3$.

But take care!

You are asked about the volume of *air*, not of oxygen. Air is only approximately 1/5 oxygen – and so you need 5 times more air than you would need oxygen. The amount of air needed is $2500\,cm^3$

Problem • 1

Hydrogen and oxygen react according to the equation:

$$2H_{2(g)} + O_{2(g)} \rightarrow 2H_2O_{(l)}$$

What volume of air is needed for the complete combustion of $500\,cm^3$ of hydrogen?

Problem • 2

What volume of carbon dioxide is produced by the complete combustion of $1\,dm^3$ of butane, C_4H_{10}?

$$2C_4H_{10(g)} + 13O_{2(g)} \rightarrow 8CO_{2(g)} + 10H_2O_{(l)}$$

Using Avogadro's Law to work out equations and unknown formulae

Suppose you had an unknown hydrocarbon, C_xH_y, whose formula you wanted to find. One way of doing it is to burn the hydrocarbon completely in oxygen, measuring the volumes of everything used and produced. The next two examples show how the results would be processed, but are not concerned with how you would obtain the results. Example 6 shows how this might be done.

Example 4

A simple example

> **Note:** In calculations of this sort, pay attention to the temperature quoted. If it is 100 °C or more, any water produced will be a gas, and so Avogadro's Law applies to it. At room temperature, it will be a liquid, and Avogadro's Law will not apply.

$20\,cm^3$ of an unknown hydrocarbon, C_xH_y, needed $70\,cm^3$ of oxygen for complete combustion. $40\,cm^3$ of CO_2 were produced as well as $60\,cm^3$ of steam. All volumes were measured at 100 °C and the same laboratory pressure. Write the equation for the reaction and so find the formula of the hydrocarbon.

All the volumes are simple multiples of $10\,cm^3$, so let's assume that $10\,cm^3$ contains "n" molecules – and because of Avogadro's Law, this will be true of all of the gases in the reaction. It follows that $2n$ molecules of C_xH_y react with $7n$ molecules of oxygen to give $4n$ molecules of CO_2 and $6n$ molecules of water as steam:

$$2nC_xH_y + 7nO_2 \rightarrow 4nCO_2 + 6nH_2O$$

You can divide the whole equation by "n" to simplify it to:

> With experience, most people would miss out the stage involving the "n"s and jump straight to the second version of the equation just by looking at the ratios of the volumes, i.e. 2:7:4:6.

$$2C_xH_y + 7O_2 \rightarrow 4CO_2 + 6H_2O$$

Now you take advantage of the fact that you have a balanced equation to find x and y.

Look at the balancing of the carbons: $2x = 4$ $x = 2$
and now the hydrogens: $2y = 12$ $y = 6$

The hydrocarbon is C_2H_6 (ethane).

Example 5

Making it slightly more awkward

You can solve this problem with one less bit of information. You don't actually need the volume of the steam produced – which means that you could equally find a solution if the volumes were quoted at room temperature, where the water would be liquid.

$10\,cm^3$ of an unknown hydrocarbon, C_xH_y, required $30\,cm^3$ of oxygen for complete combustion. $20\,cm^3$ of CO_2 was formed. (All volumes were measured at room temperature and pressure.) Write the equation for the reaction and so find the formula of the hydrocarbon.

> We are using the normal short cut here. If you aren't happy about it, work it through in the same way as example 4, taking "n" molecules to be in $10\,cm^3$. You should end up with the same equation after cancelling the "n"s.

Equal volumes of gases contain equal numbers of molecules at the same temperature and pressure. You therefore use 3 times as many molecules of oxygen as there are of hydrocarbon, and produce twice as many molecules of CO_2 as you had molecules of hydrocarbon. You can't say anything at all about the water that is formed.

$$C_xH_y + 3O_2 \rightarrow 2CO_2 + \text{some } H_2O$$

It is easy to find x from the balanced equation: $x = 2$

You have to find the number of hydrogens in a roundabout way via the oxygens. There are 6 oxygens on the left, and so there must be a total of 6 on the right. 4 of those are in the $2CO_2$, leaving 2 to be accounted for in water. There must therefore be $2H_2O$. The equation now reads:

$$C_xH_y + 3O_2 \rightarrow 2CO_2 + 2H_2O$$

Now you can easily count the hydrogens: $y = 4$

The hydrocarbon is C_2H_4 (ethene).

Example 6

> **Exposing the products to sodium hydroxide:** CO_2 is an acidic gas which reacts with sodium hydroxide (an alkali). The drop in volume at this stage is due solely to the carbon dioxide being removed.

This example shows how these results might be produced

$20\,cm^3$ of an unknown hydrocarbon, C_xH_y, was mixed with $80\,cm^3$ of oxygen (an excess) in a graduated tube. A spark was passed through the mixture, and the resulting gases were allowed to cool back to room temperature. $60\,cm^3$ of gas was left. When this gas was exposed to sodium hydroxide solution, the volume fell to $40\,cm^3$. (See side note.) Write the equation for the combustion, and so find the formula of the hydrocarbon.

You need to pick out the information that you were given in the last problem. Why is there $40\,cm^3$ left over at the end of the sequence? There won't be any hydrocarbon left, the CO_2 has reacted with the sodium hydroxide solution, and any water will have condensed to just a drop or so of liquid. The remaining gas is the excess oxygen.

$20\,cm^3$ of hydrocarbon was used.

> **Hint:** You started with $80\,cm^3$ of oxygen, but had $40\,cm^3$ left over.
>
> The volume fell by $20\,cm^3$ when the gases were exposed to sodium hydroxide solution.

$40\,cm^3$ of oxygen must have been used up in the combustion process.

$20\,cm^3$ of CO_2 was formed.

This time the ratio of volumes (and so of molecules) is

$$1C_xH_y : 2O_2 : 1CO_2$$
$$C_xH_y + 2O_2 \rightarrow CO_2 + \text{some } H_2O$$

There must be $2H_2O$ to balance the oxygens, which gives $x = 1$ and $y = 4$. The hydrocarbon is CH_4 (methane).

Problem . 3

20 cm³ of an unknown hydrocarbon needed 120 cm³ of oxygen for complete combustion. 80 cm³ of CO_2 was produced. All volumes were measured at room temperature and pressure. Find the formula of the hydrocarbon.

Problem . 4

10 cm³ of an unknown hydrocarbon was sparked with 90 cm³ of oxygen (an excess). When the resulting gases were cooled back to the original room temperature, they had a volume of 70 cm³. Exposure of the gases to sodium hydroxide solution reduced the volume to 40 cm³. Find the formula of the hydrocarbon.

The molar volume of a gas

Avogadro's Law says that equal volumes of gases at the same temperature and pressure contain the same number of molecules.

Turning this around: at the same temperature and pressure, equal numbers of molecules of a gas are contained in the same volume.

If you have 1 mole of any gas, it will contain the Avogadro Number of molecules (approximately 6×10^{23} molecules). The number doesn't really matter, but if you have 1 mole of any gas it will contain the same number of molecules and therefore occupy the same volume. This volume is called the **molar volume**.

Another note on units

Densities or **concentrations** are measured in units like grams per cubic centimetre or moles per cubic decimetre. You write these as:

■ $g\,cm^{-3}$

■ $mol\,dm^{-3}$

You should read the minus sign in the unit as "per" – so that $mol\,dm^{-3}$ is read as "moles **per** cubic decimetre".

> $mol\,dm^{-3}$ is the same as writing $\dfrac{mol}{dm^3}$.

Example 7

Calculating the volume of 1 mole of oxygen, O_2

The density of oxygen at 25 °C and 1 atmosphere is $1.33\,g\,dm^{-3}$. This is simply a way of saying that 1.33 g occupies a volume of $1\,dm^3$. (O = 16)

> 1 mol of oxygen, O_2, weighs 32 g.
>
> The volume occupied by 1 mol is therefore $\dfrac{32}{1.33}\,dm^3 = 24.1\,dm^3$

> Hint: You need to find out how many lots of 1.33 g (each of which occupies 1 dm³) there are in 32 g of oxygen (which is the mass of 1 mole).

If you work out the volume occupied by 1 mole of **any gas** at room temperature and pressure (**rtp**) it turns out to be very close to $24\,dm^3$ ($24\,000\,cm^3$). So we can make the following useful generalisation.

> *1 mole of any gas at room temperature and pressure (rtp) occupies a volume of 24 dm³. This is called the molar volume.*

The molar volume varies with temperature and pressure. Another value sometimes quoted for it is $22.4\,dm^3$ at 0 °C and 1 atmosphere pressure.

Simple calculations using the molar volume

In all the examples that follow, we will assume a value of $24\,dm^3$ for the molar volume at room temperature and pressure (rtp).

Example 8

> **Hint:** It may help to insert an extra step:
> 2 g of hydrogen occupies 24 dm^3
> 1 g of hydrogen occupies 12 dm^3
> 0.01 g of hydrogen occupies 0.01 × 12 dm^3 = 0.12 dm^3

Calculating the volume of a given mass of gas

Calculate the volume of 0.01 g of hydrogen at rtp. (H = 1)
1 mol H_2 weighs 2 g and occupies 24 dm^3.

If 2 g of hydrogen occupies 24 dm^3

then 0.01 g of hydrogen occupies $\frac{0.01}{2} \times 24\,dm^3$
$= 0.12\,dm^3$

Example 9

Calculating the mass of a given volume of gas

Calculate the mass of 100 cm^3 of CO_2 at rtp. (C = 12; O = 16)
24 dm^3 (24 000 cm^3) of CO_2 at rtp weighs 44 g (1 mol)

> **Hint**: Work out the mass of 1 cm^3 (by dividing by 24 000) and then multiply by 100.

100 cm^3 of CO_2 weighs $\frac{100}{24\,000} \times 44\,g$
$= 0.183\,g$

Problem • 5

Take the molar volume to be 24.0 dm^3 at rtp.

(a) Calculate the mass of 200 cm^3 of chlorine gas (Cl_2) at rtp.
(b) Calculate the density of argon (Ar) at rtp.
(c) Calculate the volume occupied by 0.16 g of oxygen (O_2) at rtp.
(d) If a gas has a density of 1.42 $g\,dm^{-3}$ at rtp, calculate the mass of 1 mole of the gas.

(O = 16; Cl = 35.5; Ar = 40)

Problem • 6

Calculate the volume occupied by 1 mole of nitrogen (N_2) at 0 °C and 1 atmosphere pressure if its density under those conditions is 1.25 $g\,dm^{-3}$. (N = 14)

Calculations from equations involving gases

Example 10

Calculate the volume of carbon dioxide evolved at room temperature and pressure when an excess of dilute hydrochloric acid is added to 1.00 g of calcium carbonate:

> The commonest mistake in a sum of this kind is to work out the mass of 1 mole of CO_2. Once you have that figure of 44 g, you feel you have to do something with it and will probably work out the mass of CO_2 produced instead of the volume.
> There are two things you can do to stop yourself making this sort of mistake. Read the question carefully, and notice that it asks you for the *volume* of CO_2 produced. Realise that you are given a value for the *molar volume*. If the examiner gives you this, then you must use it somewhere. If you get to the end of the question without using it, you've done it wrong!

$$CaCO_3 + 2HCl \rightarrow CaCl_2 + CO_2 + H_2O$$

(C = 12; O = 16; Ca = 40. Molar volume = 24 dm^3 at rtp.)

Interpret the equation in terms of moles:

1 mol $CaCO_3$ gives 1 mol CO_2

Substitute masses and volumes where appropriate:

100 g $CaCO_3$ (1 mol) gives 24 dm^3 CO_2 at rtp

Do the simple proportion sum:

If 100 g $CaCO_3$ (1 mol) gives 24 dm^3 CO_2 at rtp
then 1 g $CaCO_3$ gives 1/100 × 24 dm^3
$= 0.24\,dm^3$

Example 11

A student carried out an experiment in which she had to produce some hydrogen from the reaction between aluminium and excess dilute hydrochloric acid. In order to measure the volume evolved at room temperature and pressure, she collected the hydrogen in a $100\,cm^3$ gas syringe. What is the maximum mass of aluminium she could have used so that she did not exceed the $100\,cm^3$ capacity of the gas syringe?

$$2Al + 6HCl \rightarrow 2AlCl_3 + 3H_2$$

(Al = 27. Molar volume = $24\,000\,cm^3$ at rtp)

Interpret the equation in terms of moles:

2 mol Al gives 3 mol H_2

Substitute masses and volumes where appropriate:

$2 \times 27\,g$ Al gives $3 \times 24\,000\,cm^3$ H_2
54 g Al gives $72\,000\,cm^3$ H_2

Do the simple proportion sum:

(You need to work out how much aluminium would give $100\,cm^3$ of hydrogen – the maximum allowable.)

If $72\,000\,cm^3$ H_2 comes from 54 g Al

then $100\,cm^3$ H_2 comes from $54 \times \dfrac{100}{72\,000}$ g Al = 0.075 g Al

> **Maths a bit weak?** Use the extra step:
>
> $72\,000\,cm^3$ H_2 comes from 54 g of Al
>
> $1\,cm^3$ H_2 comes from $\dfrac{54}{72\,000}$ g of Al
>
> $100\,cm^3$ H_2 comes from
>
> $\dfrac{54}{72\,000} \times 100$ g = 0.075 g of Al

Problem • 7

Take the molar volume of a gas to be $24\,dm^3$ at room temperature and pressure.

Chlorine can be prepared by heating manganese(IV) oxide with an excess of concentrated hydrochloric acid. What is the maximum volume of chlorine (measured at room temperature and pressure) that could be obtained from 2.00 g of manganese(IV) oxide?

$$MnO_2 + 4HCl \rightarrow MnCl_2 + Cl_2 + 2H_2O$$

(O = 16; Mn = 55)

Problem • 8

What mass of potassium nitrate would you have to heat in order to produce $1.00\,dm^3$ of oxygen at rtp?

$$2KNO_3 \rightarrow 2KNO_2 + O_2$$

(N = 14; O = 16; K = 39)

The ideal gas equation

> **Note!** Check your syllabus. Not all examination boards require you to know about this.

The molar volume lets you convert from volumes of gases to numbers of moles (and vice versa) at a particular temperature and pressure. The ideal gas equation lets you do this at any temperature and pressure (see Figure 3.1).

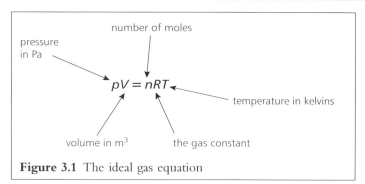

> ➤ **Ideal gases** are those which obey the ideal gas equation. There is no such thing as an ideal gas, but real gases obey the equation reasonably well at ordinary pressures and temperatures. Higher temperatures and lower pressures make gases more ideal. For an explanation of this, see a standard text book.

Figure 3.1 The ideal gas equation

Notes on the various terms in the equation

Pressure

This is measured in pascals (Pa). An alternative name for the pascal is "newton per square metre" ($N\,m^{-2}$). Examiners sometimes give the pressure in kPa (kilopascals). If this happens, you must remember to multiply by 1000 to convert it into pascals. For example, you would have to put 100 kPa into the equation as 100 000 Pa.

Volume

This is the most confusing part. The volume has to be in cubic metres – not cm^3 or dm^3. If the volume is given in the wrong units, you must convert it.

$$1\,m^3 = 1000\,dm^3 = 1\,000\,000\,cm^3$$

To convert from:

    dm^3 to m^3 divide by 1000 (that is the same as multiplying by 10^{-3})
    cm^3 to m^3 divide by 1 000 000 (or multiply by 10^{-6})

Examples: $2\,dm^3$ is the same as $2 \times 10^{-3}\,m^3$.
                 $25\,cm^3$ is the same as $25 \times 10^{-6}\,m^3$.

> ➤ **Hint:** You can usually tell that you've forgotten one of these conversions if you end up with a very silly answer – wrong by a factor of a thousand or a million.

Temperature

This has to be in kelvins. To convert from °C to kelvins, add 273.

Examples: $100\,°C = 373\,K$
           $25\,°C = 298\,K$

The gas constant

> ➤ The **units** are sometimes expressed in the order $J\,mol^{-1}\,K^{-1}$. Don't worry about this. As long as these three units are attached to the number, you are talking about the same constant.

A value for this will always be given in an exam. To 3 significant figures its value is $8.31\,J\,K^{-1}\,mol^{-1}$. Data books give other values for this as well, but in different units (e.g. $cm^3\,atm\,K^{-1}\,mol^{-1}$). These other values apply if you use units like atmospheres for pressure or cm^3 for volumes. You can ignore them.

Number of moles

Remember that:

$$\text{Number of moles} = \frac{\text{mass (g)}}{\text{mass of 1 mole (g)}}$$

It is often convenient to merge this equation into the ideal gas equation, giving:

$$pV = \frac{\textbf{mass (g)}}{\textbf{mass of 1 mole (g)}} \times \textbf{RT}$$

➤ It is **essential** for you to be able to work out this version of the ideal gas equation. Almost every sum that you do will involve you having to convert $pV = nRT$ into this form before you do anything else.

Example 12

Find the volume occupied by 2.20 g of carbon dioxide, CO_2, at 298 K and a pressure of 100 kPa. (C = 12, O = 16. $R = 8.31\,J\,K^{-1}\,mol^{-1}$)

It helps to rearrange the ideal gas equation before you start:

$$pV = nRT$$

$$pV = \frac{\text{mass (g)}}{\text{mass of 1 mole (g)}} \times RT$$

$$V = \frac{\text{mass (g)}}{\text{mass of 1 mole (g)}} \times \frac{RT}{p}$$

➤ If you are happier putting the numbers in first, and then rearranging to find V, do it that way i.e.

$$100\,000 \times V = \frac{2.20}{44} \times 8.31 \times 298$$

etc.

It doesn't matter how you handle the equation as long as you get the right answer. If you want to use a different method, do so – just check that your answer is the same at the end.

Now substitute in the numbers. Remember to check the units. Everything is OK except for the pressure. This has to be entered as 100 000 Pa. The mass of 1 mole of CO_2 is 44 g.

$$V = \frac{\text{mass (g)}}{\text{mass of 1 mole (g)}} \times \frac{RT}{p}$$

$$= \frac{2.20}{44} \times \frac{8.31 \times 298}{100\,000}$$

$$= 1.24 \times 10^{-3}\,m^3$$

You could convert this into dm^3 by multiplying by 1000 if you wanted to. There's probably no point.

Example 13

What pressure is exerted by 1.60 g of oxygen, O_2, in a volume of $2.00\,dm^3$ at a temperature of 80 °C? (O = 16. $R = 8.31\,J\,K^{-1}\,mol^{-1}$)

Again, rearrange the ideal gas equation:

$$pV = nRT$$

$$pV = \frac{\text{mass (g)}}{\text{mass of 1 mole (g)}} \times RT$$

$$p = \frac{\text{mass (g)}}{\text{mass of 1 mole (g)}} \times \frac{RT}{V}$$

➤ See the previous side note if you aren't comfortable with this.

Now put the numbers in, checking the units as you go. The volume is in the wrong units, and so is the temperature. $V = 2.00 \times 10^{-3}\,m^3$ and $T = 353\,K$. 1 mole of oxygen, O_2, weighs 32 g.

$$p = \frac{mass\ (g)}{mass\ of\ 1\ mole\ (g)} \times \frac{RT}{V}$$

$$= \frac{1.60}{32} \times \frac{8.31 \times 353}{2.00 \times 10^{-3}}\ Pa$$

$$= 73\,300\ Pa$$

Example 14

This is an example of one of the most important uses of the ideal gas equation – which is finding the relative formula masses of gases. Remember that the mass of 1 mole of something is simply the relative formula mass expressed in grams. In the equations we've been using, the "mass of 1 mole (g)" is numerically the same as the relative formula mass.

$56.0\,cm^3$ of an unknown gas X, measured at a temperature of $90\,°C$ and a pressure of 101 kPa, was found to weigh 0.135 g. Find the relative formula mass of the gas. $(R = 8.31\,J\,K^{-1}\,mol^{-1})$

Rearrange the ideal gas equation to find the mass of 1 mole:

$$pV = nRT$$

$$pV = \frac{mass\ (g)}{mass\ of\ 1\ mole\ (g)} \times RT$$

$$Mass\ of\ 1\ mole\ (g) = mass\ (g) \times \frac{RT}{pV}$$

➤ Once again, if you aren't comfortable with this approach to rearranging the equation, see the side note for example 12.

Again, slot the numbers in, checking the units as you go. This time everything needs to be corrected except the mass! Make sure that you understand the reasons for the numbers in the next equation.

$$Mass\ of\ 1\ mole\ (g) = mass\ (g) \times \frac{RT}{pV}$$

$$= 0.135 \times \frac{8.31 \times 363}{101\,000 \times 56 \times 10^{-6}}\ g$$

$$= 72.0\,g$$

The relative formula mass is therefore 72.0.

$R = 8.31\,J\,K^{-1}\,mol^{-1}$

Problem • 9

Find the volume occupied by 0.100 g of hydrogen, H_2, at 293 K and a pressure of 100 kPa. (H = 1)

Problem • 10

Find the mass of $200\,cm^3$ of carbon monoxide, CO, at $17\,°C$ and a pressure of 98 900 Pa. (C = 12; O = 16)

Problem • 11

1.25 g of an unknown gas occupied $923\,cm^3$ at a pressure of 102 kPa and a temperature of 290 K. Find the relative formula mass of the gas.

End of chapter checklist

Can you do the following things?

■ State and use Avogadro's Law.

■ Understand and use the concept of the molar volume, including calculations from equations involving working out volumes of gases produced.

■ State and use the ideal gas equation (if required by your syllabus).

Revision problems

Numerical answers are provided for these problems, but no worked solutions.

Problem • 12

Ethane burns in oxygen according to the equation:

$$2C_2H_6 + 7O_2 \rightarrow 4CO_2 + 6H_2O$$

(a) What volume of oxygen would be required to burn $1\,dm^3$ of ethane?
(b) What volume of carbon dioxide would be produced?

Problem • 13

During the manufacture of nitric acid from ammonia, ammonia gas is oxidised by passing it with air over a red-hot platinum–rhodium catalyst:

$$4NH_3 + 5O_2 \rightarrow 4NO + 6H_2O$$

(a) What volume of air is required by $1.00\,m^3$ of ammonia? (Take air to be 20% oxygen and 80% nitrogen.)
(b) Assuming the reaction is complete, what volumes of what gases will be present in the mixture leaving the catalyst for an input of $1.00\,m^3$ of ammonia? (Assume the gas volumes are all measured at the temperature of the catalyst.)

Problem • 14

$20\,cm^3$ of a hydrocarbon needed $90\,cm^3$ of oxygen for complete combustion. $60\,cm^3$ of CO_2 was produced. All volumes were measured at room temperature and pressure. Find the formula of the hydrocarbon.

Problem • 15

$10\,cm^3$ of an unknown hydrocarbon was sparked with $100\,cm^3$ of oxygen (an excess). When the resulting gases were cooled back to the original room temperature, they had a volume of $75\,cm^3$. Exposure of the gases to sodium hydroxide solution reduced the volume to $35\,cm^3$. Find the formula of the hydrocarbon.

Problem • 16

(a) Calculate the density of carbon dioxide, CO_2, at rtp.
(b) Calculate the volume occupied by $0.100\,g$ of hydrogen chloride, HCl, at rtp.
(c) Calculate the mass of $137\,cm^3$ of nitrogen, N_2, at rtp.
(d) If $1.00\,g$ of a gas occupies $375\,cm^3$ at rtp, calculate the mass of 1 mole of the gas.
(e) A gas has a density of $2.96\,g\,dm^{-3}$ at rtp. Calculate the mass of 1 mole of the gas.

(H = 1; C = 12; N = 14; O = 16; Cl = 35.5; molar volume of a gas = $24.0\,dm^3$ at rtp)

Problem • 17

Calculate the volume of hydrogen (measured at room temperature and pressure) obtainable by reacting 0.240 g of magnesium with an excess of dilute sulphuric acid.

$$Mg + H_2SO_4 \rightarrow MgSO_4 + H_2$$

(Mg = 24; molar volume of a gas = $24\,000\,cm^3$ at rtp)

Problem • 18

Sulphur dioxide can be removed from flue gases by reacting it with calcium carbonate (limestone). If a flue gas contains 1.00% sulphur dioxide by volume, what mass of calcium carbonate is needed to remove the sulphur dioxide from $1000\,m^3$ of the flue gas?

$$CaCO_3 + SO_2 \rightarrow CaSO_3 + CO_2$$

(C = 12; O = 16; Ca = 40. Assume that the gas volumes are measured at room temperature and pressure, and that the molar volume under these conditions is $24.0\,dm^3$. $1\,m^3 = 1000\,dm^3$)

Problem • 19

2.76 g of a carbonate, X_2CO_3, was treated with an excess of dilute hydrochloric acid, and the carbon dioxide evolved was collected and measured. $480\,cm^3$ was produced at room temperature and pressure.

$$X_2CO_3 + 2HCl \rightarrow 2XCl + CO_2 + H_2O$$

Calculate (a) the number of moles of X_2CO_3 in the experiment, (b) the mass of 1 mole of X_2CO_3, and (c) the relative atomic mass of X.

(C = 12; O = 16. The molar volume at rtp = $24\,000\,cm^3$)

Problem • 20

These questions involve the ideal gas equation. $R = 8.31\,J\,K^{-1}\,mol^{-1}$.

(a) Calculate the mass of $130\,cm^3$ of fluorine, F_2, at 21 °C and 101 kPa.
(b) 5.00 g of water (about a teaspoonful) was vaporised at 100°C and a pressure of 100 kPa. What volume of steam was produced at this temperature and pressure?
(c) What pressure will be exerted by 1.25 g of carbon dioxide, CO_2, contained in a volume of $500\,cm^3$ at a temperature of 298 K?
(d) At what temperature will 1.00 g of chlorine, Cl_2, in a container of volume $1.00\,dm^3$ exert a pressure of 100 kPa?
(e) 0.230 g of a volatile liquid was vaporised at a temperature of 363 K and a pressure of 101 000 Pa. The volume of vapour measured under these conditions was $149\,cm^3$. Calculate the relative formula mass of the liquid.

(H = 1; C = 12; O = 16; F = 19; Cl = 35.5)

Problem • 21

(a) Calculate the number of moles of gas molecules in a laboratory of volume $969\,m^3$ (not including the volume taken up by benches, etc.) at a temperature of 290 K and a pressure of 99.5 kPa.
(b) Assuming that air contains 0.93% by volume of argon, calculate the number of moles of argon in the lab, and hence the number of argon molecules in the lab.

($R = 8.31\,J\,K^{-1}\,mol^{-1}$. The Avogadro Constant, $L = 6.02 \times 10^{23}\,mol^{-1}$)

Problem • 22

A sample of ammonia was made by heating 1.07 g of ammonium chloride with an excess of calcium hydroxide. What volume of ammonia gas would be produced if it was collected at a temperature of 292 K and a pressure of 1.02×10^5 Pa?

$$2NH_4Cl + Ca(OH)_2 \rightarrow CaCl_2 + 2H_2O + 2NH_3$$

(H = 1; N = 14; Cl = 35.5. The gas constant, $R = 8.31\,J\,K^{-1}\,mol^{-1}$.)

Problem • 23

Limestone is impure calcium carbonate. Excess hydrochloric acid was added to 1.50 g of crushed limestone, and the carbon dioxide evolved was collected. 330 cm^3 of carbon dioxide was collected at a temperature of 295 K and a pressure of 1.01×10^5 Pa. Assume that no carbon dioxide was lost by solution in the hydrochloric acid.

$$CaCO_3 + 2HCl \rightarrow CaCl_2 + CO_2 + H_2O$$

Calculate:

(a) the number of moles of carbon dioxide formed
(b) the mass of calcium carbonate in the limestone
(c) the percentage of calcium carbonate in the limestone.

(C = 12; O = 16; Ca = 40. The gas constant, $R = 8.31\,J\,K^{-1}\,mol^{-1}$.)

Problem • 24

An element X formed a chloride XCl_n, which was gaseous at room temperature. The mass spectrum of X showed two isotopes, ^{10}X 18.7% and ^{11}X 81.3%. 0.735 g of XCl_n occupied a volume of 151 cm^3 at 17°C and 100 kPa.

(a) Use the mass spectrum to calculate the relative atomic mass of X.
(b) Calculate the mass of 1 mole of XCl_n. The molar volume = 24.1 dm^3 at this temperature and pressure, and $R = 8.31\,J\,K^{-1}\,mol^{-1}$. You may use either piece of information.
(c) Hence calculate n in XCl_n. (Cl = 35.5)

4 Basic Calculations Involving Solutions

In the two previous chapters we have looked at calculations from equations involving masses of solids and volumes of gases. Many reactions are done in solution, and this chapter looks at how you handle problems involving concentrations of solutions. The level of chemistry and maths required is no greater than anything you have already come across.

How to work with solution concentrations

Concentrations of solutions

Two different units for concentration

Concentrations can be measured in:

- $g\,dm^{-3}$
- $mol\,dm^{-3}$

and you have to be able to convert between them. This isn't hard! You have already practised converting moles into grams and vice versa. When you are doing the conversions in concentration sums, the only thing that is different is that the amount of substance you are talking about happens to be dissolved in $1\,dm^3$ of solution. This does not affect the sum in any way.

> The concentration of a solution in $mol\,dm^{-3}$ is sometimes called the **molarity** of the solution, and given the symbol M.
>
> For example, a solution of HCl with a concentration of $2\,mol\,dm^{-3}$ is described as 2 M HCl. You would read this as ''2 molar HCl''.
>
> A solution of NaOH with a concentration of $0.1\,mol\,dm^{-3}$ is described as 0.1 M NaOH. You would read this as ''0.1 molar NaOH''.

Example 1

A solution of sodium hydroxide, NaOH, had a concentration of $4\,g\,dm^{-3}$. What is its concentration in $mol\,dm^{-3}$? (H = 1; O = 16; Na = 23)

    1 mol NaOH weighs 40 g

    4 g is 4/40 mol = 0.1 mol

    $4\,g\,dm^{-3}$ is therefore $0.1\,mol\,dm^{-3}$

> The term molarity is dropping out of use. It saves a bit of writing in describing the concentration of a solution (M is quicker to write than $mol\,dm^{-3}$), but it obscures what you are talking about. Be aware of it, but avoid using it yourself! If you see ''M'' in a book or a question, read it as ''$mol\,dm^{-3}$''.

Example 2

What is the concentration of a $0.0500\,mol\,dm^{-3}$ solution of sodium carbonate, Na_2CO_3, in $g\,dm^{-3}$? (C = 12; O = 16; Na = 23)

    1 mol Na_2CO_3 weighs 106 g

    0.0500 mol weighs $0.0500 \times 106\,g = 5.30\,g$

    $0.0500\,mol\,dm^{-3}$ is therefore $5.30\,g\,dm^{-3}$.

> **Remember:**
> Number of moles
> $$= \frac{mass(g)}{mass\ of\ 1\ mole(g)}$$

55

Example 3

What is the concentration in $mol\,dm^{-3}$ of a solution containing 2.10 g of sodium hydrogencarbonate, $NaHCO_3$, in $250\,cm^3$ of solution? (This is about as hard as you can make it!) (H = 1; C = 12; O = 16; Na = 23)

$250\,cm^3$ is 1/4 of $1000\,cm^3$ (1 dm^3)

Therefore a solution containing 2.10 g in $250\,cm^3$ has the same concentration as one containing 4×2.10 g in $1000\,cm^3$.

4×2.10 g is 8.40 g

1 mol $NaHCO_3$ weighs 84 g

8.40 g is $8.40/84\,mol = 0.100\,mol$

The concentration is therefore $0.100\,mol\,dm^{-3}$.

(H = 1; C = 12; O = 16; Na = 23; S = 32; K = 39)

Problem • 1

Some dilute sulphuric acid, H_2SO_4, had a concentration of $4.90\,g\,dm^{-3}$. What is its concentration in $mol\,dm^{-3}$?

Problem • 2

What is the concentration in $g\,dm^{-3}$ of some potassium hydroxide, KOH, solution with a concentration of $0.200\,mol\,dm^{-3}$?

Problem • 3

What mass of sodium carbonate, Na_2CO_3, would be dissolved in $100\,cm^3$ of solution in order to get a concentration of $0.100\,mol\,dm^{-3}$?

Basic calculations from equations involving solutions

Example 4

What mass of barium sulphate would be produced by adding excess barium chloride solution to $20.0\,cm^3$ of copper(II) sulphate solution of concentration $0.100\,mol\,dm^{-3}$? (O = 16; S = 32; Ba = 137)

$$BaCl_{2(aq)} + CuSO_{4(aq)} \rightarrow BaSO_{4(s)} + CuCl_{2(aq)}$$

1 mol $CuSO_4$ gives 1 mol $BaSO_4$

Up to now, questions of this sort would have started with some mass of copper(II) sulphate. You would also have been given the relative atomic mass of copper so that you could work out the mass of 1 mole of $CuSO_4$.

This time you are given the volume of copper(II) sulphate solution and its concentration. What you can do with that is work out the number of moles of copper(II) sulphate you are starting with:

$$\text{Number of moles of } CuSO_4 = \frac{20.0}{1000} \times 0.100$$

$$= 0.002\,00\,mol$$

➤ If the answer appears on your calculator as 2.00×10^{-3}, there is no reason why you can't quote it in that form. Either notation is perfectly valid.

It is *essential* that you can see the logic of this step, because it underpins everything else we shall do in this section. Let's explore the logic.

A concentration of $0.100 \, mol \, dm^{-3}$ means that every $1 \, dm^3$ ($1000 \, cm^3$) contains $0.100 \, mol$. How you get to the result from here depends on how comfortable you are with numbers.

If you are at ease with numbers:

$$20.0 \, cm^3 \text{ is } \frac{20.0}{1000} \text{ of } 1000 \, cm^3$$

Therefore the number of moles in $20.0 \, cm^3$ is $\dfrac{20.0}{1000} \times 0.100$

If you do not find numbers so easy:

$1000 \, cm^3$ contains $0.100 \, mol$

$1 \, cm^3$ contains $\dfrac{0.100}{1000} \, mol$

$20.0 \, cm^3$ contains $20.0 \times \dfrac{0.100}{1000} \, mol$

Although this expression looks different, it is actually exactly the same as the first one. Both work out to be $0.002 \, 00 \, mol$.

Back to the question again!

$$BaCl_{2(aq)} + CuSO_{4(aq)} \rightarrow BaSO_{4(s)} + CuCl_{2(aq)}$$

$$\text{Number of moles of } CuSO_4 = \frac{20.0}{1000} \times 0.100$$

$$= 0.002 \, 00 \, mol$$

1 mol $CuSO_4$ gives 1 mol $BaSO_4$

$0.002 \, 00$ mol $CuSO_4$ gives $0.002 \, 00$ mol $BaSO_4$ (RFM = 233)

$$= 0.002 \, 00 \times 233 \, g$$

$$= 0.466 \, g$$

> If you need to use more steps to get the answer, use them. Do it your own way. As long as you get the same answer, it doesn't matter. The same thing applies to **all** the questions which follow.

Example 5

What is the maximum mass of calcium carbonate which will react with $25.0 \, cm^3$ of $2.00 \, mol \, dm^{-3}$ hydrochloric acid? (C = 12; O = 16; Ca = 40)

$$CaCO_3 + 2HCl \rightarrow CaCl_2 + H_2O + CO_2$$

$$\text{Number of moles of } HCl = \frac{25.0}{1000} \times 2.00$$

$$= 0.0500 \, mol$$

1 mol $CaCO_3$ reacts with 2 mol HCl

> In all examples of this kind, where you are given the volume and concentration of a solution, start by working out how many moles of that substance you have got. It is almost always the best starting place.

Therefore you only use half as many moles of $CaCO_3$ as HCl.

$$\text{Number of moles of } CaCO_3 = \frac{0.0500}{2}$$

$$= 0.0250 \, mol$$

1 mol $CaCO_3$ weighs $100\,g$

$0.0250\,mol$ weighs $0.0250 \times 100\,g = 2.50\,g$

The maximum mass of calcium carbonate which you could react with this amount of hydrochloric acid is therefore $2.50\,g$.

Example 6

> In this and all the following calculations in this chapter, you might wonder why numbers like 0.500 and 0.240 are used instead of the simpler 0.5 and 0.24. Why does the number 0.0100 mol H_2SO_4 appear half way through the sum – rather than just 0.01? Why is the answer 20.0 cm³ rather than simply 20 cm³?

The numbers in the question itself represent the accuracy to which the experiment was done. For example, 0.240 g means that the magnesium was weighed on a 3 decimal place balance. 0.500 mol dm⁻³ sulphuric acid means that the concentration was accurate to 3 significant figures. These numbers define the accuracy with which you can quote your final answer – which in this case should not exceed 3 significant figures.

The answer, 20.0 cm³, reflects the accuracy of the rest of the sum. In an exam, you probably wouldn't lose any marks by quoting this as 20 cm³, but you could lose a mark for quoting an answer to more significant figures than the data in the question allowed. Be careful if you write down numbers in the middle of the sum which are not specifically asked for by the examiners. Do not round these too much. If your final answer is going to be quoted to 3 significant figures, your intermediate numbers should be carried through to **at least** this accuracy to avoid introducing small errors into your final answer.

What is the minimum volume of $0.500\,mol\,dm^{-3}$ sulphuric acid needed to react with $0.240\,g$ of magnesium? ($Mg = 24$)

$$Mg + H_2SO_4 \rightarrow MgSO_4 + H_2$$

1 mol Mg reacts with 1 mol H_2SO_4

24 g Mg reacts with 1 mol H_2SO_4

So $0.240\,g$ Mg reacts with $\dfrac{0.240}{24}$ mol H_2SO_4

$$= 0.0100\,mol\ H_2SO_4$$

The sulphuric acid contains $0.500\,mol$ in every $1\,dm^3$ ($1000\,cm^3$). Where you go from here depends on your feel for numbers.

If you are comfortable with numbers:

You need a fraction $\dfrac{0.0100}{0.500}$ of $1\,dm^3 = 0.0200\,dm^3$ ($20.0\,cm^3$)

So, the volume of sulphuric acid required is $20.0\,cm^3$.

If you are not comfortable with numbers:

Use a formula based on the fact that concentration is measured in $mol\,dm^{-3}$:

$$\textbf{Concentration} = \frac{\textbf{\textit{moles}}}{\textbf{dm}^3}$$

You can rearrange this to give:

$$\text{Volume in dm}^3 = \frac{\text{moles}}{\text{concentration}}$$

If you aren't happy with the rearrangement, learn the triangle of Figure 4.1 and make sure you understand how it relates to the equations above.

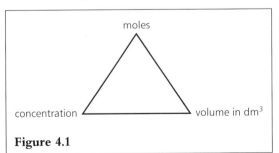

Figure 4.1

Using the formula:

$$\text{Volume in dm}^3 = \frac{\text{moles}}{\text{concentration}}$$

$$= \frac{0.0100}{0.500}$$

$$= 0.0200$$

You can convert this into $20.0\,\text{cm}^3$ if you want to, but it isn't important unless you really need the volume in cm^3.

Problem • 4

A student set out to make some copper(II) oxide from copper(II) sulphate. He took $20.0\,\text{cm}^3$ of $0.400\,\text{mol dm}^{-3}$ copper(II) sulphate solution, added an excess of sodium hydroxide to give a precipitate of copper(II) hydroxide and then boiled the mixture to convert the copper(II) hydroxide into copper(II) oxide. What is the maximum mass of copper(II) oxide that he could obtain?

$$CuSO_4 + 2NaOH \rightarrow Cu(OH)_2 + Na_2SO_4$$
$$Cu(OH)_2 \rightarrow CuO + H_2O$$

$(O = 16; Cu = 64)$

Problem • 5

What volume of hydrochloric acid of concentration $2.00\,\text{mol dm}^{-3}$ would have to be added to $25.0\,\text{cm}^3$ of $0.500\,\text{mol dm}^{-3}$ sodium carbonate solution to give a neutral solution of sodium chloride?

$$Na_2CO_3 + 2HCl \rightarrow 2NaCl + CO_2 + H_2O$$

Deriving equations from experiments

> **Stoichiometry** simply refers to numerical proportions. For example, you could have an equation in which the stoichiometry was 1 mole of A reacting with 2 moles of B to give 2 moles of C. You can also talk about the stoichiometry of a compound. In water, for example, the stoichiometry is 2 atoms of hydrogen to 1 atom of oxygen.

So far we have been looking at how you can calculate reacting amounts from given equations. It is perfectly possible to reverse this and work out equations from experimental data. We talk about "finding the stoichiometry of a reaction".

You might say: "Why bother? Why not just balance the equation?" But this assumes that you know everything about what is reacting and what is formed. At some time all equations have had to be validated by doing experiments.

Example 7

Hydrochloric acid (HCl) was added to sodium carbonate solution (Na_2CO_3) in the presence of the indicator phenolphthalein. Phenolphthalein is bright pink in alkaline solutions and colourless in acids. $25.0\,\text{cm}^3$ of $0.0500\,\text{mol dm}^{-3}$ sodium carbonate solution was placed in a flask with some indicator and $0.100\,\text{mol dm}^{-3}$ hydrochloric acid was added from a burette. The indicator changed colour after $12.5\,\text{cm}^3$ of acid had been added. During the addition there had been no CO_2 evolved.

➤ **Don't worry** if you are daunted at first by the complexity of a problem like this. The trick is simply to find somewhere to start. After that things will usually flow along easily.

In almost all these questions, start by looking for something whose volume and concentration you know – and then work out how many moles of it you've got.

The problem is to find the equation for the reaction.

In this sum, we have enough information to work out the number of moles of both the sodium carbonate and the hydrochloric acid – so let's do it.

$$\text{Number of moles of sodium carbonate} = \frac{25.0}{1000} \times 0.0500$$

$$= 1.25 \times 10^{-3}$$

$$\text{Number of moles of hydrochloric acid} = \frac{12.5}{1000} \times 0.100$$

$$= 1.25 \times 10^{-3}$$

So they react 1:1. The left hand side of the equation must read:

$$Na_2CO_3 + HCl \rightarrow$$

(and you can't change these proportions). You now either have to do more experiments to establish the right hand side, or make reasonable guesses. In this case, no CO_2 was given off, so the carbon must remain as a part of some other compound. It is probable that sodium chloride solution was formed – so if you take out NaCl, what does that leave? It leaves $NaHCO_3$, sodium hydrogencarbonate.

The overall equation might be:

$$Na_2CO_3 + HCl \rightarrow NaHCO_3 + NaCl$$

All you know for certain, though, is the left hand side.

If the reaction had been done in the presence of the indicator methyl orange, twice as much hydrochloric acid would have been needed and this time carbon dioxide would have been given off.

The reacting proportions this time would be $1Na_2CO_3 : 2HCl$

$$Na_2CO_3 + 2HCl \rightarrow$$

and you know that CO_2 appears on the right hand side. Sensible guesswork this time would lead to:

$$Na_2CO_3 + 2HCl \rightarrow 2NaCl + CO_2 + H_2O$$

You could improve this experiment by measuring the volume of CO_2 evolved to find out how many moles of that were produced, and also evaporating the solution to dryness to establish the mass and therefore the number of moles of NaCl.

Example 8

$20.0\,cm^3$ of $0.100\,mol\,dm^{-3}$ lead(II) nitrate solution was mixed with $10.0\,cm^3$ of $0.400\,mol\,dm^{-3}$ potassium iodide solution to give a bright yellow precipitate of lead(II) iodide. The precipitate was filtered, washed, dried, and weighed. 0.922 g of lead(II) iodide had been produced. The remaining solution was tested for lead(II) ions and iodide ions, both of which were absent. Confirm that the equation for the reaction is

$$Pb(NO_3)_{2(aq)} + 2KI_{(aq)} \rightarrow PbI_{2(s)} + 2KNO_{3(aq)}$$

$(I = 127;\ Pb = 207)$

➤ Once again, **don't panic!** Start by working out the number of moles of anything that you know both the volume and concentration of. Worry about the rest of the question as you go along.

The old advice to read and understand the whole question before you start often doesn't work in these sums! It could cause you to give up in complete confusion. Find a familiar point to start with, and then see what happens.

➤ **Hint:** Since you are told the mass of PbI_2 and the RAMs of Pb and I, you are obviously expected to work out the number of moles of it. Look carefully at a question for hints of this sort.

The absence of the lead(II) ions and the iodide ions from the final solution showed that the lead(II) nitrate and potassium iodide had been added in exactly the right proportions.

Work out how many moles of everything there were in the reaction.

$$\text{Number of moles of lead(II) nitrate} = \frac{20.0}{1000} \times 0.100$$
$$= 2.00 \times 10^{-3}$$

$$\text{Number of moles of potassium iodide} = \frac{10.0}{1000} \times 0.400$$
$$= 4.00 \times 10^{-3}$$

1 mole of PbI_2 weighs 461 g

$$0.922 \text{ g is } \frac{0.922}{461} \text{ mol} = 2.00 \times 10^{-3}$$

The reacting proportions are therefore

1 mol $Pb(NO_3)_2$ to 2 mol KI giving 1 mol PbI_2

That is exactly what the equation says. You would have to deduce the potassium nitrate by balancing what you have left over in the equation. There is actually a long-winded calculation you could do to confirm the potassium nitrate if you wanted to. You could calculate the mass of potassium nitrate remaining (and hence the number of moles), on the basis that the total mass of chemicals at the end must be the same as the total mass at the beginning. You would find the masses of lead(II) nitrate and potassium iodide from their numbers of moles. You've probably got better things to do!

Problem • 6

25.0 cm³ of 0.100 mol dm⁻³ sodium hydrogencarbonate solution, $NaHCO_3$, was placed in a flask together with some methyl orange indicator. 0.100 mol dm⁻³ sulphuric acid, H_2SO_4, was run in from a burette until the indicator changed colour. 12.5 cm³ of acid was needed.

In a second experiment, the same quantities of sodium hydrogencarbonate and sulphuric acid were mixed and the carbon dioxide evolved was collected and measured. 60.0 cm³ of gas was collected at room temperature and pressure. The solution from this experiment was evaporated to dryness and the mass of sodium sulphate, Na_2SO_4, produced was found to be 0.178 g.

Determine the equation for this reaction.

(O = 16; Na = 23; S = 32. The molar volume of a gas at rtp is 24 000 cm³)

Titration calculations

Basic titration sums

This work on solutions has been leading up to what is one of the key A level chemistry calculation types – using the known concentration of one solution to find an unknown concentration of a second solution.

A solution whose concentration is known is called a **standard** solution. Finding the concentration of the second solution is called **standardising** it.

Example 9

$25.0 \, \text{cm}^3$ of $0.100 \, \text{mol dm}^{-3}$ NaOH solution required $23.5 \, \text{cm}^3$ of dilute hydrochloric acid for neutralisation. Calculate the concentration of the hydrochloric acid.

$$\text{NaOH} + \text{HCl} \rightarrow \text{NaCl} + \text{H}_2\text{O}$$

The concentration might be required in either mol dm^{-3} or g dm^{-3}.

Before you start, it is often useful to extract the essential information from the question.

$25.0 \, \text{cm}^3$ of $0.100 \, \text{mol dm}^{-3}$ NaOH $\equiv 23.5 \, \text{cm}^3$ of unknown HCl

("$\equiv$" means "is equivalent to".)

What do you know most about?

In titration calculations it is always best to start from what you know most about. In this case, you know everything about the sodium hydroxide – both its volume and its concentration.

How many moles of sodium hydroxide went into the experiment?

The experiment used $25.0 \, \text{cm}^3$ of $0.100 \, \text{mol dm}^{-3}$ NaOH solution.

$0.100 \, \text{mol dm}^{-3}$ means that in every $1 \, \text{dm}^3$ ($1000 \, \text{cm}^3$) there is $0.100 \, \text{mol}$ of sodium hydroxide.

In $25.0 \, \text{cm}^3$, there will be $\dfrac{25.0}{1000} \times 0.100 \, \text{mol NaOH} = 0.00250 \, \text{mol NaOH}$.

> ➤ **If your maths is weak,** put in an extra step. Work out how many moles there are in $1 \, \text{cm}^3$ by dividing by 1000, and then multiply by 25 to find out how many there are in $25 \, \text{cm}^3$.

How many moles of hydrochloric acid will this react with?

$$\text{NaOH} + \text{HCl} \rightarrow \text{NaCl} + \text{H}_2\text{O}$$

1 mol NaOH reacts with 1 mol HCl

Therefore $0.002\,50 \, \text{mol NaOH}$ reacts with $0.002\,50 \, \text{mol HCl}$.

What is the concentration of the HCl in mol dm^{-3}?

Think about what you know at this stage:

■ You know that it needs $0.002\,50 \, \text{mol HCl}$ to neutralise the NaOH.

■ You know that you actually added $23.5 \, \text{cm}^3$ of dilute hydrochloric acid to neutralise the NaOH.

It follows that the $23.5 \, \text{cm}^3$ must contain $0.00250 \, \text{mol HCl}$.

All you now need to do is to find out how many moles there would be in $1000 \, \text{cm}^3$ ($1 \, \text{dm}^3$) of this solution.

> ➤ **If your maths is weak:** again, insert an extra step. Work out the number of moles in $1 \, \text{cm}^3$ by dividing by 23.5, and then multiply by 1000 to find out how many moles there are in $1000 \, \text{cm}^3$.

If $23.5 \, \text{cm}^3$ contain $0.002\,50 \, \text{mol HCl}$

$1000 \, \text{cm}^3$ contain $\dfrac{1000}{23.5} \times 0.002\,50 \, \text{mol HCl} = 0.106 \, \text{mol}$

The concentration is therefore $0.106 \, \text{mol dm}^{-3}$.

What is the concentration of the HCl in g dm^{-3}?

(H = 1; Cl = 35.5)

> 1 mol HCl weighs 36.5 g
>
> Therefore 0.106 mol weighs 0.106×36.5 g = 3.87 g
>
> The concentration is 3.87 g dm^{-3}.

What the sum ends up looking like:

Most of the above never gets written down on paper – you are thinking it out in your head.

$$\text{Number of moles of NaOH} = \frac{25.0}{1000} \times 0.100$$

$$= 0.002\,50 \text{ mol}$$

NaOH + HCl $\rightarrow$ NaCl + H$_2$O

0.002 50 mol NaOH reacts with 0.002 50 mol HCl, which is in 23.5 cm^3

$$\text{Concentration of HCl} = \frac{1000}{23.5} \times 0.002\,50 \text{ mol dm}^{-3}$$

$$= 0.106 \text{ mol dm}^{-3}$$

1 mol HCl weighs 36.5 g

Therefore 0.106 mol weighs 0.106×36.5 g = 3.87 g

The concentration is 3.87 g dm^{-3}.

Example 10

25 cm^3 of sodium hydroxide solution of unknown concentration was titrated with dilute sulphuric acid of concentration 0.050 mol dm^{-3}. 20.0 cm^3 of the acid was required to neutralise the alkali. Find the concentration of the sodium hydroxide solution in mol dm^{-3}.

$$2\text{NaOH} + \text{H}_2\text{SO}_4 \rightarrow \text{Na}_2\text{SO}_4 + 2\text{H}_2\text{O}$$

Extracting the main information in just one line:

> 25 cm^3 of unknown NaOH $\equiv$ 20.0 cm^3 of 0.050 mol dm^{-3} H$_2$SO$_4$

What do you know most about?

In this case, you know everything about the sulphuric acid.

How many moles of sulphuric acid went into the experiment?

The experiment used 20.0 cm^3 of 0.050 mol dm^{-3} H$_2$SO$_4$.

$$\text{Moles of sulphuric acid used} = \frac{20.0}{1000} \times 0.050$$

$$= 0.0010 \text{ mol}$$

How many moles of sodium hydroxide will this react with?

The equation says that each mole of sulphuric acid reacts with 2 moles of sodium hydroxide.

$$\text{Moles of sodium hydroxide} = 2 \times 0.0010$$
$$= 0.0020$$

What is the concentration of the NaOH in $mol\,dm^{-3}$?

There is 0.0020 mol in $25\,cm^3$.

$$\text{Concentration} = \frac{1000}{25} \times 0.0020\,mol\,dm^{-3}$$
$$= 0.080\,mol\,dm^{-3}$$

Example 11 $25.0\,cm^3$ of $0.100\,mol\,dm^{-3}$ sodium hydrogencarbonate solution was titrated with dilute sulphuric acid of unknown concentration. $17.6\,cm^3$ of the acid was required to neutralise the sodium hydrogencarbonate. Find the concentration of the sulphuric acid in $g\,dm^{-3}$.

$$2NaHCO_3 + H_2SO_4 \rightarrow Na_2SO_4 + 2H_2O + 2CO_2$$

Extracting the main information in just one line:

$$25.0\,cm^3 \text{ of } 0.100\,mol\,dm^{-3}\,NaHCO_3 \equiv 17.6\,cm^3 \text{ of unknown } H_2SO_4$$

What do you know most about?

In this case, you know everything about the sodium hydrogencarbonate.

How many moles of sodium hydrogencarbonate were used?

The experiment used $25.0\,cm^3$ of $0.100\,mol\,dm^{-3}\,NaHCO_3$.

$$\text{Moles of NaHCO}_3 \text{ used} = \frac{25.0}{1000} \times 0.100$$
$$= 0.002\,50\,mol$$

How many moles of sulphuric acid will this react with?

The equation says that you only need half as many moles of sulphuric acid as sodium hydrogencarbonate.

$$\text{Moles of } H_2SO_4 = 0.5 \times 0.002\,50$$
$$= 0.001\,25$$

What is the concentration of H_2SO_4 in $mol\,dm^{-3}$?

There is 0.001 25 mol in $17.6\,cm^3$.

$$\text{Concentration} = \frac{1000}{17.6} \times 0.001\,25\,mol\,dm^{-3}$$
$$= 0.0710\,mol\,dm^{-3}$$

What is the concentration of the H_2SO_4 in $g\,dm^{-3}$?

(H = 1; O = 16; S = 32)

> 1 mol H_2SO_4 weighs 98 g
> Therefore 0.0710 mol weighs $0.0710 \times 98\,g = 6.96\,g$
> The concentration is $6.96\,g\,dm^{-3}$.

Example 12

What happens if concentrations are not given in $mol\,dm^{-3}$?

2.10 g of sodium hydrogencarbonate was dissolved in water and the solution made up to 250 cm^3. 25.0 cm^3 of this solution was pipetted into a conical flask and some methyl orange indicator added. This solution was neutralised by 25.9 cm^3 of dilute hydrochloric acid added from a burette. Calculate the concentration of the acid in $g\,dm^{-3}$. (H = 1; C = 12; O = 16; Na = 23; Cl = 35.5)

> $NaHCO_3 + HCl \rightarrow NaCl + CO_2 + H_2O$

The problem here is that although you know both the volume and concentration of the sodium hydrogencarbonate, the concentration units are not $mol\,dm^{-3}$. You can't do the sort of calculations you have been doing unless the units are right!

The units are wrong on two counts:

■ They are in grams rather than in moles.

■ The volume is 250 cm^3 rather than 1 dm^3 (1000 cm^3).

You need to put both of these right before you start the main titration calculation. Sort the volume out first because it is easier.

250 cm^3 is a quarter of 1000 cm^3. So if you wanted to make up a solution of the same concentration you would have to dissolve 4 times as much in 1 dm^3.

> Concentration of sodium hydrogencarbonate = $2.10 \times 4\,g\,dm^{-3}$
> $= 8.40\,g\,dm^{-3}$

We now have the volume units right, so it remains to convert grams into moles.

> 1 mole of $NaHCO_3$ weighs 84 g
> Therefore, 8.40 g of $NaHCO_3$ = 0.100 mol
> The concentration of the sodium hydrogencarbonate is $0.100\,mol\,dm^{-3}$.

Now the calculation is straightforward again.

> 25.0 cm^3 of $0.100\,mol\,dm^{-3}$ $NaHCO_3$ ≡ 25.9 cm^3 of unknown HCl
>
> Number of moles of $NaHCO_3 = \dfrac{25.0}{1000} \times 0.100$
>
> $= 0.002\,50\,mol$

From the equation:

> 1 mol $NaHCO_3$ ≡ 1 mol HCl
> Number of moles of HCl = 0.00250 mol (in 25.9 cm^3)
>
> Therefore concentration of HCl = $\dfrac{1000}{25.9} \times 0.00250\,mol\,dm^{-3}$
>
> $= 0.0965\,mol\,dm^{-3}$

1 mole of HCl weighs 36.5 g

0.0965 moles of HCl weighs $0.0965 \times 36.5\,\text{g} = 3.52\,\text{g}$

The concentration of the HCl is therefore $3.52\,\text{g}\,\text{dm}^{-3}$

So you see – the heart of the sum is exactly the same as before. You just need to read the question carefully to check the units you are given and those that you are asked to give the answer in.

Simple titration sums using more complicated reactions

There is no reason why you have to limit titrations to reactions between acids and alkalis. Any reaction between two solutions could be used, provided there is some way of knowing when exactly the right amounts have been added. As long as you have an equation, there is no problem. The calculations are identical. There is no reason why you should be put off by unfamiliar reactions.

Example 13

$25.0\,\text{cm}^3$ of iron(II) sulphate solution of concentration $0.100\,\text{mol}\,\text{dm}^{-3}$ was acidified with an equal volume of dilute sulphuric acid (an excess), and then titrated with potassium manganate(VII) solution. It required $20.6\,\text{cm}^3$ of potassium manganate(VII) solution to reach the end-point of the titration. Find the concentration of the potassium manganate(VII) solution in $\text{mol}\,\text{dm}^{-3}$.

$$\text{MnO}_4{}^-{}_{(aq)} + 8\text{H}^+{}_{(aq)} + 5\text{Fe}^{2+}{}_{(aq)} \rightarrow \text{Mn}^{2+}{}_{(aq)} + 5\text{Fe}^{3+}{}_{(aq)} + 4\text{H}_2\text{O}_{(l)}$$

$25.0\,\text{cm}^3$ of $0.100\,\text{mol}\,\text{dm}^{-3}$ FeSO$_4$ $\equiv 20.6\,\text{cm}^3$ of unknown KMnO$_4$

or $25.0\,\text{cm}^3$ of $0.100\,\text{mol}\,\text{dm}^{-3}$ Fe$^{2+}{}_{(aq)}$ $\equiv 20.6\,\text{cm}^3$ of unknown MnO$_4{}^-{}_{(aq)}$

You obviously know everything there is to know about the Fe^{2+} ions – so that is where you start.

$$\text{Number of moles of Fe}^{2+}{}_{(aq)} = \frac{25.0}{1000} \times 0.100$$
$$= 0.002\,50\,\text{mol}$$

Looking at the equation, you only need 1/5 as much MnO$_4{}^-{}_{(aq)}$ as you do of Fe$^{2+}{}_{(aq)}$.

$$\text{Number of moles of MnO}_4{}^-{}_{(aq)} = \frac{1}{5} \times 0.002\,50$$
$$= 0.000\,500\,\text{mol (contained in } 20.6\,\text{cm}^3)$$

$$\text{Concentration of MnO}_4{}^-{}_{(aq)} = \frac{1000}{20.6} \times 0.000\,500\,\text{mol}\,\text{dm}^{-3}$$
$$= 0.0243\,\text{mol}\,\text{dm}^{-3}$$

The chemistry may look difficult, but the sum is the same!

> **Note:** You might need to re-read pages 6 to 14 on ionic equations. For now you need to realise:
>
> The MnO$_4{}^-$ ions come from the potassium manganate(VII) solution, KMnO$_4$. Each mole of KMnO$_4$ gives 1 mole of MnO$_4{}^-$ ions. This means that the concentrations (in $\text{mol}\,\text{dm}^{-3}$) of the KMnO$_4$ and MnO$_4{}^-$ are exactly the same. If you work out the concentration of the MnO$_4{}^-$ you have automatically worked out the concentration of the KMnO$_4$.
>
> A similar idea applies to the iron(II) sulphate solution. The concentration of the FeSO$_4$ solution (in $\text{mol}\,\text{dm}^{-3}$) is exactly the same as the concentration of the Fe^{2+} ions because each FeSO$_4$ gives one Fe^{2+} ion.
>
> The hydrogen ions are provided by the sulphuric acid. There is an excess of these, so you don't have to worry about them.

Example 14

An excess of potassium iodide solution was added to $25.0\,\text{cm}^3$ of copper(II) sulphate solution, and the iodine liberated was titrated with standard sodium thiosulphate solution. $15.7\,\text{cm}^3$ of $0.200\,\text{mol}\,\text{dm}^{-3}$ sodium thiosulphate solution, Na$_2$S$_2$O$_3$, was needed to react with all the iodine. Find the concentration of the copper(II) sulphate solution in grams of CuSO$_4$ per dm^3. (O = 16; S = 32; Cu = 64)

$$2CuSO_4 + 4KI \rightarrow 2K_2SO_4 + 2CuI + I_2$$

$$2Na_2S_2O_3 + I_2 \rightarrow 2NaI + Na_2S_4O_6$$

Does the fact that there are two equations cause problems? Not at all! You simply need to trace the relationships through the equations.

$$2 \text{ mol } CuSO_4 \equiv 1 \text{ mol } I_2 \equiv 2 \text{ mol } Na_2S_2O_3$$

In other words, every 1 mole of copper(II) sulphate eventually needs 1 mole of sodium thiosulphate.

You know everything about the sodium thiosulphate – so start there.

$$\text{Number of moles of } Na_2S_2O_3 = \frac{15.7}{1000} \times 0.200$$

$$= 0.003\,14 \text{ mol}$$

The equations say that every mole of $Na_2S_2O_3$ reacts (indirectly) with 1 mole of $CuSO_4$.

Number of moles of $CuSO_4 = 0.003\,14$ (contained in 25.0 cm^3)

$$\text{Concentration of } CuSO_4 = \frac{1000}{25.0} \times 0.003\,14 \text{ mol dm}^{-3}$$

$$= 0.1256 \text{ mol dm}^{-3}$$

1 mol $CuSO_4$ weighs 160 g

0.1256 mol weighs $0.1256 \times 160 \text{ g} = 20.1 \text{ g}$

The concentration is therefore 20.1 g dm^{-3}.

Again, the chemistry may be more complicated, but it is still the same basic calculation.

Problem • 7

25.0 cm^3 of $0.200 \text{ mol dm}^{-3}$ sodium carbonate solution was neutralised by 20.0 cm^3 of dilute hydrochloric acid. Find the concentration (in g dm^{-3}) of the hydrochloric acid.

$$Na_2CO_3 + 2HCl \rightarrow 2NaCl + CO_2 + H_2O$$

($H = 1$; $Cl = 35.5$)

Problem • 8

Strontium hydroxide, $Sr(OH)_2$, is only sparingly soluble in water at room temperature ($20\,°C$). In an experiment to measure its solubility, a student shook some solid strontium hydroxide with some de-ionised water for several minutes to ensure that as much dissolved as possible. She filtered off the excess solid to leave a colourless saturated solution of strontium hydroxide.

She pipetted 25.0 cm^3 of this solution into a conical flask, added a few drops of methyl orange indicator, and then titrated it with $0.100 \text{ mol dm}^{-3}$ hydrochloric acid from a burette. She needed to add 32.8 cm^3 of the acid to neutralise the strontium hydroxide:

$$Sr(OH)_2 + 2HCl \rightarrow SrCl_2 + 2H_2O$$

Calculate the concentration of the saturated strontium hydroxide solution in g dm^{-3}.

($H = 1$; $O = 16$; $Sr = 88$)

Problem • 9

In an experiment to find the concentration of some dilute sulphuric acid, a student diluted it exactly 10 times to give a concentration suitable for titration. He made up some standard sodium hydroxide solution by dissolving 1.00 g of it in 250 cm^3 of solution. He then found that 25.0 cm^3 of the sodium hydroxide solution required 23.5 cm^3 of the diluted sulphuric acid for neutralisation. Calculate the concentration of the original dilute sulphuric acid in mol dm^{-3}.

$$2NaOH + H_2SO_4 \rightarrow Na_2SO_4 + 2H_2O$$

(H = 1; O = 16; Na = 23)

Problem • 10

In an experiment to find the concentration of a solution of iodine, 25.0 cm^3 of the solution was titrated with 0.100 mol dm^{-3} sodium thiosulphate solution. 18.8 cm^3 of sodium thiosulphate solution was required to reach the end-point. Find the concentration of the iodine solution in g dm^{-3}.

$$I_2 + 2Na_2S_2O_3 \rightarrow 2NaI + Na_2S_4O_6$$

(I = 127)

Problem • 11

25.0 cm^3 of hydrogen peroxide solution, H_2O_2, was acidified with an excess of dilute sulphuric acid and then titrated with 0.0200 mol dm^{-3} potassium manganate(VII) solution, KMnO$_4$. 28.1 cm^3 of the potassium manganate(VII) solution was required to reach the end-point. Find the concentration of the hydrogen peroxide in mol dm^{-3}:

$$5H_2O_{2(aq)} + 2MnO_4{}^-{}_{(aq)} + 6H^+{}_{(aq)} \rightarrow 2Mn^{2+}{}_{(aq)} + 5O_{2(g)} + 8H_2O_{(l)}$$

(**Hint**: If the equation bothers you, read the note on page 66. Think very carefully about the reacting ratio in this case.)

. . . .

Using titrations to find other things

Up to now we have been doing titration calculations to find the concentrations of various solutions, but you can use similar sums to find other things as well. Some examples will make this clear.

You are strongly advised not to start this section until you are confident that you can do most of the last set of problems without too much difficulty.

Example 15

A fairly simple introductory example

The following experiment was done in order to **estimate the percentage purity** of a sample of sodium hydrogencarbonate.

2.50 g of impure sodium hydrogencarbonate was dissolved in pure water and the volume made up to 250 cm^3. 25.0 cm^3 of this solution was pipetted into a conical flask, a few drops of methyl orange added, and sulphuric acid of concentration 0.0500 mol dm^{-3} was run in from a burette until the solution became orange. 28.3 cm^3 of the acid were needed. What is the percentage purity of the sodium hydrogencarbonate? (H = 1; C = 12; O = 16; Na = 23)

As with all calculations, the problem is knowing where to start. Once you have decided where to start there is usually no difficulty.

You have information about two things: the sodium hydrogencarbonate and the acid.

You do not, however, know *everything* about the sodium hydrogencarbonate. It is **impure** and you don't know how much of the 2.50 g is actually sodium hydrogencarbonate and how much is junk. You do, however, know everything about the acid – so start there.

As a general rule in these more complicated calculations, start at the end and work back. It is very rare indeed for you to be able to begin at the beginning!

So, start from the acid . . .

$$\text{Number of moles of } H_2SO_4 = \frac{28.3}{1000} \times 0.0500$$

$$= 1.415 \times 10^{-3}$$

$$2NaHCO_3 + H_2SO_4 \rightarrow Na_2SO_4 + 2CO_2 + 2H_2O$$

You need twice as much $NaHCO_3$ as H_2SO_4.

$$\text{Number of moles of } NaHCO_3 = 2 \times 1.415 \times 10^{-3}$$

$$= 2.83 \times 10^{-3} \text{ (in 25.0 cm}^3 \text{ of solution)}$$

At this stage you would normally go on to work out the concentration in $mol\,dm^{-3}$. You could still do this and eventually you would get an answer, but by a rather roundabout route. There is a short cut that is almost always used in questions of this kind. Notice that all of the impure sodium hydrogencarbonate was originally dissolved in 250 cm^3 of water and that the experiment used a 25.0 cm^3 sample of that.

If you multiplied the number of moles in 25.0 cm^3 by 10, that would tell you how many moles of sodium hydrogencarbonate there was in your total sample:

$$\text{Number of moles of } NaHCO_3 \text{ in total} = 10 \times 2.83 \times 10^{-3}$$

$$= 0.0283$$

Now we can work out the total mass of sodium hydrogencarbonate in the original sample:

1 mole of $NaHCO_3$ weighs 84 g

Therefore mass of $NaHCO_3 = 0.0283 \times 84$ g

$$= 2.377 \text{ g}$$

So the calculated mass of sodium hydrogencarbonate is 2.377 g, whereas the amount dissolved was actually 2.50 g.

$$\text{The percentage purity} = \frac{2.377}{2.50} \times 100\%$$

$$= 95.1\%$$

Example 16

Another similar example

1.15 g of impure iron wire was dissolved in 30 cm³ of dilute sulphuric acid (a large excess) under such conditions that iron(II) sulphate solution was formed:

$$Fe_{(s)} + 2H^+_{(aq)} \rightarrow Fe^{2+}_{(aq)} + H_{2(g)}$$

➤ If you are still worried about ionic equations, re-read pages 6 to 14.

The resulting solution was made up to a total of 250 cm³ with pure water. 25.0 cm³ of the diluted solution was further acidified and titrated with 0.0200 mol dm⁻³ potassium manganate(VII) solution. 20.0 cm³ of potassium manganate(VII) solution were required to reach the end-point of the titration.

$$5Fe^{2+}_{(aq)} + MnO_4^-_{(aq)} + 8H^+_{(aq)} \rightarrow 5Fe^{3+}_{(aq)} + Mn^{2+}_{(aq)} + 4H_2O_{(l)}$$

Find the percentage purity of the iron wire. (Fe = 56)

As always, **start from what you know everything about.** Worry about everything else as you go along. In this case, you know everything about the potassium manganate(VII) solution.

$$\text{Number of moles of KMnO}_4 = \frac{20.0}{1000} \times 0.0200$$

$$= 4.00 \times 10^{-4}$$

Now worry about the equations. You aren't interested in the first equation for now.

The second equation says that 5 mol $Fe^{2+}_{(aq)}$ reacts with 1 mol $MnO_4^-_{(aq)}$. Here you need to realise that the concentrations of $MnO_4^-_{(aq)}$ and $KMnO_4$ (potassium manganate(VII)) are the same because each $KMnO_4$ contains one $MnO_4^-_{(aq)}$ ion.

Each mole of $MnO_4^-_{(aq)}$ reacts with 5 times as much $Fe^{2+}_{(aq)}$.

$$\text{Number of moles of Fe}^{2+}_{(aq)} = 5 \times 4.00 \times 10^{-4}$$

$$= 2.00 \times 10^{-3} \text{ (in 25.0 cm}^3 \text{ of solution)}$$

This was a sample from the total solution of 250 cm³, which therefore contains 10 times as much $Fe^{2+}_{(aq)}$.

$$\text{Total moles of Fe}^{2+}_{(aq)} = 10 \times 2.00 \times 10^{-3}$$

$$= 0.0200$$

The first equation says that 1 mol Fe gives 1 mol $Fe^{2+}_{(aq)}$.

Therefore the iron wire contained 0.0200 moles of Fe.

$$\text{Mass of iron in the wire} = 0.0200 \times 56 \text{ g}$$

$$= 1.12 \text{ g}$$

The mass of the impure wire was 1.15 g.

$$\text{Percentage purity of wire} = \frac{1.12}{1.15} \times 100\%$$

$$= 97.4\%$$

Example 17   A nasty looking problem

Sodium carbonate crystals contain water of crystallisation. The formula of the crystals is $Na_2CO_3.nH_2O$, where "n" is a whole number. 2.86 g of sodium carbonate crystals were dissolved in pure water and the solution made up to 250 cm^3. A 25.0 cm^3 sample of this solution was pipetted into a conical flask and some methyl orange added as indicator. 0.100 mol dm^{-3} hydrochloric acid was added from a burette until the indicator turned orange. 20.0 cm^3 of the acid was required. Calculate "n" in the formula above. (H = 1, C = 12, O = 16, Na = 23)

$$Na_2CO_3 + 2HCl \rightarrow 2NaCl + CO_2 + H_2O$$

Your first response to a question like this? Don't panic!

You may not have the first idea of how you are going to get all the way through to the answer, but that does not matter at this stage.

Start from what you know most about . . . and again bear in mind that this will probably be towards the end of the question. Having made a start, ideas will occur to you as you go along. There is usually a sort of inevitability about the whole thing – the question leads you to an answer.

What you know everything about is the hydrochloric acid, so start in the now familiar way:

$$\text{Number of moles of HCl} = \frac{20.0}{1000} \times 0.100$$

$$= 2.00 \times 10^{-3}$$

$$Na_2CO_3 + 2HCl \rightarrow 2NaCl + CO_2 + H_2O$$

The amount of sodium carbonate needed is therefore only a half of that of the hydrochloric acid.

$$\text{Number of moles of } Na_2CO_3 = 1.00 \times 10^{-3} \text{ (in 25.0 cm}^3 \text{ of solution)}$$

Just as in the previous examples, it will save time and produce a more logical solution if we now work out how much sodium carbonate there was in the whole 250 cm^3 of solution (instead of per dm^3), because this then ties in with the total amount of crystals that were dissolved in the water. Obviously there will be 10 times as much.

$$\text{Total number of moles of } Na_2CO_3 = 10 \times 1.00 \times 10^{-3}$$

$$= 0.0100 \text{ moles}$$

Everything so far has just been following the routine. Now you might be forced to think.

We've got this number (0.0100 moles of sodium carbonate). What can we do with it? In the question it talks about the mass of sodium carbonate crystals dissolved measured in grams. You could always try converting this number of moles into grams and see if that leads anywhere . . .

1 mol Na_2CO_3 weighs 106 g.

0.0100 mol Na_2CO_3 = 0.0100 × 106 g

$$= 1.06 \text{ g}$$

➤ It may well be that, left to your own devices, you wouldn't have got all the way through this calculation at first sight, but **never just give up and abandon it without giving it a try**. Even if you only got half way through – did the initial titration bit, and perhaps worked out the masses of a mole of sodium carbonate and a mole of water – you could actually score most of the marks. If you don't even attempt it, you are bound to score nothing.

In an exam, you would probably be guided through a calculation like this by the examiners – so the difficulties are much less than you might think anyway. In a structured paper, focus entirely on what the examiner is asking you to find in that particular tiny part of the question – and ignore everything else for the time being.

Looking at the question again, you should see that there is a discrepancy between this figure and the weight of sodium carbonate crystals dissolved. What causes the difference? It must be the water in the crystals.

In the absence of any other bright ideas, you could always work out the mass of this extra water:

$$\text{Mass of water in crystals} = 2.86 - 1.06\,g$$
$$= 1.80\,g$$

We have now used up all the numbers given in the question, so we are obviously nearly there. All you need to do now is to have a think about what is meant by the formula $Na_2CO_3.nH_2O$.

It tells you that 1 mole of Na_2CO_3 is combined with "n" moles of water. We already worked out that we've got 0.0100 moles of sodium carbonate. If we worked out how many moles of water there were combined with it, then the ratio follows without difficulty.

$$1.80\,g \text{ of water is } \frac{1.80}{18} \text{ moles of water} = 0.100\,mol$$

So, if 0.0100 mol of Na_2CO_3 combines with 0.100 mol of H_2O

1 mol of Na_2CO_3 combines with 10 mol of H_2O

The formula is therefore: $Na_2CO_3.10H_2O$

Back titrations

What is a back titration?

The easiest way of explaining how a back titration works is to outline the first example that is coming up – to find the percentage of calcium carbonate in a sample of limestone.

A known mass of limestone is dissolved in some acid of known volume and concentration. The acid is in excess. A titration is then done to find out how much acid is left over. From that you can work out how much acid has been used up by the limestone, and hence back to the amount of calcium carbonate in the limestone.

All back titrations work in this way – you use an excess of something and then do a titration to find out how much is left over.

Example 18

1.25 g of crushed limestone was added to 50.0 cm³ of 1.00 mol dm⁻³ hydrochloric acid (an excess). The mixture was left until all bubbling stopped and was then made up carefully to 250 cm³ with pure water. A 25.0 cm³ sample of this was pipetted into a conical flask and some methyl orange indicator was added. Sodium hydroxide solution of concentration 0.100 mol dm⁻³ was added from a burette. 30.0 cm³ were needed to reach the end-point of the indicator. Calculate the percentage of calcium carbonate in the limestone. (C = 12; O = 16; Ca = 40)

$$NaOH + HCl \rightarrow NaCl + H_2O$$

$$CaCO_3 + 2HCl \rightarrow CaCl_2 + CO_2 + H_2O$$

On the same principle that we used for the last example, don't worry too much about the whole question at the beginning. Start from what you know about and see where it leads you.

■ You **don't** know everything about the limestone, only that some unknown amount of it is calcium carbonate.

■ You **do** know everything about the acid you dissolved it in.

■ You **do** know everything about the sodium hydroxide solution.

This time, then, you have got 2 possible starting points. Confused? Don't be. Work out how many moles you have got of both! We will do the sodium hydroxide first on the principle that it is usually best to start as near the end of the question as possible!

$$\text{Number of moles of NaOH} = \frac{30.0}{1000} \times 0.100$$

$$= 3.00 \times 10^{-3}$$

$$\text{NaOH} + \text{HCl} \rightarrow \text{NaCl} + \text{H}_2\text{O}$$

From the equation, you need the same number of moles of HCl and NaOH.

Therefore, number of moles of HCl $= 3.00 \times 10^{-3}$ (in $25.0\,\text{cm}^3$ of solution)

This was a $25.0\,\text{cm}^3$ sample from the whole $250\,\text{cm}^3$ of the reaction mixture.

Therefore, number of moles of HCl left over in the
whole mixture after reacting with the limestone $\quad = 10 \times 3.00 \times 10^{-3}$

$$= 0.0300\,\text{mol}$$

Now that is as far as we can go with these numbers for a while: we know how much hydrochloric acid was left over after the reaction. We also have enough information in the question to work out how much acid there was at the beginning. We started off with $50.0\,\text{cm}^3$ of $1.00\,\text{mol}\,\text{dm}^{-3}$ HCl.

$$\text{Number of moles of HCl originally} = \frac{50.0}{1000} \times 1.00$$

$$= 0.0500\,\text{mol}$$

So, we started with 0.0500 moles of HCl and ended up with 0.0300 moles. The missing HCl was used up by the calcium carbonate in the limestone.

$$\text{Number of moles of HCl used up} = 0.0500 - 0.0300$$

$$= 0.0200\,\text{mol}$$

Now we need the equation for the acid–carbonate reaction:

$$\text{CaCO}_3 + 2\text{HCl} \rightarrow \text{CaCl}_2 + \text{CO}_2 + \text{H}_2\text{O}$$

In other words, there are only half as many moles of calcium carbonate as there are of hydrochloric acid.

Number of moles of $\text{CaCO}_3 = 0.5 \times 0.0200 = 0.0100\,\text{mol}$

1 mole of CaCO_3 weighs $100\,\text{g}$

Therefore mass of $\text{CaCO}_3 = 0.0100 \times 100 = 1.00\,\text{g}$

Finally, because the original mass of limestone was $1.25\,\text{g}$,

$$\text{Percentage of CaCO}_3 = \frac{1.00}{1.25} \times 100\% = 80.0\%$$

➤ **Note:** In an examination, particularly on a structured paper, you would almost certainly be guided through a question like this in easy steps.

Example 19   6.60 g of a fertiliser containing ammonium sulphate was boiled with an excess of sodium hydroxide solution. All of the ammonia gas (NH_3) liberated was absorbed in $50.0 \, cm^3$ of $1.00 \, mol \, dm^{-3}$ hydrochloric acid (an excess). The resulting solution was diluted carefully to exactly $250 \, cm^3$ to give a solution of suitable concentration for titration. A $25.0 \, cm^3$ portion of this solution was titrated with $0.100 \, mol \, dm^{-3}$ sodium hydroxide solution. $20.0 \, cm^3$ of the sodium hydroxide solution was required for neutralisation. Calculate the percentage of ammonium sulphate in the fertiliser. (H = 1; N = 14; O = 16; S = 32)

$$(NH_4)_2SO_4 + 2NaOH \rightarrow Na_2SO_4 + 2NH_3 + 2H_2O$$

$$NH_3 + HCl \rightarrow NH_4Cl$$

$$NaOH + HCl \rightarrow NaCl + H_2O$$

We are going to do this example entirely without comment. Nothing is substantially different from anything that has gone before.

$$\text{Number of moles of NaOH} = \frac{20.0}{1000} \times 0.100$$

$$= 0.002\,00$$

1 mol NaOH reacts with 1 mol HCl

Number of moles of HCl = 0.002 00 (in $25.0 \, cm^3$ of solution)

Number of moles of HCl in the total $250 \, cm^3$ of solution = $10 \times 0.002\,00$

$$= 0.0200$$

i.e. number of moles of HCl left over after reaction with ammonia = 0.0200

$$\text{Number of moles of HCl at start} = \frac{50.0}{1000} \times 1.00$$

$$= 0.0500$$

Number of moles of HCl used up by the ammonia = 0.0500 − 0.0200

$$= 0.0300$$

1 mol HCl reacts with 1 mol NH_3

Number of moles of NH_3 produced = 0.0300

$$(NH_4)_2SO_4 + 2NaOH \rightarrow Na_2SO_4 + 2NH_3 + 2H_2O$$

The number of moles of ammonium sulphate is half the number of moles of ammonia produced.

$$\text{Number of moles of } (NH_4)_2SO_4 = 0.5 \times 0.0300$$

$$= 0.0150$$

1 mol $(NH_4)_2SO_4$ weighs 132 g

$$\text{Mass of } (NH_4)_2SO_4 = 0.0150 \times 132 \, g$$

$$= 1.98 \, g$$

$$\text{Percentage of } (NH_4)_2SO_4 = \frac{1.98}{6.60} \times 100\%$$

$$= 30.0\%$$

Problem • 12

➤ **Note!** These are not intended to be easy. Do not attempt them until you can do questions like those earlier in this chapter without difficulty, and fully understand the recent worked examples.
In an exam, you are quite likely to be helped through questions of this sort, which should make life much easier.

2.00 g of impure potassium sulphite, K_2SO_3, was dissolved in water and the solution made up to 250 cm^3. A 25.0 cm^3 portion of this solution was acidified with an excess of dilute sulphuric acid and then titrated with 0.0200 mol dm^{-3} potassium manganate(VII) solution. 24.0 cm^3 of this solution was required to reach the end-point of the titration. Calculate the percentage purity of the potassium sulphite.

$$5K_2SO_3 + 2KMnO_4 + 3H_2SO_4 \rightarrow 6K_2SO_4 + 2MnSO_4 + 3H_2O$$

(O = 16; S = 32; K = 39)

Problem • 13

A sample of zinc was claimed to be at least 98% pure. The following experiment was carried out to check that claim. 0.462 g of the zinc was added to 50.0 cm^3 of 0.500 mol dm^{-3} sulphuric acid (an excess), and the mixture was warmed carefully until no further reaction occurred. The resulting solution was made up to 250 cm^3 with pure water. A 25.0 cm^3 sample of this solution needed 18.0 cm^3 of 0.200 mol dm^{-3} sodium hydroxide solution to neutralise the excess sulphuric acid. Assuming that none of the impurities in the zinc reacted with the original sulphuric acid, confirm that the zinc was more than 98% pure.

$$Zn + H_2SO_4 \rightarrow ZnSO_4 + H_2$$
$$H_2SO_4 + 2NaOH \rightarrow Na_2SO_4 + 2H_2O$$

(Zn = 65)

Problem • 14

A solution contained sodium hydroxide which was reacting slowly with other things present. In order to find the amount of sodium hydroxide present at a particular time, 100 cm^3 of 1.00 mol dm^{-3} hydrochloric acid (an excess) was added to neutralise the sodium hydroxide and stop the reaction. The mixture was made up to exactly 250 cm^3 with pure water. A 25.0 cm^3 sample of the diluted mixture was titrated with 0.100 mol dm^{-3} sodium hydrogencarbonate solution. 40.0 cm^3 was required to produce a neutral solution. Calculate the number of moles of sodium hydroxide in the original solution.

$$NaOH + HCl \rightarrow NaCl + H_2O$$
$$NaHCO_3 + HCl \rightarrow NaCl + H_2O + CO_2$$

- -

"Double indicator" titrations

➤ **Check your syllabus.** Not all syllabuses expect you to be able to do these sums.

When an excess of dilute hydrochloric acid is added to sodium carbonate solution, carbon dioxide is evolved, and the overall equation is:

$$Na_2CO_3 + 2HCl \rightarrow 2NaCl + CO_2 + H_2O$$

If you do the reaction in the presence of different indicators, though, you find that the reaction actually happens in two quite distinct stages.

Stage 1: In the presence of phenolphthalein

Phenolphthalein is bright pink in solutions with a pH greater than 10.0. As the pH falls below 10.0, the colour of the indicator fades, and it becomes colourless at about pH 8.3. This is almost exactly the pH of solutions of sodium hydrogencarbonate, $NaHCO_3$, at the sort of concentrations we normally use.

If dilute hydrochloric acid is run into sodium carbonate solution until phenolphthalein just becomes colourless, no carbon dioxide is given off. A solution of sodium hydrogencarbonate is formed:

$$Na_2CO_3 + HCl \rightarrow NaCl + NaHCO_3$$

Stage 2: In the presence of methyl orange

Methyl orange is yellow in solutions with a pH greater than 4.4 and is red when the pH falls below 3.1. In between, it shows various shades of orange. You normally titrate until there is the first trace of orange in the original yellow.

When the phenolphthalein has become colourless in stage 1, a few drops of methyl orange are added and the titration is continued until the solution changes from yellow to show the first trace of orange. This time carbon dioxide is produced as the sodium hydrogencarbonate reacts with the hydrochloric acid:

$$NaHCO_3 + HCl \rightarrow NaCl + CO_2 + H_2O$$

The volumes of acid used

Each of these two stages represents exactly half of the overall reaction. Whatever amount of acid is added from the burette in the first stage, you will need to add *exactly* the same amount again to complete the second stage. So if, for example, you needed $20.4 \, cm^3$ of acid in the presence of the phenolphthalein, you would need to add another $20.4 \, cm^3$ after you had added the methyl orange to reach the final end-point.

➤ You need to be convinced of this. If you look at the two equations, for every mole of Na_2CO_3 you need a mole of HCl to complete the first stage, producing a mole of $NaHCO_3$. That mole of $NaHCO_3$ needs another mole of HCl to complete the second stage. So, however much acid you need for the first stage, you need the same amount again for the second stage.

Using the double indicator method to solve real problems

You can use the fact that the reaction between sodium carbonate and hydrochloric acid takes place in two stages to analyse two different mixtures.

Example 20

➤ Sodium carbonate may well become contaminated with sodium hydrogencarbonate by reaction with carbon dioxide in the air:

$Na_2CO_3 + CO_2 + H_2O \rightarrow 2NaHCO_3$

Analysing mixtures of Na_2CO_3 and $NaHCO_3$

$25.0 \, cm^3$ of a solution containing sodium carbonate contaminated with sodium hydrogencarbonate required $20.0 \, cm^3$ of $0.100 \, mol \, dm^{-3}$ hydrochloric acid to reach the end-point in the presence of phenolphthalein, and an additional $25.0 \, cm^3$ of the acid when methyl orange was added. Find the concentrations of both sodium carbonate and sodium hydrogencarbonate.

A1 $Na_2CO_3 + HCl \rightarrow NaCl + NaHCO_3$ needs 20.0 cm³ HCl

A2 $NaHCO_3 + HCl \rightarrow NaCl + CO_2 + H_2O$ ⎫

B *$NaHCO_3 + HCl \rightarrow NaCl + CO_2 + H_2O$* ⎬ needs 25.0 cm³ HCl

If reaction A1 needs 20.0 cm³ of acid, then reaction A2 needs the same amount because these represent the two stages of the sodium carbonate/HCl reaction.

Reactions A2 and B together need 25.0 cm³.

Reaction A2 needs 20.0 cm³.

So reaction B needs $(25.0 - 20.0)$ cm³ $= 5.0$ cm³.

What we have now done is to split this into two simple titration calculations.

(a) 25.0 cm³ of sodium carbonate solution needs 20.0 cm³ of 0.100 mol dm⁻³ HCl for the reaction

$$Na_2CO_3 + HCl \rightarrow NaCl + NaHCO_3$$

$$\text{Number of moles of HCl} = \frac{20.0}{1000} \times 0.100$$

$$= 0.002\,00 \text{ mol}$$

The equation shows that the Na_2CO_3 and HCl react 1:1 in this stage of the reaction.

Therefore number of moles of $Na_2CO_3 = 0.002\,00$ (in 25.0 cm³)

$$\text{Concentration of } Na_2CO_3 = 0.002\,00 \times \frac{1000}{25.0}$$

$$= 0.0800 \text{ mol dm}^{-3}$$

(b) 25.0 cm³ of sodium hydrogencarbonate solution needs 5.0 cm³ of 0.100 mol dm⁻³ HCl for the reaction

$$NaHCO_3 + HCl \rightarrow NaCl + CO_2 + H_2O$$

$$\text{Number of moles of HCl} = \frac{5.0}{1000} \times 0.100$$

$$= 5.00 \times 10^{-4} \text{ mol}$$

The equation shows that the $NaHCO_3$ and HCl react 1:1.

Therefore number of moles of $NaHCO_3 = 5.00 \times 10^{-4}$ (in 25.0 cm³)

$$\text{Concentration of } NaHCO_3 = 5.00 \times 10^{-4} \times \frac{1000}{25.0}$$

$$= 0.0200 \text{ mol dm}^{-3}$$

Example 21

Analysing mixtures of NaOH and Na_2CO_3

What happens this time with the two indicators is slightly different, and you need to think very carefully in order not to get the two cases confused.

Remember that the phenolphthalein turns colourless when the pH has fallen to about 8.3. This cannot possibly happen until all the sodium hydroxide has been neutralised, because sodium hydroxide is strongly alkaline.

The phenolphthalein therefore picks up the completion of these *two* reactions:

$NaOH + HCl \rightarrow NaCl + H_2O$

$Na_2CO_3 + HCl \rightarrow NaCl + NaHCO_3$

The methyl orange then tells you when the second stage of the sodium carbonate reaction is complete:

$$NaHCO_3 + HCl \rightarrow NaCl + CO_2 + H_2O$$

$25.0 \, cm^3$ of a solution containing sodium hydroxide contaminated with sodium carbonate required $28.0 \, cm^3$ of $0.100 \, mol \, dm^{-3}$ HCl in the presence of phenolphthalein, and an additional $4.3 \, cm^3$ of acid when methyl orange was added. Find the concentrations of both the sodium hydroxide and the sodium carbonate.

A $NaOH + HCl \rightarrow NaCl + H_2O$

B1 $Na_2CO_3 + HCl \rightarrow NaCl + NaHCO_3$ $\left.\right\}$ needs $28.0 \, cm^3$ HCl

B2 $NaHCO_3 + HCl \rightarrow NaCl + CO_2 + H_2O$ needs $4.3 \, cm^3$ HCl

If reaction B2 needs $4.3 \, cm^3$ of acid, then reaction B1 needs the same amount because these represent the two stages of the sodium carbonate/HCl reaction.

Reactions A and B1 together need $28.0 \, cm^3$.
Reaction B1 needs $4.3 \, cm^3$.
So reaction A needs $(28.0 - 4.3) \, cm^3 = 23.7 \, cm^3$.

Again we have split the question into two simple titration calculations.

(a) $25.0 \, cm^3$ of sodium hydroxide solution needs $23.7 \, cm^3$ of $0.100 \, mol \, dm^{-3}$ HCl for the reaction:

$$NaOH + HCl \rightarrow NaCl + H_2O$$

$$\text{Number of moles of HCl} = \frac{23.7}{1000} \times 0.100$$

$$= 0.002\,37 \, mol$$

The equation shows that the NaOH and HCl react 1:1.

Therefore number of moles of NaOH $= 0.002\,37$ (in $25.0 \, cm^3$)

$$\text{Concentration of NaOH} = 0.002\,37 \times \frac{1000}{25.0}$$

$$= 0.0948 \, mol \, dm^{-3}$$

(b) $25.0 \, cm^3$ of sodium carbonate solution needs $4.3 \, cm^3$ of $0.100 \, mol \, dm^{-3}$ HCl for the reaction:

$$Na_2CO_3 + HCl \rightarrow NaCl + NaHCO_3$$

$$\text{Number of moles of HCl} = \frac{4.3}{1000} \times 0.100$$

$$= 4.30 \times 10^{-4} \, mol$$

The equation shows that the Na_2CO_3 and HCl react 1:1 in this stage of the reaction.

Therefore number of moles of $Na_2CO_3 = 4.30 \times 10^{-4}$ (in $25.0 \, cm^3$)

$$\text{Concentration of } Na_2CO_3 = 4.30 \times 10^{-4} \times \frac{1000}{25.0}$$

$$= 0.0172 \, mol \, dm^{-3}$$

Problem • 15

25.0 cm³ of a solution containing a mixture of sodium carbonate and sodium hydrogencarbonate was titrated with 0.250 mol dm⁻³ hydrochloric acid. 12.7 cm³ of the acid was required to reach the end-point with phenolphthalein, and a further 20.9 cm³ when methyl orange was used. Calculate the concentrations of the sodium carbonate and sodium hydrogencarbonate in mol dm⁻³.

Problem • 16

1.0 m³ of air was passed slowly over some solid sodium hydroxide to absorb the carbon dioxide. The sodium hydroxide (now contaminated with sodium carbonate) was then dissolved in water and made up to a volume of 1.00 dm³. A 25.0 cm³ sample of this solution was titrated with 0.100 mol dm⁻³ hydrochloric acid. 46.9 cm³ of acid was needed to reach the end-point in the presence of phenolphthalein, and a total of 50.0 cm³ was needed when methyl orange was used.

(a) Calculate the concentration of sodium carbonate in the solution in mol dm⁻³.

(b) How many moles of carbon dioxide were there in 1.0 m³ of air? The equation for the reaction between sodium hydroxide and carbon dioxide is:

$$2NaOH + CO_2 \rightarrow Na_2CO_3 + H_2O$$

(c) If the volume of 1 mole of a gas is 0.024 m³ at room temperature and pressure, calculate the percentage of carbon dioxide in the air.

End of chapter check list

Can you do the following things?

■ Convert concentrations in g dm⁻³ to mol dm⁻³ and vice versa.

■ Work out the number of moles contained in a particular volume given the concentration in mol dm⁻³.

■ Work out the concentration in mol dm⁻³ given the number of moles contained in a particular volume.

■ Work out equations from information about the quantities of substances involved.

■ Interpret equations (full or ionic) to establish reacting proportions with confidence.

■ Do titration calculations to find concentrations of solutions in familiar and unfamiliar cases, where concentrations may be measured in mol dm⁻³ or g dm⁻³.

■ Use titration results to calculate things such as percentage purity.

■ Do simple back titration sums (possibly with some guidance).

■ Understand how to use the "double indicator" method to work out the concentrations of the components of mixtures like sodium carbonate and sodium hydrogencarbonate, or sodium hydroxide and sodium carbonate (if your syllabus demands it).

Revision problems

Numerical answers are provided for these problems, but no worked solutions.

Problem • 17

(a) What is the concentration in $mol\,dm^{-3}$ of a solution of potassium hydroxide, KOH, containing $4.13\,g\,dm^{-3}$?

(b) What is the concentration in $g\,dm^{-3}$ of a solution of potassium manganate(VII), $KMnO_4$, containing $0.0200\,mol\,dm^{-3}$?

(c) What is the concentration in $mol\,dm^{-3}$ of a solution containing $3.77\,g$ of sodium hydrogencarbonate, $NaHCO_3$, in $250\,cm^3$ of solution?

(d) What mass of sodium carbonate crystals, $Na_2CO_3.10H_2O$, must be dissolved in $250\,cm^3$ of solution in order to give a concentration of $0.0500\,mol\,dm^{-3}$?

($H = 1$; $C = 12$; $O = 16$; $Na = 23$; $K = 39$; $Mn = 55$)

Problem • 18

(a) Calculate the volume of carbon dioxide released at room temperature and pressure when $25.0\,cm^3$ of $2.00\,mol\,dm^{-3}$ hydrochloric acid is added to an excess of calcium carbonate.

$$CaCO_3 + 2HCl \rightarrow CaCl_2 + CO_2 + H_2O$$

(b) What mass of calcium carbonate would be used up during the reaction?

(Molar volume of a gas $= 24.0\,dm^3$ at rtp; $C = 12$; $O = 16$; $Ca = 40$)

Problem • 19

What is the minimum volume of $2.00\,mol\,dm^{-3}$ hydrochloric acid needed to react with $1.25\,g$ of magnesium carbonate, $MgCO_3$?

$$MgCO_3 + 2HCl \rightarrow MgCl_2 + CO_2 + H_2O$$

($C = 12$; $O = 16$; $Mg = 24$)

Problem • 20

What volume of oxygen (measured at room temperature and pressure) could be obtained from decomposition of $50\,cm^3$ of $2.0\,mol\,dm^{-3}$ hydrogen peroxide?

$$2H_2O_2 \rightarrow 2H_2O + O_2$$

(The molar volume of a gas at rtp is $24\,dm^3$)

Problem • 21

When an excess of silver nitrate solution was added to $10.0\,cm^3$ of sodium chloride solution, $0.780\,g$ of silver chloride was precipitated. Find the concentration of the sodium chloride solution in $g\,dm^{-3}$.

$$AgNO_3 + NaCl \rightarrow AgCl + NaNO_3$$

($Na = 23$; $Cl = 35.5$; $Ag = 108$)

Problem • 22

$0.800\,g$ of a metal Y (RAM $= 40$) reacted with $40.0\,cm^3$ of $1.00\,mol\,dm^{-3}$ hydrochloric acid to produce a neutral solution of Y chloride and $480\,cm^3$ of hydrogen gas (H_2) collected at room temperature and pressure. Evaporating the solution to dryness produced $2.22\,g$ of solid Y chloride.

(a) Find the empirical formula for Y chloride.

(b) Use the given information to construct the equation for the reaction.

($Cl = 35.5$. Molar volume of a gas at rtp $= 24.0\,dm^3$)

Problem . 23

In each of these questions concerning simple titrations, calculate the unknown concentration in $mol\,dm^{-3}$.

(a) $25.0\,cm^3$ of $0.125\,mol\,dm^{-3}$ sodium hydroxide was neutralised by $17.5\,cm^3$ of dilute nitric acid of unknown concentration:

$$NaOH + HNO_3 \rightarrow NaNO_3 + H_2O$$

(b) $25.0\,cm^3$ of sodium carbonate solution of unknown concentration was neutralised by $22.2\,cm^3$ of $0.100\,mol\,dm^{-3}$ nitric acid:

$$Na_2CO_3 + 2HNO_3 \rightarrow 2NaNO_3 + CO_2 + H_2O$$

(c) $25.0\,cm^3$ of $0.250\,mol\,dm^{-3}$ potassium carbonate solution was neutralised by $31.7\,cm^3$ of ethanoic acid of unknown concentration:

$$2CH_3COOH + K_2CO_3 \rightarrow 2CH_3COOK + CO_2 + H_2O$$

Problem . 24

Lime water is calcium hydroxide solution. In an experiment to find the concentration of calcium hydroxide in lime water, $25.0\,cm^3$ of lime water needed $18.8\,cm^3$ of $0.0400\,mol\,dm^{-3}$ hydrochloric acid to neutralise it. Calculate the concentration of the calcium hydroxide in $g\,dm^{-3}$.

$$Ca(OH)_2 + 2HCl \rightarrow CaCl_2 + 2H_2O$$

$(H = 1; O = 16; Ca = 40)$

Problem . 25

(a) Some potassium manganate(VII) solution was made up to a concentration of approximately $0.02\,mol\,dm^{-3}$. In order to standardise it, it was titrated against hot sodium ethanedioate solution containing $0.0500\,mol\,dm^{-3}$ of ethanedioate ions, $C_2O_4^{2-}$. $25.0\,cm^3$ of sodium ethanedioate solution was pipetted into a conical flask and acidified with about $25\,cm^3$ of dilute sulphuric acid (a large excess). The solution was heated carefully to a temperature greater than $60\,°C$, and the potassium manganate(VII) solution was added from a burette until the first trace of a permanent pink colour was seen. $24.3\,cm^3$ of potassium manganate(VII) solution was required. Calculate the concentration of the potassium manganate(VII) solution in $mol\,dm^{-3}$.

$$5C_2O_4^{2-} + 2MnO_4^- + 16H^+ \rightarrow 2Mn^{2+} + 10CO_2 + 8H_2O$$

(b) The standardised potassium manganate(VII) solution from part (a) was used to find the concentration of some iron(II) sulphate solution, $FeSO_4$. $25.0\,cm^3$ of the iron(II) sulphate solution was acidified with an equal volume of dilute sulphuric acid. $27.9\,cm^3$ of the potassium manganate(VII) solution was required to reach the end-point. Calculate the concentration of the iron(II) sulphate solution in $mol\,dm^{-3}$.

$$MnO_4^- + 5Fe^{2+} + 8H^+ \rightarrow Mn^{2+} + 5Fe^{3+} + 4H_2O$$

Problem . 26

In order to find the concentration of some dilute hydrochloric acid, a student took $25.0\,cm^3$ and diluted it accurately to $250\,cm^3$. She made up a standard solution of sodium hydrogencarbonate by dissolving $2.25\,g$ of it in water, and making up the solution to $250\,cm^3$. A $25.0\,cm^3$ sample of this solution required $25.6\,cm^3$ of the diluted hydrochloric acid to react to completion. Find the concentration of the original acid in $mol\,dm^{-3}$.

$$NaHCO_3 + HCl \rightarrow NaCl + CO_2 + H_2O$$

$(H = 1; C = 12; O = 16; Na = 23)$

Problem • 27

In an experiment to find the percentage of sodium chloride in a sample of rock salt, 1.50 g of the rock salt was crushed and dissolved in water in a beaker. The mixture was filtered, and washings from the beaker were also run through the filter paper. The residue on the filter paper was washed thoroughly and the washings added to the filtrate. The solution formed was made up to 250 cm^3 with pure water. A 25.0 cm^3 sample of this was titrated with 0.100 mol dm^{-3} silver nitrate solution using potassium chromate(VI) solution as indicator. 23.5 cm^3 of the silver nitrate solution was needed. Find the percentage of sodium chloride in the rock salt.

$$NaCl + AgNO_3 \rightarrow AgCl + NaNO_3$$

(Na = 23; Cl = 35.5)

Problem • 28

The concentration of some ammonium chloride solution was found in the following way. 25.0 cm^3 of the solution was mixed with 25.0 cm^3 of 1.00 mol dm^{-3} sodium hydroxide solution (an excess), and the mixture boiled gently in a fume cupboard to remove all the ammonia. 20.0 cm^3 of 0.200 mol dm^{-3} hydrochloric acid was needed to neutralise the excess sodium hydroxide:

$$NH_4Cl + NaOH \rightarrow NaCl + NH_3 + H_2O$$
$$NaOH + HCl \rightarrow NaCl + H_2O$$

Calculate

(a) the number of moles of sodium hydroxide originally;
(b) the number of moles of sodium hydroxide left after reaction with the ammonium chloride;
(c) the number of moles of ammonium chloride in 25.0 cm^3 of solution;
(d) the concentration of the ammonium chloride in g dm^{-3}.

(H = 1; N = 14; Cl = 35.5)

Problem • 29

The mineral cerussite consists of lead(II) carbonate, PbCO$_3$. A particular lead ore consisted only of cerussite and inert rocky material. 1.00 g of crushed ore was added to 25.0 cm^3 of 1.00 mol dm^{-3} nitric acid (an excess) in a beaker. When no more reaction was observed, the mixture was filtered, and washings from the beaker were also run through the filter paper. The residue on the filter paper was washed thoroughly and the washings added to the filtrate. The solution formed was made up to 250 cm^3 with water. A 25.0 cm^3 sample of this was titrated with 0.100 mol dm^{-3} sodium hydroxide solution. 20.5 cm^3 was required to produce a neutral solution.

$$PbCO_3 + 2HNO_3 \rightarrow Pb(NO_3)_2 + CO_2 + H_2O$$
$$HNO_3 + NaOH \rightarrow NaNO_3 + H_2O$$

(a) Calculate the number of moles of nitric acid present in the original 25.0 cm^3 of 1.00 mol dm^{-3} acid.
(b) Calculate the number of moles of nitric acid left after reaction with the ore.
(c) Calculate the number of moles of lead(II) carbonate in 1.00 g of the ore.
(d) Calculate the mass of lead which could be obtained from 1 tonne of the ore, assuming 100% extraction was possible.

(Pb = 207)

Problem • 30

The following experiment was carried out to find the formula for an ionic chloride, MCl_n, containing M^{n+} and Cl^- ions. 1.21 g of the chloride was dissolved in water and made up to 250 cm^3 of solution. 25.0 cm^3 of this solution was titrated with silver nitrate solution containing 0.0500 mol dm^{-3} of $Ag^+_{(aq)}$, using potassium chromate(VI) solution as indicator. 20.0 cm^3 of silver nitrate solution was required to reach the end-point.

$$Ag^+_{(aq)} + Cl^-_{(aq)} \rightarrow AgCl_{(s)}$$

(a) Calculate the number of moles of silver ions used in the titration.
(b) Calculate the mass of Cl^- and hence of M in the chloride.
(c) Find the empirical formula of the chloride.

(Cl = 35.5; M = 85.5)

Problem • 31

25.0 cm^3 of a solution containing a mixture of sodium carbonate and sodium hydrogencarbonate was titrated with 0.100 mol dm^{-3} hydrochloric acid. 12.5 cm^3 of the acid was required to reach the end-point with phenolphthalein, and a further 32.5 cm^3 when methyl orange was used. Calculate the concentrations of the sodium carbonate and sodium hydrogencarbonate in mol dm^{-3}.

Problem • 32

25.0 cm^3 of a solution containing a mixture of sodium carbonate and sodium hydroxide was titrated with 0.200 mol dm^{-3} hydrochloric acid. 20.0 cm^3 of the acid was required to reach the end-point using phenolphthalein as the indicator. However, when methyl orange was used instead of phenolphthalein, 25.0 cm^3 of acid was needed to reach the end-point. Calculate the concentrations of the sodium carbonate, Na_2CO_3, and sodium hydroxide, NaOH, in g dm^{-3}.

(H = 1; C = 12; O = 16; Na = 23)

Thermochemistry

This chapter starts by looking at how you process the results of experiments to measure the amount of heat evolved or absorbed during reactions which are easy to do in the laboratory. The bulk of the chapter then looks at how you can estimate the heat evolved or absorbed for all sorts of changes by working from published data. The level of maths needed for processing experimental results is similar to that needed for basic mole calculations. Most of the rest of the chapter involves little more than addition and subtraction.

Processing the results from thermochemistry experiments

A neutralisation reaction

This is chosen because it is typical of the sort of reaction that you can easily do with a minimal amount of apparatus, and yet still produce good results. It measures the amount of heat evolved when an acid and an alkali react together to give a salt and water. For example:

$$NaOH_{(aq)} + HCl_{(aq)} \rightarrow NaCl_{(aq)} + H_2O_{(l)}$$

The equation shows that the alkali and acid react 1 mole to 1 mole. If their concentrations were the same, you would have to take equal volumes of the two solutions – for example, $25\,cm^3$ of each at $1.0\,mol\,dm^{-3}$.

The experiment

An expanded polystyrene cup is used (see Figure 5.1) because it is a good insulator – helping to prevent heat losses – and because it absorbs hardly any heat itself.

Leave both solutions in the laboratory to reach the same temperature if possible because it makes the calculation very slightly easier! (We will consider what to do if they aren't the same temperature later.) Measure out $25\,cm^3$ of the sodium hydroxide solution and place it in the cup. Record the temperature. Add $25\,cm^3$ of the acid, stir, and record the highest temperature reached.

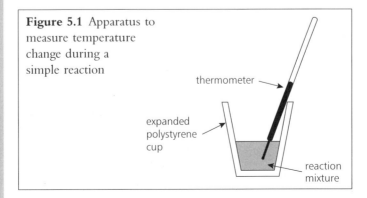

Figure 5.1 Apparatus to measure temperature change during a simple reaction

thermometer

expanded polystyrene cup

reaction mixture

The sum

The heat evolved is worked out using:

> **heat evolved = mass × specific heat × temperature rise**

This is sometimes written as:

> **heat evolved or absorbed = $ms\,\Delta T$**

where m is the mass, s is the specific heat and ΔT is the change in temperature. If there is a drop in temperature, then heat has been absorbed during the reaction; an increase shows that heat has been evolved.

The mass in this case is 50 g. This is because you have a total of 50 cm³ of solutions with densities of 1 g cm⁻³. (This is only an approximation, of course. In reality, the density will not be **exactly** the same as water.)

The specific heat can be taken as the same as that of water: $4.18\,\mathrm{J\,g^{-1}\,K^{-1}}$.

The temperature rise is whatever you have just measured. If the temperature rise was, say, 6.7 °C:

$$\text{Heat evolved} = 50 \times 4.18 \times 6.7\,\mathrm{J}$$
$$= 1400\,\mathrm{J}$$

What if the temperatures of the two solutions at the start were different?

Suppose:

Temperature of hydrochloric acid	= 17.9 °C
Temperature of sodium hydroxide solution	= 18.3 °C
Maximum temperature reached	= 24.8 °C

In this case you would split the sum into two parts. 25 g of solution had its temperature raised by 6.9 °C (24.8 − 17.9). The other 25 g had its temperature raised by 6.5 °C (24.8 − 18.3).

$$\text{Heat evolved} = (25 \times 4.18 \times 6.9) + (25 \times 4.18 \times 6.5)$$
$$= 1400\,\mathrm{J}$$

Making the sum more useful

We have worked out the amount of heat in joules evolved when the reaction happened between the arbitrary amounts of chemicals we chose. It is more usual to standardise this by working out the amount of heat which would have been evolved if mole quantities of substances had reacted.

In the case of neutralisation reactions, heat evolved is calculated "per mole of water formed".

Each mole of sodium hydroxide gives one mole of water (look back at the equation). We started with 25 cm³ of sodium hydroxide solution containing 1 mole in every 1000 cm³. 25 cm³ is 1/40 of 1000 cm³, and so we have 1/40 of a mole of sodium hydroxide that will have produced 1/40 of a mole of water.

To work out how much heat would have been evolved if we had produced 1 mole rather than 1/40 of a mole, we simply multiply our answer for the amount of heat evolved by 40.

Using the figure of 1400 J calculated above, this would give 40×1400 J for each mole of water produced. That is 56 000 J.

To show that heat is evolved during the reaction, the number is given a negative sign (the logic behind this will be explained later in this chapter), and because of the large numbers involved, it is usually expressed in kilojoules – where 1 kJ is 1000 J.

The answer would normally be quoted as -56 kJ mol^{-1} where, in a neutralisation reaction, the "per mole" (mol^{-1}) means "per mole of water formed".

Improving the experiment – plotting a cooling curve

Although the neutralisation reaction is virtually instantaneous, the temperature recorded on the thermometer does not instantly reach a peak. Time is needed for the thermometer to respond to changes in the temperature of the solution. During that time, heat is being lost to the surroundings. It would be useful to be able to estimate how much heat was being lost, so that we could work out what the maximum temperature should have been. To do this, the temperature is recorded at a series of times during the experiment.

For example, suppose the temperature of the solution in the cup was measured at 1 minute intervals. The second solution was added a few seconds after the 2 minute temperature reading in the table that follows.

Time (mins)	0	1	2	3	4	5	6
Temperature (°C)	18.1	18.1	18.1	24.8	24.7	24.6	24.5

If you look at the figures in the table, you can see that after the temperature reached its peak, it fell at a steady 0.1°C per minute because heat was being lost to the surroundings. It would therefore be reasonable to assume that it fell by a similar amount between the point of mixing (at minute 2) and the maximum temperature recorded (at minute 3). The true maximum temperature should have been 24.9 °C if there had been no heat losses. This corrected temperature can be used in the calculations.

These are made-up numbers, of course. In reality, the pattern isn't likely to be so obvious, and so a graph is plotted (see Figure 5.2).

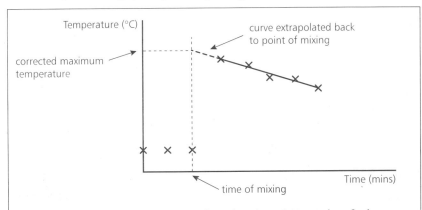

Figure 5.2 Graph of temperature plotted against time used to find maximum temperature

A combustion reaction

Heat is evolved when things burn, and it is quite easy to measure the amount of heat evolved when a liquid like ethanol burns – although the results tend to be very inaccurate using simple apparatus. Ethanol and other alcohols are frequently used because they burn cleanly and completely without producing soot.

The experiment – quick and inaccurate version

The calorimeter can be made of copper or glass (or can be as simple as an old baked bean tin) and contains a known mass of water (see Figure 5.3). The whole apparatus is surrounded by some sort of shielding to prevent draughts. The water will need to be stirred – either with the thermometer or with an extra stirrer.

The initial temperature of the water is measured. The spirit burner containing the flammable liquid (ethanol, perhaps) is weighed, and then lit and placed under the calorimeter. The temperature is allowed to rise a few degrees, and then the flame is blown out and the maximum temperature recorded. A cap is placed over the wick to prevent loss of liquid vapour, and then the spirit burner is reweighed.

Sample results

Mass of water = 250 g
Original temperature of water = 19.5 °C
Final temperature of water = 23.7 °C
Original mass of burner + ethanol = 41.36 g
Final mass of burner + ethanol = 41.18 g

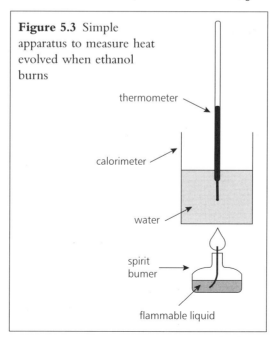

Figure 5.3 Simple apparatus to measure heat evolved when ethanol burns

thermometer

calorimeter

water

spirit bumer

flammable liquid

➤ Temperature rise =
23.7 −19.5 = 4.2 °C or 4.2 K
(the degree size is the same on
both scales).

The value of 4389 J is quoted
too accurately, but it is not
the final answer. Don't round
numbers off too soon.

➤ You may be confused
about how a number can
suddenly become negative. It
depends on how you describe
it. If you use the statement
that the heat **evolved** during a
reaction is 1100 kJ, then you
don't really need the negative
sign. If you talk about the heat
change (properly called the
enthalpy change) during the
reaction, then the negative
sign shows that heat has been
evolved. The logic behind this
will be dealt with shortly.

The sum

The specific heat of water is $4.18 \, \text{J} \, \text{g}^{-1} \, \text{K}^{-1}$. For the moment, we are going to ignore the heat absorbed by the calorimeter and the thermometer.

Heat evolved = mass × specific heat × temperature rise

$$= 250 \times 4.18 \times 4.2 \, \text{J}$$

$$= 4389 \, \text{J (or 4.389 kJ)}$$

Mass of ethanol burnt $= 41.36 - 41.18 \, \text{g}$

$$= 0.18 \, \text{g}$$

1 mole of ethanol (C_2H_5OH) weighs 46 g.

The heat evolved per mole of ethanol burnt

$$= 4.389 \times \frac{46}{0.18} \, \text{kJ}$$

$$= 1100 \, \text{kJ (to 2 significant figures)}$$

The answer should properly be recorded as $-1100 \, \text{kJ} \, \text{mol}^{-1}$. The negative sign shows that heat is evolved; the "mol^{-1}" means "per mole of ethanol".

Comments

The accepted value for the amount of heat evolved when 1 mole of ethanol burns is $-1367 \, \text{kJ} \, \text{mol}^{-1}$. The answer that these results produce is therefore much too low. We have not allowed for the heat absorbed by the calorimeter and the thermometer (and, perhaps, the stirrer), and we have made no allowance for the heat losses to the atmosphere. Plotting a cooling curve will not work this time, because the heat wasn't all evolved in one instant – there is no obvious time that you could extrapolate a curve back to.

Improving the experiment in a simple way

Suppose you knew the amount of heat given out when 1 mole of methanol (CH_3OH) burns. The value is $-726 \, \text{kJ} \, \text{mol}^{-1}$. To find a more accurate value for ethanol, you would do the experiment twice, once with methanol and once with ethanol, in each case keeping the amount of water identical and the temperature rise much the same, so that similar heat losses are involved in both cases.

Results with methanol

Mass of water	= 250 g
Original temperature of water	= 19.1 °C
Final temperature of water	= 23.8 °C
Original mass of burner + methanol	= 42.56 g
Final mass of burner + methanol	= 41.30 g

Results with ethanol

Mass of water	= 250 g
Original temperature of water	= 19.5 °C
Final temperature of water	= 24.0 °C
Original mass of burner + ethanol	= 40.87 g
Final mass of burner + ethanol	= 40.67 g

The sum

The methanol results are used to find the **heat capacity** of the apparatus – that is the amount of heat needed to raise the temperature by $1\,°C$ (the same as $1\,K$).

> ➤ 1 mole of methanol weighs 32 g.
>
> **Remember:**
>
> Number of moles
> $$= \frac{\text{mass (g)}}{\text{mass of 1 mole (g)}}$$

Mass of methanol used $= 0.26\,g$

Number of moles of methanol used $= \dfrac{0.26}{32}$

$$= 8.125 \times 10^{-3}$$

Each mole evolves $726\,kJ$ of heat when it burns.

Total heat evolved $= 8.125 \times 10^{-3} \times 726\,kJ$

This raised the temperature by $4.7\,°C$. The heat capacity of the apparatus is the amount of heat needed to raise the temperature by $1\,°C$.

Heat capacity $= \dfrac{8.125 \times 10^{-3} \times 726}{4.7}\,kJ\,°C^{-1}$

$$= 1.26\,kJ\,°C^{-1}$$

In the ethanol experiment, the temperature rose by $4.5\,°C$. The heat capacity of the apparatus is unchanged, provided the amount of water is still the same. Every degree increase in temperature needed $1.26\,kJ$ of heat to be evolved.

Heat evolved in ethanol case $= 4.5 \times 1.26\,kJ$
$$= 5.67\,kJ$$

Mass of ethanol used $= 0.20\,g$

If $46\,g$ of ethanol (1 mole) had been burnt, the heat evolved would have been

$$\frac{46}{0.20} \times 5.67 = 1300\,kJ \text{ (to 2 significant figures)}$$

The heat evolved when ethanol burns is therefore $-1300\,kJ\,mol^{-1}$. Notice that this answer is closer to the accepted one ($-1376\,kJ\,mol^{-1}$), but the experiment is still full of errors. The practical details could be improved further, but there would be no difference in the way the calculation is done.

Problem • 1

A student carried out an experiment to measure the heat evolved when sodium hydroxide solution was neutralised with dilute sulphuric acid:

$$2NaOH + H_2SO_4 \rightarrow Na_2SO_4 + 2H_2O$$

He placed $50\,cm^3$ of $1.0\,mol\,dm^{-3}$ sodium hydroxide solution in a plastic cup and recorded its steady temperature. He poured $25\,cm^3$ of $1.0\,mol\,dm^{-3}$ sulphuric acid into a measuring cylinder and recorded the temperature of that. Then he added the sulphuric acid to the sodium hydroxide and started timing at the point of mixing, recording temperatures at 1 minute intervals for 5 minutes.

Results:
Temperature of sodium hydroxide solution $= 20.5\,°C$
Temperature of dilute sulphuric acid $= 20.8\,°C$

Time (mins)	0	1	2	3	4	5
Temp of mixture (°C)		29.5	29.3	29.1	28.9	28.7

Assume that the density of all solutions is $1\,g\,cm^{-3}$ and their specific heats are all $4.18\,J\,g^{-1}\,K^{-1}$.

(a) Estimate the maximum temperature which would have been reached in the absence of any heat losses.
(b) Calculate the total amount of heat evolved during this reaction.
(c) Calculate the amount of heat evolved per mole of water formed during the neutralisation.

The apparatus shown in Figure 5.3 was used to measure the amount of heat evolved when 1 mole of hexane, C_6H_{14}, burns completely to give carbon dioxide and water. The heat capacity of the apparatus had been previously found to be $1.15\,kJ\,^{\circ}C^{-1}$, and everything was kept the same in this experiment.

Results:
Mass of burner + hexane before experiment = 45.63 g
Mass of burner + hexane after experiment = 45.50 g
Original temperature of water   = 19.7 °C
Final temperature of water   = 24.9 °C

(a) Calculate the heat evolved during this experiment.
(b) Calculate the heat evolved when 1 mole of hexane burns.

(H = 1; C = 12)

Hess's Law cycles

Defining some terms

We are going on now to look at how you can estimate the amount of heat evolved or absorbed during reactions from published data. You can't do this until you know what all the words mean.

Enthalpy changes

During almost all chemical reactions there are changes in the energy of the system, and you normally see this as heat either being evolved or absorbed. Energy is needed to break bonds in the original materials, and energy is released when new bonds are made in the products. It is very, very unlikely that these two processes will be exactly in balance, and so some energy will either be released to the surroundings, or absorbed from the surroundings.

The heat evolved or absorbed during a reaction is known as the **enthalpy change** for the reaction and is given the symbol ΔH – read as "delta H". You can't actually measure the heat content (or **enthalpy**) of a particular substance – just the **change in enthalpy** when it reacts to form something new.

If heat is evolved during a reaction, the reaction is said to be **exothermic**, and the value of ΔH is given a negative sign (for example, $-200\,kJ$).

If heat is absorbed during a reaction, the reaction is **endothermic**, and ΔH is given a positive sign (for example, $+100$ kJ). The "+" must always be written – you cannot just assume it.

> ➤ **Beyond A level:** Strictly speaking, the enthalpy change is a measure of the heat evolved or absorbed if the reaction is done at **constant pressure**. Because almost all reactions in the lab are done open to the atmosphere (and therefore at constant atmospheric pressure), this is a sensible measure to use. When an experiment is done in a closed container of fixed volume, the heat evolved or absorbed in these conditions is called the **internal energy change** and is given the symbol ΔU.

For reactions involving no change in volume (for example, if no gases are evolved), the two measures are identical, but in other cases, there is a slight difference. If you want to find out more, you will need to refer to a reasonably advanced text book.

The reason for these signs is that the reactions are looked at from the point of view of the substances reacting (the reactants). This is more readily seen on an enthalpy diagram (see Figure 5.4).

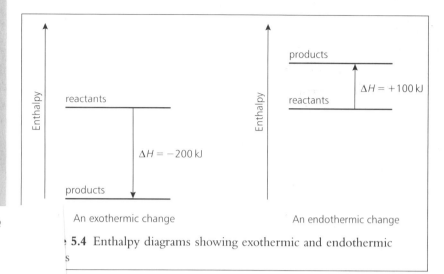

An exothermic change   An endothermic change

5.4 Enthalpy diagrams showing exothermic and endothermic

othermic change, the reactants lose heat energy to the surroundings; in
hermic change, they gain it from the surroundings.

othermic case, for example, you could perhaps do an experiment
owed that 200 kJ of heat energy was evolved when particular
of substances reacted. You would not know what the actual enthalpy
tent) of either the reactants or the products was – but you would
the products had an enthalpy of 200 kJ less than the reactants. All
erested in is enthalpy **changes**.

d conditions

y change quoted under standard conditions is given the symbol
ich you read as "delta H standard" or as "delta H nought". Even
reaction does not take place under standard conditions, the
measured value under other conditions is corrected to give a standard one. At
A level this doesn't really concern you – all values quoted will be standard
ones.

Standard conditions include:

■ 298 K (unless some other temperature is specifically stated);

■ a pressure of 1 atmosphere;

■ solution concentrations of 1 mol dm^{-3};

■ substances present in their standard states.

"Standard state" means the physical state that you would expect a substance to
be in under these conditions. For example, water as a liquid, $H_2O_{(l)}$; sodium
as a solid, $Na_{(s)}$; hydrogen as gaseous molecules, $H_{2(g)}$.

> ➤ You may find standard pressure quoted as 100 KPa which is slightly less than 1 atmosphere. Find out which your examiners want.

91

➤ **Note:** These various **enthalpy changes** are sometimes called by slightly different terms. The correct term is "enthalpy change of . . ." (reaction or combustion or formation or neutralisation). Frequently the word "change" is missed out, so that "enthalpy of . . ." (reaction, etc.) means the same thing.

In older text books, you may find the original term "heat of . . ." (reaction, etc.).

➤ **Dynamic equilibrium:** In the example quoted, the reaction combining nitrogen and hydrogen is happening at exactly the same rate as that splitting up the ammonia. The result is a mixture of nitrogen, hydrogen and ammonia – called an equilibrium mixture.

Standard enthalpy change of reaction, $\Delta H^{\ominus}$

This is the enthalpy change when substances react under standard conditions in quantities given by the equation for the reaction.

Instead of using the term "enthalpy change", you can also use the phrase "the heat evolved or absorbed when . . .". For example, suppose

$$2A + B \rightarrow C + D \qquad \Delta H^{\ominus} = -153\, kJ\, mol^{-1}$$

This means that if 2 moles of A react with 1 mole of B under standard conditions, 153 kJ of heat is evolved. The use of the unit "mol^{-1}" in this context is a bit odd. It isn't "per mole of A" or "per mole of B". It relates to the whole equation expressed in mole quantities.

If you have a reversible reaction in a state of dynamic equilibrium, the standard enthalpy change of reaction is calculated on the assumption that the reaction goes completely to the right hand side. For example,

$$N_2 + 3H_2 \rightleftharpoons 2NH_3 \qquad \Delta H^{\ominus} = -92\, kJ\, mol^{-1}$$

This means that if 1 mole of nitrogen and 3 moles of hydrogen reacted **completely** to give 2 moles of ammonia, 92 kJ of heat would be evolved (see Figure 5.5). In reality, only about 15% usually combines under the conditions used industrially, but the standard enthalpy change is still quoted as $-92\, kJ\, mol^{-1}$.

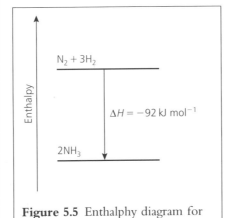

Figure 5.5 Enthalphy diagram for the formation of ammonia

If the reaction is written in the reverse direction:

$$2NH_3 \rightleftharpoons N_2 + 3H_2$$

the sign of the enthalpy change is also reversed, i.e. $\Delta H^{\ominus} = +92\, kJ\, mol^{-1}$. This is important: if you reverse the direction of a reaction, the sign of the enthalpy change reverses as well. This is all fairly obvious if you look at the enthalpy diagram. If 92 kJ is evolved when nitrogen and hydrogen combine to make ammonia, then 92 kJ must be put back in to make ammonia split up again.

Standard enthalpy change of combustion, $\Delta H^{\ominus}_c$

This is the enthalpy change when 1 mole of a substance is burned completely in oxygen under standard conditions.

Be careful if you use the alternative phraseology for this. You could say "the heat evolved when . . . ". Be careful not to say "heat evolved or absorbed when . . . " – a combustion reaction absorbing heat is a contradiction in terms!

> ➤ This is a good example of the case where a standard enthalpy change has to be calculated from a reaction done under non-standard conditions. Hardly anything will actually burn at a temperature of 298 K (25 °C). Don't worry about this at A level – just use the standard value given to you.

$$\text{e.g.} \quad S_{(s)} + O_{2(g)} \rightarrow SO_{2(g)} \qquad\qquad \Delta H^{\ominus}_c = -297\,\text{kJ mol}^{-1}$$

$$H_{2(g)} + \tfrac{1}{2}O_{2(g)} \rightarrow H_2O_{(l)} \qquad\qquad \Delta H^{\ominus}_c = -286\,\text{kJ mol}^{-1}$$

$$C_4H_{10(g)} + 6\tfrac{1}{2}O_{2(g)} \rightarrow 4CO_{2(g)} + 5H_2O_{(l)} \quad \Delta H^{\ominus}_c = -2877\,\text{kJ mol}^{-1}$$

Notice that you will often have to write halves into combustion equations. The definition must have 1 mole of the substance you are burning, and if this means that the rest of the equation needs to contain halves, then so be it.

Standard enthalpy change of neutralisation, $\Delta H^{\ominus}_{neut}$

This is the enthalpy change when an acid and an alkali react together under standard conditions to give one mole of water.

Heat is always **evolved** when an acid and an alkali neutralise each other, so the alternative phraseology would be "the heat evolved when . . . ".

$$\text{e.g.} \quad NaOH_{(aq)} + HCl_{(aq)} \rightarrow NaOH_{(aq)} + H_2O_{(l)} \quad \Delta H^{\ominus}_{neut} = -58\,\text{kJ mol}^{-1}$$

In this case, the "mol^{-1}" refers to the 1 mole of water being formed. We looked at how this enthalpy change could be measured earlier in this chapter.

Standard enthalpy change of formation, $\Delta H^{\ominus}_f$

This is the enthalpy change when 1 mole of a substance is formed from its elements under standard conditions.

In this case, you can replace the term "enthalpy change" in the definition by "heat evolved or absorbed". Some substances have positive enthalpy changes of formation, others negative.

This is a very important term, and a large proportion of calculations will need you to use it somewhere.

$$\text{e.g.} \quad Na_{(s)} + \tfrac{1}{2}Cl_{2(g)} \rightarrow NaCl_{(s)} \qquad\qquad \Delta H^{\ominus}_f = -411\,\text{kJ mol}^{-1}$$

$$C_{(s)} + O_{2(g)} \rightarrow CO_{2(g)} \qquad\qquad \Delta H^{\ominus}_f = -394\,\text{kJ mol}^{-1}$$

$$2C_{(s)} + 1\tfrac{1}{2}H_{2(g)} + \tfrac{1}{2}N_{2(g)} \rightarrow CH_3CN_{(l)} \quad \Delta H^{\ominus}_f = +31\,\text{kJ mol}^{-1}$$

Notes

In some cases, an enthalpy change can be called by different names. For example, the enthalpy change of formation of CO_2 is also the enthalpy change of combustion of carbon.

> ➤ We have not done any calculations for several pages now, but it is a complete waste of time trying to do the thermochemistry calculations which follow if you do not fully understand the meanings of all the terms we have discussed, and how to write equations for things like enthalpy change of combustion or formation.
>
> If you aren't reasonably happy about writing or balancing the sorts of equations we have been using, now is a good time to go back and do some revision.

In all cases, the equation must be written so that 1 mole of the substance is formed, even if this means writing fractions into the equation. You must also start from **elements** – the only compound in the equation is the one being formed.

Everything must be present in its standard state, which is the state you would expect it to be in at 298 K and 1 atmosphere pressure. This is not just the physical state, but also implies the fact that hydrogen is H_2 molecules, nitrogen is N_2 molecules, and so on. It is important that you do not write the hydrogens as "$3H_{(g)}$". You must show the hydrogens as H_2 molecules – not as individual atoms – because this is how they exist at 298 K.

Enthalpy changes of formation can be quoted for substances which you can't make directly from the elements. For example, in the third equation above, there is no way that you can persuade carbon, hydrogen and nitrogen to combine together to make CH_3CN (ethanenitrile) directly. The value can, however, be calculated in ways that we will look at shortly.

The enthalpy change of formation of any element in its standard state is zero. This is fairly obvious if you think about it. How much heat is going to be evolved or absorbed if you make $O_{2(g)}$ from $O_{2(g)}$, for example, or $Na_{(s)}$ from $Na_{(s)}$? Not a lot!

Problem • 3

The enthalpy change of combustion of ethane, C_2H_6, is represented by the equation:

$$C_2H_{6(g)} + 3\tfrac{1}{2}O_{2(g)} \rightarrow 2CO_{2(g)} + 3H_2O_{(l)}$$

Write equations representing the enthalpy change of combustion of:

(a) carbon,
(b) methane, $CH_{4(g)}$
(c) ethanol, $C_2H_5OH_{(l)}$
(d) octane, $C_8H_{18(l)}$

Problem • 4

The enthalpy change of formation of methane is represented by the equation:

$$C_{(s)} + 2H_{2(g)} \rightarrow CH_{4(g)}$$

Write equations representing the enthalpy change of formation of:

(a) sodium iodide, $NaI_{(s)}$
(b) water, $H_2O_{(l)}$
(c) ethanol, $C_2H_5OH_{(l)}$
(d) calcium carbonate, $CaCO_{3(s)}$
(e) sodium chlorate(V), $NaClO_{3(s)}$

Hess's Law

> *The enthalpy change accompanying a chemical change is independent of the route by which the chemical change occurs.*

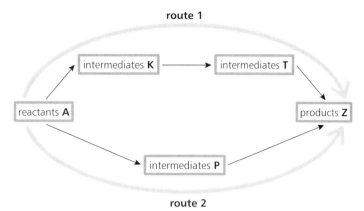

This means that if you convert reactants **A** into products **Z** in one step or in many steps, the overall enthalpy change is always the same.

The overall enthalpy change is determined by the gap between the reactants and the products on an enthalpy diagram, and that gap is not affected in any way by the route you use to get from one to the other (see Figure 5.6). Whichever route you use, the overall enthalpy change is the same, ΔH.

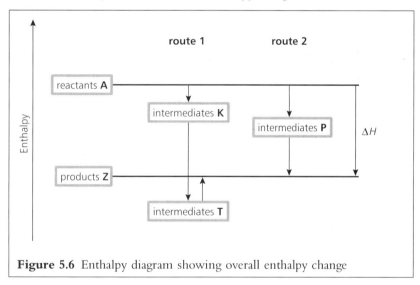

Figure 5.6 Enthalpy diagram showing overall enthalpy change

Using Hess's Law to calculate enthalpy changes

A typical question will give you an enthalpy change to find, together with a list of relevant data.

Step 1

Write down the equation for the enthalpy change you are asked to find. Write ΔH over the top of the arrow. Take care at this stage that you have got the equation properly balanced. If your equation is wrong, your final answer will almost certainly be wrong as well. Get into the habit of putting state symbols in the equation. In some cases, they matter.

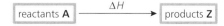

> ➤ **Note!** With the exception of Born–Haber cycles (see later) which are usually drawn in a way similar to Figure 5.6, all enthalpy change calculations can be done using the method described in the main body of the text. Provided you don't try to take short cuts, this method is virtually foolproof.
>
> You may come across other ways of doing these calculations which are sometimes slightly quicker, but these other methods need you to learn several different techniques depending on what you are asked to do, and what information you are given. This is potentially confusing. Practice **one** method which will cover **all** sums.

Step 2

Now use the information you are given in the question to complete a cycle (often, but not always a triangle) that you can apply Hess's Law to.

Your diagram will often end up looking like one of the following:

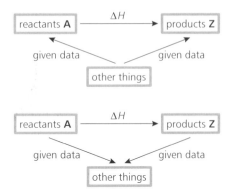

Which way the arrows point in the bottom part of the diagram will depend entirely on what information you are given. Examples coming up shortly will make this clear.

Step 3

Apply Hess's Law. You need to find two routes within the diagram **which do not go against the flow of any arrows**. The starting point for the two routes will be a corner of the diagram that arrows are leaving from. The end point of the two routes is the corner where arrow heads are arriving.

For the two diagrams above, the routes would be:

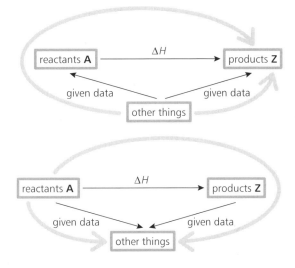

> ➤ **Note!** You must be sure that you go with the flow of the arrows. It is possible to reverse the flow of an arrow, but if you do that you must also reverse the sign of the enthalpy change. It is confusing, and you are likely to forget to do it. It also means that you will have to stop and think! Just accept the arrows the way they are, and find two routes which don't involve changing anything.

Notice that the pattern of the two routes is quite different in the two cases. You must not try to learn a particular pattern – it varies too much. Work out what the two routes are in each new situation. It will not take you more than a few seconds anyway!

Hess's Law says that the total enthalpy change on the two routes will be identical – so add together the enthalpy changes on each route, and equate them. This gives you an equation in which the only unknown is ΔH.

Examples will make this process very obvious.

Example 1

Calculate the standard enthalpy change for the reaction:

$$C_2H_{4(g)} + H_{2(g)} \rightarrow C_2H_{6(g)}$$

given the following standard enthalpy changes of combustion:

$$\Delta H^{\ominus}_c(C_2H_{4(g)}) = -1411 \text{ kJ mol}^{-1}$$
$$\Delta H^{\ominus}_c(H_{2(g)}) \quad = -286 \text{ kJ mol}^{-1}$$
$$\Delta H^{\ominus}_c(C_2H_{6(g)}) = -1560 \text{ kJ mol}^{-1}$$

You are given the equation, so write it down with ΔH written over the arrow:

$$C_2H_{4(g)} + H_{2(g)} \xrightarrow{\Delta H} C_2H_{6(g)}$$

Now slot in the information you have been given. Think carefully about what it means. Enthalpy change of combustion is about burning 1 mole of the substance completely in oxygen – in other words, you start from the substance and turn it into something else. In this case, then, your arrows will start from the ethene, hydrogen and ethane and go towards the bottom corner of the diagram.

Start with the ethene value (because that's the first one you are given):

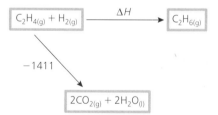

Notice that we have not bothered to write the oxygens into the equation – we simply assume that we can obtain all we need from the air. You must however, be careful to balance the carbons and hydrogens – hence the $2CO_2$ and $2H_2O$.

Now add in the value for hydrogen:

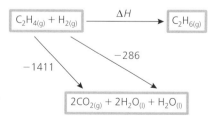

This leaves the value for the ethane. If you burn ethane, you get the same $2CO_2 + 3H_2O$ as before – you are bound to, because you have still got

97

exactly the same number of carbons and hydrogens. Putting in the ethane value gives:

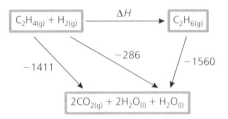

Now all you need to do is find two routes around the diagram without going against the flow of any arrows. In this case, the routes will start in the top left hand corner, because that is where arrows are leaving from. The routes end in the bottom corner, because that is where all the arrow heads end up.

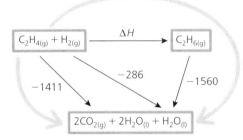

Now use Hess's Law, which says that the total enthalpy changes on the two routes are equal:

$$\Delta H - 1560 = -1411 - 286$$

Solving for ΔH gives:

$$\Delta H = +1560 - 1411 - 286$$
$$\Delta H = -137 \, \text{kJ mol}^{-1}$$

This has taken a lot of paper to describe, but most of it goes on in your mind. The final answer in an exam would look like this:

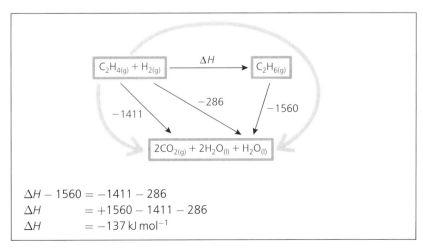

$$\Delta H - 1560 = -1411 - 286$$
$$\Delta H \quad = +1560 - 1411 - 286$$
$$\Delta H \quad = -137 \, \text{kJ mol}^{-1}$$

Example 2   Calculate the enthalpy change of combustion of ethene, C_2H_4, given the following standard enthalpy changes of formation:

$$\Delta H^{\ominus}{}_f(C_2H_{4(g)}) = +52\ \text{kJ mol}^{-1}$$

$$\Delta H^{\ominus}{}_f(CO_{2(g)}) = -394\ \text{kJ mol}^{-1}$$

$$\Delta H^{\ominus}{}_f(H_2O_{(l)}) = -286\ \text{kJ mol}^{-1}$$

Start by writing the equation with ΔH over the top of the arrow. Be careful to get it balanced properly, otherwise your sum is bound to be wrong.

$$C_2H_{4(g)} + 3O_{2(g)} \xrightarrow{\ \Delta H\ } 2CO_{2(g)} + 2H_2O_{(l)}$$

This time you are given enthalpy changes of formation. This is about making 1 mole of substance from the elements – with everything being in its standard state (the state you would expect to find it in under standard conditions).

This time, the arrows will point towards the substances in the equation, and at the bottom corner of the diagram will be the elements. Start with the first bit of information you are given and put it into the diagram:

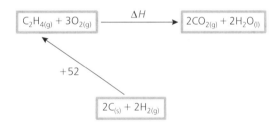

> The hydrogen is $2H_2$ – **not** $4H$. Hydrogen exists as H_2 molecules under standard conditions.

Now add in the values for carbon dioxide and water. **Be very careful at this point!** In both cases you are making **2 moles** of compound. The $\Delta H^{\ominus}{}_f$ values relate to making **1 mole**. You must remember to multiply both values by 2. Forgetting to do this is one of the commonest mistakes in this type of calculation.

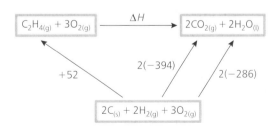

> This is a good example of a case where it is useful to draw boxes around substances – especially the collection of elements at the bottom. It is impossible to draw arrows from the correct combination of elements to all the substances. Think of the bottom corner as a box of elements that you can draw on as you need.

What about the oxygen? This is already an element in its standard state. There will be no enthalpy change involved in taking the oxygen from the bottom corner to the top left. You could include it by writing (0) over a dotted arrow if you wished. At least you would be forced to stop and think about it – and not just casually leave it out!

99

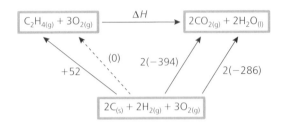

Finally find two routes around the diagram without going against the flow of an arrow, and then apply Hess's Law.

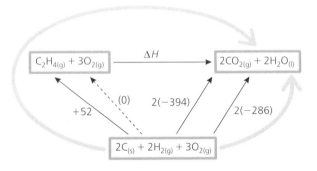

$$\Delta H + 52 = 2(-394) + 2(-286)$$
$$\Delta H \quad = -52 + 2(-394) + 2(-286)$$
$$\Delta H \quad = -1412 \, \text{kJ mol}^{-1}$$

Once again, all you would write down in an exam is the final diagram and the sum.

> **Hint:** Read your calculator instruction book so that you understand how to do this simple sum as quickly as possible. It could save you a lot of time fiddling around with brackets or memory if you understand the order that your calculator does things in.

Example 3

> This is a simple example of a way of finding an enthalpy change of formation for a compound which can't actually be made directly from its elements. This doesn't matter. You can draw a valid Hess's Law cycle even if one of the steps is an imaginary one. Most compounds, in fact, can't be made directly from their elements, but they can still have a calculated enthalpy change of formation assigned to them – and this can be used to calculate other enthalpy changes involving that compound.

Calculate the standard enthalpy change of formation of methane from the following enthalpy changes of combustion:

$$\Delta H^{\ominus}_c(CH_{4(g)}) = -890 \, \text{kJ mol}^{-1}$$
$$\Delta H^{\ominus}_c(H_{2(g)}) = -286 \, \text{kJ mol}^{-1}$$
$$\Delta H^{\ominus}_c(C_{(s)}) = -394 \, \text{kJ mol}^{-1}$$

Start by writing the equation for the enthalpy change you want, with ΔH written over the top of the arrow:

Then slot in all the information you have been given. In this case, we are burning everything, and so arrows will start from the substances in the equation and go down to combustion products in the bottom corner. The final diagram will look like this:

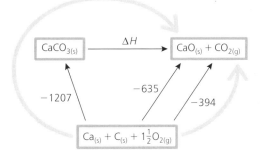

$$\Delta H - 890 = -394 + 2(-286)$$

$$\Delta H = +890 - 394 + 2(-286)$$

$$\Delta H = -76 \, kJ \, mol^{-1}$$

> **Note!** There are 2 moles of hydrogen being burnt – the value for hydrogen therefore has to be multiplied by 2.

Example 4

Calculate the enthalpy change for the reaction:

$$CaCO_{3(s)} \rightarrow CaO_{(s)} + CO_{2(g)}$$

Standard enthalpy changes of formation:

$$\Delta H^{\ominus}{}_f(CaCO_{3(s)}) = -1207 \, kJ \, mol^{-1}$$

$$\Delta H^{\ominus}{}_f(CaO_{(s)}) = -635 \, kJ \, mol^{-1}$$

$$\Delta H^{\ominus}{}_f(CO_{2(g)}) = -394 \, kJ \, mol^{-1}$$

This time you are given the equation – so write it down again with ΔH over the top of the arrow and then construct the rest of the cycle using the information you have been given. In this case, the bottom corner of the diagram will consist of the elements because you have been given standard enthalpies of formation.

> This is a simple example of a problem involving an enthalpy change of formation of a compound (the calcium carbonate) that can't be made directly from its elements. The −1207 value will have been worked out using the sort of calculations we've been doing. You can then use this value to work out the enthalpy change in familiar reactions like the example on the right.

$$\Delta H - 1207 = -635 - 394$$

$$\Delta H = +1207 - 635 - 394$$

$$\Delta H = +178 \, kJ \, mol^{-1}$$

> **Note!** You **must** include the + sign in the answer. It isn't enough just to write 178. It has to be +178.

101

Example 5 Calculate the standard enthalpy change of formation of solid ammonium chloride, NH_4Cl, using the following data:

$$\Delta H^{\ominus}_{f}(NH_{3(g)}) = -46.1 \text{ kJ mol}^{-1}$$

$$\Delta H^{\ominus}_{f}(HCl_{(g)}) = -92.3 \text{ kJ mol}^{-1}$$

$$NH_{3(g)} + HCl_{(g)} \rightarrow NH_4Cl_{(s)} \qquad \Delta H^{\ominus} = -176.0 \text{ kJ mol}^{-1}$$

➤ **Remember:** Enthalpy change of formation must start from **elements**. Although ammonium chloride is being made when ammonia and HCl react, this does not fit the definition for enthalpy change of formation.

As always, write down the equation for the enthalpy change you want, with ΔH written over the top of the arrow:

$$\frac{1}{2}N_{2(g)} + 2H_{2(g)} + \frac{1}{2}Cl_{2(g)} \xrightarrow{\Delta H} NH_4Cl_{(s)}$$

Now use the information to complete a cycle:

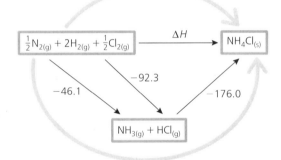

➤ **You have an unusual assortment of information in this example, but just think about what each piece means, and slot it onto the diagram, taking care that the arrows point in the right direction. The two routes this time do not correspond to ones we've come across before. This doesn't matter – you just work them out as you need them. Don't leave this example until you are sure that you understand why the cycle is drawn as it is.**

$$\Delta H = -46.1 - 92.3 - 176.0$$

$$\Delta H = -314.4 \text{ kJ mol}^{-1}$$

(Strictly speaking this should be written as $\Delta H^{\ominus}_{f} = -314.4 \text{ kJ mol}^{-1}$.)

Problem • 5 Calculate the enthalpy change for the reaction:

$$2NaNO_{3(s)} \rightarrow 2NaNO_{2(s)} + O_{2(g)}$$

given the following standard enthalpy changes of formation in kJ mol^{-1}: $NaNO_3$ −468; $NaNO_2$ −359

Problem • 6 The standard enthalpy change of combustion of carbon in the form of graphite is −393.5 kJ mol^{-1}; for carbon in the form of diamond it is −395.4 kJ mol^{-1}. Calculate the enthalpy change for the reaction

$$C_{(s,graphite)} \rightarrow C_{(s,diamond)}$$

Problem • 7 Calculate the standard enthalpy change of formation of sucrose, $C_{12}H_{22}O_{11}$, given the following standard enthalpy changes of combustion: carbon −394 kJ mol^{-1}; hydrogen −286 kJ mol^{-1}; sucrose −5640 kJ mol^{-1}.

Problem • 8

Calculate the standard enthalpy change of the reaction:

$$4FeS_{2(s)} + 11O_{2(g)} \rightarrow 2Fe_2O_{3(s)} + 8SO_{2(g)}$$

Standard enthalpy changes of formation in kJ mol^{-1}:

$$FeS_{2(s)} = -178; \ Fe_2O_{3(s)} = -824; \ SO_{2(g)} = -297$$

Problem • 9

Calculate the standard enthalpy change of formation of liquid hydrogen peroxide, H_2O_2, from the following information:

$$2H_{2(g)} + O_{2(g)} \rightarrow 2H_2O_{(l)} \qquad \Delta H^{\ominus} = -572 \ kJ \ mol^{-1}$$
$$2H_2O_{2(l)} \rightarrow 2H_2O_{(l)} + O_{2(g)} \qquad \Delta H^{\ominus} = -196 \ kJ \ mol^{-1}$$

> ➤ **Note!** Remember that mol^{-1} refers to mole quantities of the whole equation as it is written – not to 1 mole of H_2 or 1 mole of H_2O_2.

- -

Defining some more terms

Bond enthalpy or bond energy

To break a bond needs an input of energy – an endothermic process. When a bond is made, energy is evolved – an exothermic change. Bond energy is a measure of the amount of energy needed to **break** a bond.

Unfortunately (for simple understanding) there are two confusingly similar terms used, and one of these can have somewhat different meanings depending on the context! Fortunately this doesn't turn out to be a problem as far as actually doing the sums is concerned.

Bond dissociation energy (or enthalpy)

If you have a simple diatomic molecule (one containing only two atoms) like hydrogen, H_2, or hydrogen bromide, HBr, the energy needed to break one mole of the bond is called the bond dissociation energy (or bond dissociation enthalpy):

$$H_{2(g)} \rightarrow 2H_{(g)} \qquad \text{Bond dissociation energy} = +436 \ kJ \ mol^{-1}$$
$$HBr_{(g)} \rightarrow H_{(g)} + Br_{(g)} \qquad \text{Bond dissociation energy} = +366 \ kJ \ mol^{-1}$$

You must always start from the original compound in the gas state, and what you end up with must also be in the gas state.

> ➤ **Radical** is an atom or group of atoms which contains an unpaired electron. The dot in $CH_3\cdot$ shows this unpaired electron. The hydrogen atom formed is also a radical, of course. With atoms, the dot isn't usually written, unless you are trying to make a particular point – it is not relevant here.

This term becomes more problematic if you start with a compound containing more than 2 atoms – for example, in methane, CH_4. If you break off one mole of hydrogen atoms, you will end up with methyl **radicals**, $CH_3\cdot$:

$$CH_{4(g)} \rightarrow CH_{3(g)}\cdot + H_{(g)}$$

The hydrogen atoms left attached to the carbon are no longer in exactly the same environment as they were in methane, and so the strength of the bond will be different in $CH_3\cdot$ than in CH_4. Breaking off a second mole of hydrogen atoms will require a different bond dissociation enthalpy from the first. Taking the third one off will need a different amount of energy again, and so will the fourth.

It is much more convenient to take an average value.

➤ **Hint:** When you are doing problems involving bond enthalpies, it is usually a good idea to draw the full structural formula of the compounds involved. By doing this, it is easy to count the numbers of bonds being broken. It is surprisingly easy to get the number of bonds wrong if you work from a formula like C_2H_5OH, for example.

Mean (or average) bond enthalpies (or energies)

Suppose $+1662\,kJ$ are needed to break all the bonds in a mole of methane to produce gaseous carbon atoms and gaseous hydrogen atoms:

$$H-\underset{\underset{H}{|}}{\overset{\overset{H}{|}}{C}}-H_{(g)} \longrightarrow C_{(g)} + 4H_{(g)} \qquad \Delta H = +1662\,kJ\,mol^{-1}$$

4 moles of C–H bonds are being broken, and so the mean bond enthalpy is

$$\frac{+1662}{4} = +415.5\,kJ\,mol^{-1}$$

Mean bond enthalpies are the ones you will almost always use in calculations. Mean bond enthalpies are also known as **bond energy terms**. Throughout the rest of this topic, they will simply be called bond enthalpies.

Important

When you are using bond enthalpies, you must start from the compound in the gas state, and end up with individual atoms of the elements, also in the gas state. If you are given a problem which involves a liquid, you first have to convert it into a gas before you can do any bond enthalpy sums. If you need to do this, the examiners will give you the necessary enthalpy change information.

Standard enthalpy change of vaporisation, $\Delta H^{\ominus}{}_v$

This is the heat needed to convert one mole of substance from liquid to gas. The substance should be at its boiling point and a pressure of 1 atmosphere.

For example, $\Delta H^{\ominus}{}_v$ for water is $+41\,kJ\,mol^{-1}$. This means that if you have 1 mole of water at $100\,°C$, it will take $41\,kJ$ to convert it entirely to steam.

Standard enthalpy change of atomisation, $\Delta H^{\ominus}{}_a$

This is the heat needed to produce 1 mole of gaseous atoms from the element in its standard state.

It is essential to remember that the "per mole" in this case refers to a mole of gaseous atoms – and not a mole of the original element. All the following changes represent enthalpy changes of atomisation:

$$\tfrac{1}{2}\,H_{2(g)} \rightarrow H_{(g)} \qquad\qquad \Delta H^{\ominus}{}_a = +218\,kJ\,mol^{-1}$$

$$K_{(s)} \rightarrow K_{(g)} \qquad\qquad \Delta H^{\ominus}{}_a = \ \ +89\,kJ\,mol^{-1}$$

$$\tfrac{1}{2}\,Br_{2(l)} \rightarrow Br_{(g)} \qquad\qquad \Delta H^{\ominus}{}_a = +112\,kJ\,mol^{-1}$$

$$\tfrac{1}{4}\,P_{4(s)} \rightarrow P_{(g)} \qquad\qquad \Delta H^{\ominus}{}_a = +315\,kJ\,mol^{-1}$$

Calculations involving bond enthalpies

> There is considerable variation in values quoted for **bond enthalpies** depending on what source you use. Often, there is even inconsistency within a single book – a value used on one page being inconsistent with one used a page or two later.

Part of the problem is that there are two different meanings of the word "average" (or "mean"). We have just calculated the average C–H bond enthalpy in methane to be +415.5 kJ mol^{-1}. But "average" can also be taken to apply to an average value for all C–H bonds – whatever their environment, for example, in ethane or ethene or benzene or ethanal or whatever. Because the hydrogen is bonded slightly differently in all of these (a problem largely beyond A level), the strength will not be exactly the same as the average value in methane. To make life easier, an average value is taken which is approximately right for all C–H bonds (but not exactly right for any of them!). The average value which we shall take in the calculations which follow is +413 kJ mol^{-1}.

Because of this averaging, calculations using bond enthalpies only ever give an approximate answer. Little of this need really concern you for exam purposes. Just use whatever values you are given, but bear in mind the inaccuracies which are bound to be present in bond enthalpy sums.

There are two different approaches to these calculations. There is a quick, short-cut method for which you will need to learn a different technique, and which will present you with some difficulties if a slightly unusual problem comes up. Or, you can use exactly the same technique that we have used up to now. Each question will take a little longer to do, but you will be able to cope with any problem you may be given, with the minimum amount of thinking in an exam! This is the way we are going to do it.

Example 6

Estimate the enthalpy change for the reaction:

$$C_2H_{4(g)} + H_2O_{(g)} \rightarrow CH_3CH_2OH_{(g)}$$

given the following bond enthalpies:

C–C	+ 347 kJ mol^{-1}
C=C	+ 612 kJ mol^{-1}
C–H	+ 413 kJ mol^{-1}
O–H	+ 464 kJ mol^{-1}
C–O	+ 358 kJ mol^{-1}

Notice that the water and the ethanol are not in their standard states, which should be liquid. This is partly because, when the reaction is done industrially, they would be gases anyway, but mainly it is to make the sum more straightforward.

Start by writing the equation with ΔH over the arrow exactly as before. Show the structures of **all** the molecules to make counting bonds easier.

Now stop and think about the information you are given. Mean bond enthalpies measure the energy needed to break 1 mole of a particular bond in a gaseous compound to give gaseous atoms. In this example, all the compounds are gaseous, so this isn't a problem. Your arrows will run from the compounds down to gaseous atoms in the bottom corner.

Make sure that you understand the reason for every single number on the following cycle.

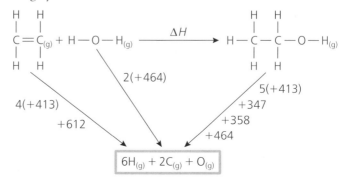

Now find two routes around the diagram without going against the flow of an arrow, and equate them according to Hess's Law.

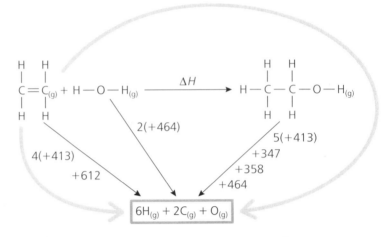

$$\Delta H + 5(+413) + 347 + 358 + 464 = 4(+413) + 612 + 2(+464)$$

Solving for ΔH gives:

$$\Delta H = -42 \text{ kJ mol}^{-1}.$$

Example 7

Calculate the mean bond enthalpy of the Si$-$F bond in SiF$_{4(g)}$, given the following enthalpy changes:

Formation of $SiF_{4(g)}$:	-1615 kJ mol^{-1}
Atomisation of silicon:	$+456$ kJ mol^{-1}
Atomisation of fluorine:	$+79$ kJ mol^{-1}

Start by writing an equation for the change you are interested in:

$$\begin{array}{c} F \\ | \\ F-Si-F_{(g)} \\ | \\ F \end{array} \xrightarrow{\Delta H} Si_{(g)} + 4F_{(g)}$$

You could work out a value for ΔH exactly as before, but you would have to remember to divide it by 4 at the end of the calculation, because you are breaking 4 bonds. This time, then, it would make life easier to write something different over the arrow – not ΔH, but 4(Si–F), where (Si–F) represents the mean bond enthalpy of the Si–F bond, which is what you are trying to find.

$$\begin{array}{c} F \\ | \\ F-Si-F_{(g)} \\ | \\ F \end{array} \xrightarrow{4(Si-F)} Si_{(g)} + 4F_{(g)}$$

To complete the diagram, use the information you are given. The enthalpy change of formation of SiF$_4$ concerns making the compound from its elements in their standard states – silicon as Si$_{(s)}$ and fluorine as F$_{2(g)}$. The enthalpy changes of atomisation take the elements in their standard states and turn them into gaseous atoms.

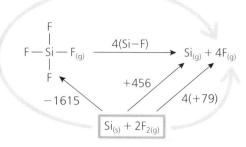

Notice that fluorine's atomisation enthalpy has been multiplied by 4. This is because of the 4 moles of fluorine atoms that are being formed. Remember that it is the number of moles of atoms formed that matters – not how many moles of molecules of element you start from.

$$4(Si-F) - 1615 = +456 + 4(+79)$$

Which solves to give $(Si-F) = +597 \, kJ \, mol^{-1}$

Example 8

Estimate the enthalpy change of formation of but-1-ene, $CH_2{=}CHCH_2CH_{3(g)}$, given the following information:

Enthalpy changes of atomisation:	carbon:	$+717 \, kJ \, mol^{-1}$
	hydrogen:	$+218 \, kJ \, mol^{-1}$
Mean bond enthalpies:	C—H:	$+413 \, kJ \, mol^{-1}$
	C—C:	$+347 \, kJ \, mol^{-1}$
	C=C:	$+612 \, kJ \, mol^{-1}$

> **"Estimate"** In bond enthalpy calculations the word "estimate" is often used rather than "calculate". This reflects the inaccuracies involved when you use mean bond enthalpies. The answer will only be an approximation to the correct value.

As always, write the equation for the change you are going to calculate. You must remember to start from the elements in their standard states.

$$4C_{(s)} + 4H_{2(g)} \xrightarrow{\Delta H} \underset{\substack{| \;\; | \;\; | \;\; | \\ H \qquad H \; H}}{\overset{\substack{H \;\; H \;\; H \;\; H \\ | \;\; | \;\; | \;\; |}}{C{=}C-C-C}}-H_{(g)}$$

At the bottom corner of the diagram will be the gaseous atoms, formed by atomising the two elements, or taking the compound to pieces.

> **Think about this!** Make sure that you understand the reason for every single number on this diagram.

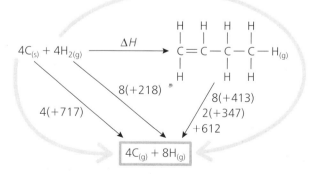

$$\Delta H + 8(+413) + 2(+347) + 612 = 4(+717) + 8(+218)$$
$$\Delta H = 4(+717) + 8(+218) - 8(+413) - 2(+347) - 612$$
$$\Delta H = +2 \, kJ \, mol^{-1}$$

Example 9   Estimate the bond enthalpy for the C–C bond in ethane, $C_2H_{6(g)}$, given the following information:

Standard enthalpy of formation of ethane:		$-85\,kJ\,mol^{-1}$
Mean bond enthalpy of C–H:		$+413\,kJ\,mol^{-1}$
Enthalpy changes of atomisation:	carbon:	$+717\,kJ\,mol^{-1}$
	hydrogen:	$+218\,kJ\,mol^{-1}$

The problem this time is that there isn't an equation you can write which only involves breaking a C–C bond. The C–C bond enthalpy is a **part** of the enthalpy change involved if you break ethane up to produce gaseous atoms – and this is as close as you can get to what you actually want.

$$\underset{(g)}{H-\overset{\overset{\displaystyle H}{|}}{C}-\overset{\overset{\displaystyle H}{|}}{\underset{\underset{\displaystyle H}{|}}{C}}-H} \xrightarrow{\;(C-C) + 6(+413)\;} 2C_{(g)} + 6H_{(g)}$$

Once you are over this hurdle, the problem then becomes like all the others. The bottom corner of the diagram this time will consist of the elements in their standard states:

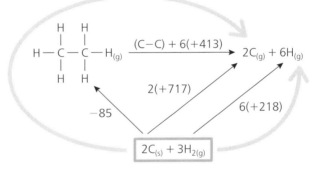

$$-85 + (C{-}C) + 6(+413) = 2(+717) + 6(+218)$$
$$(C{-}C) \qquad\qquad = 2(+717) + 6(+218) + 85 - 6(+413)$$
$$(C{-}C) \qquad\qquad = +349\,kJ\,mol^{-1}$$

Example 10   This final worked example involving bond enthalpies shows you how to cope if liquids are present in your equation. Remember that bond enthalpies can only be used if everything is in the gas state.

Estimate the enthalpy change when hydrogen peroxide decomposes to water and oxygen according to the equation:

$$2H_2O_{2(l)} \rightarrow 2H_2O_{(l)} + O_{2(g)}$$

The structural formula of hydrogen peroxide is H–O–O–H.

Bond enthalpies:	H—O	$+464\,kJ\,mol^{-1}$
	O—O	$+144\,kJ\,mol^{-1}$
	O=O	$+498\,kJ\,mol^{-1}$
Enthalpy changes of vaporisation	$H_2O_{2(l)}$	$+43\,kJ\,mol^{-1}$
	$H_2O_{(l)}$	$+41\,kJ\,mol^{-1}$

There aren't any problems at the beginning this time. You are given the equation – just rewrite it showing all the bonds, and with ΔH over the arrow:

$$2H-O-O-H_{(l)} \xrightarrow{\Delta H} 2H-O-H_{(l)} + O=O_{(g)}$$

You **cannot** use bond enthalpies on either the hydrogen peroxide or the water if they are liquids, but you do have the information to convert them into gases.

$$2H-O-O-H_{(l)} \xrightarrow{\Delta H} 2H-O-H_{(l)} + O=O_{(g)}$$

$2(+43)$ $2(+41)$

$$2H-O-O-H_{(g)} \qquad\qquad 2H-O-H_{(g)}$$

Now you can use the bond enthalpy data. The bottom corner of the diagram will consist of gaseous atoms of hydrogen and oxygen:

> **Note!** You need to be very careful counting the number of bonds when you have more than one mole of substances. Don't be afraid actually to draw the molecules the correct number of times (in this case 2 of each), and then physically count the bonds.

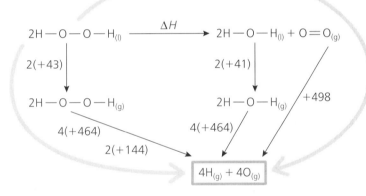

$$\Delta H + 2(+41) + 4(+464) + 498 = 2(+43) + 4(+464) + 2(+144)$$

Solving this for ΔH gives:

$$\Delta H = -206\,\text{kJ mol}^{-1}$$

Problem • 10

Estimate the enthalpy change in the following reaction between methane and chlorine:

$$CH_{4(g)} + Cl_{2(g)} \rightarrow CH_3Cl_{(g)} + HCl_{(g)}$$

Mean bond enthalpies:

C—H	$+413\,\text{kJ mol}^{-1}$
Cl—Cl	$+243\,\text{kJ mol}^{-1}$
C—Cl	$+346\,\text{kJ mol}^{-1}$
H—Cl	$+432\,\text{kJ mol}^{-1}$

Problem • 11

Calculate the mean bond enthalpy of the H—S bond in hydrogen sulphide, $H_2S_{(g)}$.

Standard enthalpy change of formation of $H_2S_{(g)}$: $-21\,\text{kJ mol}^{-1}$

Enthalpy changes of atomisation:

sulphur:	$+279\,\text{kJ mol}^{-1}$
hydrogen:	$+218\,\text{kJ mol}^{-1}$

Problem • 12

Estimate the enthalpy change of combustion of propane, $C_3H_{8(g)}$.

Mean bond enthalpies:

C—C	$+347\,\text{kJ mol}^{-1}$
C—H	$+413\,\text{kJ mol}^{-1}$
O=O	$+498\,\text{kJ mol}^{-1}$
C=O(in CO_2)	$+805\,\text{kJ mol}^{-1}$
H—O	$+464\,\text{kJ mol}^{-1}$

Enthalpy change of vaporisation of water: $\quad +41\,\text{kJ mol}^{-1}$

Problem • 13

Estimate the enthalpy change of formation of tetrachloromethane, $CCl_{4(l)}$.

Mean bond enthalpies:

C—Cl	$+346\,\text{kJ mol}^{-1}$
Cl—Cl	$+243\,\text{kJ mol}^{-1}$

Enthalpy change of vaporisation of $CCl_{4(l)}$: $\quad +30\,\text{kJ mol}^{-1}$
Enthalpy change of atomisation of carbon: $\quad +717\,\text{kJ mol}^{-1}$

Defining even more terms

First ionisation energy

The first ionisation energy is the energy required to remove the most loosely held electron from one mole of gaseous atoms to produce 1 mole of gaseous ions each carrying a charge of 1+:

$$X_{(g)} \; \rightarrow \; X^+{}_{(g)} + e^-$$

Successive ionisation energies

The second ionisation energy is defined by the equation:

$$X^+{}_{(g)} \; \rightarrow \; X^{2+}{}_{(g)} + e^-$$

It is the energy needed to remove a second electron from each ion in 1 mole of gaseous 1+ ions to give gaseous 2+ ions.

You can then have as many successive ionisation energies as there are electrons in the original atom.

The first three ionisation energies of aluminium, for example, are given by:

$$Al_{(g)} \rightarrow Al^+{}_{(g)} + e^- \qquad \text{1st IE} = +577\,\text{kJ mol}^{-1}$$
$$Al^+{}_{(g)} \rightarrow Al^{2+}{}_{(g)} + e^- \qquad \text{2nd IE} = +1820\,\text{kJ mol}^{-1}$$
$$Al^{2+}{}_{(g)} \rightarrow Al^{3+}{}_{(g)} + e^- \qquad \text{3rd IE} = +2740\,\text{kJ mol}^{-1}$$

In order to form an $Al^{3+}{}_{(g)}$ ion from $Al_{(g)}$, you would have to supply:

$$+577 + 1820 + 2740 = +5137\,\text{kJ mol}^{-1}$$

First electron affinity

The first electron affinity is the energy released when 1 mole of gaseous atoms each acquire an electron to form 1 mole of gaseous 1− ions:

$$X_{(g)} + e^- \; \rightarrow \; X^-{}_{(g)}$$

Whereas ionisation energies always have positive values, first electron affinities have negative values. For example, the first electron affinity of chlorine is $-364\,\text{kJ mol}^{-1}$.

Second electron affinity

The second electron affinity is defined by the equation:

$$X^-_{(g)} + e^- \rightarrow X^{2-}_{(g)}$$

It is the energy needed to add a second electron to each ion in 1 mole of gaseous 1− ions to give gaseous 2− ions.

Notice that second electron affinities are positive. Energy is needed to force an electron into an already negative ion. For example, the second electron affinity of oxygen is $+844 \, \text{kJ mol}^{-1}$.

Lattice enthalpy

> ➤ The terms "**lattice enthalpy**" and "**lattice energy**" are often used as if they mean exactly the same thing. In fact there is a slight difference between them which relates to the conditions under which they are defined. You don't need to worry about this at A level.

Lattice enthalpy is a measure of the enthalpy difference between a solid ionic crystal and its scattered gaseous ions. The enthalpy diagram in Figure 5.7 shows the lattice enthalpy for sodium chloride.

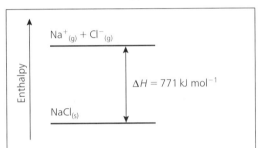

Figure 5.7 Simple enthalpy diagram showing lattice enthalpy of sodium chloride

You could, of course, define lattice enthalpy either as the exothermic change as you go from gaseous ions to solid crystal, or as the endothermic change as the crystal is split into its separated gaseous ions. Unfortunately **both** definitions are in current use.

> *Before you read on, find out which version of the definition your syllabus uses, and then stick to that in all the examples you do.*

Definition 1

Lattice enthalpy is the heat evolved when 1 mole of solid crystal is formed from its scattered gaseous ions:

> ➤ "**Scattered gaseous ions**" The gaseous ions have to be far enough apart for there to be no residual attractions between them. Lattice enthalpy is a measure of the attractive forces within the crystal.

$$\text{e.g.} \quad Na^+_{(g)} + Cl^-_{(g)} \rightarrow NaCl_{(s)} \qquad LE = -771 \, \text{kJ mol}^{-1}$$

Definition 2

Lattice enthalpy is the heat needed to convert 1 mole of solid crystal into its scattered gaseous ions:

$$\text{e.g.} \quad NaCl_{(s)} \rightarrow Na^+_{(g)} + Cl^-_{(g)} \qquad LE = +771 \, \text{kJ mol}^{-1}$$

If you look at the sign of the lattice enthalpy given to you in a question, it will be obvious which of these definitions is being used. The problem only arises if you are asked to define lattice enthalpy or to calculate a lattice enthalpy – in which case you need to be in tune with your examiners.

Born–Haber cycles

A Born–Haber cycle is a particular form of Hess's Law cycle which relates to the formation of ionic crystals. Born–Haber cycles are drawn differently from the cycles we have used up to now, but there is no difference in the way the sums are done. It is easier to explain how a Born–Haber cycle works by using a specific example.

The Born–Haber cycle for sodium chloride

The enthalpy change of formation of sodium chloride is $-411\ kJ\ mol^{-1}$:

$$Na_{(s)} + \tfrac{1}{2}Cl_{2(g)} \rightarrow NaCl_{(s)} \qquad \Delta H^{\ominus}_{f} = -411\ kJ\ mol^{-1}$$

A Born–Haber cycle looks in detail at all the individual changes which contribute to this. For convenience, we will look at the changes affecting the sodium first, and the chlorine afterwards.

The sodium ends up as sodium ions, Na^{+}. To go from sodium atoms to sodium ions involves the first ionisation energy of the sodium. But ionisation energies apply only to gaseous atoms – so first the sodium has to be atomised. You need the enthalpy change of atomisation:

$$Na_{(s)} \rightarrow Na_{(g)} \qquad \Delta H^{\ominus}_{a} = +109\ kJ\ mol^{-1}$$

Now you can make the ions. You need the first ionisation energy of sodium:

$$Na_{(g)} \rightarrow Na^{+}_{(g)} + e^{-} \qquad 1st\ IE = +494\ kJ\ mol^{-1}$$

Repeating the process for the chlorine, you need to atomise the chlorine, and then form the negative ion. This time you need the enthalpy change of atomisation and the electron affinity:

$$\tfrac{1}{2}Cl_{2(g)} \rightarrow Cl_{(g)} \qquad \Delta H^{\ominus}_{a} = +121\ kJ\ mol^{-1}$$
$$Cl_{(g)} + e^{-} \rightarrow Cl^{-}_{(g)} \qquad 1st\ EA = -364\ kJ\ mol^{-1}$$

Putting this onto an enthalpy diagram we get Figure 5.8 (which is not to scale)

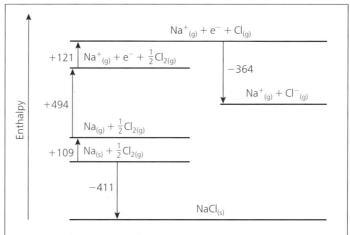

Figure 5.8 Enthalpy diagram showing Born–Haber cycle for formation of sodium chloride

You could now use this cycle to find the lattice enthalpy of sodium chloride. Diagrams are given for both definitions of lattice enthalpy, in Figures 5.9 and 5.10. Refer **only** to the one which corresponds to your syllabus.

Either:

> ➤ **Use this diagram and calculation if your syllabus defines lattice enthalpy as the exothermic change making the crystal from the gaseous ions.**
> When you have worked out the lattice enthalpy, you will find that it has a negative sign showing that heat has been evolved. As long as you point the arrow in the right direction, the calculation automatically works out the correct sign.
>
> Do not be tempted to write ''−LE'' into your equation or cycle (because you think that the lattice enthalpy should be negative). The symbol ''LE'' already includes that negative sign. In this case, LE = −771.

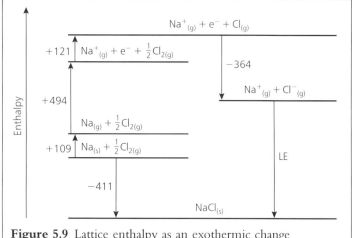

Figure 5.9 Lattice enthalpy as an exothermic change

Finding two routes around the diagram in Figure 5.9 without going against the flow of any arrows gives:

$$+109 + 494 + 121 - 364 + LE = -411$$

Solving this gives

$$LE = -771 \, kJ \, mol^{-1}$$

Or:

> ➤ **Use this diagram and calculation if your syllabus defines lattice enthalpy as the endothermic change splitting the crystal into its gaseous ions.**
>
> When you have worked out the lattice enthalpy, you will find that it has a positive sign showing that heat was needed to split the crystal into its scattered gaseous ions. As long as you point the arrow in the right direction, the calculation automatically works out the correct sign.

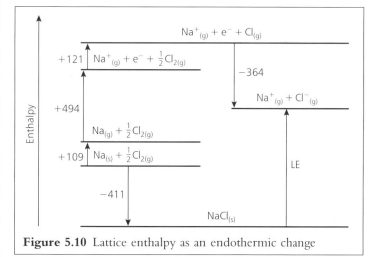

Figure 5.10 Lattice enthalpy as an endothermic change

Finding two routes around the diagram in Figure 5.10 without going against the flow of any arrows gives:

$$+109 + 494 + 121 - 364 = -411 + LE$$

Solving this gives

$$LE = +771 \, kJ \, mol^{-1}$$

You can perfectly well use a Born–Haber cycle to find any one of the terms which make it up. You might, for example, be asked to draw a Born–Haber cycle and then find the electron affinity of bromine from the following data:

$$Na_{(s)} \rightarrow Na_{(g)} \qquad\qquad \Delta H^{\ominus}{}_a = +109\,kJ\,mol^{-1}$$
$$Na_{(g)} \rightarrow Na^+{}_{(g)} + e^- \qquad\qquad 1st\ IE = +494\,kJ\,mol^{-1}$$
$$\tfrac{1}{2}Br_{2(l)} \rightarrow Br_{(g)} \qquad\qquad \Delta H^{\ominus}{}_a = +112\,kJ\,mol^{-1}$$
$$Na_{(s)} + \tfrac{1}{2}Br_{2(l)} \rightarrow NaBr_{(s)} \qquad\qquad \Delta H^{\ominus}{}_f = -360\,kJ\,mol^{-1}$$

and **either**

$$Na^+{}_{(g)} + Br^-{}_{(g)} \rightarrow NaBr_{(s)} \qquad LE = -733\,kJ\,mol^{-1}$$

or

$$NaBr_{(s)} \rightarrow Na^+{}_{(g)} + Br^-{}_{(g)} \qquad LE = +733\,kJ\,mol^{-1}$$

The cycle has just the same form as for sodium chloride (see Figure 5.11).

> ➤ It would be a good idea to redraw this (and other similar diagrams) showing only the arrow corresponding to the definition of lattice enthalpy that your particular syllabus wants.

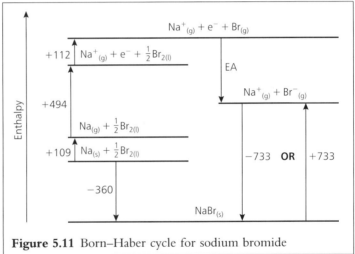

Figure 5.11 Born–Haber cycle for sodium bromide

Depending on which definition of lattice enthalpy you are using, you will use one of the following equations:

either

$$+109 + 494 + 112 + EA - 733 = -360$$

or

$$+109 + 494 + 112 + EA = -360 + 733$$

If you look carefully at these, you will see that they are variations on the same expression. Whichever you use, the answer comes out as:

$$EA = -342\,kJ\,mol^{-1}$$

> ➤ Take some time! Be sure that you understand exactly how the expression which matches your definition of lattice enthalpy arises from the Born–Haber cycle.

Some more complicated Born–Haber cycles

Any compound which consists of 1+ and 1− ions will have a Born–Haber cycle of exactly the same form as the sodium chloride or sodium bromide one. The complication comes if you have ions with charges greater than 1.

The Born–Haber cycle for magnesium oxide

Magnesium oxide contains Mg^{2+} and O^{2-} ions. The cycle will have to include a first plus a second ionisation energy to make the 2+ ion, and a first plus a second electron affinity to make the 2− ion. Remember that second electron affinities are positive, and so the diagram looks more complicated (see Figure 5.12).

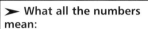

What all the numbers mean:
+150 is the enthalpy change of atomisation of magnesium.
+736 and +1450 are the first and second ionisation energies of magnesium.
+248 is the enthalpy change of atomisation of oxygen.
−142 is the first electron affinity of oxygen.
+844 is the second electron affinity of oxygen.
−602 is the enthalpy change of formation of magnesium oxide.

Your lattice enthalpy arrow won't be double ended. Yours will either point up or down according to which definition of lattice enthalpy you are using. It would be a good idea to redraw this diagram to avoid getting confused.

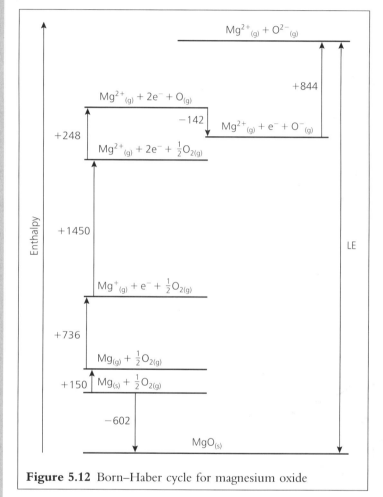

Figure 5.12 Born–Haber cycle for magnesium oxide

Although the cycle looks more complicated, you can simply find two routes around it which don't go against the flow of any arrows.

If your lattice enthalpy arrow points downwards

$$+150 + 736 + 1450 + 248 - 142 + 844 + LE = -602$$

Solving to give: $LE = -3888 \, kJ \, mol^{-1}$

If your lattice enthalpy arrow points upwards

$$+150 + 736 + 1450 + 248 - 142 + 844 = -602 + LE$$

Solving to give: $LE = +3888 \, kJ \, mol^{-1}$

Once again, you could work out **any** of the changes in this cycle, as long as you knew all the other ones.

The cycle for magnesium chloride

Magnesium chloride is $MgCl_2$, containing Mg^{2+} ions and $2Cl^-$ ions. The changes for the magnesium will be the same as the last cycle – atomisation and then first plus second ionisation energies. This time the two electrons that are released are given one each to two chlorine atoms. Because you are only adding one electron to each chlorine atom, you only need the first electron affinity, but you have to remember to multiply it by 2. The cycle is shown in Figure 5.13.

> ➤ **What all the numbers mean:**
> +150 is the enthalpy change of atomisation of magnesium.
> +736 and +1450 are the first and second ionisation energies of magnesium.
> +121 is the enthalpy change of atomisation of chlorine. It has to be multiplied by 2 because of the 2 chlorine atoms formed.
> −364 is the first electron affinity of chlorine. This also has to be multiplied by 2 because you are adding an electron to each of 2 chlorine atoms.
> −642 is the enthalpy change of formation of magnesium chloride.

> ➤ Once again it would be a good idea to redraw this so that the lattice enthalpy arrow points in the direction required by your syllabus.

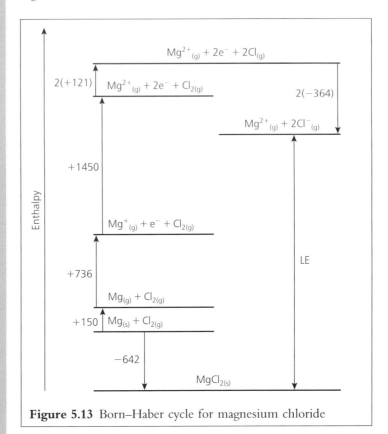

Figure 5.13 Born–Haber cycle for magnesium chloride

In exactly the same way as the previous examples, you could work out the lattice enthalpy of the magnesium chloride. If you do this, you should find it comes to either $-2492\,kJ\,mol^{-1}$ or $+2492\,kJ\,mol^{-1}$, depending on which definition of lattice enthalpy you are working from.

The cycle for sodium oxide

Sodium oxide is Na_2O, containing $2Na^+$ ions and an O^{2-} ion. This time the terms relating to sodium will have to be multiplied by two: 2 times the enthalpy change of atomisation, and 2 times the first ionisation energy (because you are removing 1 electron from each of 2 atoms). In the oxygen case, because 1 atom is accepting both electrons, you will need the first plus second electron affinities.

The cycle is shown in Figure 5.14.

➤ **Draw** the lattice enthalpy arrow so that it points in the direction required by your syllabus.

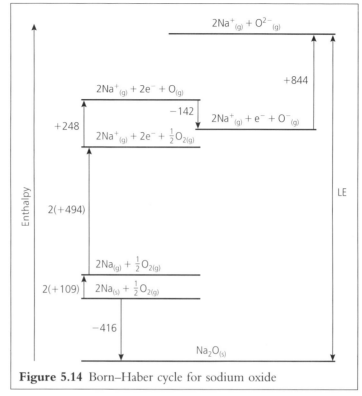

Figure 5.14 Born–Haber cycle for sodium oxide

And again, you can simply find two routes around the diagram which don't go against the flow of any arrows.

If your lattice enthalpy arrow points downwards

$2(+109) + 2(+494) + 248 - 142 + 844 + LE = -416$

Solving to give: $LE = -2572 \, kJ \, mol^{-1}$

If your lattice enthalpy arrow points upwards

$2(+109) + 2(+494) + 248 - 142 + 844 = -416 + LE$

Solving to give: $LE = +2572 \, kJ \, mol^{-1}$

Problem • 14

Draw a Born–Haber cycle for potassium iodide, KI, and use it to find the lattice enthalpy of KI.

Enthalpy changes of atomisation: potassium $+90 \, kJ \, mol^{-1}$; iodine $+107 \, kJ \, mol^{-1}$. First ionisation energy of potassium $+418 \, kJ \, mol^{-1}$. First electron affinity of iodine $-314 \, kJ \, mol^{-1}$. Enthalpy change of formation of $KI_{(s)}$ $-328 \, kJ \, mol^{-1}$.

Problem • 15

Draw a Born–Haber cycle for strontium chloride, $SrCl_2$, and use it to find the enthalpy change of formation of $SrCl_{2(s)}$.

Enthalpy changes of atomisation: strontium $+164 \, kJ \, mol^{-1}$; chlorine $+121 \, kJ \, mol^{-1}$. Ionisation energies of strontium: first $+548 \, kJ \, mol^{-1}$; second $+1060 \, kJ \, mol^{-1}$. First electron affinity of chlorine $-364 \, kJ \, mol^{-1}$. Lattice enthalpy of strontium chloride
(defined in the sense $Sr^{2+}_{(g)} + 2Cl^-_{(g)} \rightarrow SrCl_{2(s)}$) $-2112 \, kJ \, mol^{-1}$;
(defined in the sense $SrCl_{2(s)} \rightarrow Sr^{2+}_{(g)} + 2Cl^-_{(g)}$) $+2112 \, kJ \, mol^{-1}$.

117

Enthalpy changes when ionic compounds dissolve in water

Enthalpy change of solution

This is the enthalpy change when 1 mole of ionic substance dissolves in water to give a solution of infinite dilution. "Infinitely dilute" is not meant literally! It simply means that you have used enough water so that adding some more doesn't result in any more heat being evolved or absorbed. The equation for the reaction would be written as, for example:

$$NaCl_{(s)} + (aq) \rightarrow Na^+_{(aq)} + Cl^-_{(aq)}$$

The sodium and chloride ions were already there in the crystal, of course. The process of dissolving in water frees them from the lattice and wraps them in water molecules.

Hydration enthalpy (enthalpy change of hydration)

The hydration enthalpy of an ion refers to the process:

$$X^{n\pm}_{(g)} + (aq) \rightarrow X^{n\pm}_{(aq)}$$

It is the enthalpy change when 1 mole of gaseous ions dissolve in sufficient water to produce an infinitely dilute solution. It applies equally to positive or negative ions, and irrespective of the number of charges – hence the symbol, $X^{n\pm}$. Hydration enthalpies are always negative. The heat is evolved because of the formation of attractive forces between the ions and water molecules.

e.g. $Mg^{2+}_{(g)} + (aq) \rightarrow Mg^{2+}_{(aq)}$ $\Delta H = -1920 \, kJ \, mol^{-1}$

$Cl^-_{(g)} + (aq) \rightarrow Cl^-_{(aq)}$ $\Delta H = -364 \, kJ \, mol^{-1}$

Calculating enthalpy changes of solution

You can set up a simple Hess's Law cycle involving lattice enthalpies and hydration enthalpies. For example, for sodium chloride:

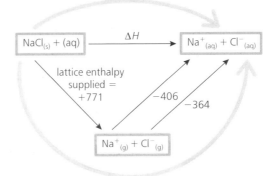

This gives

$\Delta H = +771 - 406 - 364$

$\Delta H = +1 \, kJ \, mol^{-1}$

In other words, when 1 mole of sodium chloride dissolves in water to give an infinitely dilute solution, 1 kJ is absorbed from the surroundings – the solution becomes slightly colder.

Notice that whichever definition of lattice enthalpy you are working with, it is usual on these diagrams to draw the arrow from the solid to the gaseous ions – in other words, to consider how much heat you have to supply to split the lattice up, before you recover heat again as the ions become hydrated.

Nobody, of course, is suggesting that when sodium chloride dissolves in water, it first splits into gaseous ions scattered all over the universe, which then become hydrated as they dive back into the water – which is what the enthalpy changes we are using imply. We have calculated the enthalpy change using an imaginary route, but according to Hess's Law, it will produce exactly the same overall enthalpy change as the processes the ions really undergo.

| **Problem • 16** | Calculate the enthalpy change of solution of barium chloride, $BaCl_2$, given: |

$$BaCl_{2(s)} \rightarrow Ba^{2+}_{(g)} + 2Cl^-_{(g)} \qquad \Delta H = +2018 \, kJ \, mol^{-1}$$

$$Ba^{2+}_{(g)} + (aq) \rightarrow Ba^{2+}_{(aq)} \qquad \Delta H = -1360 \, kJ \, mol^{-1}$$

$$Cl^-_{(g)} + (aq) \rightarrow Cl^-_{(aq)} \qquad \Delta H = -364 \, kJ \, mol^{-1}$$

End of chapter checklist

Can you do the following things?

■ Calculate enthalpy changes (heat evolved or absorbed) from simple experimental results.

■ Relate the sign of an enthalpy change to whether it is exothermic or endothermic.

■ Define the term standard as applied to enthalpy changes.

■ Define the following standard enthalpy changes: formation, combustion, neutralisation, vaporisation, atomisation, solution, hydration.

■ State Hess's Law.

■ Define mean bond enthalpy, first (and successive) ionisation energy, first (and successive) electron affinity, lattice enthalpy.

■ Use the above terms in simple calculations involving Hess's Law cycles – either as triangular (or occasionally more complicated) diagrams or as Born–Haber cycles as appropriate.

Revision problems

Numerical answers are provided for these problems, but no worked solutions.

Problem • 17

An experiment was carried out to find the enthalpy change of neutralisation of ethanoic acid with sodium hydroxide:

$$CH_3COOH + NaOH \rightarrow CH_3COONa + H_2O$$

50 cm³ of 2.0 mol dm⁻³ sodium hydroxide solution was placed in a plastic cup and its temperature recorded. 50 cm³ of 2.0 mol dm⁻³ ethanoic acid was placed in a measuring cylinder and its temperature was recorded. The acid was added to the sodium hydroxide solution and the temperature recorded at 1 minute intervals for 5 minutes.

Results:
Temperature of sodium hydroxide solution = 19.4 °C
Temperature of ethanoic acid solution = 18.8 °C

Time (mins)	0	1	2	3	4	5
Temp of mixture (°C)		31.5	31.0	30.5	30.1	29.6

Assume that the density of all solutions is 1 g cm⁻³ and their specific heats are all 4.18 J g⁻¹ K⁻¹.

(a) Estimate the maximum temperature which would have been reached in the absence of any heat losses.
(b) Calculate the total amount of heat evolved during this reaction.
(c) Calculate the amount of heat evolved per mole of water formed during the neutralisation.

Problem • 18

The apparatus in Figure 5.3 was used to determine the enthalpy change of combustion of propanone, CH_3COCH_3. It was first calibrated by burning ethanol, CH_3CH_2OH, which has a known enthalpy change of combustion of -1367 kJ mol⁻¹.

Results with ethanol:
Mass of water = 250 g
Original temperature of water = 18.5 °C
Final temperature of water = 23.3 °C
Original mass of burner + ethanol = 48.295 g
Final mass of burner + ethanol = 48.100 g

Results with propanone:
Mass of water = 250 g
Original temperature of water = 19.2 °C
Final temperature of water = 23.5 °C
Original mass of burner + propanone = 49.623 g
Final mass of burner + propanone = 49.454 g

(a) Use the ethanol results to calculate the heat capacity of the apparatus in kJ °C⁻¹.
(b) Calculate the enthalpy change of combustion of propanone.

(H = 1; C = 12; O = 16)

Problem • 19

Calculate the enthalpy change of hydrogenation of benzene to cyclohexane:

$$C_6H_{6(l)} + 3H_{2(g)} \rightarrow C_6H_{12(l)}$$

Standard enthalpy changes of combustion in kJ mol^{-1}: benzene -3267, hydrogen -286, cyclohexane -3920.

Problem • 20

Calculate the enthalpy changes for the thermal decomposition of (a) lithium carbonate, (b) sodium carbonate.

$$Li_2CO_{3(s)} \rightarrow Li_2O_{(s)} + CO_{2(g)}$$
$$Na_2CO_{3(s)} \rightarrow Na_2O_{(s)} + CO_{2(g)}$$

Standard enthalpy changes of formation in kJ mol^{-1}: lithium carbonate -1216, lithium oxide -598, sodium carbonate -1131, sodium oxide -414, carbon dioxide -394.

Problem • 21

Calculate the standard enthalpy change of formation of ethanol, $CH_3CH_2OH_{(l)}$ from the following standard enthalpy changes of combustion (all in kJ mol^{-1}): carbon -394, hydrogen -286, ethanol -1367.

Problem • 22

Calculate the standard enthalpy change of combustion of ethyne, $C_2H_{2(g)}$, from the following data (all in kJ mol^{-1}): standard enthalpy change of formation of ethyne $+228$; standard enthalpy changes of combustion: hydrogen -286, carbon -394.

Problem • 23

Hydrazine, $N_2H_{4(l)}$, is used as a rocket fuel. It burns in oxygen to produce nitrogen and steam:

$$N_2H_{4(l)} + O_{2(g)} \rightarrow N_{2(g)} + 2H_2O_{(g)}$$

(a) Calculate the enthalpy change when 1 mole of hydrazine burns. Standard enthalpy changes of formation (in kJ mol^{-1}): hydrazine $+50.6$, $H_2O_{(g)}$ -242.
(b) How much heat is evolved if 1 tonne of hydrazine burns completely in this way? (H = 1; N = 14. 1 tonne = 1000 kg.)

Problem • 24

Calculate the enthalpy change of formation of bromoethane, $C_2H_5Br_{(l)}$ from the following data:

$$2C_{(s)} + 2H_{2(g)} \rightarrow C_2H_{4(g)} \qquad \Delta H = +52.2 \text{ kJ mol}^{-1}$$
$$\tfrac{1}{2}H_{2(g)} + \tfrac{1}{2}Br_{2(l)} \rightarrow HBr_{(g)} \qquad \Delta H = -36.4 \text{ kJ mol}^{-1}$$
$$C_2H_{4(g)} + HBr_{(g)} \rightarrow C_2H_5Br_{(l)} \qquad \Delta H = -106.3 \text{ kJ mol}^{-1}$$

Problem • 25

Estimate the enthalpy change for the reactions between hydrogen and the halogens, fluorine and chlorine:

$$H_{2(g)} + X_{2(g)} \rightarrow 2HX_{(g)} \qquad \text{where X = F or Cl}$$

Bond enthalpies (in kJ mol^{-1}): H—H $+436$, F—F $+158$, Cl—Cl $+243$, H—F $+568$, H—Cl $+432$

Problem • 26

Under some circumstances, methane reacts explosively with chlorine to give carbon and hydrogen chloride:

$$CH_{4(g)} + 2Cl_{2(g)} \rightarrow C_{(s)} + 4HCl_{(g)}$$

Estimate the enthalpy change for this reaction.

Mean bond enthalpies: C—H +413, Cl—Cl +243, H—Cl +432. Enthalpy change of atomisation of carbon: +717. (All values in kJ mol^{-1}.)

Problem • 27

Estimate the mean bond enthalpies of (a) the S—F bond in $SF_{6(g)}$, (b) the P—Cl bond in $PCl_{3(l)}$.

Enthalpy changes of formation: $SF_{6(g)}$ −1209, $PCl_{3(l)}$ −320. Enthalpy changes of atomisation: sulphur +279, fluorine +79, phosphorus +315, chlorine +122. Enthalpy change of vaporisation: $PCl_{3(l)}$ +33. (All values in kJ mol^{-1}.)

Problem • 28

Estimate the enthalpy change of formation of ethanol, $CH_3CH_2OH_{(l)}$, from the following information (all values in kJ mol^{-1}).

Enthalpy changes of atomisation: carbon +717, hydrogen +218, oxygen +249. Mean bond enthalpies: C—H +413, C—C +347, C—O +358, O—H +464. Enthalpy change of vaporisation: $CH_3CH_2OH_{(l)}$ +38.6. (All values in kJ mol^{-1}.)

Problem • 29

(a) Construct a Born–Haber cycle for caesium fluoride, CsF, and use it to find the electron affinity of fluorine.
(b) Construct a Born–Haber cycle for barium chloride, $BaCl_2$, and use it to find the enthalpy change of formation of barium chloride.

Data (all values in kJ mol^{-1}):

Enthalpy changes of atomisation:		
	caesium	+79
	barium	+176
	fluorine	+79
	chlorine	+121
Ionisation energies:	caesium (1st)	+376
	barium (1st)	+502
	barium (2nd)	+966
First electron affinity:	chlorine	−364
Enthalpy change of formation:	caesium fluoride	−531

$$Cs^+_{(g)} + F^-_{(g)} \rightarrow CsF_{(s)} \qquad -716$$
$$Ba^{2+}_{(g)} + 2Cl^-_{(g)} \rightarrow BaCl_{2(s)} \qquad -2018$$

Problem • 30

Calculate the enthalpy change of solution of lithium fluoride, LiF, given the following information (all values in kJ mol^{-1}):

$$LiF_{(s)} \rightarrow Li^+_{(g)} + F^-_{(g)} \quad \Delta H = +1022.$$

Hydration enthalpies: $Li^+_{(g)}$ −519, $F^-_{(g)}$ −506.

This chapter looks at how you process the results of rates of reaction experiments. The level of maths needed for most syllabuses is fairly low – much of it hardly even needs a calculator. Some syllabuses may want you to draw and interpret simple graphs. You might have to learn to use a function on your calculator that you have not used before – but it isn't difficult.

The effect of concentration on rates of reaction

At GCSE the argument goes: "If you increase the concentration of one of the reactants, the rate of reaction increases. This is because there will be more particles in a given volume, and therefore a greater chance of them hitting each other and so reacting."

The situation is not quite as simple as this. Changing the concentration does not **necessarily** have a simple effect on the rate of the reaction. The reason is that reactions usually take place in more than one step – and some steps are fast and others are slow. How fast the reaction happens depends on the speed of the **slowest** step.

A simple analogy makes this fairly obvious.

A travel example

Suppose you wanted to travel from Newquay in Cornwall to New York. You can think of this as a two-step process – you first have to get to Heathrow, and then catch a plane.

Suppose you **walked** from Newquay to Heathrow, and then caught an ordinary plane across the Atlantic. Because of the time taken to get to London, this will take at least two or three weeks altogether, and perhaps much longer (depending on how fit you are, and how much luggage you are carrying). Trying to speed it up by flying by Concorde is going to make virtually no difference to your total time. In other words, doing something to speed up an already fast stage of a reaction makes little difference to the overall time that the reaction takes.

If, however, you caught a train from Newquay to Heathrow (thereby speeding up the slow step), the total time taken would be cut down to less than one day. In terms of reactions, only things which affect the slow step will have any significant effect on the rate of the reaction.

The slow step of a reaction is known as the **rate-determining step**.

A chemical example

Suppose you have a chemical reaction which takes place in two steps:

Overall:	$A + B \rightarrow C + D$
Slow step:	$A \rightarrow$ intermediate $+ C$
Fast step:	intermediate $+ B \rightarrow D$

> ➤ This argument only works if there is a big difference in the rates of the two steps. If you travelled to Heathrow by train and then caught Concorde instead of an ordinary plane, speeding up the second step would now make a significant percentage difference to the overall time taken, because the two steps now have similar rates.
>
> The examples of chemical reactions quoted at A level in this topic will have one step which is far slower than the others – one step which is obviously **rate determining** – so there is no problem.

If you increase the concentration of A, there are more molecules which can potentially fall apart in the slow step, and so the reaction will speed up.

Increasing the concentration of B, however, will make no noticeable difference to how fast the overall reaction happens. Supposing that the second step is already virtually instantaneous, speeding it up is not going to make a lot of difference!

In this example:

■ increasing the concentration of A speeds up the reaction;

■ increasing the concentration of B has no effect.

Could we have predicted this?

NO! You could only predict this if you knew in advance what the steps in the reaction were – in other words, the **mechanism** of the reaction. But this is putting the cart before the horse! Mechanisms are in part deduced by finding out which concentrations affect the rate of the reaction – in other words which things are taking part in slow or fast steps. You have to do **experiments** in order to find this out.

Explaining orders of reaction

It is quite difficult to define orders of reaction in words – it is more usually done mathematically.

Suppose you have a chemical reaction with the equation:

$$x A + y B + z C + \ldots \rightarrow \text{products}$$

and that by doing experiments you find that the rate of reaction is related to the concentrations of the reactants by the mathematical equation:

$$\text{Rate} = k[A]^a[B]^b[C]^c \ldots$$

> **Don't panic!** All the terms in this equation are going to be explained in detail.

This is called the **rate equation** or **rate expression** for the reaction.

Rate

The rate of a reaction is usually measured in terms of how fast the concentration of one of the reactants is falling (although you could also measure it in terms of how fast the concentration of one of the products is increasing). It has units of **$mol\,dm^{-3}\,s^{-1}$**, "moles per cubic decimetre per second". If the rate at one particular time during the reaction was measured as $0.01\,mol\,dm^{-3}\,s^{-1}$, it means that at that time the concentration of one of the reactants was falling by $0.01\,mol\,dm^{-3}$ every second.

The rate constant k

> The relationship between the rate constant k and temperature and activation energy is given by the **Arrhenius Equation**. This is explored later in the chapter, although it isn't required by most syllabuses.

Although k is described as a constant, it is only constant if the temperature and the activation energy of the reaction stay constant. Increasing the temperature increases k, and so would adding a catalyst.

However, for the moment, where we are only considering changes in concentration, k can be taken as constant. Its units vary depending on the exact form of the equation. This will become clear when we do some simple sums later.

The concentration terms

Rate $= k[A]^a[B]^b[C]^c \ldots$

[A] (etc.) simply means "the concentration of A in $mol\,dm^{-3}$".

If you doubled the concentration of A and the rate of the reaction doubled as well, you could say that the rate was proportional to the concentration of A:

Rate $\propto [A]$

You would normally write this as:

Rate $= k[A]$

where k is some constant number – in this case, the rate constant.

The equation says that if you do something to A, you are doing the same thing to the rate.

Suppose, however, that when you doubled the concentration of A, the rate of reaction increased **four times**. In other words doubling the concentration of A caused the rate to go up $2^2(= 4)$ times. You could write this as:

Rate $= k[A]^2$

Or you could have found from experiments that doubling the concentration of A caused the rate of reaction to increase eight times. Eight is 2^3. You could write that into the rate expression as

Rate $= k[A]^3$

Going back to the rate equation:

Rate $= k[A]^a[B]^b[C]^c \ldots$

The little numbers in the rate equation (a, b, c, etc.) help to relate the change in concentration to the actual change in the rate of reaction. These numbers are called **orders of reaction** with respect to the various substances:

"a" is the order of reaction with respect to A
"b" is the order of reaction with respect to B
"c" is the order of reaction with respect to C
and so on . . .

If you add together all the individual orders of reaction ($a + b + c + \ldots$), the sum is called the **overall order of reaction** – or simply the **order of reaction**. If you are told that a reaction has an order of 2, it means that the sum of all the individual orders is 2.

Orders of reaction

Orders of reaction are usually small numbers, and can be fractional – for example, 1.4. However, at A level you will only have to deal with orders of 0, 1 or 2.

125

> A **zero order** arises because the substance is taking part in a fast step of the reaction. Obviously, if you were to decrease the concentration of this substance a lot, eventually you would slow down this fast step so much that it wasn't fast any more! At this point, its concentration would matter, and would affect the rate of reaction. In other words, orders can change if you change the concentration of one of the reactants by very large amounts. As long as you stick to the normal doubling or tripling of concentrations which are common in A level questions, this will not be a problem.

Zero order

An order of **0** is called zero order. If a reaction is zero order with respect to a particular reactant, it means that the concentration of that substance does not affect the rate of the reaction. That substance would not appear in the rate equation.

You might wonder why you don't write it as, for example:

Rate = $k[A]^0$

Mathematically, any number raised to the power of 0 is equal to 1. In other words, $[A]^0 = 1$. You don't write unnecessary 1s into equations.

First order

An order of **1** is called first order. This means that whatever you do to the concentration, exactly the same thing happens to the rate. For example, doubling the concentration doubles the rate; tripling the concentration triples the rate and so on. If a reaction is first order with respect to a particular substance, it would be written into the rate equation as, for example:

Rate = $k[A]$

You might wonder why it isn't written as: Rate = $k[A]^1$. Again, you don't write unnecessary 1s into equations. [A] means $[A]^1$.

Second order

An order of **2** is called second order. In this case, whatever you do to the concentration, the **square** of that happens to the rate. For example, if you double the concentration, the rate will increase four times (2^2). If you triple the concentration, the rate goes up nine times (3^2). It would be written into the rate equation as, for example:

Rate = $k[A]^2$

Putting this all together

Suppose you had a reaction with the equation:

2A + 3B + C → D + 2E

and you found by doing experiments that doubling the concentration of

A had no effect on the rate of reaction
B increased the rate of reaction four times
C doubled the rate of reaction

The reaction is   zero order with respect to A
                   second order with respect to B
                   first order with respect to C

The rate expression is therefore: Rate = $k[B]^2[C]$

The overall order of the reaction is 3 (because the sum of the individual orders, $0 + 2 + 1$, is 3).

Notice that the orders have no particular relationship to the numbers in the chemical equation. You cannot predict orders of reaction – they can only be found from experiment.

Finding orders of reaction from initial rate experiments

What are initial rate experiments?

The easiest way of working out orders of reaction is from **initial rate** experiments. In these, mixtures of reactants are made up and the rate is measured at the very beginning of the reaction. This has the advantage that you already know the concentrations of everything. During the course of the reaction these concentrations decrease and you would have to find some way of measuring them.

A series of experiments is carried out in which the concentrations of the various reactants are changed one at a time, but everything else is left the same.

How to process the results

You may be given tables of information showing what happens to the initial rate of the reaction as you change various concentrations. It will show the results of perhaps 3 or 4 experiments.

Find any 2 experiments where the only difference between them is that one (**and only one**) concentration has changed. Then look at the effect that the concentration change has had on the rate of reaction.

For example:

Change in concentration	Change in rate	Order of reaction
×2	no change	0
×2	×2	1
×2	×4	2

Change in concentration	Change in rate	Order of reaction
×3	no change	0
×3	×3	1
×3	×9	2

There may well be other possibilities. Look for changes in rate which:

do not change	zero order
are the same as the change in concentration	first order
are the square of the change in concentration	second order

Worked examples

In all the examples in this chapter, chemical reactions will be given in general terms (A, B, C, etc.) rather than with real substances. The reason for this is that it is much easier to make up simple examples, rather than using real data. In exams, you may either get this sort of general case or real reactions. It makes no difference whatsoever to the way you work things out.

Example 1

Using the data in the following table, find the order of reaction with respect to A, B and C, and the overall order of reaction. Write the rate equation and calculate a value for the rate constant including units.

Experiment	Concentrations (mol dm^{-3})			Rate of loss of A (mol dm^{-3} s^{-1})
	A	B	C	
1	0.1	0.1	0.1	2.0×10^{-4}
2	0.2	0.1	0.1	4.0×10^{-4}
3	0.2	0.2	0.1	1.6×10^{-3}
4	0.1	0.1	0.2	2.0×10^{-4}

Finding the orders of reaction

Work systematically. Start by checking out A, and look for two experiments where the concentrations of everything else have remained unchanged, but the concentration of A is different. In this case, you obviously need to look at experiments 1 and 2.

The concentration of A has doubled and so has the rate of reaction. The reaction is therefore **first order** with respect to A.

Now look at B. Between experiments 2 and 3 the concentration of B has doubled whereas everything else has stayed the same. What has happened to the rate?

The rate has changed from 4×10^{-4} to 1.6×10^{-3}. Non-mathematicians frequently get confused at this point, but there is no reason to. If you can't see the relationship easily, use your calculator and divide the bigger number by the smaller one. Not sure which is the bigger one? The one at the higher concentration is bound to be bigger – but if you divide by the wrong number you will get an obviously silly answer and will have to try again!

> **Note:** If you did the division the wrong way around you would get an answer of 0.25. Doubling the concentration of B can't possibly make the rate smaller – so you know that you have done it wrong!

So: $\dfrac{1.6 \times 10^{-3}}{4 \times 10^{-4}} = 4$

A doubling of the concentration of B has caused the rate to go up four times. The reaction is **second order** with respect to B.

Finally to C. In this case you need to look at experiments 1 and 4. Doubling the concentration of C while everything else stays the same has made no difference to the rate. The reaction is **zero order** with respect to C.

The overall order is the sum of the individual orders. $1 + 2 + 0$ is equal to 3. The reaction is **third order** overall.

The rate equation

Rate $= k[A][B]^2$

Notice that C is not written into the equation. C has no effect on the rate of reaction. Its order is zero.

Finding the rate constant k

k is a constant and its value will be the same for all of the experiments. To find k, you simply rearrange the rate equation to give an expression for k, and then slot in the numbers relating to any **one** experiment. Most people usually choose the first experiment, but it doesn't matter in the least!

Rearranging the rate expression gives:

$$k = \frac{\text{Rate}}{[A][B]^2}$$

Substituting in the numbers for the first experiment gives:

$$k = \frac{2.0 \times 10^{-4}}{(0.1) \times (0.1)^2} = 0.2$$

Working out the units for k

Working out units is not difficult, but it is easy to make careless errors. Just take your time over it. Instead of substituting numbers into the expression for k, you substitute the units for the various terms, and then cancel them exactly as if they were ordinary fractions. Having done that you tidy them all up so that they are arranged on one line.

The expression for k is:

$$k = \frac{\text{Rate}}{[A][B]^2}$$

Substitute the various units for rate or concentration instead of the numbers you substituted to get the numerical value for k:

$$k = \frac{\text{mol dm}^{-3}\,\text{s}^{-1}}{(\text{mol dm}^{-3})(\text{mol dm}^{-3})^2}$$

You can cancel a mol dm^{-3} term from the top and bottom exactly as if it were any other fraction:

$$k = \frac{\text{s}^{-1}}{(\text{mol dm}^{-3})^2}$$

Now you need to tidy this all up into a single line, and it is here that you are likely to make mistakes if you aren't careful.

Working with powers

This box is included in case your maths is a bit rusty.

$$a^2 \times a^3 = a^5$$

Multiplying two terms together like this, you add the indices. The logic of this is that a^2 is $a \times a$; a^3 is $a \times a \times a$. Multiplying them together gives $a \times a \times a \times a \times a$ which is a^5.

$$a^3 \div a^2 = a$$

Dividing two terms like this, you subtract the indices. The logic of this is that a^3 is $a \times a \times a$. If you divide this by a^2 ($a \times a$), you are just left with a.

$$(a^3)^2 = a^6$$

To save having to remember a third rule, think of $(a^3)^2$ as $a^3 \times a^3$.

Finally, if you have terms on the bottom of a fraction, and you want to put them on the top, reverse the sign of their indices. For example,

$$1/a^2 = a^{-2} \qquad 1/a^{-2} = a^2$$

This is simply a result of the way the negative sign in an index is defined. a^{-2} is defined to mean $1/a^2$.

➤ If you would rather substitute the numbers in the rate equation first and then rearrange it afterwards, there is no reason why you can't do it that way. It does, however, make it slightly easier to work out the units for k if you have the rate equation rearranged as shown here.

➤ **Note!** Do not leave this example until you are **sure** that you understand the algebra involved. There are several places in the A level course where you might be asked to work out units for things, and although each example is probably only going to be worth 1 mark, it isn't worth wasting. Do not be put off by the amount of time this takes. In an exam you will probably be working at a rate of about 1 mark per minute, and with practice, it should not take anything like 1 minute to work out units in most cases.

Back to the problem again:

$$k = \frac{s^{-1}}{(mol\,dm^{-3})^2}$$

$$= \frac{s^{-1}}{mol^2\,dm^{-6}}$$

$$= mol^{-2}\,dm^6\,s^{-1}$$

The value for k is therefore $0.2\,mol^{-2}\,dm^6\,s^{-1}$.

Example 2   Using the data in the following table, find the order of reaction with respect to A, B and C, and the overall order of reaction. Write the rate equation and calculate a value for the rate constant including units.

Experiment	Concentrations (mol dm^{-3})			Rate of loss of A (mol dm^{-3} s^{-1})
	A	B	C	
1	0.010	0.020	0.0050	1.4×10^{-6}
2	0.010	0.010	0.0050	7.0×10^{-7}
3	0.020	0.020	0.0050	1.4×10^{-6}
4	0.020	0.020	0.015	4.2×10^{-6}

Try to work this out yourself before you read any further.

Finding the orders of reaction

Compare experiments 1 and 3. The concentration of A has doubled but the other concentrations have not changed. There is no change in the rate.

The reaction is **zero order** with respect to A.

Now compare experiments 1 and 2 – all that has changed is the concentration of B. The concentration of B has halved between the two experiments, and so has the rate. (Check this on your calculator if you aren't sure.) Because what you do to the concentration of B has the same effect on the rate, the reaction is **first order** with respect to B.

➤ **Hint:** If halving concentrations worries you, think of the reactions the other way around. Start from experiment 2 and notice that the concentration of B and the rate have doubled as you go from experiment 2 to experiment 1.

Finally compare experiments 3 and 4. The only difference is that the concentration of C has tripled. So has the rate. The reaction is **first order** with respect to C.

The **overall order** is $0 + 1 + 1$, i.e. **second order** overall.

The rate equation

Rate = k[B][C]

Finding the rate constant k

Rearranging the rate equation gives:

$$k = \frac{Rate}{[B][C]}$$

> There is no reason why you have to use the values from the first experiment. You could equally well choose any other experiment. Try it just to convince yourself that you get the same answer.

> The **units** for k are different from the first example. The units depend on the overall order of the reaction. The first example turned out to be third order; this one was second order.

Substituting values from the first experiment gives:

$$k = \frac{1.4 \times 10^{-6}}{0.020 \times 0.0050}$$

$$= 0.014$$

Finding the units for k

$$k = \frac{\text{Rate}}{[B][C]}$$

$$= \frac{\text{mol dm}^{-3}\,\text{s}^{-1}}{(\text{mol dm}^{-3})(\text{mol dm}^{-3})}$$

$$= \frac{\text{s}^{-1}}{\text{mol dm}^{-3}}$$

$$= \text{mol}^{-1}\,\text{dm}^3\,\text{s}^{-1}$$

The value for k is therefore $0.014\,\text{mol}^{-1}\,\text{dm}^3\,\text{s}^{-1}$.

Example 3

This is an example of a badly designed experiment in which too many things seem to be varying at once. Only A level chemistry examiners would ever think of designing a series of experiments like this!

Using the data in the following table, find the order of reaction with respect to A and B, and the overall order of reaction. Write the rate equation and calculate a value for the rate constant including units.

Experiment	Concentrations (mol dm^{-3})		Rate of loss of A (mol dm^{-3} s^{-1})
	A	B	
1	0.10	0.10	2.5×10^{-5}
2	0.20	0.10	2.5×10^{-5}
3	0.30	0.20	5.0×10^{-5}

Finding the orders of reaction

The concentration of A doubles between experiments 1 and 2 with no effect on the rate. The reaction is **zero order** with respect to A.

The problem is that the concentration of A never stays constant for you to examine the effect of B. However, this time that doesn't actually matter, because the concentration of A has no effect on the rate. You can therefore ignore the values in the A column – whether the concentration is 0.10 or 0.30 makes no difference to the rate.

The concentration of B doubles between experiments 1 and 3 (or 2 and 3 – it doesn't matter because A is not affecting the rate). The rate also doubles. The reaction is **first order** with respect to B.

It is also **first order overall**, because $0 + 1 = 1$.

The rate equation

$$\text{Rate} = k[B]$$

Finding the rate constant k

Rearranging the rate equation gives:

$$k = \frac{\text{Rate}}{[B]}$$

Substituting values for the first experiment:

$$k = \frac{2.5 \times 10^{-5}}{0.10}$$

$$= 2.5 \times 10^{-4}\ \text{s}^{-1}$$

> ➤ Working out the **units** for an overall first order reaction is very quick and easy. Try it yourself to confirm that the unit is in fact s^{-1}.

Example 4

This is another example of a poorly designed series of experiments. This time it is made slightly more awkward because nothing turns out to be zero order.

Using the data in the table, find the order of reaction with respect to A and B.

Experiment	Concentrations (mol dm^{-3})		Rate of loss of A ($\text{mol dm}^{-3}\ \text{s}^{-1}$)
	A	B	
1	0.10	0.10	1.0×10^{-3}
2	0.10	0.20	2.0×10^{-3}
3	0.30	0.30	9.0×10^{-3}

Finding the orders of reaction

Where to start? You cannot actually start with A this time because there isn't a pair of experiments in which the concentration of A changes while that of B remains the same – so you will have to start with B.

Between experiments 1 and 2, the concentration of B doubles and so does the rate. The reaction is **first order** with respect to B.

Now consider reactions 1 and 3. Both concentrations have changed, but you now know what effect the change in B would have. The concentration of B has tripled. That would triple the rate because the reaction is first order with respect to B.

In fact the rate has increased 9 times – 3 times due to B, and therefore 3 times again due to A. This was caused by a tripling of the concentration of A, and so the reaction is **first order** with respect to A.

> ➤ If you have trouble with the **units**, see example 2.

You could now go on to calculate k if you were asked to, but there is nothing new in this. If you want to practise doing it, the answer is $0.10\ \text{mol}^{-1}\ \text{dm}^3\ \text{s}^{-1}$.

Example 5

People frequently become quite good at working out orders of reaction, but then get completely thrown if the examiners do something as simple as turn the table of results through 90°! This example is included so that you can meet and defeat this challenge before it really matters in an exam. There is nothing new at all in the calculation.

Using the data in the following table, find the order of reaction with respect to A and B, and the overall order of reaction. Write the rate equation and calculate a value for the rate constant including units.

	Experiment 1	Experiment 2	Experiment 3
[A] $(mol\,dm^{-3})$	0.12	0.36	0.36
[B] $(mol\,dm^{-3})$	0.04	0.04	0.20
Rate of loss of A $(mol\,dm^{-3}\,s^{-1})$	9.0×10^{-5}	8.1×10^{-4}	8.1×10^{-4}

Finding the orders of reaction

Between experiments 1 and 2, the concentration of B has stayed the same but that of A has tripled. The rate has gone up nine times. $9 = 3^2$. The reaction is **second order** with respect to A.

Changing the concentration of B between experiments 2 and 3 has made no difference to the rate. The reaction is **zero order** with respect to B.

Overall the reaction is **second order** $(2 + 0 = 2)$.

The rate equation

$$Rate = k[A]^2$$

Finding the rate constant k

Rearranging the rate equation gives:

$$k = \frac{Rate}{[A]^2}$$

Substituting values for the first experiment:

$$k = \frac{9.0 \times 10^{-5}}{(0.12)^2}$$

$$= 6.25 \times 10^{-3}\,mol^{-1}\,dm^3\,s^{-1}$$

➤ Work out the **units** yourself. If you have trouble with them, they are derived in a similar way to those in example 2.

Example 6

It is perfectly possible to reverse the calculations we have done so far – to be given a rate equation and be asked to calculate things from it. This example is perhaps the easiest thing you could be asked to do.

The reaction between P and Q has the rate equation

$$Rate = k[P][Q]^2$$

The rate constant was found to be $1.60 \times 10^{-6}\,mol^{-2}\,dm^6\,s^{-1}$ at a particular temperature.

Calculate the rate of the reaction at that temperature if the concentration of P was $0.15\,mol\,dm^{-3}$ and that of Q was $0.30\,mol\,dm^{-3}$.

➤ You could be given this information in a different way. For example, you could be told that the reaction was first order with respect to P and second order with respect to Q. You would first have to translate this into the rate equation given in the main text.

All you have to do is substitute the given values in the rate equation:

$$Rate = 1.60 \times 10^{-6} \times 0.15 \times (0.30)^2$$

$$= 2.16 \times 10^{-8}\,mol\,dm^{-3}\,s^{-1}$$

Example 7

You could, of course, equally well be given a rate equation and a rate constant, and be asked what concentration would be needed to achieve a particular rate.

A reaction between N and M was first order with respect to each. The rate constant was found to be $0.048\,mol^{-1}\,dm^3\,s^{-1}$ at a particular temperature. If the concentration of N was $0.10\,mol\,dm^{-3}$, what concentration of M would be needed to give a rate of reaction of $2.4 \times 10^{-4}\,mol\,dm^{-3}\,s^{-1}$?

$$Rate = k[N][M]$$

➤ If you would rather substitute the numbers first and do the rearrangement after, there is no reason why you can't do it that way.

Rearrange this to find the concentration of M:

$$[M] = \frac{Rate}{k[N]}$$

$$= \frac{2.4 \times 10^{-4}}{0.048 \times 0.10}$$

$$= 0.050\,mol\,dm^{-3}$$

Example 8

Another possibility is to give you a table of results of the kind we have worked from several times in this chapter, but with gaps which have to be filled in. You would either be given the rate equation, or you might have just found it from other data in the table – exactly as in examples 1 to 5. You already know how to find rate equations, so in this example we will assume that you are given it.

➤ Once again, you might simply be told that the reaction was first order with respect to D and second order with respect to E and be left to construct your own rate equation.

The rate equation for the reaction between D and E had the form:

$$Rate = k[D][E]^2$$

Fill in the blanks in the following table.

➤ There is an **alternative way** of doing this if you want to use it. It involves a lot more maths and a bit less thought. Use experiment 1 to find a value for the rate constant k. You will find that it comes to 0.012. This means that:

$$rate = 0.012[D][E]^2$$

If you slot the given values for each of the other experiments into this equation in turn, you can rearrange it and calculate the value you want, e.g. in experiment 2,

$$rate = 0.012 \times 0.200 \times (0.100)^2$$

and in experiment 3,

$$1.08 \times 10^{-4} = 0.012 \times 0.100 \times [E]^2$$

This is all so time consuming that it is really a "last resort" method!

Experiment	Concentrations (mol dm^{-3})		Rate of loss of D (mol dm^{-3} s^{-1})
	D	E	
1	0.100	0.100	1.20×10^{-5}
2	0.200	0.100	(blank a)
3	0.100	(blank b)	1.08×10^{-4}
4	(blank c)	0.100	6.00×10^{-5}

Blank a

The concentration of D has doubled between experiments 1 and 2. Because the reaction is first order with respect to D, the rate will also double. That new rate would be $2.40 \times 10^{-5}\,mol\,dm^{-3}\,s^{-1}$.

Blank b

Comparing experiments 1 and 3 (so that the concentration of D remains the same), the rate has increased 9 times due to the change in the concentration of E. The reaction is second order with respect to E, so the concentration of E must have gone up 3 times (because $9 = 3^2$). The new concentration of E is $0.300\,mol\,dm^{-3}$.

Blank c

Compare reactions 1 and 4, so that you keep the concentration of E the same. The rate has gone up 5 times. Because the reaction is first order with respect to D, its concentration must also have increased 5 times. Its new concentration is 0.500 mol dm^{-3}.

Problem • 1

Using data from the following table, find the orders of reaction with respect to A and B, write the rate equation, and calculate a value for the rate constant including its units.

Experiment	Concentrations (mol dm^{-3})		Rate of loss of A (mol dm^{-3} s^{-1})
	A	B	
1	0.010	0.010	1.0×10^{-5}
2	0.010	0.030	1.0×10^{-5}
3	0.030	0.030	9.0×10^{-5}

Problem • 2

(a) Using data from experiments 1 to 4 in the following table, find the orders of reaction with respect to D, E and F, write the rate equation, and calculate a value for the rate constant including its units. (The question marks in experiments 5 and 6 represent values that you will be expected to calculate in part (b).)

Experiment	Concentrations (mol dm^{-3})			Rate of loss of D (mol dm^{-3} s^{-1})
	D	E	F	
1	0.10	0.10	0.20	4.40×10^{-6}
2	0.10	0.10	0.40	8.80×10^{-6}
3	0.10	0.050	0.20	4.40×10^{-6}
4	0.30	0.10	0.20	1.32×10^{-5}
5	0.20	0.20	0.20	?
6	?	0.10	0.10	8.80×10^{-6}

(b) Calculate (i) the rate of loss of D in experiment 5, and (ii) the concentration of D in experiment 6.

Problem • 3

Using data from the following table, find the orders of reaction with respect to R and S, write the rate equation, and calculate a value for the rate constant including its units.

Experiment	Concentrations (mol dm^{-3})		Rate of loss of S (mol dm^{-3} s^{-1})
	R	S	
1	0.20	0.10	1.6×10^{-7}
2	0.30	0.10	1.6×10^{-7}
3	0.40	0.40	6.4×10^{-7}

Problem . 4

Using data from the following table, find the orders of reaction with respect to L, M and N, write the rate equation, and calculate a value for the rate constant including its units.

	Expt 1	Expt 2	Expt 3	Expt 4
[L] $(mol\,dm^{-3})$	0.10	0.20	0.20	0.20
[M] $(mol\,dm^{-3})$	0.15	0.15	0.30	0.30
[N] $(mol\,dm^{-3})$	0.10	0.10	0.10	0.20
Rate of loss of M $(mol\,dm^{-3}\,s^{-1})$	9.60×10^{-5}	3.84×10^{-4}	3.84×10^{-4}	7.68×10^{-4}

Problem . 5

A reaction involving only X was second order with respect to X. The rate constant for the reaction at a particular temperature was found to be $1.44 \times 10^{-4}\,mol^{-1}\,dm^3\,s^{-1}$.

(a) Calculate the rate of the reaction when the concentration of X is $0.200\,mol\,dm^{-3}$.

(b) What concentration of X is needed to give a rate of $1.20 \times 10^{-5}\,mol\,dm^{-3}\,s^{-1}$?

Finding orders of reaction graphically

Rate–concentration graphs

Real experiments do not produce results which are as tidy as those we have used in the examples so far. Experimental error would force you to do more than simply double the concentration of one of the reactants in order to find its effect on the rate of the reaction. You would have to take a series of readings at different concentrations, and then interpret them graphically.

In the following examples, we are going to assume that we are changing the concentration of one of the reactants, A, keeping everything else the same. The initial rate of reaction is measured for each value of the concentration.

Zero order with respect to A

If the reaction is zero order with respect to A, the concentration of A does not appear in the rate equation, and so the equation reads:

Rate = k[other concentration terms]

These "other concentration terms", which might include B, C and so on, will be constant throughout these experiments because we have chosen only to change the concentration of A. So if

[other concentration terms] = constant

then the whole of the right hand side of the rate equation is constant. Putting that into words: "The rate of reaction is constant (independent of the concentration of A)."

> Later on we could do another series of experiments which involved changing the concentrations of B or C (etc.) if we wanted to. In these, the concentration of A would then be kept constant.

If you measured the rate of reaction at various concentrations of A, you would get a graph like Figure 6.1.

Allowing for experimental error (hence the slight fluctuations in the points), the rate is constant – independent of the value of [A].

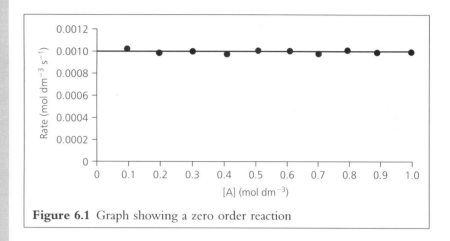

Figure 6.1 Graph showing a zero order reaction

Finding a value for the rate constant k

This is only simply done **if A is the only substance taking part in the reaction**. This means that there will not be any other concentration terms in the rate equation, and so it would simplify to:

Rate = k

The value of k can be read off the graph. In the example above, k has the value of $0.0010 \, mol \, dm^{-3} \, s^{-1}$, because the rate remains constant at that value.

Summary

A horizontal straight line on one of these graphs shows a zero order reaction.

First order with respect to A

In this case the rate equation reads:

Rate = k[A][other concentration terms]

Once again, we are going to keep everything constant apart from the concentration of A – which again means that the other concentration terms are constant. This time the rate equation will simplify to:

Rate = constant × [A]

where the constant is a combination of k and the other concentration terms.

You can read this as "The rate of reaction is proportional to the concentration of A." If you plot this you will get a straight line like Figure 6.2.

137

➤ **Maths a bit rusty?** To find the slope of a straight line graph like this, choose a point **on the line** (**not** one of the plotted points – unless it falls exactly on the best-fit line) and trace back to the horizontal and vertical axes. Divide the vertical by the horizontal value – in this case, the rate value by the concentration value.

The dotted lines could have been drawn to meet the best-fit line **anywhere** along its length – the further to the right the better, because it cuts down the percentage errors in reading the graph. In this case, they were not drawn at the extreme right of the graph to make it clear that they were not being aimed at the last plotted point, but at some random place **on the line.**

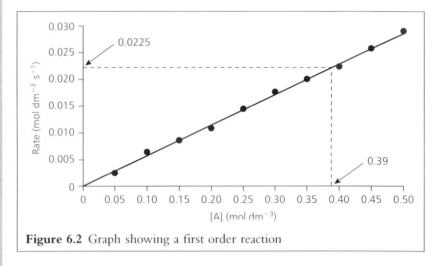

Figure 6.2 Graph showing a first order reaction

This graph shows that the rate is proportional to the concentration of A – in other words that the reaction is first order with respect to A. The dotted lines and the values of 0.0225 and 0.39 are added in order to find the slope of the line.

Finding a value for the rate constant k

Again, this is only easily done if A is the only substance present in the reaction. In that case, the rate equation simplifies to:

Rate = k[A]

The rate constant, k, is the slope of the graph.

The slope is given by $0.0225/0.39 = 0.058$.

The value for k is therefore $0.058\,s^{-1}$.

➤ **Worried about the units?** Rearranging the equation gives $k = $ rate/[A]. So the units are $mol\,dm^{-3}\,s^{-1}/mol\,dm^{-3}$. The $mol\,dm^{-3}$ terms cancel, leaving s^{-1}.

Summary

A sloping straight line through the origin (0,0) on one of these graphs shows that the reaction is first order.

Second order with respect to A

The rate equation would be:

Rate = k[A]^2[other concentration terms]

Again, everything will be constant apart from the concentration of A. This time the rate equation will simplify to:

Rate = constant $\times$ [A]^2

where the constant is a combination of k and the other concentration terms.

You can read this as "The rate of reaction is proportional to the square of the concentration of A." If you plot a graph of rate against [A], you get a curve, as in Figure 6.3.

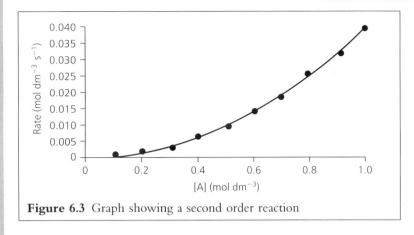

Figure 6.3 Graph showing a second order reaction

You must not assume because you get a curve that the reaction is second order with respect to A. All you can say is that it is not zero or first order. It could be some odd fractional order. The only way of being sure that it is second order is to replot a graph of rate against $[A]^2$ (see Figure 6.4).

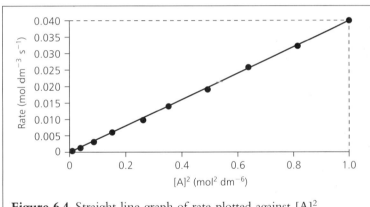

Figure 6.4 Straight line graph of rate plotted against $[A]^2$ confirms a second order reaction

This time you do get a straight line showing that the rate is proportional to $[A]^2$ – in other words that the reaction is second order with respect to A.

Finding a value for the rate constant k

Again, this can be done if A is the only substance present in the reaction. In this case, the rate equation simplifies to:

Rate $= k[A]^2$

The rate constant, k, is the slope of the last graph. You would find the slope in the same way as before. From the graph,

$k = 0.040/1.0$
$\quad = 0.040\,\text{mol}^{-1}\,\text{dm}^3\,\text{s}^{-1}$

➤ If you replotted this and found that you did not get a straight line – what then? All you could say for sure was that the reaction was not zero, first or second order with respect to A. To find the order you would need some more sophisticated maths.

➤ **Units?** $k = \text{rate}/[A]^2$.
Substituting units:
$k = \text{mol}\,\text{dm}^{-3}\,\text{s}^{-1}/(\text{mol}\,\text{dm}^{-3})^2$
Cancelling a $\text{mol}\,\text{dm}^{-3}$ term top and bottom of the fraction leaves:
$k = \text{s}^{-1}/\text{mol}\,\text{dm}^{-3}$
Organising this into one line gives:
$k = \text{mol}^{-1}\,\text{dm}^3\,\text{s}^{-1}$

Concentration–time graphs

So far we have been finding orders of reaction using initial rate methods. This means that you make up a mixture with reactants of known concentrations and measure the initial rate of the reaction. Then you throw away that mixture, and make up new ones in which the concentrations of the reactants vary in a systematic way – each time measuring the initial rate of the reaction.

You can also find orders of reaction by making up one mixture and measuring what happens to the concentration of one of the reactants during the course of that single reaction. The orders we are now measuring will be **overall orders** – and to make the discussion simpler, we will assume throughout this section that there is only a single reactant, A.

During the course of a single reaction, the concentration of A will fall as it is converted into products. The way it falls differs depending on the order of the reaction.

Zero order reactions

The rate of reaction is independent of the concentration of A. So even as A is used up, the rate of reaction will not change – the concentration of A will fall in a steady way (see Figure 6.5).

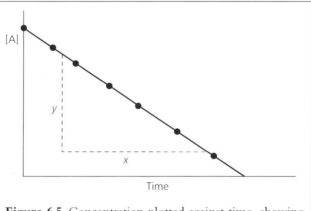

Figure 6.5 Concentration plotted against time, showing a zero order reaction

> ➤ **To be precise:** Technically, the slope of this graph is negative – in other words, the slope is $-y/x$. This is because the concentration of A **decreases** with time. Since the slope is negative, then the rate of reaction should really be reported as a negative amount, for example $-0.01 \, \text{mol} \, \text{dm}^{-3} \, \text{s}^{-1}$. This would show that the concentration of A was **falling** by $0.01 \, \text{mol} \, \text{dm}^{-3}$ every second.
>
> For most purposes, though, the rate is normally quoted as $0.01 \, \text{mol} \, \text{dm}^{-3} \, \text{s}^{-1}$, with the decrease shown in the way the change is described – for example, "the rate of **fall** in concentration of A is $0.01 \, \text{mol} \, \text{dm}^{-3} \, \text{s}^{-1}$".
>
> Do not worry about this – it is not likely to be an issue in an exam.

The straight line shows that the rate of fall of concentration of A is constant. If it varied you would get a curve. You can find the rate at which [A] falls by measuring the slope of the line – that is, by working out y/x. Where you choose to draw your dotted lines is entirely up to you.

Because for a zero order reaction, "rate $= k$", by measuring the rate you are automatically measuring the rate constant, k.

First and second order reactions

For a first order reaction, the rate is proportional to the concentration of A, and for a second order reaction it is proportional to the square of the concentration of A. This means that as the concentration of A falls, the reaction will get slower. This results in a curve rather than a straight line (see Figure 6.6).

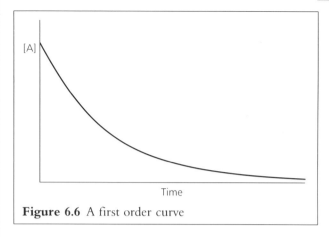

Figure 6.6 A first order curve

Can you tell that this is a first order curve just by looking at it? **No!** Although a second order curve looks different (see Figure 6.7), you could not be **certain** which you had – or if you had some fractional order like 1.2.

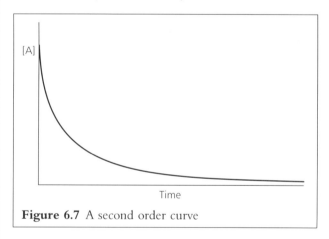

Figure 6.7 A second order curve

How to tell if you have a first order curve by measuring half life

Half life

The half life of a reaction is the time it takes for the concentration to fall to half of its initial value – whatever that is. Half life is given the symbol $t_{1/2}$.

> *For a first order reaction, the half life is constant – independent of the initial concentration.*

Suppose that the half life of a first order reaction is 10 minutes and that the initial concentration was $1.000 \, mol \, dm^{-3}$. It will take 10 minutes for the concentration to fall to $0.500 \, mol \, dm^{-3}$. It will take a further 10 minutes for the concentration to fall by half again – to $0.250 \, mol \, dm^{-3}$. In another 10 minutes it will be down to $0.125 \, mol \, dm^{-3}$, and so on.

Equally, it would take that same reaction 10 minutes for the concentration to fall from 0.800 to $0.400 \, mol \, dm^{-3}$, or from 0.600 to $0.300 \, mol \, dm^{-3}$. It makes

141

no difference at all what concentration you start from – it will take 10 minutes for it to fall by half.

> **Only first order reactions have constant half lives.**

In all other cases, the half life depends on the initial concentration. For a second order reaction, for example, it will take a different length of time for the concentration to fall from 1.000 to 0.500 mol dm^{-3} than it does to fall from 0.500 to 0.250 mol dm^{-3}.

So having plotted what you think might be a first order concentration–time curve, use it to find several half lives (see Figure 6.8). If these are constant to within experimental error, then the reaction is first order.

➤ How do you know if your half lives are constant to within experimental error? If they all fluctuate around one value, then they are probably constant. If, however, they tend to drift in one direction (getting gradually smaller or larger as you move along the curve), then they are probably not constant.

➤ **If you are interested:** There is a simple relationship between the half life of a first order reaction and the rate constant, k:

$$k = \frac{\ln 2}{t_{1/2}}$$

"ln" means "natural logarithm". You do not need to understand what that means – just find the "ln" button on your calculator. If you enter it correctly you will find that ln 2 has a value of 0.6931 (etc.). Divide that by $t_{1/2}$ (in seconds) to find k (in units of s^{-1}).

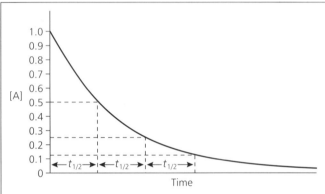

Figure 6.8 Using a concentration–time curve to find half lines

You do not have to work out successive half lives (for example, 1.0 to 0.5, 0.5 to 0.25, 0.25 to 0.125, and so on) – you could perfectly well choose 1.0 to 0.5, 0.8 to 0.4, 0.6 to 0.3 and so on, but you should sample as much of your curve as possible.

If you are asked to quote a value for half life, average the readings from your graph.

Simple sums with half lives

Example 9 A first order reaction has a half life of 15 minutes. If the initial concentration is 0.80 mol dm^{-3}, how long will it take for the concentration to fall to 0.10 mol dm^{-3}?

These sums are so trivial that it is tempting to do them in your head, but that risks making silly mistakes. Sketch a simple table:

Time (mins)	Concentration (mol dm^{-3})
0	0.80
15	0.40
30	0.20
45	0.10

The concentration falls to 0.10 mol dm^{-3} in 45 minutes (3 half lives).

Example 10 — A first order reaction has a half life of 5 minutes. If the initial concentration is $1.200\ \text{mol dm}^{-3}$, what will the concentration be after 20 minutes?

Time (mins)	Concentration (mol dm^{-3})
0	1.200
5	0.600
10	0.300
15	0.150
20	0.075

The concentration will fall to $0.075\ \text{mol dm}^{-3}$ in 20 minutes.

Example 11 — Two first order reactions were started at the same time. Reaction A had an initial concentration of $1.0\ \text{mol dm}^{-3}$ and a half life of 20 minutes. Reaction B had an initial concentration of $4.0\ \text{mol dm}^{-3}$ and a half life of 10 minutes. At what time would the concentrations in the two reactions become equal?

Time (mins)	Concentration in A (mol dm^{-3})	Concentration in B (mol dm^{-3})
0	1.0	4.0
10	?	2.0
20	0.5	1.0
30	?	0.5
40	0.25	0.25

> **Note:** You can only work out what the concentrations are at whole numbers of half lives – hence the "?" in the A column at 10 and 30 minutes. For example, the value at 10 minutes is **not** 0.75. This would imply a straight line graph of concentration against time. For a first order reaction, it isn't a straight line – it's a curve! The concentration at 10 minutes can be calculated using more sophisticated maths, or it can be found from a graph. It turns out to be $0.71\ \text{mol dm}^{-3}$.

You can see that the concentrations become equal at 40 minutes.

Finding rates from concentration–time graphs

This is something which is so time consuming that it is almost inconceivable that you would be asked to do it in an A level exam. You might, however, need to know how to do it as a part of a practical exercise.

A steep slope on the curve means that the concentration is falling rapidly; a shallow slope means a slow reaction. To find the rate of the reaction at any time (or for any concentration), you can measure the slope of the curve at that point (see Figure 6.9).

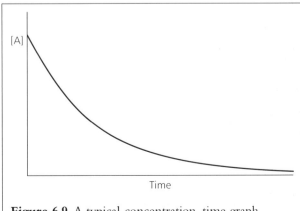

Figure 6.9 A typical concentration–time graph

> If you plotted the original concentration–time graph, and then found several rates from it, and then plotted a rate–concentration graph, and then deduced things from that, the whole process could take the best part of an hour. There is no way you could be asked to do this in a modern A level chemistry exam. You might need to know how to do it **in principle**, but not **in practice**.

Measure the slope by drawing a tangent to the curve at the point you are interested in, and find the slope of the tangent.

The slope of the curve (and therefore the rate of reaction at that point) is given by y/x (see Figure 6.10).

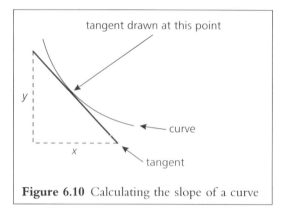

Figure 6.10 Calculating the slope of a curve

If you found the rate of the reaction at a number of different concentrations, you would get enough data to plot a rate–concentration curve of the sort we discussed earlier in this chapter.

To make the rate–concentration graph easier to plot, it obviously makes sense to determine the rate at simple values for concentration – 0.8, 0.6, 0.4, etc.

Problem • 6

Using the data in the following table, plot a graph of rate of reaction (y-axis) against concentration of X (x-axis) and determine the order of reaction with respect to X. Use your graph to find a value for the rate constant (including units).

[X] (mol dm^{-3})	0.100	0.210	0.285	0.420	0.540	0.700
Rate (mol dm^{-3} s^{-1})	0.0055	0.0116	0.0157	0.0231	0.0297	0.0385

Problem • 7

Using the data in the following table, plot a suitable graph to find the order of reaction with respect to Y. Use your graph to find a value of the rate constant (including units).

[Y] (mol dm^{-3})	0.120	0.200	0.320	0.445	0.560
Rate (mol dm^{-3} s^{-1})	1.73×10^{-6}	4.80×10^{-6}	12.9×10^{-6}	23.8×10^{-6}	37.6×10^{-6}

Problem • 8

Plot a graph of concentration of Z (y-axis) against time (x-axis) and use it to find the order of reaction with respect to Z. What is the value of the rate constant (including units)?

Time (secs)	0	20	40	60	80	100
[Z] (mol dm^{-3})	1.00	0.85	0.70	0.55	0.40	0.25

Problem • 9

Plot a graph of concentration of R (y-axis) against time (x-axis). Use the graph to show that the reaction is first order, and give an average value for the half life of the reaction.

Time (secs)	0	150	300	450	750	1150	1450	1750
[R] (mol dm^{-3})	1.000	0.812	0.659	0.535	0.353	0.202	0.133	0.088

Problem • 10

(a) A first order reaction has a half life of 5 minutes. What percentage of the original concentration of the reactant will remain after 20 minutes?

(b) The concentration of a reactant in a first order reaction fell to a quarter of its original value in 36 minutes. What is the half life of the reaction?

(c) A first order reaction has a half life of 8 minutes. If the original concentration of the reactant was $0.64\,mol\,dm^{-3}$, how long would it take for the concentration to fall to $0.01\,mol\,dm^{-3}$?

(d) Two first order reactions were started at the same time. Reaction A had an initial concentration of $1.00\,mol\,dm^{-3}$ and a half life of 15 minutes. Reaction B had an initial concentration of $2.00\,mol\,dm^{-3}$ and a half life of 10 minutes. At what time would the concentrations of the two reactions become equal?

The effect of temperature on rates

> **Note!** Most syllabuses do not expect you to know the work in this section. Check yours now before you go any further.

So far we have been looking at the effect of concentrations on rates of reaction, and have produced rate equations like: rate $= k[A][B]^2$

Changing the temperature or adding a catalyst also changes rates of reaction, and the rate equation does not at first sight seem to allow for this. In fact, both of these changes affect the value of the rate constant, k.

The Arrhenius Equation

The Arrhenius Equation shows the effect that changing the temperature or the activation energy of the reaction has on the rate constant. The activation energy is changed if you add a catalyst.

$$k = Ae^{-(E_A/RT)}$$

■ k is the rate constant.

■ E_A is the activation energy.

■ T is the temperature (in kelvins).

■ R is the gas constant ($8.31\,J\,K^{-1}\,mol^{-1}$).

■ A is approximately constant, and is taken as constant over small temperature ranges.

■ e is a mathematical entity (rather like π).

A more useful form of the same equation is:

$$\ln k = \ln A - \frac{E_A}{R}(1/T)$$

"ln k" and "ln A" are a form of logarithm of the numbers. For A level chemistry purposes, you do not need to understand this – you just have to find the "ln" button on your calculator. Do not confuse it with the "log" button. Try it now. $\ln 2 = 0.6931\ldots$ Your calculator will probably want you to enter "2" and then press the "ln" button. If this does not give you the answer $0.6931\ldots$, try entering it the other way round or read your calculator instruction book!

145

The last equation can be simplified even more, because ln A will be constant:

$$\ln k = c - \frac{E_A}{R}(1/T)$$

You can also modify this equation to show the effect of changes in temperature directly on the rate of the reaction:

$$\ln (rate) = c - \frac{E_A}{R}(1/T)$$

All that happens is that the constant c changes.

Using these equations to find activation energy

If you are given values of either the rate constant or the rate of reaction at various temperatures, it is quite easy to find the activation energy of a reaction by drawing a graph. A straight line graph has an equation:

$$y = c + mx$$

where c and m are both constants. m is the slope of the graph. Compare this with one of the equations above.

> It doesn't matter which equation you choose to compare with $y = c + mx$. Both the other equations are of exactly the same form.

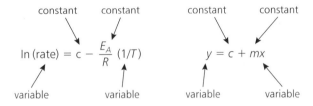

The equation on the left will also give a straight line provided you plot ln(rate) on the y axis against $(1/T)$ on the x axis. The slope of the line will be $-(E_A/R)$, because this corresponds to "m" in the right hand equation.

Example 12

Plot the following values of ln(rate) on the y axis against $1/T$ on the x axis, and use the graph to find a value for the activation energy of the reaction.

$1/T \times 10^3$	3.448	3.333	3.226	3.125	3.030
ln (rate)	−0.748	−0.056	0.591	1.197	1.767

> That top row could also be labelled as $(1/T)/10^{-3}$ – in other words each value of $1/T$ has been divided by 10^{-3}. $3.448 \times 10^{-3}/10^{-3}$ becomes 3.448, of course. If you take numbers from the graph, you have to remember to multiply them by 10^{-3} in order to get a proper value.

Before plotting the graph, look carefully at the heading for the top row. What does $1/T \times 10^3$ mean? Each value of $1/T$ has been multiplied by 10^3. This is to make plotting the graph easier – to avoid having to plot values like 3.448×10^{-3}. The only problem is that you have to remember to divide by 10^3 (or multiply by 10^{-3}, which is the same thing) when you use these values to find the gradient of the graph (see Figure 6.11).

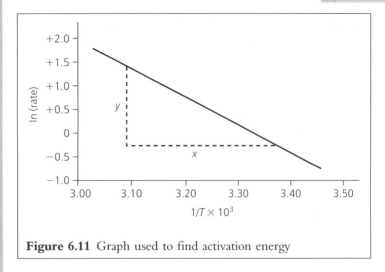

Figure 6.11 Graph used to find activation energy

Because this graph slopes downwards, the slope is negative. Measure the slope by working out $-y/x$, placing your triangle anywhere convenient.

If you plot the graph, you should find that the slope is $-6020\,K$. (Remember to multiply the x value by 10^{-3} or divide by 10^3.)

We have already shown that the slope is given by $-E_A/R$.

$$-\frac{E_A}{R} = -6020$$

$$-E_A = -6020 \times 8.31$$

$$E_A = 50\,000\,J\,mol^{-1}$$

This would more normally be quoted as $50\,kJ\,mol^{-1}$.

> **Units for slope?** ln(rate) doesn't have units. $1/T$ has units of K^{-1}. The units are therefore $1/K^{-1} = K$.

> **Units for E_A?** The slope has units of K. R has units of $J\,K^{-1}\,mol^{-1}$. Multiplying them together leaves $J\,mol^{-1}$.

Example 13

> **Units for k?** These would vary depending on the overall order of the reaction. You do not need to worry about these. Whatever the units are, when you calculate a logarithm, the units disappear anyway.

> **Do this!** In particular, check your values for ln k. Calculate values to a number of decimal places that you could reasonably plot on your graph.

The first example was simplified by giving you values ready to plot. You are more likely to have to work those values out first from T, and either the rate constant or the rate. For example, suppose you were given the following values of temperature and rate constant:

T(K)	293	313	333	353
k	0.0030	0.0216	0.122	0.567

You need to redraw this as a table of values of $1/T$ and ln k:

$1/T$	3.413×10^{-3}	3.195×10^{-3}	3.003×10^{-3}	2.833×10^{-3}
ln k	-5.81	-3.84	-2.10	-0.57

Now plot the graph as before (see Figure 6.12).

147

> We have plotted the $1/T$ value as $1/T \times 10^3$ to avoid having to write all the 10^{-3} terms in. When you measure the slope, don't forget to reconvert the x value into its true value.

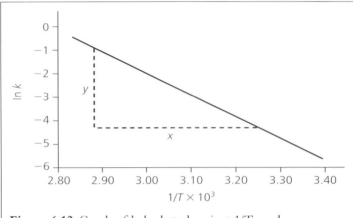

Figure 6.12 Graph of $\ln k$ plotted against $1/T$ used to find activation energy

The slope is again given by $-y/x$. It is negative because the line is sloping downwards. You will find that the slope is about $-9000\,\text{K}$. So, as above:

$$-\frac{E_A}{R} = -9000$$

$$-E_A = -9000 \times 8.31$$

$$E_A = 75\,000\,\text{J}\,\text{mol}^{-1} \text{ (to 2 significant figures)}$$

Problem • 11

The rate constant of a reaction was found to vary with temperature as follows.

$T(\text{K})$	290	310	330	350
$k \times 10^3$	1.01	5.04	20.7	72.2

By plotting a suitable graph, find the activation energy of the reaction. ($R = 8.31\,\text{J}\,\text{K}^{-1}\,\text{mol}^{-1}$)

End of chapter checklist

> You may not need to do all these things. Check your syllabus and past exam papers.

Can you do the following things?

■ Understand what is meant by the order of a reaction with respect to a particular substance, and by the overall order of the reaction.

■ Write a rate equation if you are given values for the individual orders of reaction.

■ Find the rate equation from tables of initial rate data.

■ Find a value for the rate constant k given a rate equation and values for concentrations and rate of reaction.

■ Know the units for rate, and for concentration, and determine the units for k given the rate equation.

■ Use a rate equation to calculate a value for rate of reaction or concentration of reactant if you are given values for the other terms in the equation.

- Recognise the shape of a rate–concentration graph for zero and first order reactions, and know how to find a value for the rate constant from such a graph.

- Know that a second order reaction gives a straight line graph if you plot rate against the square of concentration. Know how to find a value for the rate constant from such a graph.

- Recognise the shape of a concentration–time graph for a zero order reaction and know how to find a value for the rate constant from such a graph.

- Understand the concept of half life, know that a first order reaction has a constant half life, and be able to determine half life from a concentration–time graph for a first order reaction.

- Do simple calculations involving the half life of first order reactions.

- Know how to determine the rate of the reaction at any particular concentration from a concentration–time graph.

- Plot a suitable graph and use it to find activation energy given values for rate of reaction or rate constant varying with temperature.

Revision problems

Numerical answers are provided for these problems, but no worked solutions.

Problem • 12

Using data from the following table, find the orders of reaction with respect to K and L, write the rate equation, and calculate a value for the rate constant including its units.

Experiment	Concentrations ($mol\,dm^{-3}$)		Rate of loss of K ($mol\,dm^{-3}\,s^{-1}$)
	K	L	
1	0.10	0.10	5.5×10^{-5}
2	0.20	0.10	1.1×10^{-4}
3	0.20	0.20	2.2×10^{-4}

Problem • 13

(a) Using data from the following table, find the orders of reaction with respect to A, B and C, write the rate equation, and calculate a value for the rate constant including its units.

Experiment	Concentrations ($mol\,dm^{-3}$)			Rate of loss of A ($mol\,dm^{-3}\,s^{-1}$)
	A	B	C	
1	0.100	0.100	0.100	2.10×10^{-6}
2	0.200	0.100	0.100	2.10×10^{-6}
3	0.300	0.200	0.100	8.40×10^{-6}
4	0.400	0.200	0.200	1.68×10^{-5}

(b) Calculate the initial rate of the reaction if each reactant had a concentration of $0.250\,mol\,dm^{-3}$.

Problem • 14

A reaction between G and F was first order with respect to both. The rate constant for the reaction was 1.4×10^{-3} mol^{-1} dm^3 s^{-1}.

(a) Write the rate equation for the reaction.
(b) What would the initial rate of the reaction be if the concentrations of G and F were 0.50 and 0.20 mol dm^{-3} respectively?
(c) If the initial concentration of G was 0.40 mol dm^{-3}, what concentration of F would be required to give an initial rate of 2.8×10^{-4} mol dm^{-3} s^{-1}?

Problem • 15

The reaction between A, B and C had the rate equation:

$$\text{Rate} = k[A]^2[C]$$

Work out the values which should go into the following table to replace the letters a, b and c.

Experiment	Concentrations (mol dm^{-3})			Rate of loss of A (mol dm^{-3} s^{-1})
	A	B	C	
1	0.10	0.20	0.10	2.5×10^{-4}
2	a	0.20	0.10	1.0×10^{-3}
3	0.10	0.40	0.20	b
4	0.20	0.30	c	3.0×10^{-3}

Problem • 16

Four reactions U, V, W and X each involved only one reactant. Assuming that they can only have orders of 0, 1 or 2, use the following data to find the order of each reaction, and a value for its rate constant, including units.

Reaction U

[U] (mol dm^{-3})	0.180	0.390	0.550	0.765	0.935
Rate (mol dm^{-3} s^{-1})	3.60×10^{-4}	7.80×10^{-4}	11.0×10^{-4}	15.3×10^{-4}	18.7×10^{-4}

Reaction V

[V] (mol dm^{-3})	0.155	0.360	0.514	0.706	0.912
Rate (mol dm^{-3} s^{-1})	0.0160	0.0160	0.0160	0.0160	0.0160

Reaction W

[W] (mol dm^{-3})	0.220	0.400	0.565	0.680	0.845
Rate (mol dm^{-3} s^{-1})	4.84×10^{-6}	16.0×10^{-6}	31.9×10^{-6}	46.2×10^{-6}	71.4×10^{-6}

Reaction X

[X] (mol dm^{-3})	0.160	0.370	0.525	0.695	0.882
Rate (mol dm^{-3} s^{-1})	7.20×10^{-4}	16.7×10^{-4}	23.6×10^{-4}	31.3×10^{-4}	39.7×10^{-4}

Problem • 17

By plotting a suitable graph, show that the following reaction is first order. What is the half life of the reaction?

Time (secs)	0	100	200	300	400	500	600	700	800
[X] (mol dm^{-3})	1.000	0.749	0.561	0.420	0.315	0.236	0.177	0.132	0.099

Problem • 18

(a) If, during a first order reaction, the concentration fell to 12.5% of its original value in 24 minutes, what is the half life of the reaction?

(b) If the initial concentration in a first order reaction with a half life of 12 minutes was 0.400 mol dm^{-3}, what would the concentration be after 48 minutes?

Problem • 19

Use data from the following table showing how the rate constant for a reaction varies with temperature to plot a suitable graph to calculate the activation energy of the reaction.

T(K)	288	313	338	363
k	5.99×10^{-5}	9.59×10^{-4}	0.0102	0.0782

$(R = 8.31\,\text{J}\,\text{K}^{-1}\,\text{mol}^{-1})$

This chapter introduces straightforward equilibrium calculations. There isn't any complicated maths involved, although in some cases you will need to be able to do some very simple algebra. If your algebra is not very good, it's not a disaster!

Introduction – reminding you what the words mean

Dynamic homogeneous equilibrium

Homogeneous means that all the substances involved are in the same phase.

Phase is a better term than **physical state**. Phases are physically distinct parts of a system – parts that you can see boundaries between. If you had a solid and a gas, these are clearly two different parts of the total system and there is an obvious boundary between them. If, on the other hand, you had a mixture of gases, these would be a single phase because there would be no boundary.

The advantage of the term **phase** over physical state comes when you think of mixtures of liquids (or mixtures of solids). If you have two miscible liquids (for example, ethanol and water), these form a single phase with no boundary. But if you had two immiscible liquids (for example, petrol and water), one floats on top of the other with an obvious boundary between them. You would only have one physical state (liquid), but two phases.

A **dynamic equilibrium** involves a reversible reaction in a closed system – one from which nothing escapes (except heat) and to which nothing is added (except heat). For example, the Haber Process for the manufacture of ammonia involves the dynamic equilibrium:

$$N_{2(g)} + 3H_{2(g)} \rightleftharpoons 2NH_{3(g)}$$

At equilibrium, the rate of the forward reaction (between nitrogen and hydrogen) becomes exactly equal to the rate of the back reaction (the splitting up of the ammonia).

So from then on there is no further change in the total amounts of nitrogen, hydrogen or ammonia present, because the ammonia is being formed at exactly the same rate as it is splitting up. There will only be a change in amounts if one of the conditions of the reaction (like temperature or pressure) is changed.

Dynamic implies that the reaction is still continuing. **Equilibrium** implies the constant amounts of everything.

Dynamic heterogeneous equilibrium

In this case a dynamic equilibrium exists where the substances are not all in the same phase. Typical examples include cases where mixtures of solids and gases are involved.

> ➤ **Note:** This is not a substitute for a standard text book. If you are unsure about any of the routine descriptive parts relating to equilibria, get them sorted out before you attack the calculations. All we are doing here is explaining a few key words which come up in numerical problems.

Dynamic homogeneous equilibria

The equilibrium constant, K_c

You will become familiar with two equilibrium constants, K_c and K_p. K_c is a constant derived from the concentrations of things present – which may be gases or liquids. K_p is derived from pressures, and only applies to gases. For now, we are going to consider K_c – the equilibrium constant in terms of concentrations.

Writing an expression for K_c

Suppose you have a dynamic homogeneous equilibrium with the equation:

$$aA + bB \rightleftharpoons cC + dD$$

A, B, C and D are either all gases or all liquids – hence "homogeneous".

Suppose you allowed this reaction to reach equilibrium and then measured the steady concentrations of everything present. Irrespective of how much A or B or C or D you started with, you can write an expression involving them which always gives the same answer (provided you keep the temperature constant).

That constant answer is called the **equilibrium constant** for the reaction and is given by the expression:

$$K_c = \frac{[C]^c[D]^d}{[A]^a[B]^b}$$

[A], [B], [C] and [D] are simply the concentrations of the various substances in $mol\,dm^{-3}$.

The powers (a, b, c and d) are the numbers which appear in front of the substances in the equation. If there isn't a number, the power is 1 – and the concentration term would just be written as, for example, [A].

> *Notice that equilibrium constants are always expressed by writing the right hand side terms on top and the left hand side terms underneath.*

You must write down the equation for the reaction to which the equilibrium constant applies, otherwise you cannot see which is the right hand side and which the left hand side. You could, for example, write the above reaction the other way around. That's fair enough – it's a reversible reaction, and you could just as well have produced an equilibrium mixture by starting from C and D:

$$cC + dD \rightleftharpoons aA + bB$$

The equilibrium constant for this reaction is

$$K_c = \frac{[A]^a[B]^b}{[C]^c[D]^d}$$

➤ From here on the word "dynamic" will be omitted. You can assume that any mention of the word "equilibrium" implies "dynamic equilibrium".

➤ **Note!** Do not confuse the use of the powers in the equilibrium constant expression with the apparently similar use in the rate equations in Chapter 6. In the equilibrium constant expression, the powers are simply the numbers which appear in the equation. In the rate equations, the powers represent the orders of reaction, which can only be found from experiment, and which do not necessarily bear any relation to the numbers in the equation.

➤ If you look carefully at the two K_c expressions, you will see that the second one is simply the first one turned upside down. Suppose K_c for the reaction written one way is, say, 4. If the reaction was written the other way around, K_c would be 1/4 (or 0.25).

153

Both equilibrium constant expressions are perfectly valid. Both match the equations that accompany them. In an exam, you will probably be asked to write an expression for K_c for a reaction given to you by the examiners – in which case there's no problem. The equation will be written on the exam paper.

If you have to write your own equation, take care to get it properly balanced. You cannot write a correct expression for K_c from an incorrect equation.

Equilibrium constants are constant (at a particular temperature)

Nothing changes the value of the equilibrium constant except a change in temperature. Changing the pressure or the concentration of something or adding a catalyst makes no difference to the equilibrium constant, but a change in temperature will give it a different value. Calculating the new value is beyond A level, but you should be able to deduce whether it will increase or decrease. Use Le Chatelier's Principle to find out how the balance of the right hand side and left hand side of the equation changes.

> ➤ **Hazy about Le Chatelier?** You shouldn't really be reading a chapter on equilibrium calculations if you haven't got the basic descriptive ideas properly under control. Stop now and do some revision.

e.g. $N_{2(g)} + 3H_{2(g)} \rightleftharpoons 2NH_{3(g)}$ $\qquad \Delta H = -92 \text{ kJ mol}^{-1}$

If you decrease the temperature, according to Le Chatelier the system will respond by favouring the reaction which will raise it again. It can do that by producing more ammonia because that reaction is exothermic. There will therefore be more ammonia and less nitrogen and hydrogen at equilibrium.

$$K_c = \frac{[NH_3]^2}{[N_2][H_2]^3}$$

Because there will now be a bigger number on the top and smaller numbers on the bottom of the fraction, K_c will increase if you lower the temperature in this case.

The units of K_c

> ➤ **Working out units:** If you are not familiar with how to work out units, stop now and read pages 129 to 130 in Chapter 6.

The units of K_c vary from case to case, and you will have to work them out every time you calculate a value for K_c in a question. Write down the expression for K_c and then substitute units into it rather than numbers.

Example 1

$$N_{2(g)} + 3H_{2(g)} \rightleftharpoons 2NH_{3(g)}$$

$$K_c = \frac{[NH_3]^2}{[N_2][H_2]^3}$$

$$= \frac{(\text{mol dm}^{-3})^2}{(\text{mol dm}^{-3})(\text{mol dm}^{-3})^3}$$

$$= \frac{1}{(\text{mol dm}^{-3})^2}$$

$$= \frac{1}{\text{mol}^2 \text{ dm}^{-6}}$$

$$= \text{mol}^{-2} \text{ dm}^6$$

Example 2

$$C_2H_{4(g)} + H_2O_{(g)} \rightleftharpoons C_2H_5OH_{(g)}$$

$$K_c = \frac{[C_2H_5OH]}{[C_2H_4][H_2O]}$$

$$= \frac{mol\,dm^{-3}}{(mol\,dm^{-3})(mol\,dm^{-3})}$$

$$= \frac{1}{mol\,dm^{-3}}$$

$$= mol^{-1}\,dm^3$$

Example 3

$$CH_3COOC_2H_{5(l)} + H_2O_{(l)} \rightleftharpoons CH_3COOH_{(l)} + C_2H_5OH_{(l)}$$

$$K_c = \frac{[CH_3COOH][C_2H_5OH]}{[CH_3COOC_2H_5][H_2O]}$$

$$= \frac{(mol\,dm^{-3})(mol\,dm^{-3})}{(mol\,dm^{-3})(mol\,dm^{-3})}$$

In this case, the units all cancel out and so K_c has no units – it is just a number. This will happen whenever there are exactly the same number of molecules on both sides of the equation. Look for this situation in examples – if you recognise it, you won't need to waste time working out non-existent units.

Problem • 1

Write down an expression for K_c and work out its units in each of the following examples:

(a) $2SO_{2(g)} + O_{2(g)} \rightleftharpoons 2SO_{3(g)}$
(b) $N_2O_{4(g)} \rightleftharpoons 2NO_{2(g)}$
(c) $2HI_{(g)} \rightleftharpoons H_{2(g)} + I_{2(g)}$
(d) $2NH_{3(g)} \rightleftharpoons N_{2(g)} + 3H_{2(g)}$

Calculating values for K_c

Example 4

At its most trivial, all you might be asked to do is to write an expression for K_c and then substitute given values in it. This question relates to the equilibrium:

$$H_{2(g)} + I_{2(g)} \rightleftharpoons 2HI_{(g)}$$

When equilibrium had been established at 764 K, the mixture was found to contain: hydrogen 2.484×10^{-3} mol dm^{-3}; iodine 2.514×10^{-3} mol dm^{-3}; hydrogen iodide 1.695×10^{-2} mol dm^{-3}. Calculate a value for K_c at this temperature.

First write an expression for K_c:

$$K_c = \frac{[HI]^2}{[H_2][I_2]}$$

➤ You might perhaps wonder why the concentrations of hydrogen and iodine are different. In fact, there isn't the slightest reason why they should be the same. They would only be the same if you mixed them initially in exactly the right proportions, or if you started from hydrogen iodide.

155

> **Note:** If there aren't any units, say so! It shows the examiners that you haven't just forgotten to work them out.

Example 5

> Dilute hydrochloric acid is often used as a convenient source of both water and acid catalyst. 18 g of dilute hydrochloric acid contains almost exactly 1 mole of water.

Then substitute the given values:

$$K_c = \frac{(1.695 \times 10^{-2})^2}{(2.484 \times 10^{-3})(2.514 \times 10^{-3})}$$

$$= 46.0 \text{ (no units)}$$

There are no units in this case, because there are the same number of molecules on both sides of the equation.

Most questions will need a bit more effort than the last one. This example is more typical.

If an ester like ethyl ethanoate reacts with water in the presence of an acid catalyst, the following equilibrium is established:

$$CH_3COOC_2H_{5(l)} + H_2O_{(l)} \rightleftharpoons CH_3COOH_{(l)} + C_2H_5OH_{(l)}$$

ethyl ethanoate   ethanoic acid   ethanol

Exactly 1 mole of ethyl ethanoate was mixed with exactly 1 mole of water (from dilute hydrochloric acid) and allowed to reach equilibrium. The equilibrium mixture was analysed and found to contain 0.300 moles of ethanoic acid. Calculate a value for K_c at the temperature of the reaction.

To work out a value for K_c, you need to know the concentrations of everything at equilibrium. To find the concentrations, you need to know the number of moles of everything and the total volume. Draw up a little table to make clear what we actually know at the moment.

	$CH_3COOC_2H_{5(l)}$	$+ H_2O_{(l)}$	$\rightleftharpoons$	$CH_3COOH_{(l)}$	$+ C_2H_5OH_{(l)}$
Start (moles)	1	1		0	0
Equilibrium (moles)	?	?		0.300	?

You would not write the question marks down. These represent blanks that we need to think about before we put real values in.

Look at the relationships shown by the equation. Focus on one particular pair of substances at a time, and ignore everything else. Start with the ethanoic acid and the ethanol (because this is the easiest to see!).

The equation says that for every mole of ethanoic acid that is produced, you will also get one mole of ethanol. If 0.300 mole of ethanoic acid is formed, there will also be 0.300 mole of ethanol. You can slot that number into your table.

Now forget entirely about that relationship, and focus instead on the relationship between the ethanoic acid and the ethyl ethanoate. The equation says that 1 mole of ethyl ethanoate will react to produce 1 mole of ethanoic acid. Since 0.300 mole of ethanoic acid has been formed, 0.300 mole of ethyl ethanoate must have reacted. That leaves 0.700 mole. Slot that number into the table.

Now focus on the relationship between ethanoic acid and water. 1 mole of water reacts to produce 1 mole of ethanoic acid. 0.300 mole of water must have reacted, leaving 0.700 mole.

➤ When you draw up this table, show how you derived the values of 0.700 by writing down $1 - 0.300 = 0.700$. It shows the examiner what you are doing, but also forces you to think carefully and not just make snap guesses.

Most equilibrium calculations will involve drawing up a similar table – and it is essential that you get this "equilibrium (moles)" line right.

Your table now looks like this:

	$CH_3COOC_2H_{5(l)}$	$+$	$H_2O_{(l)}$	$\rightleftharpoons$	$CH_3COOH_{(l)}$	$+ C_2H_5OH_{(l)}$
Start (moles)	1		1		0	0
Equilibrium (moles)	$1 \quad 0.300$ $= 0.700$		$1 - 0.300$ $= 0.700$		0.300	0.300

Now we have a bit of a problem. In order to feed numbers into the equilibrium constant expression we need **concentrations** (in $mol\,dm^{-3}$), not numbers of moles. We are not told the volume of the mixture, and can't possibly guess it. Certainly we cannot assume that it will be $1\,dm^3$. We can't just ignore it either! So for now, call it "V", and hope something turns up later. The total calculation now looks like this:

	$CH_3COOC_2H_{5(l)}$	$+$	$H_2O_{(l)}$	$\rightleftharpoons$	$CH_3COOH_{(l)}$	$+ C_2H_5OH_{(l)}$
Start (moles)	1		1		0	0
Equilibrium (moles)	$1 - 0.300$ $= 0.700$		$1 - 0.300$ $= 0.700$		0.300	0.300
Equilibrium concentrations ($mol\,dm^{-3}$)	$0.700/V$		$0.700/V$		$0.300/V$	$0.300/V$

➤ **Units?** There aren't any. This is another example of an equilibrium with the same number of molecules on each side of the equation.

$$K_c = \frac{[CH_3COOH][C_2H_5OH]}{[CH_3COOC_2H_5][H_2O]}$$

$$= \frac{(0.300/V)(0.300/V)}{(0.700/V)(0.700/V)}$$

$$= \frac{0.300 \times 0.300}{0.700 \times 0.700}$$

$$= 0.184 \text{ (no units)}$$

➤ **Worried** about the apparent length of this problem? Don't be! Most of it is describing thought processes. All that would appear on paper is the final version of the calculation given on this page.

Conveniently, all the "V" terms cancel out. This happens because there are the same number of molecules on both sides of the equation. If there were different numbers of molecules on the right hand side and the left hand side, the volumes would not cancel. How would you cope with that problem? There would not be a problem, because the examiners would have to tell you the volume of the system in the question.

So was there any point in writing all the "V"s into the calculation if they were only going to cancel out again? YES! You must get into the habit of putting them in **every time**. Otherwise you are going to forget to do it when it really matters.

Example 6

This problem relates to the gaseous equilibrium:

$$B_{(g)} + C_{(g)} \rightleftharpoons A_{(g)}$$

0.500 mole of B and 0.300 mole of C were mixed in a container of volume $10.0\,dm^3$ at a temperature of 400 K. At equilibrium there was found to be 0.100 mole of A present. Calculate the value for K_c at this temperature.

	$B_{(g)}$	$+$	$C_{(g)}$	$\rightleftharpoons$	$A_{(g)}$
Start (moles)	0.500		0.300		0
Equilibrium (moles)	0.500 − 0.100 = 0.400		0.300 − 0.100 = 0.200		0.100
Equilibrium concentration $(mol\,dm^{-3})$	0.400/10.0 = 0.0400		0.200/10.0 = 0.0200		0.100/10.0 = 0.0100

> **Note!** If 0.100 mole of A are formed, 0.100 mole of both B and C will have been used up.

> **This time** you are given the volume ($10.0\,dm^3$), so there's no problem.

$$K_c = \frac{[A]}{[B][C]}$$

$$= \frac{0.0100}{0.0400 \times 0.0200}$$

$$= 12.5\,mol^{-1}\,dm^3$$

> **Units?** If you have trouble with the units, see example 2 on page 155.

Example 7

So far, working out the "equilibrium (moles)" line has been straightforward because all the relationships involved in the equations have been 1:1. Where they are different (1:2, for example), there is more chance of making mistakes. This example illustrates the thinking involved.

The question refers to the gaseous equilibrium:

$$A_{(g)} \rightleftharpoons 2B_{(g)}$$

4.00 moles of A was placed in a $20.0\,dm^3$ container and heated to 320 K until equilibrium had been established. The equilibrium mixture was found to contain 1.50 moles of A. Calculate the value for K_c at this temperature.

	$A_{(g)}$	$\rightleftharpoons$	$2B_{(g)}$
Start (moles)	4.00		0
Equilibrium (moles)	1.50		?

Thinking

2.50 moles of A has been used up (4.00 − 1.50).
Each mole of A used up produces two moles of B.
So at equilibrium there must be 2 × 2.50 moles of B present.

So the complete answer looks like this:

	$A_{(g)}$	$\rightleftharpoons$	$2B_{(g)}$
Start (moles)	4.00		0
Equilibrium (moles)	1.50		2 × (4.00 − 1.50) = 5.00
Equilibrium concentration $(mol\,dm^{-3})$	1.50/20.0 = 0.0750		5.00/20.0 = 0.250

> **Hint:** The volume of the system was $20.0\,dm^3$.

$$K_c = \frac{[B]^2}{[A]}$$

$$= \frac{(0.250)^2}{0.0750}$$

$$= 0.833\,mol\,dm^{-3}$$

Example 8

Making life more difficult!

If you were going to work out an equilibrium constant from a real experiment, you would necessarily have to do more calculations than we have been doing. You would have to work out how many moles of starting substances you had, and find out how many moles of something you had at equilibrium. You could be asked to do the same thing in an exam – probably with some guidance.

> **Note:** This example includes a titration calculation. If you haven't practised these recently, now would be a good time to go back and do some revision.

24.0 g of ethanoic acid and 23.0 g of ethanol were mixed in a stoppered bottle and left for several days to reach equilibrium at room temperature. At the end of that time, the mixture was poured into pure water and made up to a total volume of $250 \, cm^3$. A $25.0 \, cm^3$ sample of this needed $26.5 \, cm^3$ of $0.400 \, mol \, dm^{-3}$ sodium hydroxide solution to neutralise the remaining ethanoic acid. Calculate a value for K_c for the reaction:

$$CH_3COOH_{(l)} + C_2H_5OH_{(l)} \rightleftharpoons CH_3COOC_2H_{5(l)} + H_2O_{(l)}$$
ethanoic acid   ethanol   ethyl ethanoate

(H = 1; C = 12; O = 16. The equation for the reaction between ethanoic acid and sodium hydroxide is:

$$CH_3COOH + NaOH \rightarrow CH_3COONa + H_2O)$$

Finding the starting numbers of moles of ethanoic acid and ethanol is straightforward:

> **Remember:**
> Number of moles
> $$= \frac{mass \, (g)}{mass \, of \, 1 \, mole \, (g)}$$

Number of moles of ethanoic acid = 24.0/60 = 0.400 moles

(1 mole weighs 60 g)

Number of moles of ethanol = 23.0/46 = 0.500 moles

(1 mole weighs 46 g)

Now you have to use the titration results to work out the number of moles of ethanoic acid at equilibrium. Start with what you know everything about – the sodium hydroxide.

$$\text{Number of moles of NaOH} = \frac{26.5}{1000} \times 0.400$$

$$= 0.0106$$

$$CH_3COOH + NaOH \rightarrow CH_3COONa + H_2O$$

1 mole of NaOH reacts with 1 mole of ethanoic acid.

> ➤ Start by working out how much ethanoic acid has been used up. This will be the same as the amount of ethyl ethanoate formed because of the 1:1 relationship between them in the equation.
>
> The amount of water formed will be the same as the amount of ethyl ethanoate formed, because they are also in a 1:1 relationship.
>
> The amount of ethanol used up will be the same as the amount of ethanoic acid used up – again a 1:1 relationship.
>
> We do not know what the volume of the original mixture is. It was **not** $250 \, cm^3$ – that was after you diluted it so that it could be titrated. The "*V*"s eventually cancel out.

Therefore there are 0.0106 moles of ethanoic acid in the $25 \, cm^3$ sample.

In the whole $250 \, cm^3$ of solution there were 10×0.0106 moles of ethanoic acid = 0.106 moles.

This solution contained all of the equilibrium mixture. The equilibrium mixture therefore contained 0.106 moles of ethanoic acid.

Now we are back to the K_c calculations that we have been practising:

	$CH_3COOH_{(l)}$	$+ C_2H_5OH_{(l)}$	$\rightleftharpoons$	$CH_3COOC_2H_{5(l)}$	$+ H_2O_{(l)}$
Start (moles)	0.400	0.500		0	0
Equilibrium (moles)	0.106	0.500 − 0.294 = 0.206		0.400 − 0.106 = 0.294	0.294
Equilibrium concentration (mol dm⁻³)	0.106/*V*	0.206/*V*		0.294/*V*	0.294/*V*

$$K_c = \frac{[CH_3COOC_2H_5][H_2O]}{[CH_3COOH][C_2H_5OH]}$$

$$= \frac{(0.294/V)(0.294/V)}{(0.106/V)(0.206/V)}$$

$$= \frac{0.294 \times 0.294}{0.106 \times 0.206}$$

$$= 3.96 \text{ (no units)}$$

➤ There are no units because there are equal numbers of molecules on each side of the equation.

Problem • 2

This question relates to the reaction:

$$2M_{(g)} \rightleftharpoons N_{(g)}$$

At equilibrium, the concentrations of M and N were respectively 0.141 mol dm^{-3} and 0.872 mol dm^{-3}. Calculate the value for K_c at the temperature of the reaction.

Problem • 3

On heating, X decomposes reversibly according to the equation:

$$X_{(g)} \rightleftharpoons Y_{(g)} + Z_{(g)}$$

This reaction was allowed to reach equilibrium at two different temperatures.

(a) When 1.00 mole of X was heated at 200 °C in a container of volume 25.0 dm^3, the equilibrium mixture was found to contain 0.200 mole of Y. Calculate the value of K_c at this temperature.

(b) When the equilibrium constant was measured at 500 °C, K_c was found to have a value of 4.00×10^{-3} mol dm^{-3}. Is the decomposition of X exothermic or endothermic? Explain your answer.

Problem • 4

A mixture of 2.00 mole of A and 1.00 mole of B was allowed to reach equilibrium according to the equation:

$$A_{(l)} + B_{(l)} \rightleftharpoons C_{(l)} + D_{(l)}$$

The equilibrium mixture was found to contain 0.400 mole of B. Calculate the value for K_c at the temperature of the reaction.

Problem • 5

1.00 mole of hydrogen iodide was heated in a container of volume 20.0 dm^3 at a temperature of 765 K. At equilibrium, the mixture was found to contain 0.114 mole of iodine. Calculate K_c at this temperature for the equilibrium:

$$2HI_{(g)} \rightleftharpoons H_{2(g)} + I_{2(g)}$$

Problem • 6

A mixture of 1.00 mole of ethanoic acid, 2.00 moles of ethanol and 1.00 mole of water was allowed to reach equilibrium. On analysis, the equilibrium mixture was found to contain 0.257 mole of ethanoic acid. Find K_c for the reaction:

$$CH_3COOH_{(l)} + C_2H_5OH_{(l)} \rightleftharpoons CH_3COOC_2H_{5(l)} + H_2O_{(l)}$$

Problem • 7

44.0 g of ethyl ethanoate was mixed with 36.0 g of water containing hydrochloric acid as a catalyst and allowed to reach equilibrium over several days. The equilibrium mixture was then made up to 250 cm^3 with pure water. A 25.0 cm^3 sample of the diluted mixture was titrated with 1.00 mol dm^{-3} sodium hydroxide solution. After allowing for the acid catalyst present, the ethanoic acid in the equilibrium mixture was found to require 29.5 cm^3 of the sodium hydroxide solution for neutralisation. Find K_c for the reaction:

$$CH_3COOC_2H_{5(l)} + H_2O_{(l)} \rightleftharpoons CH_3COOH_{(l)} + C_2H_5OH_{(l)}$$

(H = 1; C = 12; O = 16. The equation for the neutralisation reaction is:

$$CH_3COOH + NaOH \rightarrow CH_3COONa + H_2O)$$

Calculating things from given values of K_c

Although you have got to think carefully – especially at the "equilibrium (moles)" stage – there isn't any difficult maths in the calculations we have done so far. Reversing the calculations to find equilibrium concentrations from given values of K_c makes them more awkward, involving some algebra. In all but the very simplest cases, the algebra needed is beyond the demands of modern A level chemistry syllabuses. If you aren't very comfortable with algebra, it doesn't matter much – as you will see.

Example 9

➤ This could be described as an **isomerisation reaction**. Isomers are molecules with the same molecular formula but with a different spatial arrangement of the atoms. An example might be

$$CH_3COCH_3 \rightleftharpoons CH_2{=}CH(OH)CH_3$$

Each molecule has the same molecular formula, C_3H_6O, but the atoms are arranged differently.

This example is about a simple equilibrium

$$A_{(l)} \rightleftharpoons B_{(l)}$$

If 1.00 mole of A was allowed to reach equilibrium, how many moles of B would be formed if K_c had a value of 0.0200 at the temperature of the reaction?

Start off in exactly the same way as before:

	$A_{(l)}$	$\rightleftharpoons$	$B_{(l)}$
Start (moles)	1.00		0
Equilibrium (moles)	?		?

Now you have a problem, because you have no information to feed into this line. You are actually being asked to **find** the number of moles of B.

So write it in as an unknown. Call it "x" – or, perhaps rather more imaginatively, "b":

	$A_{(l)}$	$\rightleftharpoons$	$B_{(l)}$
Start (moles)	1.00		0
Equilibrium (moles)	?		b

If "b" moles of B have been formed, "b" moles of A have been used up because the relationship is 1:1. The number of moles of A left at equilibrium is therefore "$1.00 - b$".

161

$$A_{(l)} \rightleftharpoons B_{(l)}$$

	$A_{(l)}$		$B_{(l)}$
Start (moles)	1.00		0
Equilibrium (moles)	1.00 − b		b
Equilibrium concentration (mol dm^{-3})	(1.00 − b)/V		b/V

➤ We do not know the volume of the system, so will have to call it "V". The "V"'s will have to cancel out.

$$K_c = \frac{[B]}{[A]}$$

$$0.0200 = \frac{b/V}{(1.00 - b)/V}$$

$$0.0200 = \frac{b}{(1.00 - b)}$$

This is where the chemistry ends! Now you've got some algebra to do to solve this for "*b*":

$$0.0200 = \frac{b}{(1.00 - b)}$$

$$0.0200 \times (1.00 - b) = b$$

$$0.0200 - 0.0200b = b$$

$$1.02b = 0.0200$$

$$b = \frac{0.0200}{1.02}$$

$$= 0.0196 \, \text{mol}$$

➤ **Hint:** Is your algebra a disaster area? Do you know that it's going to take you ages to solve this with a good chance of getting the answer wrong? Doing this last bit of algebra to get the final answer probably isn't going to earn you more than 1 mark in an exam, and so you can't afford to spend more than about 1 minute doing it.

If you have problems with algebra, once you've got to the end of the chemistry in the question, abandon the rest and spend your time more productively somewhere else on the exam paper. If you like, just guess an answer (in this case somewhere between 1 and 0), and don't forget the units – there may be a mark for them. You stand far more chance of guessing the right answer than you do of winning the National Lottery!

➤ You might well be asked to find the percentage left over. In this case start with 100 moles, or start with 1 mole, work out the fraction left, and then multiply it by 100 at the end. For example, a fraction of 0.25 is 25%. It doesn't matter which way you do it, as long as you are comfortable with your method.

➤ **Hint:** If "*f*" moles are left, (1 − *f*) moles have been used up and so (1 − *f*) moles of B have been formed because the relationship is 1:1.

Example 10 This example is very similar to the last one, except that the question is phrased differently.

The equilibrium $A_{(l)} \rightleftharpoons B_{(l)}$ has a value of K_c of 9 at a particular temperature. Calculate the fraction of the original A remaining when equilibrium is reached.

You are not told how much A to start with, but since you are asked about the **fraction** of it left over, you can start with any amount you choose.

It would make sense to start with 1 mole. If you calculated how many moles of A were left at equilibrium – say 0.25 of a mole – then 0.25 as a fraction of 1 is still 0.25. If you start with 1 mole and find the number of moles left over, you have automatically calculated the fraction left.

We'll call the fraction left "*f*".

	$A_{(l)}$		$B_{(l)}$
Start (moles)	1		0
Equilibrium (moles)	f		1 − f
Equilibrium concentration (mol dm^{-3})	f /V		(1 − f)/V

$$K_c = \frac{[B]}{[A]}$$

$$9 = \frac{(1-f)/V}{f/V}$$

$$9 = \frac{(1-f)}{f}$$

$$9f = 1 - f$$

$$10f = 1$$

$$f = \frac{1}{10} \quad (= 0.1 \text{ or } 10\%)$$

1/10 (or 0.1) of the A is left at equilibrium – or 10% if you are asked for a percentage.

Although most people would probably manage the algebra in the last two examples without too much difficulty, the problems mount up as soon as you have more than one molecule on either side of the equation.

Example 11 If K_c for the following reaction is 36 at a particular temperature, calculate the fraction of P converted into Q and R at equilibrium:

$$2P_{(g)} \rightleftharpoons Q_{(g)} + R_{(g)}$$

Again, you can start with however much P you like. Start with 1 mole, and call the fraction used up "f".

	$2P_{(g)}$	$\rightleftharpoons$	$Q_{(g)}$	$+$	$R_{(g)}$
Start (moles)	1		0		0
Equilibrium (moles)	$1-f$		$f/2$		$f/2$
Equilibrium concentrations (mol dm^{-3})	$(1-f)/V$		$(f/2)/V$ $(=0.5f/V)$		$(f/2)/V$ $(=0.5f/V)$

$$K_c = \frac{[Q][R]}{[P]^2}$$

$$36 = \frac{(0.5f/V) \times (0.5f/V)}{[(1-f)/V]^2}$$

$$36 = \frac{(0.5f) \times (0.5f)}{(1-f)^2}$$

Once you have got past the "equilibrium (moles)" line, all you are doing is substituting into the K_c expression. You will know by now that the "V"s always cancel as long as there are the same number of molecules on each side of the equation – so you ought to be able to get to this point in the calculation.

Unless your algebra is **good**, stop now! Don't waste time trying to solve it for "f". It is not likely to be worth many marks, it will take you ages, and you may well get it wrong anyway!

➤ **Warning!** Don't spend any time on the next two examples until you have checked with your syllabus to find out whether you need to be able to do questions of this kind. Read your syllabus carefully to find out what it says about solving quadratic equations. Better still, go through all the recent papers set by your Examination Board to find out what sort of questions they ask on this topic. It may well be that although the syllabus allows them to set questions involving complicated algebra, in practice they never do. At least one major Examination Board has taken this line in the past. If you are worried about it, contact your Board and ask them what their policy is. If you do need to be able to solve problems of this kind, your algebra will have to be good. If it is anything less than good, take the question as far as you can and then abandon the tricky bits.

➤ **Hint:** Consider the relationship between P and Q. For every mole of P used up you only get half as much Q formed. If "f" moles of P are used up you will get "half f" moles of Q formed. The same argument applies to R.

➤ The full solution of this problem is not given. If your algebra is good enough you will be able to do it yourself. If it isn't good enough, you shouldn't be wasting your time reading this!

There is a short cut to solving this particular equation. Notice that both sides of the equation are perfect squares. By taking the square root of both sides, you are left with:

$$\frac{0.5f}{(1-f)} = \pm 6$$

You now have to work out a value for "f" for each of the two possible roots, -6 and $+6$. You will find that the two possible answers are $f = 0.92$ and $f = 1.1$. Because "f" can't have a value greater than 1, the second answer is impossible. The fraction converted is 0.92.

Example 12

➤ **Read your syllabus.** If it says something like "Candidates will not be expected to solve quadratic equations" (possibly adding "... using the formula ...") then this example is not relevant to you.

➤ **Hint**: If "h" moles of H are formed, the same number of moles of G will be formed. If "h" moles of H are formed, that same number of moles of E and F will have been used up.

The equilibrium constant, K_c, for the following reaction is 4.0 at 20 °C.

$$E_{(l)} + F_{(l)} \rightleftharpoons G_{(l)} + H_{(l)}$$

If 2.0 moles of E and 1.0 mole of F were mixed and allowed to reach equilibrium at 20 °C, calculate the number of moles of H formed.

Call the amount of H formed "h".

	$E_{(l)}$	+	$F_{(l)}$	$\rightleftharpoons$	$G_{(l)}$	+	$H_{(l)}$
Start (moles)	2.0		1.0		0		0
Equilibrium (moles)	$2.0 - h$		$1.0 - h$		h		h
Equilibrium concentration (mol dm^{-3})	$(2.0 - h)/V$		$(1.0 - h)/V$		h/V		h/V

$$K_c = \frac{[G][H]}{[E][F]}$$

$$4.0 = \frac{(h/V) \times (h/V)}{[(2.0-h)/V] \times [(1.0-h)/V]}$$

$$4.0 = \frac{h^2}{(2.0-h) \times (1.0-h)}$$

That's the chemistry finished! Even if your syllabus expects you to solve this, unless your algebra is **good**, stop there.

To solve this for "h", you need to rearrange the expression to give an equation of the form:

$$ax^2 + bx + c = 0$$

The solution of this is given by the expression:

$$x = \frac{-b \pm \sqrt{b^2 - 4ac}}{2a}$$

Our equation rearranges to give:

$$3h^2 - 12h + 8 = 0$$

Solving this produces answers of 0.85 or 3.2, depending on whether you take the negative sign or positive sign in the expression above. You can't produce more than 1 mole of H because you are limited by the amount of F that you start with. The answer of 3.2 moles is therefore impossible, leaving you with the correct answer of 0.85 moles of H formed.

There isn't any difficult algebra in these questions apart from 10(b). You should only attempt that part if your syllabus expects you to solve quadratic equations.

Problem • 8

The equilibrium constant for the reaction:

$$A_{(l)} \rightleftharpoons B_{(l)}$$

is 39 at 100 °C. If you had 2.0 moles of A to start with, how much would be left at equilibrium at this temperature?

Problem • 9

At 50 °C, K_c is 24 for the reaction:

$$S_{(l)} \rightleftharpoons T_{(l)}$$

What percentage of S will be converted into T when equilibrium is reached at this temperature?

Problem • 10

(a) In a closed system, the hydrolysis of ethyl ethanoate reaches equilibrium according to the equation:

$$CH_3COOC_2H_{5(l)} + H_2O_{(l)} \rightleftharpoons CH_3COOH_{(l)} + C_2H_5OH_{(l)}$$

K_c has a value of 0.25 at room temperature. Suppose you started with 1 mole of ethyl ethanoate and set up a number of experiments with variable numbers ("w") of moles of water. Show that the fraction "f" of the ethyl ethanoate which reacts could be found by solving the equation:

$$\frac{f^2}{(1-f)(w-f)} = 0.25$$

(b) Find the fraction hydrolysed if $w = 1$ and if $w = 10$.

The equilibrium constant, K_p

Pressures and concentrations

Although many of the examples we have looked at involving K_c have related to gases, it is actually much easier to measure the pressure of a gas rather than its concentration. In fact, for a gas, concentration and pressure are proportional to each other. If you double the pressure for a fixed mass of gas at a constant temperature, you double the concentration. The reason is that the way you would double the pressure would be by halving the volume, and if you have the same amount of substance in half the volume, its concentration doubles.

You can also show this relationship mathematically if you are familiar with the ideal gas equation: $pV = nRT$. If you rearrange this you could produce the relationship:

$$p = \frac{n}{V} \times RT$$

n/V is just concentration – the number of moles divided by volume. As long as temperature is constant, RT is constant – and so pressure is proportional to concentration.

For gaseous equilibria it therefore makes sense to quote an equilibrium constant in terms of pressures rather than concentrations – i.e. K_p rather than K_c. There is a relationship between the two values, but you are unlikely to need it for A level purposes.

Before we can define K_p, we have to explain some other terms.

Mole fraction

This means literally what it says. If you have a mixture of gases (A, B, C, etc.) then the mole fraction of gas A is the fraction of the total number of moles which is gas A. The mole fraction of gas A is given the symbol x_A.

$$x_A = \frac{\textit{number of moles of gas A}}{\textit{total number of moles of gas}}$$

For example, if you had a mixture of 1 mole of oxygen and 4 moles of nitrogen, the total number of moles of gas is 5. The mole fraction of oxygen is therefore 1/5, and that of nitrogen 4/5.

> ➤ **Avogadro's Law** says that at the same temperature and pressure, equal volumes of gases contain equal numbers of molecules. 25% of the volume therefore means 25% of the total number of molecules. If you have 25% of the total number of molecules, you also have 25% of the total number of moles.

It is important to realise that you could be given this information in an alternative way. For example, suppose you were told that you had a mixture of nitrogen and hydrogen which contained 25% by volume of nitrogen. Saying that the nitrogen makes up 25% of the volume is exactly the same as saying that the mole fraction of nitrogen is 25% (i.e. 0.25). The hydrogen, of course, makes up the rest of the volume, and its mole fraction would be 0.75.

Partial pressure

The partial pressure of one of the gases in a mixture is the pressure which it would exert if it alone occupied the whole container. Partial pressure is given the symbol P_A or P_B (etc.).

Two important relationships

The total pressure is made up of the sum of the individual partial pressures:

$$\textit{Total pressure } P = P_A + P_B + P_C + \ldots$$

$$\textit{Partial pressure of A} = \textit{mole fraction of A} \times \textit{total pressure}$$
$$P_A = x_A \times P$$

Make sure you learn these – especially the second box. You can't do K_p calculations without them.

Writing an expression for K_p

Apart from the fact that partial pressures are used instead of concentrations, the equilibrium constant, K_p, is defined in exactly the same way as K_c. It is most easily seen using a couple of examples.

Example 13

$$2SO_{2(g)} + O_{2(g)} \rightleftharpoons 2SO_{3(g)}$$

$$K_p = \frac{P^2_{SO_3}}{P^2_{SO_2} \times P_{O_2}}$$

Notice that it is still "right hand side divided by left hand side".

Example 14

$$N_{2(g)} + 3H_{2(g)} \rightleftharpoons 2NH_{3(g)}$$

$$K_p = \frac{P^2_{NH_3}}{P_{N_2} \times P^3_{H_2}}$$

Again, K_p is right hand side partial pressures divided by left hand side partial pressures, with everything raised to the power of whatever number is in front of it in the equation.

The units of K_p

Like K_c, K_p has units unless there are equal numbers of molecules on both sides of the equation. The sort of units will depend on what units for pressure the question uses – it could be pascals (Pa), or kilopascals (kPa), or megapascals (MPa), or even atmospheres (atm). It doesn't matter. Work with whatever you are given – and don't mess around with them! If you are given the units in kPa, stick to those units – don't waste time converting them into Pa.

Revisiting the two examples above:

Example 13a Suppose you were given pressure units in kPa.

$$K_p = \frac{P^2_{SO_3}}{P^2_{SO_2} \times P_{O_2}}$$

$$= \frac{kPa^2}{kPa^2 \times kPa}$$

$$= \frac{1}{kPa}$$

$$= kPa^{-1}$$

Example 14a Suppose you were given pressure units in atmospheres (atm).

$$K_p = \frac{P^2_{NH_3}}{P_{N_2} \times P^3_{H_2}}$$

$$= \frac{atm^2}{atm \times atm^3}$$

$$= \frac{1}{atm^2}$$

$$= atm^{-2}$$

Calculating values for K_p

Example 15

When A is heated in a closed system to $400\,^{\circ}C$, the following equilibrium is set up:

$$A_{(g)} \rightleftharpoons B_{(g)} + C_{(g)}$$

The equilibrium partial pressures of the three gases were found to be: A 5.1 kPa; B 95 kPa; C 95 kPa. Calculate K_p at this temperature.

You are given all the partial pressures, so all you need to do is slot them into the K_p expression:

$$K_p = \frac{P_B \times P_C}{P_A}$$

$$= \frac{95 \times 95}{5.1}$$

$$= 1800\,kPa$$

> K_p has **units** in this case of
> $$\frac{(kPa)^2}{kPa} = kPa$$

> **Significant figures?** No more than 2, because your input numbers are only to that accuracy.

Example 16

This refers to the equilibrium

$$N_2O_{4(g)} \rightleftharpoons 2NO_{2(g)}$$

A vessel containing only dinitrogen tetroxide was held at a temperature of 350 K until equilibrium was established. The equilibrium pressure was 123 kPa and the mole fraction of nitrogen dioxide was found to be 0.800. Calculate the value of K_p at this temperature.

Stop and think what you need to know. To find K_p, you need partial pressures. Are you given them? No! To find partial pressures, you need mole fractions. Are you given them? You are given the mole fraction of NO_2 but not of N_2O_4. You need to start by finding that.

If the mole fraction of NO_2 is 0.800, the mole fraction of N_2O_4 is $1 - 0.800$.

	N_2O_4	NO_2
Mole fractions	$1 - 0.800$ $= 0.200$	0.800
Partial pressures (kPa)	0.200×123 $= 24.6$	0.800×123 $= 98.4$

> **Remember:**
> partial pressure = mole fraction × total pressure

$$N_2O_{4(g)} \rightleftharpoons 2NO_{2(g)}$$

$$K_p = \frac{P_{NO_2}^2}{P_{N_2O_4}}$$

$$= \frac{(98.4)^2}{24.6}$$

$$= 394\,kPa$$

> **Units** are exactly the same as in example 15.

Example 17

This example is about the Haber Process, where the equilibrium is:

$$N_{2(g)} + 3H_{2(g)} \rightleftharpoons 2NH_{3(g)}$$

A mixture of nitrogen and hydrogen in the mole ratio 1:3 (as required by the equation) was heated to 700 K and a pressure of 79 atmospheres in the presence of an iron catalyst. The equilibrium mixture was found to contain the following proportions of gases (by volume): N_2 21%; H_2 63%; NH_3 16%. Calculate the value for K_p at this temperature.

Do you know the partial pressures? No! Do you know the mole fractions? Yes, you do! Remember that percentages by volume are a direct measure of the mole fractions. If there is 21% by volume of nitrogen, then the mole fraction of nitrogen is 21% – usually expressed as 0.21.

	N_2	H_2	NH_3
Mole fractions	0.21	0.63	0.16
Partial pressures (atm)	0.21×79 $= 16.6$	0.63×79 $= 49.8$	0.16×79 $= 12.6$

> ➤ **Remember:**
> partial pressure = mole fraction × total pressure

> ➤ There should be no more than 2 **significant figures** in the final answer (because the percentages and pressure are only quoted to 2 figures).

> ➤ **Units?**
> $$\frac{atm^2}{atm \times atm^3} = \frac{1}{atm^2} = atm^{-2}$$

$$K_p = \frac{P^2_{NH_3}}{P_{N_2} \times P^3_{H_2}}$$

$$= \frac{(12.6)^2}{16.6 \times (49.8)^3}$$

$$= 7.7 \times 10^{-5} \ atm^{-2}$$

Example 18

This example uses exactly the same reaction with exactly the same figures as the last one, but you are given fewer of them!

This example is still about the Haber Process where the equilibrium is:

$$N_{2(g)} + 3H_{2(g)} \rightleftharpoons 2NH_{3(g)}$$

A mixture of nitrogen and hydrogen in the mole ratio 1:3 (as required by the equation) was heated to 700 K and a pressure of 79 atmospheres in the presence of an iron catalyst. The equilibrium mixture was found to contain 16% of ammonia by volume. Calculate the value for K_p at this temperature.

How do you get around the problem that you aren't told the mole fractions of nitrogen and hydrogen? If there is 16% ammonia in the equilibrium mixture, the rest must be nitrogen and hydrogen – 84%.

The nitrogen and hydrogen were in the mole ratio 1:3 at the start, and will remain in that same ratio throughout, because that is the ratio in which they are being used up.

Of every 4 moles of nitrogen/hydrogen mixture, 1 will be nitrogen (1/4 of the total) and 3 will be hydrogen (3/4 of the total).

The nitrogen is therefore 1/4 of 84% (= 21%) and the hydrogen is 3/4 of 84% (= 63%). Now the rest of the calculation is exactly the same as before.

Example 19

Hydrogen and iodine were heated in a closed container at 1100 K until equilibrium was reached:

$$H_{2(g)} + I_{2(g)} \rightleftharpoons 2HI_{(g)}$$

The equilibrium partial pressures were hydrogen 50 kPa; iodine 50 kPa; and the total equilibrium pressure was 350 kPa. Find K_p.

Do you know the partial pressures? Almost. You are given all but the hydrogen iodide value. Remember that the total pressure is the sum of the partial pressures. We can account for 100 kPa of the total (50 + 50). The missing 250 kPa must be due to the hydrogen iodide.

> ➤ There aren't any **units**. There are equal numbers of molecules on both sides of the equation. If you did substitute units into the K_p expression, they would cancel out.

$$K_p = \frac{P_{HI}^2}{P_{H_2} \times P_{I_2}}$$

$$= \frac{(250)^2}{50 \times 50}$$

$$= 25 \text{ (no units)}$$

Example 20

> ➤ When a substance **dissociates**, it splits up (decomposes) reversibly.

When phosphorus(V) chloride is heated to a sufficiently high temperature it vaporises and dissociates according to the equation:

$$PCl_{5(g)} \rightleftharpoons PCl_{3(g)} + Cl_{2(g)}$$

When 1.00 mole of PCl_5 was heated in a closed container, the equilibrium pressure was found to be 100 kPa, and the equilibrium mixture contained 0.816 mole of chlorine. Calculate K_p at the temperature of the reaction.

> ➤ Once a calculation starts to get as long as this one will turn out to be, you are likely to be given considerable guidance through it on a structured exam paper. The working here assumes that you have to think the whole thing out for yourself!

Think about what you need to know. Do you know the partial pressures? No! Do you know the mole fractions? No! What do you need to know in order to find the mole fractions? You need the number of moles of each substance at equilibrium, and the total number of moles at equilibrium. You are given the equilibrium number of moles of chlorine – so the first thing to do is to calculate the number of moles of PCl_5 and PCl_3 at equilibrium. Until you know those, it is not possible to work out the total number of moles at equilibrium.

At this point you are back to the sort of simple problem that you met in K_c calculations.

	$PCl_{5(g)}$	$\rightleftharpoons$ $PCl_{3(g)}$	+ $Cl_{2(g)}$
Start (moles)	1	0	0
Equilibrium (moles)	?	?	0.816

If 0.816 mole of chlorine are formed, there must be the same amount of PCl_3. 0.816 mole of PCl_5 must have split up.

> ➤ **Note!** You must think carefully about the way this problem develops. It starts off looking like a K_c calculation, but changes direction after a couple of lines. It would be easy to get the two confused if you weren't careful. If the examiners are guiding you through the question, this difficulty doesn't arise, of course.

	$PCl_{5(g)}$	$\rightleftharpoons$ $PCl_{3(g)}$	+ $Cl_{2(g)}$
Equilibrium (moles)	1 − 0.816 = 0.184	0.816	0.816

This is our basic information. Now we can work out the total number of moles at equilibrium, because this is needed to find the mole fractions.

Total number of moles at equilibrium = 0.184 + 0.816 + 0.816
$$= 1.816$$

Now find the mole fractions and we are back on familiar territory. Remember that the total equilibrium pressure is 100 kPa.

	PCl_5	PCl_3	Cl_2
Mole fractions	0.184/1.816 = 0.1013	0.816/1.816 = 0.4493	0.816/1.816 = 0.4493
Partial pressures (kPa)	0.1013 × 100 = 10.13	0.4493 × 100 = 44.93	0.4493 × 100 = 44.93

$$K_p = \frac{P_{PCl_3} \times P_{Cl_2}}{P_{PCl_5}}$$

$$= \frac{44.93 \times 44.93}{10.13}$$

$$= 199 \text{ kPa}$$

Example 21

This example is very similar to the last one, but is slightly trickier at the "equilibrium (moles)" stage. It relates to the equilibrium:

$$2SO_{2(g)} + O_{2(g)} \rightleftharpoons 2SO_{3(g)}$$

2.00 moles of sulphur dioxide and 1.00 mole of oxygen were mixed in the presence of a vanadium(V) oxide catalyst at a temperature of 700 K and an equilibrium pressure of 7.84 atmospheres. At equilibrium there were found to be 1.96 moles of sulphur trioxide in the mixture. Calculate K_p at this temperature.

Once again, think through what you need to know so that you can find the starting point for the calculation. Are you given partial pressures? No! Mole fractions? No! So you need to calculate the mole fractions – in which case you have to start by finding the numbers of moles of everything at equilibrium.

Try doing this before you read on.

	$2SO_{2(g)}$	+ $O_{2(g)}$	$\rightleftharpoons$ $2SO_{3(g)}$
Start (moles)	2.00	1.00	0
Equilibrium (moles)	?	?	1.96

The amount of SO_3 formed is exactly the same as the amount of SO_2 used up because their ratio in the equation is 1:1 (2:2 if you want to be fussy!).

Focusing on the relationship between the SO_3 and the oxygen, you will see that the amount of oxygen used up is only half the amount of SO_3 formed. Only half of 1.96 moles of oxygen have been used.

	$2SO_{2(g)}$	+ $O_{2(g)}$	$\rightleftharpoons$ $2SO_{3(g)}$
Equilibrium (moles)	2.00 − 1.96 = 0.04	1.00 − 1.96/2 = 0.02	1.96

The total number of moles present at equilibrium
$$= 0.04 + 0.02 + 1.96$$
$$= 2.02$$

	SO_2	O_2	SO_3
Mole fractions	0.04/2.02 = 0.01980	0.02/2.02 = 9.901×10^{-3}	1.96/2.02 = 0.9703
Partial pressures (atm)	0.01980×7.84 = 0.1552	$9.901 \times 10^{-3} \times 7.84$ = 0.07762	0.9703×7.84 = 7.607

> **Remember:**
> partial pressure = mole
> fraction × total pressure

$$K_p = \frac{P_{SO_3}^2}{P_{SO_2}^2 \times P_{O_2}}$$

$$= \frac{(7.607)^2}{(0.1552)^2 \times 0.07762}$$

$$= 31\,000 \text{ atm}^{-1}$$

Example 22

0.200 moles of dinitrogen tetroxide, N_2O_4, were allowed to reach equilibrium at 25 °C according to the equation:

$$N_2O_{4(g)} \rightleftharpoons 2NO_{2(g)}$$

The equilibrium mixture contained 4.60 g of nitrogen dioxide and the equilibrium pressure was 0.431 atmospheres. Find K_p at 25 °C. (N = 14; O = 16).

If you first find the number of moles of NO_2, the problem then becomes just like the last two. The RFM of NO_2 is 46.

4.60 g of NO_2 is 4.60/46 mol = 0.100 mol

	$N_2O_{4(g)}$	$\rightleftharpoons$	$2NO_{2(g)}$
Start (moles)	0.200		0
Equilibrium (moles)	0.200 − 0.100/2 = 0.150		0.100
The total number of moles	= 0.250		

> **Hint:** Each mole of NO_2
> formed only needs half a mole
> of N_2O_4 to break up.

	N_2O_4	NO_2
Mole fractions	0.150/0.250 = 0.600	0.100/0.250 = 0.400
Partial pressures (atm)	0.600×0.431 = 0.2586	0.400×0.431 = 0.1724

$$N_2O_{4(g)} \rightleftharpoons 2NO_{2(g)}$$

$$K_p = \frac{P_{NO_2}^2}{P_{N_2O_4}}$$

$$= \frac{(0.1724)^2}{0.2586}$$

$$= 0.115 \text{ atm}$$

Problem • 11

When phosphorus(V) chloride reached equilibrium at 200 °C according to the equation:

$$PCl_{5(g)} \rightleftharpoons PCl_{3(g)} + Cl_{2(g)}$$

the equilibrium partial pressures were: PCl_5 40 kPa; PCl_3 80 kPa; Cl_2 80 kPa. Calculate K_p at this temperature.

Problem • 12

N_2O_4 dissociates according to the equation:

$$N_2O_{4(g)} \rightleftharpoons 2NO_{2(g)}$$

When equilibrium had been established at a temperature of 298 K and an equilibrium pressure of 101 kPa, the partial pressure of N_2O_4 was found to be 72.0 kPa. Calculate K_p at this temperature.

Problem • 13

When hydrogen iodide was heated in a closed container to a temperature of 700 K, the total pressure at equilibrium was 1.00 atmosphere, and the partial pressure of the hydrogen iodide was 0.786 atmosphere. Find K_p for the reaction:

$$2HI_{(g)} \rightleftharpoons H_{2(g)} + I_{2(g)}$$

Problem • 14

1.00 mole of carbon monoxide and 1.00 mole of steam were allowed to reach equilibrium at 700 K and a pressure of 1.50 atmospheres. 0.740 mole of carbon dioxide was formed at equilibrium. Find K_p for the reaction:

$$CO_{(g)} + H_2O_{(g)} \rightleftharpoons CO_{2(g)} + H_{2(g)}$$

Problem • 15

640 g of sulphur dioxide were mixed with 256 g of oxygen and allowed to reach equilibrium in the presence of a vanadium(V) oxide catalyst at 700 K. The equilibrium pressure was 1.40 atmospheres and the mixture was found to contain 792 g of sulphur trioxide. Find the value of K_p for the equilibrium:

$$2SO_{2(g)} + O_{2(g)} \rightleftharpoons 2SO_{3(g)}$$

(O = 16; S = 32)

Calculating things from given values of K_p

The following examples all involve the same equilibrium at the same temperature (350 K):

$$N_2O_{4(g)} \rightleftharpoons 2NO_{2(g)} \qquad K_p = 3.89 \, atm$$

Example 23

When the above equilibrium was established at 350 K, the partial pressure of the NO_2 was found to be 0.700 atm. Calculate the partial pressure of the N_2O_4, and the total pressure.

Start by writing the expression for K_p, and then slot in the numbers you know:

$$K_p = \frac{P^2_{NO_2}}{P_{N_2O_4}}$$

$$3.89 = \frac{(0.700)^2}{P_{N_2O_4}}$$

$$P_{N_2O_4} = \frac{(0.700)^2}{3.89}$$

$$= 0.126 \, atm$$

The total pressure is the sum of the partial pressures:

$$Total\ pressure = 0.700 + 0.126$$
$$= 0.826 \, atm$$

Example 24

This is the same problem, but you are starting with the other partial pressure. It is possible to make a careless mistake this time.

When the above equilibrium was established at 350 K, the partial pressure of the N_2O_4 was found to be 0.200 atm. Calculate the partial pressure of the NO_2, and the total pressure.

$$K_p = \frac{P^2_{NO_2}}{P_{N_2O_4}}$$

$$3.89 = \frac{P^2_{NO_2}}{0.200}$$

$$P^2_{NO_2} = 0.200 \times 3.89$$

$$= 0.778$$

$$P_{NO_2} = \sqrt{0.778}$$

$$= 0.882 \, atm$$

➤ It is easy to forget to take the square root in the last step.

$$Total\ pressure = 0.200 + 0.882$$
$$= 1.08 \, atm$$

Example 25

We are still talking about the same equilibrium:

$$N_2O_{4(g)} \rightleftharpoons 2NO_{2(g)} \qquad K_p = 3.89 \, atm \, at \, 350 \, K$$

When 1.00 mole of dinitrogen tetroxide was heated to 350 K in a closed container, the equilibrium mixture was found to contain 0.600 mole of nitrogen dioxide. Calculate the total pressure at equilibrium, and the partial pressures of N_2O_4 and NO_2.

This is a much trickier question than the last one, and you would almost certainly be guided through it in an exam.

Work out the number of moles of dinitrogen tetroxide left at equilibrium.

➤ **Hint:** Each mole of NO_2 formed only needs half a mole of N_2O_4 to break up.

	$N_2O_{4(g)}$	$\rightleftharpoons$	$2NO_{2(g)}$
Start (moles)	1.00		0
Equilibrium (moles)	1.00 − 0.600/2 = 0.700		0.600

If the total pressure of the system at equilibrium is P, work out the partial pressures of N_2O_4 and NO_2 in terms of P.

The total number of moles at equilibrium is 1.300 (0.700 + 0.600).

	N_2O_4	NO_2
Mole fractions	0.700/1.300 = 0.5385	0.600/1.300 = 0.4615
Partial pressures (atm)	$0.5385 \times P$	$0.4615 \times P$

Write an expression for K_p and use it to calculate the total pressure P:

$$K_p = \frac{P^2_{NO_2}}{P_{N_2O_4}}$$

$$3.89 = \frac{(0.4615 \times P)^2}{0.5385 \times P}$$

$$3.89 = \frac{(0.4615)^2 \times P}{0.5385}$$

$$P = \frac{3.89 \times 0.5385}{(0.4615)^2}$$

$$= 9.84 \, \text{atm}$$

Calculate the partial pressures of N_2O_4 and NO_2.

All you have to do is to substitute P into the expressions in the bottom row of the table above:

Partial pressure of $N_2O_4 = 0.5385 \times 9.84$
$$= 5.30 \, \text{atm}$$

Partial pressure of $NO_2 = 0.4615 \times 9.84$
$$= 4.54 \, \text{atm}$$

Example 26

This problem involves doing some complicated algebra. You don't need to read it unless your syllabus expects you to solve quadratic equations.

Still the same equilibrium:

$$N_2O_{4(g)} \rightleftharpoons 2NO_{2(g)} \qquad K_p = 3.89 \, \text{atm at } 350 \, \text{K}$$

If dinitrogen tetroxide is allowed to reach equilibrium at a temperature of 350 K and an equilibrium pressure of 2.00 atmospheres, calculate the partial pressures of dinitrogen tetroxide and nitrogen dioxide in the mixture.

The first thing to notice is that you only need to calculate one of the partial pressures in the first instance. Suppose, for example, that we set out to find the partial pressure of the NO_2 – call it "p". Because the total pressure is the sum of the partial pressures, the partial pressure of N_2O_4 will be $2.00 - p$.

Write the K_p expression and then substitute into it:

$$K_p = \frac{P^2_{NO_2}}{P_{N_2O_4}}$$

$$3.89 = \frac{p^2}{(2.00 - p)}$$

> If your algebra is not good enough to cope with this, don't waste your time on it. Derive the expression involving p from K_p and leave it at that. You must, however, explain how you would obtain the partial pressure of N_2O_4. You could say something like 'If p worked out to be 0.500 atm, then the partial pressure of N_2O_4 would be $2.00 - 0.500 = 1.50$ atm.' It is obviously the wrong answer, but you should get credit for it.

Now there is some algebra to do:

$$3.89 \times (2.00 - p) = p^2$$
$$7.78 - 3.89p = p^2$$
$$p^2 + 3.89p - 7.78 = 0$$

Solve this using:

$$x = \frac{-b \pm \sqrt{b^2 - 4ac}}{2a}$$

You get two possible answers depending on whether you take the positive or negative sign. The solutions are 1.46 or −5.35. The negative answer is obviously impossible.

The partial pressure of NO_2 is 1.46 atm.

The partial pressure of N_2O_4 is $(2.00 - 1.46)$ atm $= 0.54$ atm.

Problem • 16

When hydrogen iodide is heated in a closed container, it reaches equilibrium according to the equation:

$$2HI_{(g)} \rightleftharpoons H_{2(g)} + I_{2(g)} \qquad K_p = 0.0185 \text{ at } 700\,K$$

If the partial pressure of hydrogen iodide in the mixture is 1.32 atmospheres, calculate the partial pressures of hydrogen and of iodine and the total equilibrium pressure. (Hint: The hydrogen and iodine are produced in equal amounts when the hydrogen iodide splits up.)

Problem • 17

If sulphur dioxide and oxygen are mixed in the presence of a vanadium(V) oxide catalyst, the following equilibrium can be established:

$$2SO_{2(g)} + O_{2(g)} \rightleftharpoons 2SO_{3(g)} \qquad K_p = 0.130 \text{ atm}^{-1} \text{ at } 1100\,K$$

The sulphur dioxide and oxygen were mixed in the mole ratio 2:1 (as required by the equation) and heated to 1100 K. A 50.0% conversion of SO_2 into SO_3 was required.

(a) If you started with 2.00 moles of sulphur dioxide and 1.00 mole of oxygen, calculate the numbers of moles of everything present in the equilibrium mixture assuming 50.0% conversion.
(b) If the total equilibrium pressure is P, write expressions for the partial pressures of SO_2, O_2 and SO_3 in terms of P.
(c) Write an expression for K_p and use it to calculate the total pressure P.

Problem • 18

When some dinitrogen tetroxide was allowed to reach equilibrium at 298 K in a closed container, it was found that 20.0% of it had dissociated into nitrogen dioxide according to the equation:

$$N_2O_{4(g)} \rightleftharpoons 2NO_{2(g)} \qquad K_p = 0.115 \text{ atm at } 298\,K$$

(a) Assuming that you started with 1.00 mole of N_2O_4, calculate the numbers of moles of N_2O_4 and NO_2 present at equilibrium.
(b) If the total equilibrium pressure is P, write expressions for the partial pressures of N_2O_4 and NO_2 in terms of P.
(c) Write an expression for K_p and use it to calculate the total pressure P.
(d) Work out the partial pressures of N_2O_4 and NO_2.

Problem • 19

When phosphorus(V) chloride is heated, the following equilibrium is established:

$$PCl_{5(g)} \rightleftharpoons PCl_{3(g)} + Cl_{2(g)} \qquad K_p = 160\,kPa\ at\ 200\,°C$$

(a) If the partial pressure of chlorine at equilibrium is p, calculate the partial pressures of PCl_5 and PCl_3 at equilibrium in terms of p if the total pressure is 400 kPa.
(b) Write an expression for K_p, and use it to calculate a value for p.
(c) Work out the partial pressures of each component of the equilibrium mixture.

➤ **Note:** Don't attempt this question unless your syllabus expects you to be able to solve quadratic equations.

Dynamic heterogeneous equilibria

Examples of heterogeneous equilibria

➤ **Note!** Not all syllabuses expect you to know about heterogeneous equilibria. Check your syllabus, and if you are in any doubt, look at recent exam questions, or contact the Examination Board.

In a heterogeneous equilibrium, more than one phase is present. The most common examples involve gases in contact with solids, but you could also have gases in contact with liquids, or solids in contact with liquids.

Gases in contact with solids

$$H_2O_{(g)} + C_{(s)} \rightleftharpoons H_{2(g)} + CO_{(g)}$$

$$CaCO_{3(s)} \rightleftharpoons CaO_{(s)} + CO_{2(g)}$$

$$3Fe_{(s)} + 4H_2O_{(g)} \rightleftharpoons Fe_3O_{4(s)} + 4H_{2(g)}$$

Gases in contact with liquids

$$H_2O_{(l)} \rightleftharpoons H_2O_{(g)}$$

This is the equilibrium which is established when you have some water in a closed bottle. Some of the water evaporates to give water vapour in the space above the liquid water.

Solids in contact with liquids

If you shook copper up with silver nitrate solution, you would get this equilibrium established:

$$Cu_{(s)} + 2Ag^+{}_{(aq)} \rightleftharpoons Cu^{2+}{}_{(aq)} + 2Ag_{(s)}$$

This is the sort of equilibrium which you get if you shake any sparingly soluble ionic substance with water:

$$PbCl_{2(s)} \rightleftharpoons Pb^{2+}{}_{(aq)} + 2Cl^-{}_{(aq)}$$

Equilibria like this second example are dealt with separately in Chapter 9 under "Solubility product". Check your syllabus to find out whether this is something you need to know about.

Equilibrium constants for heterogeneous equilibria

Important rule

> When writing an expression for the equilibrium constant for a heterogeneous equilibrium, terms for pure solids or pure liquids are left out of the expression.

This applies whether you are writing an expression for K_c or K_p.

Example 27

$$H_2O_{(g)} + C_{(s)} \rightleftharpoons H_{2(g)} + CO_{(g)}$$

The correct expressions	NOT
$K_c = \dfrac{[H_2][CO]}{[H_2O]}$	$\dfrac{[H_2][CO]}{[H_2O][C]}$
$K_p = \dfrac{P_{H_2} \times P_{CO}}{P_{H_2O}}$	$\dfrac{P_{H_2} \times P_{CO}}{P_{H_2O} \times P_C}$

Example 28

$$CaCO_{3(s)} \rightleftharpoons CaO_{(s)} + CO_{2(g)}$$

$$K_c = [CO_2] \qquad K_p = P_{CO_2}$$

Notice that neither of the solids is represented in the equilibrium expressions.

Example 29

$$Cu_{(s)} + 2Ag^+{}_{(aq)} \rightleftharpoons Cu^{2+}{}_{(aq)} + 2Ag_{(s)}$$

$$K_c = \frac{[Cu^{2+}]}{[Ag^+]^2}$$

➤ There is no K_p expression this time because the equilibrium doesn't involve gases.

Once again, neither solid is included in the K_c expression.

Example 30

$$H_2O_{(l)} \rightleftharpoons H_2O_{(g)}$$

$$K_p = P_{H_2O_{(g)}}$$

The liquid water is not included because it is a pure liquid phase.

Calculations involving heterogeneous equilibria

Once you know how to write expressions for the equilibrium constants, the calculations are identical to those for homogeneous equilibria. Here are two examples to illustrate this:

Example 31

When steam was heated with excess carbon to 1200 K and an equilibrium pressure of 15.5 atmospheres, 90.0% of the steam was converted into hydrogen and carbon monoxide. Calculate K_p for the equilibrium:

$$H_2O_{(g)} + C_{(s)} \rightleftharpoons H_{2(g)} + CO_{(g)}$$

Since we are given information about percentage conversion, we will start with 100 moles of steam. If you wanted to, you could start with 1 mole, but you would then have to think slightly more (for example, to convert 90% into the decimal fraction 0.9)!

➤ We are not interested in the carbon as far as the equilibrium calculation is concerned, so we leave that space blank.

	$H_2O_{(g)}$	+	$C_{(s)}$	$\rightleftharpoons$	$H_{2(g)}$	+	$CO_{(g)}$
Start (moles)	100		—		0		0
Equilibrium (moles)	$100 - 90.0$ $= 10.0$		—		90.0		90.0

The total number of moles of gas at equilibrium is $10.0 + 90.0 + 90.0 = 190$.

	H_2O	H_2	CO
Mole fractions	$10.0/190$ $= 0.05263$	$90.0/190$ $= 0.4737$	$90.0/190$ $= 0.4737$
Partial pressures (atm)	0.05263×15.5 $= 0.8158$	0.4737×15.5 $= 7.342$	0.4737×15.5 $= 7.342$

➤ Remember: partial pressure = mole fraction × total pressure

$$K_p = \frac{P_{H_2} \times P_{CO}}{P_{H_2O}}$$

$$= \frac{7.432 \times 7.432}{0.8158}$$

$$= 67.7 \text{ atm}$$

Example 32

Carbon monoxide was placed in a closed container with an excess of iron(II) oxide and heated to 1000 °C. The equilibrium pressure was 200 kPa. Calculate the partial pressures of carbon monoxide and carbon dioxide.

$$FeO_{(s)} + CO_{(g)} \rightleftharpoons Fe_{(s)} + CO_{2(g)} \qquad K_p = 0.403$$

We don't need to worry about the iron(II) oxide or the iron, because they are both solids, and won't appear in the K_p expression.

If we work out one of the partial pressures, we can easily find the other one because the total pressure is the sum of the partial pressures.

Call the partial pressure of carbon monoxide "p". The partial pressure of the carbon dioxide will then be $(200 - p)$.

$$K_p = \frac{P_{CO_2}}{P_{CO}}$$

$$0.403 = \frac{(200 - p)}{p}$$

$$0.403p = 200 - p$$

$$1.403p = 200$$

$$p = 143 \text{ kPa}$$

The partial pressure of carbon monoxide is 143 kPa.

The partial pressure of carbon dioxide is $(200 - 143)$ kPa $= 57$ kPa.

Problem • 20

When carbon is heated in the presence of carbon dioxide, the following equilibrium can be established:

$$C_{(s)} + CO_{2(g)} \rightleftharpoons 2CO_{(g)}$$

At 850 °C and an equilibrium pressure of 5.00 atmospheres, the equilibrium mixture is found to contain 21.7% carbon dioxide and 78.3% carbon monoxide. Write an expression for K_p and calculate its value at this temperature.

Problem • 21

When a solution containing 1.0 mol dm^{-3} of Pb$^{2+}_{(aq)}$ ions is shaken with some finely divided tin, the following equilibrium is set up:

$$Sn_{(s)} + Pb^{2+}_{(aq)} \rightleftharpoons Pb_{(s)} + Sn^{2+}_{(aq)} \qquad K_c = 2.2 \text{ at } 25 °C.$$

Calculate the fraction of the Pb$^{2+}_{(aq)}$ ions which is converted to solid lead.

Problem • 22

Steam was heated with an excess of carbon to 1000 K. What was the equilibrium pressure if the equilibrium mixture of gases contained 50% steam, 25% hydrogen and 25% carbon monoxide?

$$H_2O_{(g)} + C_{(s)} \rightleftharpoons H_{2(g)} + CO_{(g)} \qquad K_p = 3.7 \text{ atm at } 1000 \text{ K}$$

End of chapter checklist

➤ You may not need to do all these things. Check your syllabus and past exam papers.

Can you do the following things?

■ Write expressions for K_c and K_p for homogeneous reactions.

■ Know that for heterogeneous reactions, concentration or pressure terms for pure solid or pure liquid phases are omitted from the K_c or K_p expressions.

■ Write expressions for K_c and K_p for heterogeneous reactions.

■ Deduce the units for any given K_c or K_p expression.

■ Understand the terms mole fraction and partial pressure and state the relationship between them.

■ Calculate values for K_c or K_p given suitable data.

■ Use given values of K_p or K_c to calculate equilibrium concentrations or pressures.

Revision problems

Numerical answers are provided for these problems, but no worked solutions. None of these problems contain any difficult algebra.

Problem • 23

For the equilibrium:

$$H_{2(g)} + I_{2(g)} \rightleftharpoons 2HI_{(g)} \qquad \text{at } 700\,K$$

(a) Write an expression for K_c and calculate its value if the equilibrium concentrations are: H_2 0.214 mol dm^{-3}; I_2 0.214 mol dm^{-3}; HI 1.57 mol dm^{-3}.

(b) Write an expression for K_p and calculate its value if the equilibrium partial pressures are: H_2 0.642 kPa; I_2 0.642 kPa; HI 4.71 kPa.

Problem • 24

1.00 mol of N_2O_4 was warmed to 350 K in a container of volume 7.88 dm^3. At equilibrium, 40% of the N_2O_4 had converted into NO_2. The equilibrium pressure was 517 kPa.

$$N_2O_{4(g)} \rightleftharpoons 2NO_{2(g)}$$

(a) Calculate the numbers of moles of N_2O_4 and NO_2 present at equilibrium.

(b) Write an expression for K_c and calculate its value.

(c) Work out the partial pressures of N_2O_4 and NO_2 at equilibrium.

(d) Write an expression for K_p and calculate its value.

Problem • 25

A Haber Process plant manufacturing ammonia operated at a pressure of 100 atmospheres and a temperature of 400 °C. When the nitrogen and hydrogen were mixed in the 1:3 ratio required by the equation, the equilibrium mixture was found to contain 25.2% of ammonia by volume.

$$N_{2(g)} + 3H_{2(g)} \rightleftharpoons 2NH_{3(g)}$$

(a) Calculate the percentages of nitrogen and hydrogen in the equilibrium mixture.

(b) Calculate the partial pressures of nitrogen, hydrogen and ammonia at equilibrium.

(c) Write an expression for K_p and calculate its value at this temperature.

Problem • 26

41.7 g of phosphorus(V) chloride was heated to 200 °C in a container of volume 15.7 dm^3. When equilibrium was established, the mixture was found to contain 11.36 g of chlorine. The equilibrium pressure was found to be 90.0 kPa.

$$PCl_{5(g)} \rightleftharpoons PCl_{3(g)} + Cl_{2(g)}$$

(a) Calculate the numbers of moles of PCl_5, PCl_3 and Cl_2 present at equilibrium. (P = 31; Cl = 35.5)

(b) Write an expression for K_c and calculate its value at this temperature.

(c) Work out the partial pressures of PCl_5, PCl_3 and Cl_2 at equilibrium.

(d) Write an expression for K_p and calculate its value.

Problem • 27

1.0 mol of ethanoic acid and 2.0 mol of ethanol were mixed and allowed to reach equilibrium:

$$CH_3COOH_{(l)} + C_2H_5OH_{(l)} \rightleftharpoons CH_3COOC_2H_{5(l)} + H_2O_{(l)}$$

The equilibrium mixture was carefully diluted with pure water to a total volume of $250 \, cm^3$. A $25 \, cm^3$ sample of this required $15.5 \, cm^3$ of $1.00 \, mol \, dm^{-3}$ sodium hydroxide solution to neutralise the ethanoic acid present. Calculate K_c at the temperature of the reaction.
(The neutralisation reaction is:

$$CH_3COOH + NaOH \rightarrow CH_3COONa + H_2O)$$

Problem • 28

When steam was heated with excess carbon in a closed container to 1800 kPa, the partial pressure of steam at equilibrium was 318 kPa:

$$H_2O_{(g)} + C_{(s)} \rightleftharpoons H_{2(g)} + CO_{(g)}$$

(a) Work out the partial pressures of hydrogen and carbon monoxide.
(b) Write an expression for K_p for the heterogeneous equilibrium, and calculate its value.

Problem • 29

Solid ammonium hydrogensulphide dissociates according to the equation:

$$NH_4HS_{(s)} \rightleftharpoons NH_{3(g)} + H_2S_{(g)} \qquad K_p = 0.109 \, atm^2 \text{ at } 25 \, °C$$

If ammonium hydrogensulphide dissociates in a closed container at $25 \, °C$, calculate the equilibrium partial pressures of ammonia and hydrogen sulphide.

Problem • 30

$$N_2O_{4(g)} \rightleftharpoons 2NO_{2(g)} \qquad K_p = 0.115 \, atm \text{ at } 298 \, K$$

If the equilibrium partial pressure of N_2O_4 is 0.500 atmosphere, calculate the equilibrium partial pressure of NO_2, and the total equilibrium pressure.

Problem • 31

An excess of finely divided tin and lead was shaken with a solution containing $1.0 \, mol \, dm^{-3}$ of lead(II) ions and $0.50 \, mol \, dm^{-3}$ of tin(II) ions. Calculate the equilibrium concentrations of lead(II) and tin(II) ions:

$$Sn_{(s)} + Pb^{2+}_{(aq)} \rightleftharpoons Pb_{(s)} + Sn^{2+}_{(aq)} \qquad K_c = 2.2 \text{ at } 25 \, °C$$

Problem • 32

If solid PCl_5 is heated to $200 \, °C$, it vaporises and dissociates according to the equation:

$$PCl_{5(g)} \rightleftharpoons PCl_{3(g)} + Cl_{2(g)} \qquad K_p = 160 \, kPa \text{ at } 200 \, °C$$

90.0% of the PCl_5 is found to have dissociated.

(a) If the total equilibrium pressure is P, write expressions for the partial pressures of the gases present at equilibrium in terms of P.
(b) Write an expression for K_p and use it to calculate the total pressure P.
(c) Calculate the partial pressures of the gases present at equilibrium.

Problem • 33

Steam was heated with carbon at 1100 K until equilibrium was established. 80% of the steam was converted into hydrogen and carbon monoxide:

$$H_2O_{(g)} + C_{(s)} \rightleftharpoons H_{2(g)} + CO_{(g)} \qquad K_p = 17 \, atm \text{ at } 1100 \, K$$

Calculate the total equilibrium pressure.

Acid-Base Equilibria

This chapter explores the concept of pH. Some of it will involve doing some simple equilibrium calculations using techniques developed in Chapter 7. There isn't any difficult maths involved, although you will have to learn how to use a mathematical function on your calculator that you may not have used previously. It's not difficult!

Defining pH

$$pH = -\log_{10}[H^+]$$

$[H^+]$ has its normal meaning of "the concentration of hydrogen ions in $mol\,dm^{-3}$".

You **could** read this definition as: "pH is minus the logarithm to base 10 of the hydrogen ion concentration in moles per cubic decimetre" – but you would **never** define it in words. The statement in the box is all you need.

What are logarithms?

➤ **If you are interested:**
100 is 10^2 – the logarithm to base 10 of 100 is 2.
1000 is 10^3 – the logarithm to base 10 of 1000 is 3.
2 is $10^{0.3010}$ – the logarithm to base 10 of 2 is 0.3010.

The logarithm to base 10 of a number is the power you have to raise 10 to in order to equal that number.

Putting this process into reverse, if the logarithm to base 10 of a number is, say, 1.500, then the original number is $10^{1.500} = 31.62$. This is why you have to press the 10^x button on your calculator to "unlog" a number.

If you want to **understand** what logarithms (usually called "logs") are, you can read the information in the side box, but you do not **need** to know this for A level chemistry purposes. All you need to be able to do is to work them out. To find the logarithm to base 10 of something, use the **log** function on your calculator.

For example, to find $\log_{10}2$, you will probably have to enter **2** on your calculator and then press the **log** button. If your calculator gives an answer of 0.3010 (plus some more figures), then there is no problem. If you don't get this answer, read your calculator instruction book to find out how it wants you to enter it. It may be that you need to press **log** before you press **2**.

You will also need to know how to "unlog" things as well. For example, how do you get back from the 0.3010 on your calculator to the original number 2? You do this using the 10^x function, which you will almost certainly find is the same key as the **log** function, although you will need to press the **shift** key (or **inv** or **second function**, or whatever else your calculator calls it) first.

Try doing this – having found the log of 2, "unlog" it and make sure that you get the original 2 back again. If you don't, read your calculator instruction book.

Summary

To find the log of a number, use the **log** key. To "unlog" a number, use **shift** (or whatever it is called) and the **log** key.

Example 1

Example 2

➤ People occasionally run into problems with this sort of question because they have not learnt how to enter numbers into their calculator using scientific notation (e.g. 5.60×10^{-4}) in a simple and efficient way. If you don't quickly get the answer given for example 2, it would be worth your while spending some more time with your calculator instruction book!

➤ If a negative number has to be entered into your calculator differently, find out how to do it from the instruction book.

Calculating pH from hydrogen ion concentration

What is the pH if $[H^+] = 0.1 \, mol \, dm^{-3}$?

Find $\log_{10}(0.1)$. Your calculator should give the answer -1.

But the definition of pH is "**minus** $\log_{10}[H^+]$". "$-(-1)$" is 1. The pH is 1.

The reason for working out "**minus** $\log_{10}[H^+]$" is that when you find the log of most hydrogen ion concentrations that you are likely to work with, the answer is negative. By finding "minus log ...", you get rid of these negative signs.

What is the pH if $[H^+] = 5.60 \times 10^{-4} \, mol \, dm^{-3}$?

Enter 5.60×10^{-4} on your calculator, press the **log** button, and then reverse the sign to allow for the fact that pH is **minus** $\log_{10}[H^+]$.

You should get an answer of 3.25.

Summary

To find the pH from the hydrogen ion concentration use your calculator to find the log of the concentration, and then reverse the sign of the number your calculator gives you. In almost all cases, the calculator will produce a negative number – which means that the pH is positive.

Calculating hydrogen ion concentration from pH

There is more chance of making a careless mistake doing it this way round, but if you make that mistake, you will probably end up with a silly answer – so you can try again. It is important to remember that when you are doing pH calculations, the hydrogen ion concentrations will almost always be less than $1 \, mol \, dm^{-3}$.

Suppose the pH is 2.80; what is the hydrogen ion concentration?

$$pH = -\log_{10}[H^+]$$

Rearranging this: $\log_{10}[H^+] = -pH$

In this case, $\log_{10}[H^+] = -2.80$

Now you need to "unlog" this to find $[H^+]$. Enter 2.80 on your calculator and then press the $\pm$ button to give -2.80.

Now "unlog" this using the 10^x button. Try it! You should get an answer of $1.58 \times 10^{-3} \, mol \, dm^{-3}$.

The common mistake in doing this conversion is to forget to change the pH to a negative number before you "unlog" it. If you forgot to do that in this case, you would get an answer of $631 \, mol \, dm^{-3}$. This is an absurdly high concentration, so you would know you had done something wrong.

Summary

To find the hydrogen ion concentration from the pH, enter **minus** the pH on your calculator and then "unlog" it using the 10^x key.

Problem • 1

Convert the following hydrogen ion concentrations (all in $mol\,dm^{-3}$) into pHs:

(a) 0.0100   (b) 0.0250   (c) 3.00×10^{-4}

(d) 1.00×10^{-7} (e) 7.50×10^{-10}

Problem • 2

Convert the following pHs into hydrogen ion concentrations in $mol\,dm^{-3}$:

(a) 3.42   (b) 1.20   (c) 5.65

(d) 8.40   (e) 13.0

Problem • 3

(a) If the hydrogen ion concentration is $0.001\,00\,mol\,dm^{-3}$, what is the pH?

(b) What hydrogen ion concentration corresponds to a pH of 4.15?

(c) If the hydrogen ion concentration is $2.72 \times 10^{-3}\,mol\,dm^{-3}$, what is the pH?

(d) What hydrogen ion concentration corresponds to a pH of 10.3?

The pH of strong acids

What is a strong acid?

➤ To be precise about this, the hydrogen chloride molecules are actually reacting with water molecules:

$HCl_{(aq)} + H_2O_{(l)} \longrightarrow$
$\qquad H_3O^+{}_{(aq)} + Cl^-{}_{(aq)}$

The H_3O^+ ion can be thought of as a hydrogen ion carried by a water molecule. In these calculations, whether you write H^+ or $H^+{}_{(aq)}$ or H_3O^+ or $H_3O^+{}_{(aq)}$, you are actually talking about the same thing. For simplicity, we normally use $H^+{}_{(aq)}$ or just H^+.

In the context of these calculations, an acid is a substance which produces hydrogen ions in solution. A strong acid is one which is fully ionised in solution.

For example, hydrochloric acid is a strong acid. The hydrogen chloride molecules split up completely in water to give hydrogen ions and chloride ions:

$$HCl_{(aq)} \longrightarrow H^+{}_{(aq)} + Cl^-{}_{(aq)}$$

Other strong acids include nitric acid, HNO_3, and sulphuric acid, H_2SO_4.

Notice that sulphuric acid produces two hydrogen ions for each molecule of H_2SO_4:

$$H_2SO_{4(aq)} \longrightarrow 2H^+{}_{(aq)} + SO_4{}^{2-}{}_{(aq)}$$

Sulphuric acid is called a **diprotic acid**, because it produces 2 protons (hydrogen ions) per molecule of acid. An acid like hydrochloric acid or nitric acid, which only produce one hydrogen ion per molecule of acid, is called a **monoprotic acid**.

Calculating the pH of a strong acid

This is essentially very simple:

■ Use the concentration of the acid to find $[H^+]$.

■ Convert $[H^+]$ into pH.

Example 3

What is the pH of $0.1\,mol\,dm^{-3}$ hydrochloric acid, HCl?

Because HCl is a strong acid, every 1 mole of HCl is entirely split up into 1 mole of $H^+{}_{(aq)}$ and 1 mole of $Cl^-{}_{(aq)}$. The concentration of hydrogen ions is therefore exactly the same as the concentration of the acid.

$$[H^+] = 0.1$$
$$pH = -\log_{10}[H^+]$$
$$= -\log_{10}(0.1)$$
$$= 1$$

Example 4

➤ **Significant figures?** Be guided by the number of significant figures that your concentration is quoted to. You would not normally, however, quote pHs to more than 2 decimal places.

What is the pH of $0.00500 \, \text{mol} \, \text{dm}^{-3}$ nitric acid, HNO_3?

As before, nitric acid is a strong monoprotic acid, and so each mole of nitric acid produces 1 mole of hydrogen ions in solution.

$$[H^+] = 0.00500$$
$$pH = -\log_{10}[H^+]$$
$$= -\log_{10}(0.00500)$$
$$= 2.30$$

Example 5

What is the pH of $0.0100 \, \text{mol} \, \text{dm}^{-3}$ sulphuric acid, H_2SO_4?

You have to be very careful not to make a careless mistake with an acid like sulphuric acid. Sulphuric acid is a **diprotic acid** – each mole of acid produces 2 moles of hydrogen ions in solution:

$$H_2SO_{4(aq)} \rightarrow 2H^+{}_{(aq)} + SO_4{}^{2-}{}_{(aq)}$$

The concentration of hydrogen ions is therefore **twice** the concentration of the acid.

$$[H^+] = 2 \times 0.0100$$
$$pH = -\log_{10}[H^+]$$
$$= -\log_{10}(0.0200)$$
$$= 1.70$$

Finding the concentration of a strong acid from its pH

Simply reverse the process:

- Convert pH into $[H^+]$.

- Use $[H^+]$ to find the concentration of the acid.

Example 6

➤ Do not just accept this answer – try it yourself. If you get an answer of 39.8 when you "unlog" the pH, you forgot to make the pH negative before you pressed the 10^x button.
If you are prone to making that mistake, write the whole process down:
$$pH = -\log_{10}[H^+]$$
$$1.60 = -\log_{10}[H^+]$$
$$\log_{10}[H^+] = -1.60$$
$$[H^+] = 0.0251$$

What is the concentration of some hydrochloric acid whose pH is 1.60?

"Unlogging" the pH gives $[H^+] = 0.0251 \, \text{mol} \, \text{dm}^{-3}$.

Because hydrochloric acid, HCl, is a monoprotic acid, each mole of acid gives 1 mole of hydrogen ions in solution. The concentration of the acid is the same as the concentration of the hydrogen ions.

Example 7   What is the concentration of a strong monoprotic acid, HA, whose pH is 1.15?

"Unlogging" the pH gives $[H^+] = 0.0708 \, \text{mol} \, \text{dm}^{-3}$.

Once again, because it is a monoprotic acid, the acid concentration will be the same as the hydrogen ion concentration, because every mole of acid produces 1 mole of $H^+{}_{(aq)}$.

Example 8

What is the concentration of sulphuric acid, H_2SO_4, if its pH is 1.00?

Sulphuric acid is diprotic, so you need to be careful. "Unlogging" the pH gives $[H^+] = 0.100 \, \text{mol} \, \text{dm}^{-3}$. Now you have to stop and think:

$$H_2SO_{4(aq)} \rightarrow 2H^+{}_{(aq)} + SO_4{}^{2-}{}_{(aq)}$$

Each mole of sulphuric acid produces 2 moles of $H^+{}_{(aq)}$. There are only half the number of moles of acid as of hydrogen ions. The concentration of the acid is therefore $0.0500\,mol\,dm^{-3}$.

Problem • 4

Calculate the pHs of the following strong acids:

(a) $0.0300\,mol\,dm^{-3}$ hydrochloric acid, HCl
(b) $0.005\,00\,mol\,dm^{-3}$ sulphuric acid, H_2SO_4
(c) $0.120\,mol\,dm^{-3}$ nitric acid, HNO_3.

Problem • 5

Calculate the concentrations of the following strong acids from their pHs:

(a) hydrochloric acid, HCl, of pH 0.70
(b) sulphuric acid, H_2SO_4, of pH 1.5
(c) nitric acid, HNO_3, of pH 2.0.

The ionic product for water

> Strictly speaking, the equilibrium is

$$2H_2O_{(l)} \rightleftharpoons H_3O^+{}_{(aq)} + OH^-{}_{(aq)}$$

This does not affect the argument at all. The "concentration of water" term is going to be omitted from the final K_w expression, so the fact that our original expression for K_c would be defined differently is of no importance. The only difference is that you would end up with:

$$K_w = [H_3O^+][OH^-]$$

This means exactly the same as the expression in the main body of the text. $[H^+]$ is simply a shorthand way of writing $[H_3O^+]$.

> **Important:** You might be given a value of K_w as pK_w. The "p" in pK_w means exactly the same as in pH:

$$pK_w = -\log_{10} K_w$$

pK_w is 14.0 if K_w is 1.00×10^{-14}. Try this both ways on your calculator to be sure that you can convert one to the other.

Wherever liquid water is present, this equilibrium is established:

$$H_2O_{(l)} \rightleftharpoons H^+{}_{(aq)} + OH^-{}_{(aq)}$$

Just like any other equilibrium, you can write an expression for the equilibrium constant, K_c. You might **expect** it to look like this:

$$K_c = \frac{[H^+][OH^-]}{[H_2O]}$$

But it doesn't! Such a tiny amount of the water ionises that the concentration of the water is effectively constant. You would need to go to at least nine significant figures before you noticed any change in the concentration of the water following the ionisation!

To avoid having two constants (K_c and the concentration of water) in the same expression, a new equilibrium constant is defined. This is called the **ionic product for water** and is given the symbol K_w.

$$K_w = [H^+][OH^-]$$

The value of K_w is usually taken to be $1.00 \times 10^{-14}\,mol^2\,dm^{-6}$ at room temperature. The units are [concentration]^2 because you are multiplying two concentration terms together.

What K_w means is that whenever you have water present in a system, however impure it is, if you multiply the hydrogen ion concentration by the hydroxide ion concentration, the answer will always be 1×10^{-14} at room temperature.

> If you aren't sure about Le Chatelier's Principle, now would be a good time to go and revise it in a standard text book.

Calculating the pH of pure water

The pH of pure water varies with temperature because K_w varies with temperature. The ionisation process is endothermic, and as you raise the temperature the forward reaction is favoured according to Le Chatelier's Principle. Because more H^+ and OH^- are formed, K_w will increase with temperature.

If the water is **pure**, the concentrations of H^+ and OH^- will be equal, because each water molecule that ionises produces one of each ion:

$$H_2O_{(l)} \rightleftharpoons H^+{}_{(aq)} + OH^-{}_{(aq)}$$

If K_w is 1.00×10^{-14} mol^2 dm^{-6} (at 24 °C)

$$K_w = [H^+][OH^-]$$

and $[OH^-] = [H^+]$ because the water is pure.

So $K_w = [H^+]^2$

$$[H^+]^2 = 1.00 \times 10^{-14}$$
$$[H^+] = 1.00 \times 10^{-7}$$
$$pH = -\log_{10}[H^+]$$
$$= 7.00$$

> **Note!** 1.00×10^{-14} is exactly the same as saying 10^{-14}, so is there any point in writing it in full, and entering it in a long-winded way on your calculator?
>
> It is actually much safer to enter it in full. A surprising number of people will enter 10^{-14} on their calculators wrongly. If you enter it as 1×10^{-14} you are much less likely to get it wrong. (If you don't understand why it would make any difference, it is due to a mistaken use of the **exp** (or the equivalent) key on the calculator.)
>
> To check that you are doing it correctly, clear your calculator and then enter 1×10^{-14}. Now press the "equals" key. If the display changes to anything other than 1^{-14}, then you are doing something wrong.

This is why the pH of pure water is taken as 7 at room temperature. It is because the hydrogen ion concentration is 1.00×10^{-7} – not because it was somebody's lucky number!

If K_w is 5.13×10^{-13} mol^2 dm^{-6} (at 100 °C)

Repeating the process above using the new value for K_w gives a pH of 6.14 for pure water at 100 °C. That does not mean that the water has become slightly acidic at 100 °C – it simply means that the neutral point on the pH scale has moved from the more familiar value.

Problem • 6

Calculate the pH of pure water at

(a) 15 °C ($K_w = 4.52 \times 10^{-15}$ mol^2 dm^{-6})
(b) 50 °C ($K_w = 5.48 \times 10^{-14}$ mol^2 dm^{-6})

The pH of strong bases

What is a strong base?

A base in this context is something which combines with hydrogen ions, and a strong base is one which is fully ionised in solution. Typical strong bases include the hydroxides of Group 1 metals like sodium and potassium, and you will occasionally come across questions involving, say, calcium hydroxide or barium hydroxide from Group 2.

➤ The ions are already present in the solid hydroxides. Dissolving them in water frees them from the lattice, and they become surrounded by water molecules – "hydrated".

When these substances dissolve in water, the solutions consist of free, hydrated metal ions and hydroxide ions:

e.g. $NaOH_{(s)} + aq \rightarrow Na^+_{(aq)} + OH^-_{(aq)}$

$Ca(OH)_{2(s)} + aq \rightarrow Ca^{2+}_{(aq)} + 2OH^-_{(aq)}$

Solutions of strong bases like sodium hydroxide will have typical pHs in the region of 13 or 14. This would translate to hydrogen ion concentrations of 10^{-13} or $10^{-14}\,mol\,dm^{-3}$. Those hydrogen ions are coming from the water present in the solution:

$H_2O_{(l)} \rightleftharpoons H^+_{(aq)} + OH^-_{(aq)}$

There are far fewer hydrogen ions present than in pure water, because the extra hydroxide ions from the sodium hydroxide move the position of equilibrium to the left.

Calculating the pH of a strong base

This takes slightly longer than finding the pH of a strong acid. There are three steps rather than two:

■ Use the concentration of the base to find $[OH^-]$.

■ Use K_w to find $[H^+]$.

■ Convert $[H^+]$ into pH.

In all these examples, we will take K_w to be $1.00 \times 10^{-14}\,mol^2\,dm^{-6}$.

Example 9

What is the pH of $0.10\,mol\,dm^{-3}$ sodium hydroxide solution, NaOH?

Each mole of NaOH gives 1 mole of OH^- in solution, so the concentration of OH^- is also $0.10\,mol\,dm^{-3}$.

Now use K_w and substitute in the value for $[OH^-]$:

$$[H^+][OH^-] = 1.00 \times 10^{-14}$$

$$[H^+] \times 0.10 = 1.00 \times 10^{-14}$$

$$[H^+] = \frac{1.00 \times 10^{-14}}{0.10}$$

$$= 1.0 \times 10^{-13}$$

➤ **Note!** With a bit of practice, you could do all this on your calculator without writing anything down. Do not do that in an exam. If you make a silly mistake you won't get any credit if all you have written down is the answer.

Finally, convert $[H^+]$ into pH. You should get an answer of 13.

Example 10

What is the pH of $0.0150\,mol\,dm^{-3}$ calcium hydroxide solution, $Ca(OH)_2$?

Each mole of calcium hydroxide gives 2 moles of OH^- in solution, so the concentration of OH^- is twice $0.0150\,mol\,dm^{-3} = 0.0300\,mol\,dm^{-3}$.

➤ **Check** at least one of these problems on your calculator to make sure that you are not mis-entering anything. If you end up with an answer which is one pH unit out, then the mistake will probably lie in the way you are entering 1.00×10^{-14}.

Now use K_w and substitute in the value for $[OH^-]$:

$$[H^+][OH^-] = 1.00 \times 10^{-14}$$
$$[H^+] \times 0.0300 = 1.00 \times 10^{-14}$$
$$[H^+] = \frac{1.00 \times 10^{-14}}{0.0300}$$
$$= 3.33 \times 10^{-13}$$

Finally, convert $[H^+]$ into pH. You should get an answer of 12.5.

Finding the concentration of a strong base from its pH

Again, you reverse the process:

■ Convert pH into $[H^+]$.

■ Use K_w to find $[OH^-]$.

■ Use $[OH^-]$ to find the concentration of the base.

Example 11

What is the concentration of potassium hydroxide solution, KOH, if its pH is 12.8?

"Unlog" the pH to give $[H^+]$ in the way you have already practised:

$$pH = -\log_{10}[H^+]$$
$$12.8 = -\log_{10}[H^+]$$
$$\log_{10}[H^+] = -12.8$$
$$[H^+] = 1.585 \times 10^{-13}$$

➤ By now, you probably will not need to write down all the steps shown.

Now use K_w to find $[OH^-]$:

$$[H^+][OH^-] = 1.00 \times 10^{-14}$$
$$1.585 \times 10^{-13} \times [OH^-] = 1.00 \times 10^{-14}$$
$$[OH^-] = \frac{1.00 \times 10^{-14}}{1.585 \times 10^{-13}}$$
$$= 0.0631 \, \text{mol dm}^{-3}$$

➤ Although we have written down the value of $[H^+]$ rounded off, it would make sense to continue to use the full value which is already on your calculator in the K_w part of the calculation. Find a way of doing this on your calculator that you are comfortable with. Using the memory probably needs the least amount of thought!

Because each mole of KOH produces 1 mole of OH^-, the concentration of the KOH will also be $0.0631 \, \text{mol dm}^{-3}$.

Example 12

What is the concentration of barium hydroxide solution, $Ba(OH)_2$, if its pH is 12.0?

"Unlogging" the pH gives $[H^+] = 1.00 \times 10^{-12}$.

Now use K_w to find $[OH^-]$:

$$[H^+][OH^-] = 1.00 \times 10^{-14}$$
$$1.00 \times 10^{-12} \times [OH^-] = 1.00 \times 10^{-14}$$
$$[OH^-] = \frac{1.00 \times 10^{-14}}{1.00 \times 10^{-12}}$$
$$= 0.0100 \, \text{mol dm}^{-3}$$

Now you have to be careful. Each mole of $Ba(OH)_2$ gives 2 moles of OH^-. This means that the concentration of $Ba(OH)_2$ will be only **half** the concentration of the OH^-. The answer is therefore $0.005\,00\,mol\,dm^{-3}$.

Problem • 7

Take $K_w = 1.00 \times 10^{-14}\,mol^2\,dm^{-6}$.

Calculate the pHs of the following strong bases.

(a) $0.250\,mol\,dm^{-3}$ sodium hydroxide solution, NaOH
(b) $0.100\,mol\,dm^{-3}$ barium hydroxide solution, $Ba(OH)_2$
(c) $0.005\,00\,mol\,dm^{-3}$ potassium hydroxide solution, KOH.

Problem • 8

Calculate the concentrations of the following strong bases from their pHs:

(a) sodium hydroxide solution, NaOH, of pH 13.2
(b) strontium hydroxide solution, $Sr(OH)_2$, of pH 11.3.

Calculating the pH of mixtures produced during titrations

We are assuming in this section that the titration is a strong acid with a strong base – for example, hydrochloric acid with sodium hydroxide solution:

$$NaOH + HCl \rightarrow NaCl + H_2O$$

Suppose you are adding $0.100\,mol\,dm^{-3}$ hydrochloric acid, HCl, from a burette to $25.0\,cm^3$ of $0.100\,mol\,dm^{-3}$ sodium hydroxide solution, NaOH, in a flask. You have to calculate the pH of the solution in the flask as it changes during the titration.

There are four quite distinct problems in this. You need to find the pH:

■ before you start adding the acid;

■ when the sodium hydroxide solution is still in excess;

■ at the equivalence point;

■ when the acid is in excess.

> **Equivalence point** – the point at which you have added exactly the amounts required by the equation. In this case, because the concentrations of hydrochloric acid and sodium hydroxide are equal, and the reacting ratio is 1:1, the equivalence point comes when $25.0\,cm^3$ of the acid has been added.

Finding the pH before you start adding the acid

This is just a "pH of a strong base" calculation. The pH of $0.100\,mol\,dm^{-3}$ NaOH is found by:

$$[H^+][OH^-] = 1.00 \times 10^{-14}$$
$$[H^+] \times 0.100 = 1.00 \times 10^{-14}$$
$$[H^+] = \frac{1.00 \times 10^{-14}}{0.100}$$
$$= 1.00 \times 10^{-13}$$
$$pH = 13.0$$

Finding the pH while the sodium hydroxide solution is still in excess

Example 13

Suppose $10.0 \, cm^3$ of hydrochloric acid has been added. What will the pH be?

The solution was made by mixing $10.0 \, cm^3$ of $0.100 \, mol \, dm^{-3}$ HCl and $25.0 \, cm^3$ of $0.100 \, mol \, dm^{-3}$ NaOH.

The route through this calculation would be:

(a) Work out how many moles of H^+ and OH^- you have, so that you can work out how much excess OH^- there is.

(b) Use this value, and the total volume of the solution, to work out $[OH^-]$.

(c) Use K_w to find $[H^+]$.

(d) Convert $[H^+]$ into pH.

> Part (a) and part (b) are like parts of titration sums. If you aren't happy with what's happening, now would be a good time to do some revision from Chapter 4.

(a) Each mole of HCl produces 1 mole of H^+, so the number of moles of H^+ is the same as the number of moles of HCl.

Similarly, the number of moles of OH^- is the same as the number of moles of NaOH.

$$\text{Number of moles of } H^+ = \frac{10.0}{1000} \times 0.100$$
$$= 1.00 \times 10^{-3}$$

$$\text{Number of moles of } OH^- = \frac{25.0}{1000} \times 0.100$$
$$= 2.50 \times 10^{-3}$$

$$\text{Number of moles of excess } OH^- = 2.50 \times 10^{-3} - 1.00 \times 10^{-3}$$
$$= 1.50 \times 10^{-3}$$

> Hint: You have mixed together $10 \, cm^3$ of acid and $25 \, cm^3$ of NaOH solution.

(b) 1.50×10^{-3} moles of OH^- are contained in a total volume of $35.0 \, cm^3$.

$$[OH^-] = \frac{1000}{35.0} \times 1.50 \times 10^{-3}$$
$$= 0.04286 \, mol \, dm^{-3}$$

(c) and (d) $[H^+][OH^-] = 1.00 \times 10^{-14}$

$$[H^+] \times 0.04286 = 1.00 \times 10^{-14}$$

$$[H^+] = \frac{1.00 \times 10^{-14}}{0.04286}$$

$$= 2.333 \times 10^{-13}$$

$$pH = 12.6$$

This is all a bit long winded, but there is nothing new in it. As long as the sodium hydroxide solution is in excess, the method would be identical.

Example 14

Suppose $24.0 \, cm^3$ of hydrochloric acid has been added. What will the pH be?

The solution was made by mixing $24.0 \, cm^3$ of $0.100 \, mol \, dm^{-3}$ HCl and $25.0 \, cm^3$ of $0.100 \, mol \, dm^{-3}$ NaOH.

Try this yourself before you read on – preferably without looking at example 13!

(a) Number of moles of $H^+ = \dfrac{24.0}{1000} \times 0.100$

$$= 2.40 \times 10^{-3}$$

Number of moles of $OH^- = \dfrac{25.0}{1000} \times 0.100$

$$= 2.50 \times 10^{-3}$$

Number of moles of excess $OH^- = 2.50 \times 10^{-3} - 2.40 \times 10^{-3}$

$$= 0.10 \times 10^{-3}$$

(b) 0.10×10^{-3} moles of OH^- are contained in a total volume of $49.0\,cm^3$.

$$[OH^-] = \dfrac{1000}{49.0} \times 0.10 \times 10^{-3}$$

$$= 2.041 \times 10^{-3}\,mol\,dm^{-3}$$

(c) and (d) $[H^+][OH^-] = 1.00 \times 10^{-14}$

$$[H^+] \times 2.041 \times 10^{-3} = 1.00 \times 10^{-14}$$

$$[H^+] = \dfrac{1.00 \times 10^{-14}}{2.041 \times 10^{-3}}$$

$$= 4.90 \times 10^{-12}$$

$$pH = 11.3$$

> ➤ **Hint:** You have mixed together 24 cm³ of acid and 25 cm³ of NaOH solution.

Finding the pH at the equivalence point

The equivalence point is when you have mixed exactly the right amount of hydrochloric acid and sodium hydroxide solution according to the equation. In the case we are looking at, this will be when $25.0\,cm^3$ of $0.100\,mol\,dm^{-3}$ HCl has been added to $25.0\,cm^3$ of $0.100\,mol\,dm^{-3}$ NaOH solution.

The number of moles of H^+ and OH^- will be identical, and so you have a neutral solution of pH 7.

Finding the pH when the hydrochloric acid is in excess

This is much quicker than finding the pH when the sodium hydroxide is in excess, because you don't have to worry about K_w.

The route through these calculations would be:

(a) Work out how many moles of H^+ and OH^- you have, so that you can work out how much excess H^+ there is.

(b) Use this value, and the total volume of the solution, to work out $[H^+]$.

(c) Convert $[H^+]$ into pH.

Example 15

Suppose $26.0\,cm^3$ of hydrochloric acid has been added. What will the pH be?

The solution was made by mixing $26.0\,cm^3$ of $0.100\,mol\,dm^{-3}$ HCl and $25.0\,cm^3$ of $0.100\,mol\,dm^{-3}$ NaOH.

(a) Number of moles of $H^+ = \dfrac{26.0}{1000} \times 0.100$

$$= 2.60 \times 10^{-3}$$

Number of moles of $OH^- = \dfrac{25.0}{1000} \times 0.100$

$$= 2.50 \times 10^{-3}$$

Number of moles of excess $H^+ = 2.60 \times 10^{-3} - 2.50 \times 10^{-3}$

$$= 0.10 \times 10^{-3}$$

> **Hint:** You have mixed together 26 cm³ of acid and 25 cm³ of NaOH solution.

(b) and (c) 0.10×10^{-3} moles of H^+ are contained in a volume of $51.0\,cm^3$.

$$[H^+] = \dfrac{1000}{51.0} \times 0.10 \times 10^{-3}$$

$$= 1.961 \times 10^{-3}\,mol\,dm^{-3}$$

$$pH = 2.71$$

Example 16

Suppose $40.0\,cm^3$ of hydrochloric acid has been added. What will the pH be?

The solution was made by mixing $40.0\,cm^3$ of $0.100\,mol\,dm^{-3}$ HCl and $25.0\,cm^3$ of $0.100\,mol\,dm^{-3}$ NaOH.

Try this yourself before you read on, preferably without looking at the previous example.

(a) Number of moles of $H^+ = \dfrac{40.0}{1000} \times 0.100$

$$= 4.00 \times 10^{-3}$$

Number of moles of $OH^- = \dfrac{25.0}{1000} \times 0.100$

$$= 2.50 \times 10^{-3}$$

Number of moles of excess $H^+ = 4.00 \times 10^{-3} - 2.50 \times 10^{-3}$

$$= 1.50 \times 10^{-3}$$

(b) and (c) 1.50×10^{-3} moles of H^+ are contained in a volume of $65.0\,cm^3$.

$$[H^+] = \dfrac{1000}{65.0} \times 1.50 \times 10^{-3}$$

$$= 0.02308\,mol\,dm^{-3}$$

$$pH = 1.64$$

Variations on the theme

The methods above will cope with *any* combination of strong acid and strong base you may be given. You would, however, have to be careful in the early stages of the calculation if you were given a diprotic acid like sulphuric acid. The number of moles of hydrogen ions present in the solution would be **twice** the number of moles of sulphuric acid because each H_2SO_4 produces $2H^+$.

You would also have to be careful – for the same sort of reason – if you were given a base like barium hydroxide solution, $Ba(OH)_2$. Here, the number of moles of OH^- will be *twice* the number of moles of barium hydroxide.

Examples of these will be given in the problems which follow.

Problem • 9

Calculate the pHs of the following mixtures of strong acids and strong bases. Take $K_w = 1.00 \times 10^{-14} \, \text{mol}^2 \, \text{dm}^{-6}$.

(a) $30.0 \, \text{cm}^3$ of $1.00 \, \text{mol dm}^{-3}$ HCl and $25.0 \, \text{cm}^3$ of $1.00 \, \text{mol dm}^{-3}$ NaOH

(b) $15.0 \, \text{cm}^3$ of $1.00 \, \text{mol dm}^{-3}$ HCl and $25.0 \, \text{cm}^3$ of $1.00 \, \text{mol dm}^{-3}$ NaOH

(c) $40.0 \, \text{cm}^3$ of $0.100 \, \text{mol dm}^{-3}$ HCl and $25.0 \, \text{cm}^3$ of $0.200 \, \text{mol dm}^{-3}$ NaOH

(d) $25.0 \, \text{cm}^3$ of $0.0500 \, \text{mol dm}^{-3}$ H_2SO_4 and $10.0 \, \text{cm}^3$ of $0.100 \, \text{mol dm}^{-3}$ NaOH

(e) $20.0 \, \text{cm}^3$ of $0.100 \, \text{mol dm}^{-3}$ HNO_3 and $25.0 \, \text{cm}^3$ of $0.0500 \, \text{mol dm}^{-3}$ $Ba(OH)_2$.

Problem • 10

If you have the time, plot a pH curve for HCl and NaOH, by calculating the pH after adding different amounts of $1.00 \, \text{mol dm}^{-3}$ HCl to $25.0 \, \text{cm}^3$ of $1.00 \, \text{mol dm}^{-3}$ NaOH, and then plotting pH (vertical axis) against volume of acid added (horizontal axis). Work out the pH after the addition of the following volumes of acid (in cm^3): 0, 5, 10, 15, 20, 24, 24.5, 24.9, 25, 25.1, 25.5, 26, 30, 35, 40.

The pH of weak acids

What is a weak acid?

A weak acid is one which does not ionise to a very large extent in solution. Typical weak acids include most organic acids and some inorganic ones like hydrofluoric acid, HF.

One of the commonest weak acids is ethanoic acid, CH_3COOH. Depending on its concentration, about 1% of the ethanoic acid molecules are ionised in solution. An equilibrium is set up:

$$CH_3COOH_{(aq)} + H_2O_{(l)} \rightleftharpoons CH_3COO^-_{(aq)} + H_3O^+_{(aq)}$$

The equilibrium constant for this is called the **acidity constant** or **dissociation constant**, and is given the symbol K_a.

$$K_a = \frac{[CH_3COO^-][H_3O^+]}{[CH_3COOH]}$$

The equilibrium is often written in a shorthand version:

$$CH_3COOH_{(aq)} \rightleftharpoons CH_3COO^-_{(aq)} + H^+_{(aq)}$$

In which case, K_a would be:

$$K_a = \frac{[CH_3COO^-][H^+]}{[CH_3COOH]}$$

These two expressions are essentially identical, because H^+ is simply a shorthand way of writing H_3O^+. This short version of the equilibrium will be used in all the calculations which follow.

For a weak acid, HA:

$$HA_{(aq)} \rightleftharpoons H^+_{(aq)} + A^-_{(aq)}$$

➤ **Notice** that the water is not written into the equilibrium constant expression. The water not only takes part in the equilibrium, but is also the solvent for the reaction. As a result it is present in huge excess. If you had a litre of ethanoic acid solution, the number of moles of water present in that litre would be about 55. The amount of that water which gets used when the ethanoic acid ionises is negligible, so that the concentration of the water is effectively constant.

> The **units** are $(mol\,dm^{-3})^2$ divided by $mol\,dm^{-3}$.

$$K_a = \frac{[H^+][A^-]}{[HA]}\,mol\,dm^{-3}$$

pK_a

The values for K_a for weak acids are very small – for example, K_a for ethanoic acid is $1.74 \times 10^{-5}\,mol\,dm^{-3}$. To tidy these numbers up, pK_a is often used instead.

$$pK_a = -\log_{10}K_a$$

The relationship between pK_a and K_a is exactly the same as that between pH and $[H^+]$.

If $\quad K_a = 1.74 \times 10^{-5}$

$\quad pK_a = -\log_{10}(1.74 \times 10^{-5})$

$\quad\quad\quad = 4.76$

Going the other way, you need to "unlog" the pK_a value:

If $\quad\quad\quad pK_a = 4.76$

$\quad -\log_{10}K_a = 4.76$

$\quad\quad \log_{10}K_a = -4.76$

$\quad\quad\quad\quad K_a = 1.74 \times 10^{-5}$

If you are likely to have any difficulties with these conversions, go back and have another look at problems 1 and 2 at the beginning of this chapter.

Calculating the pH of a weak acid

The calculations are more complicated than in the case of a strong acid because, although you will know the concentration of the acid, you can't tell immediately from this what the hydrogen ion concentration is.

■ Do an equilibrium calculation to find $[H^+]$.

■ Convert $[H^+]$ into pH.

Example 17

> **Hint:** We are trying to find the hydrogen ion concentration. The CH_3COO^- concentration will be the same because equal amounts of each ion are produced when the acid ionises. For each mole of H^+ that forms, 1 mole of acid ionises – hence the acid concentration falls by whatever the hydrogen ion concentration is.

What is the pH of $0.100\,mol\,dm^{-3}$ ethanoic acid? $K_a = 1.74 \times 10^{-5}\,mol\,dm^{-3}$.

Treat this just like any other equilibrium calculation.

	$CH_3COOH_{(aq)}$	$\rightleftharpoons$	$CH_3COO^-_{(aq)}$	$+\,H^+_{(aq)}$
Start concentration ($mol\,dm^{-3}$)	0.100		0	0
Equilibrium concentration ($mol\,dm^{-3}$)	$0.100 - [H^+]$		$[H^+]$	$[H^+]$

If you take this to the next stage (substituting values into the equilibrium constant expression), you are going to end up with some nasty algebra to do. In these calculations that algebra is always simplified by making a simple approximation.

If you were to do all the algebra, you would get an answer for the concentration of H^+ of 1.310×10^{-3} mol dm^{-3}. This is quite small compared with the original concentration of the acid of 0.100 mol dm^{-3}. The approximation we make is that "$0.100 - [H^+]$" is 0.100. Obviously, that is not true, but – as you will see in a minute – it makes little difference to the final answer.

You can make this approximation in **all** the calculations to find the pH of a weak acid that you will be asked to do at A level.

The overall calculation now looks like this:

$$CH_3COOH_{(aq)} \rightleftharpoons CH_3COO^-_{(aq)} + H^+_{(aq)}$$

	CH_3COOH	CH_3COO^-	H^+
Start concentration (mol dm^{-3})	0.100	0	0
Equilibrium concentration (mol dm^{-3})	$0.100 - [H^+]$ ≈ 0.100	$[H^+]$	$[H^+]$

> "$\approx$" means "is approximately equal to".

$$K_a = \frac{[CH_3COO^-][H^+]}{[CH_3COOH]}$$

$$1.74 \times 10^{-5} = \frac{[H^+]^2}{0.100}$$

$$[H^+]^2 = 0.100 \times 1.74 \times 10^{-5}$$

$$[H^+] = \sqrt{0.100 \times 1.74 \times 10^{-5}}$$

$$= 1.319 \times 10^{-3} \text{ mol dm}^{-3}$$

$$pH = 2.88$$

Making the approximation, $[H^+]$ turns out to be 1.319×10^{-3} mol dm^{-3}. Without the approximation, and with a lot more work, $[H^+]$ should really be 1.310×10^{-3} mol dm^{-3}. There isn't much difference, and **both** of these values convert into the same pH of 2.88.

To repeat

When finding the pH of a weak acid, you can make the approximation that the equilibrium concentration of the acid is the same as the "start" concentration. It is good practice, though, to say that you are making that approximation.

Example 18

There's nothing new in this example. It is included to show what the calculation would look like without all the discussion.

Calculate the pH of 0.200 mol dm^{-3} hydrofluoric acid, HF, which has a K_a of 5.62×10^{-4} mol dm^{-3}.

$$HF_{(aq)} \rightleftharpoons H^+_{(aq)} + F^-_{(aq)}$$

	HF	H^+	F^-
Start concentrations (mol dm^{-3})	0.200	0	0
Equilibrium concentrations (mol dm^{-3})	$0.200 - [H^+]$ ≈ 0.200	$[H^+]$	$[H^+]$

$$K_a = \frac{[H^+][F^-]}{[HF]}$$

$$5.62 \times 10^{-4} = \frac{[H^+]^2}{0.200}$$

$$[H^+]^2 = 0.200 \times 5.62 \times 10^{-4}$$

$$[H^+] = \sqrt{0.200 \times 5.62 \times 10^{-4}}$$

$$= 0.010\,60\,\text{mol}\,\text{dm}^{-3}$$

$$\text{pH} = 1.97$$

Example 19

> **Note!** "Unlogging" the pK_a and then converting $[H^+]$ into pH at the end of the calculation is a bit long winded. You may come across a short-cut method of doing these calculations which involves using the formula:
>
> $$\text{pH} = \tfrac{1}{2}pK_a - \tfrac{1}{2}\log_{10}[\text{acid}]$$
>
> You will not find any examples using this formula in this book for two reasons:
> **1.** Using a formula in an exam is dangerous if there is any chance of getting the formula wrong. A calculation of this kind will probably be worth 3 or 4 marks, and if you do not remember the correct formula you will automatically lose all of those marks. There are several formulae which you may find for doing pH calculations of one sort or another, and they are all confusingly similar.
> **2.** You could be given a question which is not quite standard, and which you obviously cannot use the formula for. If you have got into the habit of using formulae instead of making sure you understand what you are doing, you are going to make major problems for yourself.
>
> If you understand what you are doing, it is much easier to be adaptable.

This example gives you the initial information differently. Instead of K_a, you are given pK_a. All you have to do is to "unlog" the pK_a value and you are back to a calculation exactly like the last two.

What is the pH of $0.0500\,\text{mol}\,\text{dm}^{-3}$ methanoic acid, HCOOH, if its pK_a is 3.75?

"Unlogging" the pK_a gives a value for K_a of $1.78 \times 10^{-4}\,\text{mol}\,\text{dm}^{-3}$. Check that you agree with this by doing it on your calculator, and then try the rest of the calculation before you read on any further.

	$HCOOH_{(aq)}$	$\rightleftharpoons$	$HCOO^-_{(aq)}$	$+$	$H^+_{(aq)}$
Start concentrations $(\text{mol}\,\text{dm}^{-3})$	0.0500		0		0
Equilibrium concentrations $(\text{mol}\,\text{dm}^{-3})$	$0.0500 - [H^+]$ ≈ 0.0500		$[H^+]$		$[H^+]$

$$K_a = \frac{[HCOO^-][H^+]}{[HCOOH]}$$

$$1.78 \times 10^{-4} = \frac{[H^+]^2}{0.0500}$$

$$[H^+]^2 = 0.0500 \times 1.78 \times 10^{-4}$$

$$[H^+] = \sqrt{0.0500 \times 1.78 \times 10^{-4}}$$

$$= 2.983 \times 10^{-3}\,\text{mol}\,\text{dm}^{-3}$$

$$\text{pH} = 2.53$$

Finding K_a or pK_a from the concentration of a weak acid and its pH

If you know the pH, you can "unlog" this to find $[H^+]$. If you also know the concentration of the acid, this gives you all the information you need to reverse the calculations we have been doing.

The pH of a weak acid, HA, of concentration $0.100\,\text{mol}\,\text{dm}^{-3}$ was found to be 4.00. Calculate the value of pK_a for the acid.

➤ **Do this!** "Unlog" the pH to make sure that you get this value for [H+].

➤ There is little point in making the approximation that $(0.100 - 1.00 \times 10^{-4})$ is 0.100. It will not save you any significant amount of time. If you do make the approximation, it probably doesn't matter as long as you say that you are doing it. Anyone solving this problem using a formula will be making this approximation anyway, although they won't realise it! The formula is derived assuming the approximation. In fact, the answer in this case is identical to 3 sig figs whether you make the approximation or not.

➤ It would be helpful if you did some revision on titration curves from a general text book before you read this section.

If the pH is 4.00, then $[H^+] = 1.00 \times 10^{-4} \, \text{mol dm}^{-3}$.

$$HA_{(aq)} \rightleftharpoons H^+_{(aq)} + A^-_{(aq)}$$

Start concentrations (mol dm^{-3}): 0.100, 0, 0

Equilibrium concentrations (mol dm^{-3}): $0.100 - 1.00 \times 10^{-4} = 0.0999$, 1.00×10^{-4}, 1.00×10^{-4}

$$K_a = \frac{[H^+][A^-]}{[HA]}$$

$$= \frac{(1.00 \times 10^{-4})^2}{0.0999}$$

$$= 1.001 \times 10^{-7} \, \text{mol dm}^{-3}$$

$$pK_a = -\log_{10} K_a$$

$$= 7.00$$

Finding pK_a from a titration curve

A titration curve shows what happens to the pH during a titration as you add increasing amounts of the solution in the burette. At the end-point of the titration, the curve suddenly becomes very steep as the pH changes very rapidly indeed.

Suppose you wanted to find pK_a for a weak acid HA. You would do a titration with the HA solution in the flask, and add sodium hydroxide solution from the burette. To find pK_a you have to add the alkali to the acid.

$$NaOH + HA \rightarrow NaA + H_2O$$

During the titration, the HA in the flask will gradually be used up and turned into NaA. To start with, there will be lots of HA and hardly any NaA, but the concentration of HA will fall continuously and the concentration of NaA will rise. Exactly half way through the titration, exactly half of the HA will have been changed into NaA, and so the two concentrations will be equal.

Half way through the titration: $[HA] = [NaA]$

Looking at the expression for K_a:

$$K_a = \frac{[H^+][A^-]}{[HA]}$$

HA is a weak acid, and so produces very few A^- ions. You can assume that virtually all the A^- ions are coming from the NaA. Therefore:

$$[A^-] = [NaA]$$

$$K_a = \frac{[H^+][NaA]}{[HA]}$$

Because [NaA] and [HA] are equal half way through the titration, the expression simplifies to

$$K_a = [H^+]$$

or $\quad pK_a = pH$

Summary

For a titration in which you add sodium hydroxide solution to a solution of a weak acid, exactly half way through the titration, the pH measured is equal to the pK_a for the acid.

How to use this in practice

> The end-point of the titration is **not** at pH 7, but lies on the steep bit of the curve. Sodium salts of weak acids are slightly alkaline with pHs typically about 8–9. Read about **salt hydrolysis** if you are interested.

- Plot the pH curve, either using a pH meter, or from data in the question.

- Find the volume of sodium hydroxide solution needed for the end-point of the titration from the steep part of the curve.

- Divide that volume by two, and use your graph to find the pH corresponding to that volume.

- The pK_a of the acid is equal to that pH.

Example 20

The end-point of the titration in Figure 8.1 corresponds to the addition of $v \, \text{cm}^3$ of sodium hydroxide solution. Divide this volume by 2 and then find the pH at $v/2 \, \text{cm}^3$.

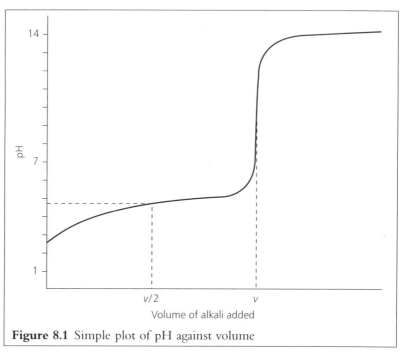

Figure 8.1 Simple plot of pH against volume

This tells you pK_a directly. In this case, pK_a is about 4.8.

Problem • 11

Write expressions for K_a (including units) for the following weak acids:

(a) hydrocyanic acid, HCN   (b) nitrous acid, HNO_2
(c) chloroethanoic acid, $CH_2ClCOOH$.

Problem • 12

Convert the following K_a values to pK_a:

(a) $1.22 \times 10^{-4} \, \text{mol dm}^{-3}$ (b) $3.75 \times 10^{-5} \, \text{mol dm}^{-3}$
(c) $5.60 \times 10^{-3} \, \text{mol dm}^{-3}$

Problem • 13

Convert the following pK_a values to K_a:

(a) 2.98   (b) 5.54   (c) 4.62

Problem • 14

Calculate the pHs of the following weak acid solutions:

(a) $0.0200\,mol\,dm^{-3}$ chloric(I) acid, HOCl. $K_a = 3.72 \times 10^{-8}\,mol\,dm^{-3}$.
(b) $0.0500\,mol\,dm^{-3}$ nitrous acid, HNO_2. $K_a = 4.57 \times 10^{-4}\,mol\,dm^{-3}$.
(c) $1.00\,mol\,dm^{-3}$ iodoethanoic acid, CH_2ICOOH.
   $K_a = 6.76 \times 10^{-4}\,mol\,dm^{-3}$.
(d) $0.100\,mol\,dm^{-3}$ propanoic acid, C_2H_5COOH. $pK_a = 4.87$.
(e) $0.250\,mol\,dm^{-3}$ hydrocyanic acid, HCN. $pK_a = 9.40$.

Problem • 15

Calculate K_a and pK_a for the following weak acids:

(a) $0.0400\,mol\,dm^{-3}$ HX if its pH is 4.50
(b) $0.125\,mol\,dm^{-3}$ HY if its pH is 3.25
(c) $0.885\,mol\,dm^{-3}$ HZ if its pH is 5.70.

Problem • 16

The data in the table show the changes in pH when $0.100\,mol\,dm^{-3}$ sodium hydroxide solution is added to $25.0\,cm^3$ of $0.100\,mol\,dm^{-3}$ ethanoic acid solution. Plot the pH curve and use it to find pK_a for ethanoic acid.

Volume of NaOH solution added (cm^3)	pH
0	2.88
3.0	3.89
6.0	4.26
9.0	4.51
12.0	4.73
15.0	4.94
18.0	5.17
21.0	5.48
24.0	6.14
24.5	6.45
24.9	7.16
25.0	8.73
25.1	11.30
25.5	12.00
27.0	12.59

The pH of weak bases

What is a weak base?

Ammonia is a typical weak base. It reacts with water to produce ammonium ions and hydroxide ions:

$$NH_{3(aq)} + H_2O_{(l)} \rightleftharpoons NH_4^+{}_{(aq)} + OH^-{}_{(aq)}$$

The ammonia is acting as a base because it is combining with a hydrogen ion from the water. Because most of it remains in solution as unreacted ammonia

201

molecules, ammonia is described as a **weak** base. The stronger the base, the further the position of equilibrium lies to the right.

Calculating the pH of a weak base

pK_a for the conjugate acid

The easiest way to find the pH of a weak base is to use a constant called K_b (sometimes in the form of pK_b). Calculations involving this are a bit long winded, but fairly simple to understand. However, K_b and pK_b are not on any of the modern A level syllabuses!

The strength of a base can also be measured in terms of the pK_a of its **conjugate acid**. The conjugate acid of any particular base is what you get if you add a hydrogen ion to it. In the case of ammonia, for example,

■ ammonia, NH_3, is the base;

■ the ammonium ion, NH_4^+, is its conjugate acid.

The pK_a value quoted relates to the equilibrium:

$$NH_4^+{}_{(aq)} \rightleftharpoons NH_3{}_{(aq)} + H^+{}_{(aq)}$$

$$K_a = \frac{[NH_3][H^+]}{[NH_4^+]}$$

$$pK_a = -\log_{10} K_a$$

Finding a way through the calculation

Let us assume that you are being asked to find the pH of some ammonia solution of a given concentration, and you are given a value for K_a for the ammonium ion, and a value for the ionic product for water, K_w.

Example 21 What is the pH of $0.100 \, mol \, dm^{-3}$ ammonia solution if K_a for the ammonium ion is $5.62 \times 10^{-10} \, mol \, dm^{-3}$? $K_w = 1.00 \times 10^{-14} \, mol^2 \, dm^{-6}$.

Think about the equations that all this refers to:

■ The equation showing ammonia acting as a base:

$$NH_3{}_{(aq)} + H_2O_{(l)} \rightleftharpoons NH_4^+{}_{(aq)} + OH^-{}_{(aq)}$$

■ The equation relating to K_a for the ammonium ion:

$$NH_4^+{}_{(aq)} \rightleftharpoons NH_3{}_{(aq)} + H^+{}_{(aq)}$$

$$K_a = \frac{[NH_3][H^+]}{[NH_4^+]}$$

$$= 5.62 \times 10^{-10}$$

■ The equation for the ionisation of water:

$$H_2O_{(l)} \rightleftharpoons H^+{}_{(aq)} + OH^-{}_{(aq)}$$
$$K_w = [H^+][OH^-]$$
$$= 1.00 \times 10^{-14}$$

These equations are all you have to work with.

Making a start

You need to find pH – which means that you first have to calculate $[H^+]$. The K_a expression contains $[H^+]$, so rearrange that:

$$\frac{[NH_3][H^+]}{[NH_4^+]} = 5.62 \times 10^{-10}$$

$$[H^+] = \frac{5.62 \times 10^{-10} \times [NH_4^+]}{[NH_3]}$$

Substituting a value for [NH₃]

Ammonia is a weak base. When we were working with weak acids, we made the approximation that so little was ionised that the equilibrium concentration was the same as the concentration we started from. You can make exactly the same approximation with weak bases.

In this case, the ammonia concentration at equilibrium can be taken to be $0.100 \, mol \, dm^{-3}$ to a reasonable approximation. Slot that value into the expression above:

$$[H^+] = \frac{5.62 \times 10^{-10} \times [NH_4^+]}{0.100}$$

Now all we need is a value for $[NH_4^+]$.

Substituting for [NH₄⁺]

This is the tricky bit! What information haven't we used yet? We have not used the equation for ammonia acting as a base, and we have not used K_w.

$$NH_{3(aq)} + H_2O_{(l)} \rightleftharpoons NH_4^+{}_{(aq)} + OH^-{}_{(aq)}$$

If you look carefully at this equation, you will see that when ammonia reacts with water it will produce exactly the same amount of both ammonium ions and hydroxide ions.

So: $[NH_4^+] = [OH^-]$

Substituting this into the last expression:

$$[H^+] = \frac{5.62 \times 10^{-10} \times [OH^-]}{0.100}$$

Why does this help? We have a way of relating $[OH^-]$ and $[H^+]$ using K_w:

$$[H^+][OH^-] = 1.00 \times 10^{-14}$$

$$[OH^-] = \frac{1.00 \times 10^{-14}}{[H^+]}$$

The final substitution

If we replace [OH$^-$] by this expression and then rearrange it, we can find [H$^+$] and then pH.

$$[H^+] = \frac{5.62 \times 10^{-10} \times [OH^-]}{0.100}$$

$$[H^+] = \frac{5.62 \times 10^{-10}}{0.100} \times \frac{1.00 \times 10^{-14}}{[H^+]}$$

$$[H^+]^2 = \frac{5.62 \times 10^{-10} \times 1.00 \times 10^{-14}}{0.100}$$

$$[H^+]^2 = 5.62 \times 10^{-23}$$

$$[H^+] = 7.497 \times 10^{-12}$$

$$pH = -\log_{10}[H^+]$$

$$= 11.1$$

Taking a short cut

There is nothing especially difficult in any of the stages of this calculation, but there are so many bits that you have to juggle with that it is quite easy to get confused and lose your way. This is one case where there may be some justification for learning and using a formula to make the calculation quick and easy.

It is extremely important that you know how your examiners are likely to ask questions about weak bases, and you can only know this by looking at past exam papers. If they always ask highly structured questions, then you have no choice but to follow their method. If, however, they simply ask you to calculate the pH of, say, ammonia solution, and give you a free hand, then you can use any valid method which gives the right answer.

If you do decide to use a formula, it would be wise to make this the **only** formula you learn on this topic. The various formulae are so similar that you stand a good chance of confusing them and using the wrong one. In that case, you would lose all the available marks.

The formula

Towards the end of the calculation we came up with the expression:

$$[H^+]^2 = \frac{5.62 \times 10^{-10} \times 1.00 \times 10^{-14}}{0.100}$$

5.62×10^{-10} was K_a for the ammonium ion. 1.00×10^{-14} is K_w. 0.100 is the concentration of the ammonia solution – call it "c".

In general terms, the expression is:

$$[H^+]^2 = \frac{K_a \times K_w}{c}$$

If you do a bit of maths on this, you end up with the formula:

$$pH = \tfrac{1}{2}pK_w + \tfrac{1}{2}pK_a + \tfrac{1}{2}\log_{10} c$$

pK_w is 14, so this can be simplified to

> You don't need to be able to deduce this formula. If you decide that it makes sense to use it, just learn it!

$$pH = 7 + \tfrac{1}{2}pK_a + \tfrac{1}{2}\log_{10}c$$

Using the formula

In the worked example above, K_a was $5.62 \times 10^{-10}\,mol\,dm^{-3}$. The concentration, c, was $0.100\,mol\,dm^{-3}$.

First convert K_a into pK_a to give 9.25.

Then put the numbers into the formula:

$$pH = 7 + \tfrac{1}{2} \times 9.25 + \tfrac{1}{2}\log_{10}0.100$$
$$= 11.1$$

This is the same answer as we got first time, but in a fraction of the time.

Warning!

You can get the right answer using the formula without having the slightest idea of what is going on. If you come to rely on the formula and are then faced with a question in which you can't use it, you will be completely lost. Use the formula as a back up to understanding, not to replace understanding.

Problem • 17

Sodium ethanoate solution is alkaline because the ethanoate ion is a weak base and reacts with water according to the equation:

$$CH_3COO^-_{(aq)} + H_2O_{(l)} \rightleftharpoons CH_3COOH_{(aq)} + OH^-_{(aq)}$$

(a) pK_a for ethanoic acid, CH_3COOH, is 4.76. Calculate a value for K_a, including the units.
(b) Write an expression for K_a for ethanoic acid, and rearrange it to give an expression for $[H^+]$.
(c) K_w is $1.00 \times 10^{-14}\,mol^2\,dm^{-6}$. Write an expression for K_w and rearrange it to give an expression for $[OH^-]$.
(d) Write an expression for the concentration of ethanoic acid at equilibrium, $[CH_3COOH]$.
(e) What is the equilibrium concentration of ethanoate ions, $[CH_3COO^-]$, in $0.200\,mol\,dm^{-3}$ sodium ethanoate solution? State any assumption you are making.
(f) By combining your answers to (b), (d) and (e), calculate the pH of $0.200\,mol\,dm^{-3}$ sodium ethanoate solution.
(g) Check your answer using the formula:
$$pH = 7 + \tfrac{1}{2}pK_a + \tfrac{1}{2}\log_{10}c$$

Problem • 18

Calculate the pHs of the following solutions of weak bases. In each case, (i) do the calculation without using the formula, (ii) check your answer using the formula. Take K_w to be 1.00×10^{-14}.

(a) $0.0500\,mol\,dm^{-3}$ 1-aminopropane solution, $C_3H_7NH_2$. pK_a for $C_3H_7NH_3^+ = 10.84$.

$$C_3H_7NH_2 + H_2O \rightleftharpoons C_3H_7NH_3^+ + OH^-$$

(b) $0.005\,00\,mol\,dm^{-3}$ phenylamine solution, $C_6H_5NH_2$. pK_a for $C_6H_5NH_3^+ = 4.62$

$$C_6H_5NH_2 + H_2O \rightleftharpoons C_6H_5NH_3^+ + OH^-$$

Buffer solutions

What are buffer solutions?

> The theory given here is a bare minimum needed to understand the calculations which follow. For a more detailed account, you may need to refer to a standard text book.

A buffer solution is a solution which resists changes in pH if small amounts of acid or alkali are added to it.

To make a buffer solution with a pH less than 7 (an acidic buffer solution), you can make up a solution containing a weak acid and one of its salts – for example, ethanoic acid and sodium ethanoate.

To make an alkaline buffer solution, you can make up a solution containing a weak base and one of its salts – for example, ammonia and ammonium chloride.

How do buffer solutions work?

Acidic buffer solutions

We will take ethanoic acid and sodium ethanoate as a typical example. The ethanoic acid is a weak acid, and so the following equilibrium is established:

$$CH_3COOH_{(aq)} \rightleftharpoons CH_3COO^-_{(aq)} + H^+_{(aq)}$$

Sodium ethanoate is an ionic salt, and in solution consists of free sodium and ethanoate ions:

$$CH_3COONa_{(s)} + aq \rightarrow CH_3COO^-_{(aq)} + Na^+_{(aq)}$$

According to Le Chatelier, the presence of the extra ethanoate ions tips the ethanoic acid equilibrium even further to the left than it was already. The solution therefore contains (amongst other things):

- lots of mainly un-ionised ethanoic acid;
- lots of ethanoate ions (almost entirely from the sodium ethanoate);
- enough H^+ to make the solution acidic.

If you add extra hydrogen ions to the solution, these will nearly all combine with the ethanoate ions, and so the pH will hardly change at all.

$$CH_3COO^-_{(aq)} + H^+_{(aq)} \rightarrow CH_3COOH_{(aq)}$$

> Why "nearly all"? The ethanoic acid formed is a weak acid, and so although we have written this equation as one way, it is in fact reversible. The presence of the ethanoate ions stops it reversing very much, so that most – but not all – of the extra hydrogen ions will be removed from the solution.

If you add hydroxide ions to the solution, almost all of these will react with the un-ionised ethanoic acid to make ethanoate ions and water:

$$CH_3COOH_{(aq)} + OH^-_{(aq)} \rightarrow CH_3COO^-_{(aq)} + H_2O_{(l)}$$

In other words, trying to alter the pH of the solution by increasing the concentration of H^+ or OH^- largely fails.

Alkaline buffer solutions

We will take ammonia and ammonium chloride as a typical example. The ammonia is a weak base, and so the following equilibrium is established:

$$NH_{3(aq)} + H_2O_{(l)} \rightleftharpoons NH_4^+_{(aq)} + OH^-_{(aq)}$$

Ammonium chloride is an ionic salt, and so its solution consists of free ammonium and chloride ions:

$$NH_4Cl_{(s)} + aq \rightarrow NH_4^+{}_{(aq)} + Cl^-{}_{(aq)}$$

The presence of the extra ammonium ions tips the ammonia equilibrium even further to the left than it was before. This solution therefore contains (amongst other things):

- lots of unreacted ammonia;

- lots of ammonium ions (almost entirely from the ammonium chloride);

- enough OH^- ions to make the solution alkaline.

If you add hydrogen ions to the solution, these will nearly all combine with the ammonia present to make more ammonium ions, and so the pH hardly changes at all.

$$NH_{3(aq)} + H^+{}_{(aq)} \rightarrow NH_4^+{}_{(aq)}$$

If you add extra hydroxide ions to the solution, most of them react with ammonium ions to produce ammonia and water:

$$NH_4^+{}_{(aq)} + OH^-{}_{(aq)} \rightarrow NH_{3(aq)} + H_2O_{(l)}$$

Once again, trying to change the pH by increasing the concentration of H^+ or OH^- largely fails.

Examples involving acidic buffer solutions

Example 22

What is the pH of a buffer solution made by making up $1.00\,dm^3$ of solution containing 1.00 mole of ethanoic acid and 1.00 mole of sodium ethanoate? K_a for ethanoic acid $= 1.74 \times 10^{-5}\,mol\,dm^{-3}$.

We need to find the hydrogen ion concentration. The hydrogen ions are coming from the ionisation of the ethanoic acid, so let's explore that.

$$CH_3COOH_{(aq)} \rightleftharpoons CH_3COO^-{}_{(aq)} + H^+{}_{(aq)}$$

$$K_a = \frac{[CH_3COO^-][H^+]}{[CH_3COOH]}$$

The difference between this and previous pH calculations is that extra ethanoate ions have been added from the sodium ethanoate. These have shifted the position of equilibrium.

Almost entirely from the sodium ethanoate

$$K_a = \frac{[CH_3COO^-][H^+]}{[CH_3COOH]}$$

These two concentrations are no longer equal

The acid is hardly ionised at all

To a very close approximation indeed, the concentration of the ethanoate ions, $[CH_3COO^-]$, is going to be the same as the concentration of the sodium ethanoate.

Similarly, the ethanoic acid is going to be so little ionised that its equilibrium concentration is whatever you put into the solution in the first place.

In this instance:

$$[CH_3COO^-] = 1.00 \, mol \, dm^{-3} \qquad [CH_3COOH] = 1.00 \, mol \, dm^{-3}$$

Substituting those values in the K_a expression gives:

$$K_a = \frac{[CH_3COO^-][H^+]}{[CH_3COOH]}$$

$$1.74 \times 10^{-5} = \frac{1.00 \times [H^+]}{1.00}$$

$$[H^+] = 1.74 \times 10^{-5} \, mol \, dm^{-3}$$

$$pH = 4.76$$

This is a special case of these calculations – where the concentrations of the two components are equal. Their concentrations will cancel out under these circumstances to leave $[H^+] = K_a$. Following this through by working out "$-\log_{10}$" of both sides, $pH = pK_a$.

Generalising

For a buffer solution made by mixing a weak acid, HA, with one of its salts – typically NaA:

$$HA_{(aq)} \rightleftharpoons H^+_{(aq)} + A^-_{(aq)}$$

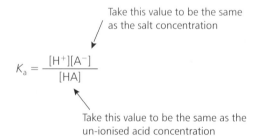

Take this value to be the same as the salt concentration

$$K_a = \frac{[H^+][A^-]}{[HA]}$$

Take this value to be the same as the un-ionised acid concentration

Example 23

Calculate the pH of a buffer solution made by dissolving 18.5 g of propanoic acid, C_2H_5COOH, and 12.0 g of sodium propanoate, C_2H_5COONa, in water and then making the volume up to 250 cm^3.
(pK_a for propanoic acid = 4.87. H = 1; C = 12; O = 16; Na = 23).

This is an irritating question, because you have to waste time finding the concentrations of everything before you can start on the pH part. If this is going to give you problems, re-read the beginning of Chapter 4.

1 mole of C_2H_5COOH weighs 74 g. 1 mole of C_2H_5COONa weighs 96 g.

> **Why times 4?** The masses given are dissolved in 250 cm^3. To get the equivalent concentration if they were dissolved in 1000 cm^3 (1 dm^3) you would have to have 4 times as much material.

$$[C_2H_5COOH] = \frac{18.5 \times 4}{74}$$

$$= 1.00 \, mol \, dm^{-3}$$

$$[C_2H_5COONa] = \frac{12.0 \times 4}{96}$$

$$= 0.500 \, mol \, dm^{-3}$$

Because virtually all the propanoate ions, $C_2H_5COO^-$, are coming from the sodium propanoate, and almost none from the propanoic acid, the propanoate concentration, $[C_2H_5COO^-]$, is also equal to $0.500\,mol\,dm^{-3}$.

We are assuming that so little of the propanoic acid ionises that its equilibrium concentration is $1.00\,mol\,dm^{-3}$.

We have now got all the information we need to slot into the K_a expression, apart from K_a itself. This comes from "unlogging" pK_a, and works out to be $1.35 \times 10^{-5}\,mol\,dm^{-3}$.

$$K_a = \frac{[C_2H_5COO^-][H^+]}{[C_2H_5COOH]}$$

$$1.35 \times 10^{-5} = \frac{0.500 \times [H^+]}{1.00}$$

$$[H^+] = \frac{1.35 \times 10^{-5}}{0.500}$$

$$= 2.70 \times 10^{-5}\,mol\,dm^{-3}$$

$$pH = 4.57$$

> **Note!** There is a formula that you can use to work out the pH of an acidic buffer solution. You may find it in one of two forms:
>
> $$pH = pK_a - log_{10}\frac{[acid]}{[salt]}$$
>
> or $pH = pK_a + log_{10}\dfrac{[salt]}{[acid]}$
>
> Although using one of these would save you a bit of time, they are not recommended for the reasons explained earlier in this chapter.

Example 24

> It would be much quicker to think about this a bit! The ethanoic acid has been diluted from $50\,cm^3$ to $150\,cm^3$ – in other words by a factor of 3. Its new concentration will be 1/3 of its original one – which is the result we've got.
>
> The sodium ethanoate has been diluted from $100\,cm^3$ to $150\,cm^3$ – by a factor of 1.5. Its new concentration will be 1/1.5 of its original one – which again is the result we've got.
>
> Do sums like this whichever way you feel most comfortable with.

A buffer solution was made by mixing $50.0\,cm^3$ of $0.300\,mol\,dm^{-3}$ ethanoic acid with $100\,cm^3$ of $0.600\,mol\,dm^{-3}$ sodium ethanoate. Calculate its pH if K_a for ethanoic acid is $1.74 \times 10^{-5}\,mol\,dm^{-3}$.

We need to start by working out the concentrations of ethanoic acid and sodium ethanoate in the final solution. The long-winded (but safe) way of doing this is to treat it almost as if you were doing titration sums.

$$\text{Number of moles of } CH_3COOH = \frac{50.0}{1000} \times 0.300$$

$$= 0.0150 \text{ (in a total volume of } 150\,cm^3)$$

$$[CH_3COOH] = \frac{1000}{150} \times 0.0150$$

$$= 0.100\,mol\,dm^{-3}$$

$$\text{Number of moles of } CH_3COONa = \frac{100}{1000} \times 0.600$$

$$= 0.0600 \text{ (in a total volume of } 150\,cm^3)$$

$$[CH_3COONa] = \frac{1000}{150} \times 0.0600$$

$$= 0.400\,mol\,dm^{-3}$$

> We are still making the same assumptions. The acid is so little ionised that its equilibrium concentration is the same as its start concentration, and it contributes virtually nothing to the concentration of the ethanoate ions.
> The concentration of the ethanoate ions is the same as the concentration of the sodium ethanoate.

Now the calculation is just the same as before:

$$K_a = \frac{[CH_3COO^-][H^+]}{[CH_3COOH]}$$

$$1.74 \times 10^{-5} = \frac{0.400 \times [H^+]}{0.100}$$

$$[H^+] = \frac{1.74 \times 10^{-5} \times 0.100}{0.400}$$

$$= 4.35 \times 10^{-6}\,mol\,dm^{-3}$$

$$pH = 5.36$$

Example 25

➤ You might think that adding only 1 cm³ of an acid or an alkali would not be expected to shift the pH very much. A simple calculation would show that if you added 1 cm³ of 10 mol dm³ hydrochloric acid (almost concentrated HCl) to 1000 cm³ of water, the pH would fall from 7 to 2. Adding 1 cm³ of sodium hydroxide solution of this concentration would increase the pH from 7 to 12. (If you want to try these calculations, work out the number of moles of H⁺ or OH⁻ in the final solutions, and then convert these to pH. For simplicity, assume that the total volume of solution is 1000 cm³ rather than 1001 cm³.)

This example looks at the effect of adding small amounts of acid or alkali to a buffer solution.

In example 22, we calculated the pH of a buffer solution which contained ethanoic acid and sodium ethanoate. The solution contained $1.00 \, mol \, dm^{-3}$ of each component. The pH turned out to be 4.76. What would be the effect of adding (a) $1.00 \, cm^3$ of $10.0 \, mol \, dm^{-3}$ hydrochloric acid and (b) $1.00 \, cm^3$ of $10.0 \, mol \, dm^{-3}$ sodium hydroxide solution to $1000 \, cm^3$ of the buffer solution? K_a for ethanoic acid $= 1.74 \times 10^{-5} \, mol \, dm^{-3}$.

(a) Adding the acid

The buffer solution works by combining the hydrogen ions from the added acid with ethanoate ions from the sodium ethanoate, turning them into ethanoic acid. This means that the concentration of the ethanoate ions will fall, while that of the ethanoic acid will rise.

$$\text{Number of moles of H}^+ \text{ added} = \frac{1.00}{1000} \times 10.0$$
$$= 0.0100 \, mol$$

0.0100 mol of ethanoate ions will be used up and 0.0100 mol of new ethanoic acid will be formed.

$$\text{Original moles of CH}_3\text{COO}^- = 1.00$$
$$\text{New moles of CH}_3\text{COO}^- = 1.00 - 0.0100$$
$$= 0.99 \, mol$$

$$\text{Original moles of CH}_3\text{COOH} = 1.00$$
$$\text{New moles of CH}_3\text{COOH} = 1.00 + 0.0100$$
$$= 1.01 \, mol$$

➤ You would get **exactly** the same answer even if you didn't make this assumption. In the K_a expression the CH₃COO⁻ value is divided by that of CH₃COOH. To find the **true** concentrations from the number of moles and the total volume, you would have to make exactly the same correction to both. When you divided one by the other, those correction terms would just cancel out.

To make the calculation simpler, we will assume that the final volume is $1000 \, cm^3$, rather than $1001 \, cm^3$.

$$\text{New } [CH_3COO^-] = 0.99 \, mol \, dm^{-3}$$
$$\text{New } [CH_3COOH] = 1.01 \, mol \, dm^{-3}$$

These numbers can go into the K_a expression:

$$K_a = \frac{[CH_3COO^-][H^+]}{[CH_3COOH]}$$

$$1.74 \times 10^{-5} = \frac{0.99 \times [H^+]}{1.01}$$

$$[H^+] = \frac{1.01 \times 1.74 \times 10^{-5}}{0.99}$$
$$= 1.775 \times 10^{-5} \, mol \, dm^{-3}$$
$$pH = 4.75$$

The pH has fallen by only 0.01.

(b) Adding the sodium hydroxide

The buffer solution works by reacting the hydroxide ions from the sodium hydroxide with ethanoic acid, producing more ethanoate ions. This means that the concentration of the ethanoate ions will rise, while that of the ethanoic acid will fall.

$$\text{Number of moles of } OH^- \text{ added} = \frac{1.00}{1000} \times 10.0$$
$$= 0.0100 \, mol$$

0.0100 mol of ethanoic acid will be used up and 0.0100 mol of new ethanoate ions will be formed.

$$\text{Original moles of } CH_3COO^- = 1.00$$
$$\text{New moles of } CH_3COO^- = 1.00 + 0.0100$$
$$= 1.01 \, mol$$

$$\text{Original moles of } CH_3COOH = 1.00$$
$$\text{New moles of } CH_3COOH = 1.00 - 0.0100$$
$$= 0.99 \, mol$$

Again to make the calculation simpler, we will assume that the final volume is $1000 \, cm^3$, rather than $1001 \, cm^3$.

$$\text{New } [CH_3COO^-] = 1.01 \, mol \, dm^{-3}$$
$$\text{New } [CH_3COOH] = 0.99 \, mol \, dm^{-3}$$

$$K_a = \frac{[CH_3COO^-][H^+]}{[CH_3COOH]}$$

$$1.74 \times 10^{-5} = \frac{1.01 \times [H^+]}{0.99}$$

$$[H^+] = \frac{0.99 \times 1.74 \times 10^{-5}}{1.01}$$
$$= 1.706 \times 10^{-5} \, mol \, dm^{-3}$$
$$pH = 4.77$$

This time the pH has **increased** by only 0.01.

Example 26

This example shows how you can calculate the proportions in which to mix an acid and one of its salts in order to produce a buffer solution of a given pH.

In what proportions should you mix ethanoic acid and sodium ethanoate in order to give a buffer solution of pH 5.00? pK_a for ethanoic acid = 4.76.

To start with, "unlog" the pK_a to give $K_a = 1.74 \times 10^{-5} \, mol \, dm^{-3}$.

"Unlog" the pH to give $[H^+] = 1.00 \times 10^{-5} \, mol \, dm^{-3}$.

Now use the K_a expression:

$$K_a = \frac{[CH_3COO^-][H^+]}{[CH_3COOH]}$$

$$1.74 \times 10^{-5} = \frac{[CH_3COO^-] \times 1.00 \times 10^{-5}}{[CH_3COOH]}$$

$$\frac{[CH_3COO^-]}{[CH_3COOH]} = \frac{1.74 \times 10^{-5}}{1.00 \times 10^{-5}}$$

$$= \frac{1.74}{1}$$

It doesn't matter what actual quantities you mix as long as the ethanoate ion to ethanoic acid ratio is 1.74:1. You could, for example, use any of the following mixtures (together with an infinite number of other possibilities – provided the ratio is 1.74:1):

■ $1000\,cm^3$ of solution containing $1.74\,mol$ sodium ethanoate and $1.00\,mol$ ethanoic acid.

■ $1000\,cm^3$ of solution containing $0.348\,mol$ sodium ethanoate and $0.200\,mol$ ethanoic acid.

■ A mixture of $174\,cm^3$ of $1.00\,mol\,dm^{-3}$ sodium ethanoate solution and $100\,cm^3$ of $1.00\,mol\,dm^{-3}$ ethanoic acid.

Examples involving alkaline buffer solutions

A mixture of ammonia and ammonium chloride solutions is a typical alkaline buffer solution. The equilibrium at the heart of the system is

$$NH_{3(aq)} + H_2O_{(l)} \rightleftharpoons NH_4^+{}_{(aq)} + OH^-{}_{(aq)}$$

To calculate the pH of the mixture, it is much easier to work from the ammonium ion, NH_4^+, than from the ammonia. The ammonium ion is called the conjugate acid of ammonia. A conjugate acid is what you get when you add a hydrogen ion to a base.

The ammonium ion is weakly acidic because it tends to lose the extra hydrogen:

$$NH_4^+{}_{(aq)} \rightleftharpoons NH_{3(aq)} + H^+{}_{(aq)}$$

The K_a expression for this is:

$$K_a = \frac{[NH_3][H^+]}{[NH_4^+]}$$

We can make the same assumptions that we've made in the previous buffer solution calculations.

Assume that the ammonia is virtually un-ionised – so take this value as the given ammonia concentration

$$K_a = \frac{[NH_3][H^+]}{[NH_4^+]}$$

Take this value to be the same as the ammonium chloride concentration

As long as you are given a K_a or pK_a value for the conjugate acid (in this case, the ammonium ion), the calculations are exactly the same as for acidic buffer solutions.

Example 27

Calculate the pH of a buffer solution containing $1.00\,mol\,dm^{-3}$ of ammonia and $0.400\,mol\,dm^{-3}$ ammonium chloride. K_a for the ammonium ion, NH_4^+, is $5.62 \times 10^{-10}\,mol\,dm^{-3}$.

$$K_a = \frac{[NH_3][H^+]}{[NH_4{}^+]} = 5.62 \times 10^{-10}$$

$$[H^+] = \frac{5.62 \times 10^{-10} \times [NH_4{}^+]}{[NH_3]}$$

$$= \frac{5.62 \times 10^{-10} \times 0.400}{1.00}$$

$$= 2.248 \times 10^{-10}$$

$$pH = 9.65$$

Example 28

Calculate the effect on the pH of adding (a) $5.00\,cm^3$ of $10.0\,mol\,dm^{-3}$ hydrochloric acid and (b) $5.00\,cm^3$ of $10.0\,mol\,dm^{-3}$ sodium hydroxide solution to $1000\,cm^3$ of the buffer solution from example 27.

(a) Adding the acid

The buffer solution works by combining the hydrogen ions from the added acid with ammonia, producing more ammonium ions. This means that the concentration of the ammonia will fall, while that of the ammonium ions rises.

$$\text{Number of moles of } H^+ \text{ added} = \frac{5.00}{1000} \times 10.0$$

$$= 0.0500 \text{ mol}$$

$0.0500\,mol$ of ammonia will be used up and $0.0500\,mol$ of new ammonium ions will be formed.

$$\text{Original moles of } NH_3 = 1.00$$
$$\text{New moles of } NH_3 = 1.00 - 0.0500$$
$$= 0.95 \text{ mol}$$
$$\text{Original moles of } NH_4{}^+ = 0.400$$
$$\text{New moles of } NH_4{}^+ = 0.400 + 0.0500$$
$$= 0.450 \text{ mol}$$

➤ You would get **exactly** the same answer even if you didn't make this assumption. Although the actual concentrations of both ammonia and ammonium ions would be slightly less than the numbers we are going to use, the ratio of the two concentrations (which is what appears in the K_a expression) would still be exactly the same.

To make the calculation simpler, we will assume that the final volume is $1000\,cm^3$, rather than $1005\,cm^3$.

$$\text{New } [NH_3] = 0.95 \text{ mol dm}^{-3}$$
$$\text{New } [NH_4{}^+] = 0.450 \text{ mol dm}^{-3}$$

Now repeat the pH calculation from example 27:

$$K_a = \frac{[NH_3][H^+]}{[NH_4{}^+]} = 5.62 \times 10^{-10}$$

$$[H^+] = \frac{5.62 \times 10^{-10} \times [NH_4{}^+]}{[NH_3]}$$

$$= \frac{5.62 \times 10^{-10} \times 0.450}{0.95}$$

$$= 2.662 \times 10^{-10}$$

$$pH = 9.57$$

The pH has fallen by just under 0.1.

(b) Adding the sodium hydroxide

The buffer solution works by reacting the hydroxide ions from the sodium hydroxide with ammonium ions, producing more ammonia:

$$NH_4{}^+{}_{(aq)} + OH^-{}_{(aq)} \rightarrow NH_{3(aq)} + H_2O_{(l)}$$

This means that the concentration of the ammonium ions falls, while that of the ammonia rises.

$$\text{Number of moles of } OH^- \text{ added} = \frac{5.00}{1000} \times 10.0$$

$$= 0.0500 \, \text{mol}$$

0.0500 mol of ammonium ions will be used up and 0.0500 mol of new ammonia will be formed.

$$\text{Original moles of } NH_3 = 1.00$$
$$\text{New moles of } NH_3 = 1.00 + 0.0500$$
$$= 1.05 \, \text{mol}$$

$$\text{Original moles of } NH_4{}^+ = 0.400$$
$$\text{New moles of } NH_4{}^+ = 0.400 - 0.0500$$
$$= 0.350 \, \text{mol}$$

Once again, to make the calculation simpler, we will assume that the final volume is $1000 \, \text{cm}^3$, rather than $1005 \, \text{cm}^3$.

$$\text{New } [NH_3] = 1.05 \, \text{mol dm}^{-3}$$
$$\text{New } [NH_4{}^+] = 0.350 \, \text{mol dm}^{-3}$$

Now for the pH calculation:

$$K_a = \frac{[NH_3][H^+]}{[NH_4{}^+]} = 5.62 \times 10^{-10}$$

$$[H^+] = \frac{5.62 \times 10^{-10} \times [NH_4{}^+]}{[NH_3]}$$

$$= \frac{5.62 \times 10^{-10} \times 0.350}{1.05}$$

$$= 1.873 \times 10^{-10}$$

$$pH = 9.73$$

This time, the pH has risen by just under 0.1.

Example 29 In what proportions should ammonia and ammonium chloride be mixed in solution to give a buffer solution of pH 10.0? pK_a for $NH_4{}^+$ is 9.25.

To start with "unlog" the pK_a to give $K_a = 5.62 \times 10^{-10} \, \text{mol dm}^{-3}$.

Now "unlog" the pH to give the desired value of $[H^+] = 1.00 \times 10^{-10} \, \text{mol dm}^{-3}$.

Now use the same expression that we have worked from in the last two examples:

$$K_a = \frac{[NH_3][H^+]}{[NH_4{}^+]} = 5.62 \times 10^{-10}$$

$$\frac{[NH_3]}{[NH_4{}^+]} = \frac{5.62 \times 10^{-10}}{[H^+]}$$

$$= \frac{5.62 \times 10^{-10}}{1.00 \times 10^{-10}}$$

$$= \frac{5.62}{1}$$

As long as you make up a solution which contains the ratio of 5.62 mol of ammonia to 1 mol of ammonium ions, the pH will be 10.0.

Problem • 19	Calculate the pH of a buffer solution which contained $0.500\,mol\,dm^{-3}$ propanoic acid, C_2H_5COOH, and $1.00\,mol\,dm^{-3}$ sodium propanoate, C_2H_5COONa. K_a for propanoic acid $= 1.35 \times 10^{-5}\,mol\,dm^{-3}$.
Problem • 20	Calculate the pH of a solution which contained $12.0\,g$ ethanoic acid, CH_3COOH, and $4.10\,g$ of sodium ethanoate, CH_3COONa dissolved in $100\,cm^3$ of solution. K_a for ethanoic acid $= 1.74 \times 10^{-5}\,mol\,dm^{-3}$. $H = 1$; $C = 12$; $O = 16$; $Na = 23$.
Problem • 21	Calculate the pH of a solution made by mixing $20.0\,cm^3$ of $0.100\,mol\,dm^{-3}$ methanoic acid, $HCOOH$, with $80.0\,cm^3$ of $0.0500\,mol\,dm^{-3}$ sodium methanoate, $HCOONa$. K_a for methanoic acid $= 1.78 \times 10^{-4}\,mol\,dm^{-3}$.
Problem • 22	A buffer solution contained $0.500\,mol\,dm^{-3}$ of a weak acid HA and $0.300\,mol\,dm^{-3}$ of its sodium salt, NaA. (a) Calculate its pH if pK_a for HA $= 4.82$. (b) Calculate the pH after adding $2.00\,cm^3$ of $5.00\,mol\,dm^{-3}$ HCl to $1000\,cm^3$ of the buffer solution. (c) Calculate the pH after adding $2.00\,cm^3$ of $5.00\,mol\,dm^{-3}$ NaOH to $1000\,cm^3$ of the buffer solution.
Problem • 23	In what proportions should you mix $1.00\,mol\,dm^{-3}$ solutions of methanoic acid, $HCOOH$, and sodium methanoate, $HCOONa$, to give a buffer solution of pH 3.50? K_a for methanoic acid $= 1.78 \times 10^{-4}\,mol\,dm^{-3}$.
Problem • 24	$500\,cm^3$ of a $1.00\,mol\,dm^{-3}$ solution of a weak base B was mixed with $500\,cm^3$ of a $1.00\,mol\,dm^{-3}$ solution of one of its salts, BH^+Cl^-. pK_a for the BH^+ ion $= 10.64$. (a) Calculate the pH of the buffer solution formed on mixing the two solutions. (b) Calculate the effect of adding (i) $4.00\,cm^3$ of $5.00\,mol\,dm^{-3}$ HCl, and (ii) $4.00\,cm^3$ of $5.00\,mol\,dm^{-3}$ NaOH solution to $1000\,cm^3$ of the buffer solution. (c) In what proportions would you have to mix the original solutions to give a buffer solution of pH 10.5?

> **Care!** Think carefully about the number of moles of B and its salt present in $1000\,cm^3$ of solution.

End of chapter checklist

Can you do the following things?

■ Define pH and convert from [H⁺] to pH and vice versa.

■ Calculate the pH of a strong acid given its concentration, and find the concentration of a strong acid from its pH.

■ Define K_w and calculate the pH of pure water given a value for K_w.

■ Calculate the pH of a strong base given its concentration, and find the concentration of a strong base from its pH.

■ Calculate the pH of mixtures produced during titrations involving strong acids and strong bases.

■ Define K_a and pK_a for a weak acid.

■ Calculate the pH of a weak acid given its concentration and K_a or pK_a.

■ Calculate K_a or pK_a for a weak acid given its concentration and pH.

■ Find pK_a for a weak acid from a titration curve.

■ Calculate the pH of a weak base given K_a or pK_a for its conjugate acid.

■ Calculate the pH of acidic or alkaline buffer solutions from suitable data.

■ Calculate the effect of adding small amounts of acid or alkali to either type of buffer solution.

■ Work out the proportions in which the components of both acidic and alkaline buffer solutions must be mixed to give a desired pH.

Revision problems

Numerical answers are provided for these problems, but no worked solutions.

Problem • 25

(a) Convert the following hydrogen ion concentrations (all in mol dm⁻³) into pHs:

    (i) 2.56×10^{-3}
    (ii) 0.850
    (iii) 8.51×10^{-12}

(b) Convert the following pHs into hydrogen ion concentrations in mol dm⁻³:

    (i)   1.91
    (ii) 6.40
    (iii) 14.3

Problem . 26

Calculate the pH of the following strong acids:

(a) 0.500 mol dm^{-3} HCl
(b) 0.0200 mol dm^{-3} H$_2$SO$_4$.

Problem . 27

Calculate the concentrations of the following strong acids from their pHs:

(a) HNO$_3$ with a pH of 1.20
(b) HCl with a pH of 0.30
(c) H$_2$SO$_4$ with a pH of 0.

Problem . 28

Calculate the pH of pure water at 20 °C, if $K_w = 6.81 \times 10^{-15}$ mol^2 dm^{-6} at this temperature.

Problem . 29

Calculate the pH of the following strong bases. Take $K_w = 1.00 \times 10^{-14}$ mol^2 dm^{-6}.

(a) 0.100 mol dm^{-3} NaOH
(b) 0.0100 mol dm^{-3} Ca(OH)$_2$.

Problem . 30

Calculate the concentrations of the following strong bases from their pHs. Take $K_w = 1.00 \times 10^{-14}$ mol^2 dm^{-6}.

(a) KOH solution with a pH of 14.3
(b) Ba(OH)$_2$ solution with a pH of 11.0.

Problem . 31

Calculate the pHs of the following mixtures of strong acids and strong bases. Take $K_w = 1.00 \times 10^{-14}$ mol^2 dm^{-6}.

(a) 15.0 cm^3 of 1.00 mol dm^{-3} HCl and 10.0 cm^3 of 1.00 mol dm^{-3} NaOH
(b) 5.00 cm^3 of 1.00 mol dm^{-3} HCl and 20.0 cm^3 of 1.00 mol dm^{-3} NaOH
(c) 10.0 cm^3 of 0.100 mol dm^{-3} H$_2$SO$_4$ and 10.0 cm^3 of 0.200 mol dm^{-3} NaOH.

Problem . 32

Calculate the pHs of the following weak acid solutions:

(a) 0.0200 mol dm^{-3} ethanoic acid, CH$_3$COOH. $K_a = 1.74 \times 10^{-5}$ mol dm^{-3}.
(b) 0.0100 mol dm^{-3} butanoic acid, C$_3$H$_7$COOH. p$K_a = 4.82$.
(c) 0.500 mol dm^{-3} chloroethanoic acid, CH$_2$ClCOOH.
$K_a = 1.38 \times 10^{-3}$ mol dm^{-3}.

Problem . 33

Ammonium chloride solution is acidic because of the presence of the ammonium ion, NH$_4^+$, which ionises slightly according to the equation:

$$NH_{4\,(aq)}^+ \rightleftharpoons NH_{3(aq)} + H^+_{(aq)}$$

pK_a for the ammonium ion is 9.25. Calculate the pH of a 1.00 mol dm^{-3} solution of ammonium chloride.

Problem . 34

Calculate pK_a for the following weak acids.

(a) 0.0200 mol dm^{-3} HNO$_2$ if its pH is 2.50
(b) 0.0125 mol dm^{-3} HCN if its pH is 5.60.

Problem • 35

Aluminium chloride solution is acidic because of the hydrated aluminium ion, $Al(H_2O)_6^{3+}{}_{(aq)}$. This establishes the following equilibrium:

$$Al(H_2O)_6^{3+}{}_{(aq)} \rightleftharpoons Al(H_2O)_5(OH)^{2+}{}_{(aq)} + H^+{}_{(aq)}$$

Calculate pK_a for the hydrated aluminium ion if the pH of a solution containing 0.100 mol of the ion in 1000 cm³ of solution has a pH of 3.00.

Problem • 36

The data in the table shows the changes in pH when 0.100 mol dm⁻³ sodium hydroxide solution is added to 25.0 cm³ of a weak acid solution (HA). Plot the pH curve and use it to find pK_a for HA.

Volume of NaOH solution added (cm³)	pH
0	2.50
3.0	3.13
6.0	3.50
9.0	3.75
12.0	3.97
15.0	4.18
18.0	4.41
21.0	4.72
24.0	5.35
24.5	5.69
24.9	6.40
25.0	8.35
25.1	11.30
25.5	12.00
27.0	12.59

Problem • 37

Calculate the pHs of the following weak base solutions. Take $K_w = 1.00 \times 10^{-14}$ mol² dm⁻⁶.

(a) 1.00 mol dm⁻³ ammonia solution, NH_3.
   K_a for $NH_4^+ = 5.62 \times 10^{-10}$ mol dm⁻³.

(b) 0.400 mol dm⁻³ methylamine solution, CH_3NH_2.

$$CH_3NH_2 + H_2O \rightleftharpoons CH_3NH_3^+ + OH^-$$

   pK_a for $CH_3NH_3^+ = 10.64$.

(c) 0.0100 mol dm⁻³ solution of a weak base B.

$$B + H_2O \rightleftharpoons BH^+ + OH^-$$

   pK_a for $BH^+ = 8.56$.

Problem • 38

Sodium ethanoate solution, CH_3COONa, is slightly alkaline because the ethanoate ion, CH_3COO^- is a weak base:

$$CH_3COO^- + H_2O \rightleftharpoons CH_3COOH + OH^-$$

pK_a for ethanoic acid is 4.76. Taking $K_w = 1.00 \times 10^{-14}$ mol² dm⁻⁶, calculate the pH of 1.00 mol dm⁻³ sodium ethanoate solution.

Problem . 39

Calculate the pHs of the following buffer solutions:

(a) A solution containing 0.400 mol ethanoic acid, CH_3COOH, and 0.500 mol sodium ethanoate, CH_3COONa, in 1000 cm^3 of solution. K_a for ethanoic acid $= 1.74 \times 10^{-5}$ mol dm^{-3}.

(b) A solution made by mixing 50.0 cm^3 of 0.300 mol dm^{-3} methanoic acid, HCOOH, with 150 cm^3 of 0.300 mol dm^{-3} sodium methanoate, HCOONa. pK_a for methanoic acid $= 3.75$.

(c) A solution containing 0.100 mol ammonia and 0.200 mol ammonium chloride in 250 cm^3 of solution. pK_a for the ammonium ion, $NH_4^+ = 9.25$.

(d) A solution made by mixing 100 cm^3 of 0.250 mol dm^{-3} methylamine solution, CH_3NH_2, with 100 cm^3 of 0.250 mol dm^{-3} methylammonium chloride, $CH_3NH_3^+Cl^-$. K_a for the methylammonium ion, $CH_3NH_3^+ = 2.29 \times 10^{-11}$ mol dm^{-3}.

Problem . 40

A buffer solution contained a mixture of 60.0 g of ethanoic acid, CH_3COOH, and 82.0 g of sodium ethanoate, CH_3COONa, in 1000 cm^3 of solution. K_a for ethanoic acid $= 1.74 \times 10^{-5}$ mol dm^{-3}.

(a) Calculate the pH of the buffer solution.

(b) Calculate the pH after adding 1.00 cm^3 of 5.00 mol dm^{-3} hydrochloric acid to 500 cm^3 of the buffer solution.

(c) Calculate the pH after adding 1.00 cm^3 of 5.00 mol dm^{-3} sodium hydroxide solution to 500 cm^3 of the buffer solution.

(H = 1; C = 12; O = 16; Na = 23.)

Problem . 41

You have available 1.00 mol dm^{-3} solutions of ammonia, ammonium chloride, ethanoic acid and sodium ethanoate. Which solutions would you mix, and in what proportions, to obtain a buffer solution of (a) pH 4.50, (b) pH 9.50?

pK_a for the ammonium ion $= 9.25$.
pK_a for ethanoic acid $= 4.76$.

Other Equilibria

This chapter investigates three sorts of equilibrium calculations which do not fit easily into other places in the book. There isn't anything difficult in the maths required.

Solubility product, K_{sp}

➤ Solubility products are included here rather than in Chapter 7, because the way questions are phrased is rather different from basic equilibrium calculations.

A solubility product is a special example of a heterogeneous equilibrium constant. If you haven't done any work on heterogeneous equilibria recently, it would help to re-read pages 177 to 179 in Chapter 7 before you go any further.

Explaining solubility product

The solubility product for lead(II) sulphate

➤ **A saturated solution** is one which contains the maximum amount of dissolved solid at a particular temperature – in the **presence of undissolved solid**. In the absence of undissolved solid, some substances can form unstable **supersaturated solutions**. As soon as you add some solid to these, all the excess dissolved material precipitates out.

Suppose you made a saturated solution of lead(II) sulphate, $PbSO_4$, by shaking the solid with water until no more would dissolve. Lead(II) sulphate is almost insoluble, so you would not notice much difference however long you shook the mixture for. You would see a white solid suspended in the water, and if you left it alone, the solid would settle to the bottom.

Lead(II) sulphate is ionic and some lead(II) ions and sulphate ions will break away from the lattice and go into solution. Others, which had broken off previously, will return to attach themselves to the solid. This equilibrium is established:

$$PbSO_{4(s)} \rightleftharpoons Pb^{2+}_{(aq)} + SO_4^{2-}_{(aq)}$$

The equilibrium constant for this heterogeneous equilibrium is called the **solubility product**, and is given the symbol K_{sp}:

$$K_{sp} = [Pb^{2+}_{(aq)}][SO_4^{2-}_{(aq)}]$$

We would normally write it missing out the state symbols as:

$$K_{sp} = [Pb^{2+}][SO_4^{2-}]$$

In common with all other heterogeneous equilibrium constants, the concentration of a solid is left out of the expression.

The solubility product for lead(II) iodide

This time the equilibrium is:

$$PbI_{2(s)} \rightleftharpoons Pb^{2+}_{(aq)} + 2I^-_{(aq)}$$
$$K_{sp} = [Pb^{2+}][I^-]^2$$

Solubility product is defined in exactly the same way as any other equilibrium constant. The concentrations of the various ions are simply raised to the power of the number in front of them in the equation.

The solubility product for bismuth sulphide

$$Bi_2S_{3(s)} \rightleftharpoons 2Bi^{3+}_{(aq)} + 3S^{2-}_{(aq)}$$

$$K_{sp} = [Bi^{3+}]^2[S^{2-}]^3$$

The units for solubility product

> ➤ **Hint:** In the first example, you are multiplying $mol\,dm^{-3}$ by $mol\,dm^{-3}$. In the second example, you are multiplying $mol\,dm^{-3}$ by $(mol\,dm^{-3})^2$ – which is $(mol\,dm^{-3})^3$ – and so on.

You will have to work out the units because they vary from example to example. The concentrations of the ions are in $mol\,dm^{-3}$. Taking the examples we have already used:

$$K_{sp} = [Pb^{2+}][SO_4^{2-}] = 1.6 \times 10^{-8}\,mol^2\,dm^{-6}$$

$$K_{sp} = [Pb^{2+}][I^-]^2 = 1.0 \times 10^{-9}\,mol^3\,dm^{-9}$$

$$K_{sp} = [Bi^{3+}]^2[S^{2-}]^3 = 1.0 \times 10^{-97}\,mol^5\,dm^{-15}$$

Limitations of solubility products

Solubility products are only constant at a particular temperature. The temperature usually quoted is 298 K.

Solubility products only apply to sparingly soluble ionic compounds. With more soluble substances (for example, sodium chloride), interactions between the ions in solution interfere with the simple equilibrium.

Solubility products only apply if the solution is in equilibrium with its solid – in other words, if the solution is saturated.

For example, in the case of lead(II) sulphate, it would be possible to multiply $[Pb^{2+}]$ by $[SO_4^{2-}]$ and get an answer **less** than $1.6 \times 10^{-8}\,mol^2\,dm^{-6}$. This would happen if the solution wasn't saturated – you haven't got equilibrium, so the equilibrium constant cannot apply.

You would never get an answer **greater** than $1.6 \times 10^{-8}\,mol^2\,dm^{-6}$, though. If you mixed solutions so that the ionic product $[Pb^{2+}][SO_4^{2-}]$ was temporarily more than $1.6 \times 10^{-8}\,mol^2\,dm^{-6}$, all the excess lead(II) sulphate would instantly precipitate out until the product came down to that value again.

Calculations

Calculating solubility products from solubility

> ➤ You might come across older ways of measuring solubility – for example, grams of solute per 100 g of water. It is by no means easy to convert from this into $g\,dm^{-3}$ of solution. You will not be faced with this problem.

For the purposes of these calculations, solubility is normally measured in $mol\,dm^{-3}$ or $g\,dm^{-3}$.

Example 1

The solubility of calcium carbonate, $CaCO_3$, at 298 K is 6.9×10^{-5} mol dm^{-3}. Calculate the solubility product at this temperature.

$$CaCO_{3(s)} \rightleftharpoons Ca^{2+}{}_{(aq)} + CO_3{}^{2-}{}_{(aq)}$$

The key to this calculation is to realise that every mole of calcium carbonate which dissolves gives 1 mole of calcium ions and 1 mole of carbonate ions in solution. So if 6.9×10^{-5} moles of calcium carbonate dissolves in 1 dm^3 of solution, then there will be 6.9×10^{-5} moles of Ca^{2+} and 6.9×10^{-5} moles of $CO_3{}^{2-}$ in 1 dm^3 of the solution.

$$[Ca^{2+}] = 6.9 \times 10^{-5} \text{ mol dm}^{-3}$$

$$[CO_3{}^{2-}] = 6.9 \times 10^{-5} \text{ mol dm}^{-3}$$

$$K_{sp} = [Ca^{2+}][CO_3{}^{2-}]$$

$$= (6.9 \times 10^{-5})^2$$

$$= 4.8 \times 10^{-9} \text{ mol}^2 \text{ dm}^{-6}$$

➤ **Take care!** Your original solubility figure was only quoted to 2 **significant figures**. Your answer must not exceed that.

Example 2

The solubility of calcium sulphate, $CaSO_4$, at 298 K is 0.67 g dm^{-3}. Calculate the solubility product at this temperature. (O = 16; S = 32; Ca = 40)

The concentration is given in inconvenient units, so the first thing to do is to convert it into mol dm^{-3}.

➤ **Remember:**

Number of moles

$$= \frac{\text{mass (g)}}{\text{mass of 1 mole (g)}}$$

1 mole of $CaSO_4$ weighs 136 g. 0.67 g is 0.67/136 mol. The solubility of calcium sulphate is:

$$\frac{0.67}{136} = 4.93 \times 10^{-3} \text{ mol dm}^{-3}$$

Each mole of calcium sulphate that dissolves produces 1 mole of Ca^{2+} and 1 mole of $SO_4{}^{2-}$ ions in solution.

$$[Ca^{2+}] = 4.93 \times 10^{-3} \text{ mol dm}^{-3}$$

$$[SO_4{}^{2-}] = 4.93 \times 10^{-3} \text{ mol dm}^{-3}$$

$$K_{sp} = [Ca^{2+}][SO_4{}^{2-}]$$

$$= (4.93 \times 10^{-3})^2$$

$$= 2.4 \times 10^{-5} \text{ mol}^2 \text{ dm}^{-6}$$

Example 3

Where the ratio of the ions in the compounds is 1:1 (as in the first two examples), the questions are fairly trivial. In other cases, you have to be rather more careful.

The solubility of lead(II) chloride, $PbCl_2$, is 0.016 mol dm^{-3} at 298 K. Calculate the solubility product at this temperature.

$$PbCl_{2(s)} \rightleftharpoons Pb^{2+}{}_{(aq)} + 2Cl^-{}_{(aq)}$$

Each mole of lead(II) chloride produces 1 mole of lead(II) ions in solution,

so $\quad [Pb^{2+}{}_{(aq)}] = 0.016 \text{ mol dm}^{-3}$

However, each mole of lead(II) chloride produces 2 moles of chloride ions in solution. If 0.016 mol of lead(II) chloride dissolves, there will be twice this amount of chloride ions present,

so $\quad [Cl^-_{(aq)}] = 0.032 \, mol \, dm^{-3}$

$K_{sp} = [Pb^{2+}][Cl^-]^2$

$\qquad = 0.016 \times (0.032)^2$

$\qquad = 1.6 \times 10^{-5} \, mol^3 \, dm^{-9}$

Example 4

The solubility of calcium phosphate, $Ca_3(PO_4)_2$, is $7.7 \times 10^{-4} \, g \, dm^{-3}$ at $25\,°C$. Calculate its solubility product at this temperature. ($O = 16$; $P = 31$; $Ca = 40$)

First, you will have to convert the concentration into $mol \, dm^{-3}$. 1 mole of calcium phosphate weighs $310\,g$. The concentration in $mol \, dm^{-3}$ is therefore

$\dfrac{7.7 \times 10^{-4}}{310} = 2.48 \times 10^{-6} \, mol \, dm^{-3}$

$Ca_3(PO_4)_{2(s)} \rightleftharpoons 3Ca^{2+}_{(aq)} + 2PO_4^{3-}_{(aq)}$

Each mole of calcium phosphate that dissolves produces 3 moles of calcium ions in solution and 2 moles of phosphate ions.

$[Ca^{2+}] = 3 \times 2.48 \times 10^{-6}$

$\qquad = 7.44 \times 10^{-6} \, mol \, dm^{-3}$

$[PO_4^{3-}] = 2 \times 2.48 \times 10^{-6}$

$\qquad = 4.96 \times 10^{-6} \, mol \, dm^{-3}$

$K_{sp} = [Ca^{2+}]^3 [PO_4^{3-}]^2$

$\qquad = (7.44 \times 10^{-6})^3 \times (4.96 \times 10^{-6})^2$

$\qquad = 1.0 \times 10^{-26} \, mol^5 \, dm^{-15}$

➤ In your answer, **do not exceed** the 2 significant figures that the solubility was quoted to in the question. Be sure that you understand why the units are $mol^5 \, dm^{-15}$.

Problem • 1

The solubility of silver(I) bromide, AgBr, at $298\,K$ is $8.8 \times 10^{-7} \, mol \, dm^{-3}$. Calculate its solubility product at this temperature.

Problem • 2

The solubility of magnesium carbonate, $MgCO_3$, at $298\,K$ is $0.27 \, g \, dm^{-3}$. Calculate its solubility product at this temperature. ($C = 12$; $O = 16$; $Mg = 24$)

Problem • 3

The solubility of aluminium hydroxide, $Al(OH)_3$, at $298\,K$ is $2.5 \times 10^{-9} \, mol \, dm^{-3}$. Calculate its solubility product at this temperature.

Problem • 4

The solubility of lead(II) iodide, PbI_2, at $298\,K$ is $0.29 \, g \, dm^{-3}$. Calculate its solubility product at this temperature. ($I = 127$; $Pb = 207$)

Problem • 5

The solubility of silver(I) sulphate, Ag_2SO_4, at $298\,K$ is $0.016 \, mol \, dm^{-3}$. Calculate its solubility product at this temperature.

Calculating solubility from solubility product

Example 5

Calculate the solubility in $mol\,dm^{-3}$ of silver chloride, AgCl, at 298 K if its solubility product is $1.8 \times 10^{-10}\,mol^2\,dm^{-6}$.

$$AgCl_{(s)} \rightleftharpoons Ag^+_{(aq)} + Cl^-_{(aq)}$$

Call the solubility of silver chloride "s" $mol\,dm^{-3}$. For every mole of silver chloride that dissolves, the solution will contain 1 mole of $Ag^+_{(aq)}$ and 1 mole of $Cl^-_{(aq)}$. So if "s" moles dissolve, the solution will contain "s" moles of each ion.

$$[Ag^+] = s\,mol\,dm^{-3} \qquad [Cl^-] = s\,mol\,dm^{-3}$$

$$K_{sp} = [Ag^+][Cl^-]$$

$$1.8 \times 10^{-10} = s \times s$$

$$s = \sqrt{1.8 \times 10^{-10}}$$

$$= 1.3 \times 10^{-5}\,mol\,dm^{-3}$$

Example 6

You need to think carefully if the ion ratio in the compound is not 1:1.

Calculate the solubility in $mol\,dm^{-3}$ of silver(I) sulphide, Ag_2S, at 298 K if its solubility product is $6.3 \times 10^{-51}\,mol^3\,dm^{-9}$.

$$Ag_2S_{(s)} \rightleftharpoons 2Ag^+_{(aq)} + S^{2-}_{(aq)}$$

Again, we will call the solubility of silver(I) sulphide "s" $mol\,dm^{-3}$. For every mole of silver(I) sulphide that dissolves, the solution will contain 2 moles of $Ag^+_{(aq)}$ and 1 mole of $S^{2-}_{(aq)}$. So if "s" moles dissolve, the solution will contain "$2s$" moles of $Ag^+_{(aq)}$ and "s" moles of $S^{2-}_{(aq)}$.

$$[Ag^+] = 2s\,mol\,dm^{-3} \qquad [S^{2-}] = s\,mol\,dm^{-3}$$

$$K_{sp} = [Ag^+]^2[S^{2-}]$$

$$6.3 \times 10^{-51} = (2s)^2 \times s$$

$$4s^3 = 6.3 \times 10^{-51}$$

$$s = \sqrt[3]{\frac{6.3 \times 10^{-51}}{4}}$$

$$= 1.2 \times 10^{-17}\,mol\,dm^{-3}$$

> ➤ During these calculations you may well need to use your calculator to find **cube roots** or **fourth roots** or whatever. With luck you will probably find a cube root button on your calculator, but for a fourth or fifth root you will have to find another way of doing it.
>
> $\sqrt[4]{16} = 16^{1/4}$
>
> The answer to this should be 2. Find out how to do this on your calculator and use this example to check your method. Use the x^y button – or better still, the $x^{1/y}$ button if you have one.

Example 7

You might, of course, be asked to calculate a solubility in $g\,dm^{-3}$.

Calculate the solubility in $g\,dm^{-3}$ of chromium(III) hydroxide, $Cr(OH)_3$, at 25 °C if its solubility product is $1.0 \times 10^{-33}\,mol^4\,dm^{-12}$.
(H = 1; O = 16; Cr = 52)

$$Cr(OH)_{3(s)} \rightleftharpoons Cr^{3+}_{(aq)} + 3OH^-_{(aq)}$$

To start, we still need to work out the solubility in $mol\,dm^{-3}$. If the solubility of the chromium(III) hydroxide is "s" $mol\,dm^{-3}$:

$$[Cr^{3+}] = s\,mol\,dm^{-3} \qquad [OH^-] = 3s\,mol\,dm^{-3}$$

$$K_{sp} = [Cr^{3+}][OH^-]^3$$

$$1.0 \times 10^{-33} = s \times (3s)^3$$

$$27s^4 = 1.0 \times 10^{-33}$$

$$s = \sqrt[4]{\frac{1.0 \times 10^{-33}}{27}}$$

$$= 2.47 \times 10^{-9}\,mol\,dm^{-3}$$

> ➤ The answer in $mol\,dm^{-3}$ is not the final answer. It is **important** not to round it off too much. Although the final answer will only be quoted to 2 significant figures, you must carry intermediate answers to more figures than that.

Now you can convert this into a solubility in $g\,dm^{-3}$. 1 mole of $Cr(OH)_3$ weighs 103 g.

The solubility is therefore $2.47 \times 10^{-9} \times 103\,g\,dm^{-3} = 2.5 \times 10^{-7}\,g\,dm^{-3}$.

As always, the final answer must not be to more significant figures than the numbers you started from.

Problem • 6

Calculate the solubilities of the following compounds in (i) $mol\,dm^{-3}$, and (ii) $g\,dm^{-3}$:

(a) barium carbonate, $BaCO_3$. $K_{sp} = 5.1 \times 10^{-9}\,mol^2\,dm^{-6}$.
(b) calcium hydroxide, $Ca(OH)_2$. $K_{sp} = 5.5 \times 10^{-6}\,mol^3\,dm^{-9}$.
(c) aluminium hydroxide, $Al(OH)_3$. $K_{sp} = 1.0 \times 10^{-33}\,mol^4\,dm^{-12}$.
(d) antimony(III) sulphide, Sb_2S_3. $K_{sp} = 1.7 \times 10^{-93}\,mol^5\,dm^{-15}$.

(H = 1; C = 12; O = 16; Al = 27; S = 32; Ca = 40; Sb = 122; Ba = 137)

The "common ion effect"

Suppose you had a saturated solution of calcium sulphate:

$$CaSO_{4(s)} \rightleftharpoons Ca^{2+}_{(aq)} + SO_4^{2-}_{(aq)}$$

$$K_{sp} = [Ca^{2+}][SO_4^{2-}] = 2.4 \times 10^{-5}\,mol^2\,dm^{-6} \text{ at } 298\,K$$

Now suppose you added another solution to this which contained an ion in common with it, for example some dilute sulphuric acid (which also contains sulphate ions).

> ➤ A "**common ion**" is an ion which is present in both substances; i.e. an ion common to both substances.

Increasing the concentration of sulphate ions will cause the position of equilibrium to move to the left according to Le Chatelier's Principle, and so more of the calcium sulphate will precipitate out. In the presence of the additional "common ion" (the sulphate in this case) the calcium sulphate becomes less soluble.

Looking at this another way, the value of the solubility product cannot be exceeded. It must remain at $2.4 \times 10^{-5}\,mol^2\,dm^{-6}$, because it is an equilibrium **constant**. Increasing the concentration of the sulphate ions by adding more of them must be compensated for by lowering the concentration of calcium ions. The only way that can be done is to turn them into solid calcium sulphate.

225

Calculations on the common ion effect

Example 8

Calculate the solubility of calcium sulphate in $mol\,dm^{-3}$ in (a) water, (b) dilute sulphuric acid of concentration $0.50\,mol\,dm^{-3}$. $K_{sp} = 2.4 \times 10^{-5}\,mol^2\,dm^{-6}$.

(a) If the solubility of calcium sulphate is "s" $mol\,dm^{-3}$,

$$[Ca^{2+}] = s\,mol\,dm^{-3} \qquad [SO_4^{2-}] = s\,mol\,dm^{-3}$$

$$K_{sp} = [Ca^{2+}][SO_4^{2-}]$$

$$2.4 \times 10^{-5} = s \times s$$

$$s = \sqrt{2.4 \times 10^{-5}}$$

$$= 4.9 \times 10^{-3}\,mol\,dm^{-3}$$

(b) Again, we will call the solubility of calcium sulphate "s" $mol\,dm^{-3}$. And again, the concentration of the calcium ions in solution will be the same, because this is the only source of the calcium ions.

So $\qquad [Ca^{2+}] = s\,mol\,dm^{-3}$

But part of the sulphate ion concentration will come from the sulphuric acid and part from the calcium sulphate. $0.50\,mol\,dm^{-3}$ sulphuric acid, H_2SO_4, has a sulphate ion concentration of $0.50\,mol\,dm^{-3}$. In addition, the dissolved calcium sulphate is supplying an extra "s" $mol\,dm^{-3}$.

So $\qquad [SO_4^{2-}] = (0.50 + s)\,mol\,dm^{-3}$

Unfortunately, if you feed these concentrations into the solubility product expression, you will end up having to do some quite nasty algebra – in fact, in cases where the ratio of the ions is not 1:1 in the original compound, you will end up with equations that there isn't any simple way of solving.

So we **always** make an approximation to simplify things. The value of "s" will be very small indeed compared with 0.50, and so we make the approximation that $(0.50 + s) \approx 0.50$.

So $\qquad [SO_4^{2-}] = 0.50\,mol\,dm^{-3}$

$$K_{sp} = [Ca^{2+}][SO_4^{2-}]$$

$$2.4 \times 10^{-5} = s \times 0.50$$

$$s = \frac{2.4 \times 10^{-5}}{0.50}$$

$$= 4.8 \times 10^{-5}\,mol\,dm^{-3}$$

You will see that the solubility is about 100 times less in the presence of the common ion.

Important generalisation

> **If you have a saturated solution of a sparingly soluble substance A, and you mix it with a solution of a substance B which contains an ion in common with A, you can assume that the concentration of the common ion is the same as its concentration in B.**

Example 9

Calculate the solubility of silver chloride, AgCl, in $0.10\,\text{mol}\,\text{dm}^{-3}$ silver nitrate solution, $AgNO_3$. $K_{sp}(AgCl) = 1.8 \times 10^{-10}\,\text{mol}^2\,\text{dm}^{-6}$ at 298 K.

Call the solubility of silver chloride "s" $\text{mol}\,\text{dm}^{-3}$.

Virtually all the silver ions present in the solution will be coming from the silver nitrate. We can make the assumption that:

$$[Ag^+] = 0.10\,\text{mol}\,\text{dm}^{-3}$$

Each mole of silver chloride dissolves to give 1 mole of chloride ions in solution. So $[Cl^-] = s\,\text{mol}\,\text{dm}^{-3}$.

$$K_{sp} = [Ag^+][Cl^-]$$
$$1.8 \times 10^{-10} = 0.10 \times s$$
$$s = \frac{1.8 \times 10^{-10}}{0.10}$$
$$= 1.8 \times 10^{-9}\,\text{mol}\,\text{dm}^{-3}$$

> ➤ Previously in this chapter we calculated the solubility of silver chloride in water. It turned out to be $1.3 \times 10^{-5}\,\text{mol}\,\text{dm}^{-3}$. You can see that it is far less soluble in the presence of silver ions from the silver nitrate solution.

Problem • 7

Calculate the solubility in $\text{mol}\,\text{dm}^{-3}$ of lead(II) sulphate, $PbSO_4$, in $0.10\,\text{mol}\,\text{dm}^{-3}$ sodium sulphate solution, Na_2SO_4. $K_{sp}(PbSO_4) = 1.6 \times 10^{-8}\,\text{mol}^2\,\text{dm}^{-6}$ at 298 K.

Problem • 8

Calculate the solubility in $\text{mol}\,\text{dm}^{-3}$ of silver(I) sulphate, Ag_2SO_4, in:

(a) water,
(b) $0.10\,\text{mol}\,\text{dm}^{-3}$ silver(I) nitrate solution, $AgNO_3$, and
(c) $0.50\,\text{mol}\,\text{dm}^{-3}$ sulphuric acid, H_2SO_4.

$K_{sp}(Ag_2SO_4) = 1.6 \times 10^{-5}\,\text{mol}^3\,\text{dm}^{-9}$ at 298 K.

Deciding whether or not precipitates will form when solutions are mixed

Example 10

Will a precipitate of lead(II) chloride be formed if $10\,\text{cm}^3$ of $0.10\,\text{mol}\,\text{dm}^{-3}$ lead(II) nitrate solution, $Pb(NO_3)_2$, is mixed with $10\,\text{cm}^3$ of $0.20\,\text{mol}\,\text{dm}^{-3}$ hydrochloric acid, HCl? $K_{sp}(PbCl_2) = 1.6 \times 10^{-5}\,\text{mol}^3\,\text{dm}^{-9}$ at 298 K.

The first thing to notice is that when you mix the solutions, all the ion concentrations will decrease. In this case each solution is being diluted from $10\,\text{cm}^3$ to a total volume of $20\,\text{cm}^3$ – so each is diluted by a factor of 2.

Before any reaction takes place, the important ion concentrations are:

$$[Pb^{2+}] = 0.050\,\text{mol}\,\text{dm}^{-3} \qquad [Cl^-] = 0.10\,\text{mol}\,\text{dm}^{-3}$$

The solubility product expression for lead(II) chloride is given by:

$$K_{sp} = [Pb^{2+}][Cl^-]^2 = 1.6 \times 10^{-5}\,\text{mol}^3\,\text{dm}^{-9}$$

If you multiply our ion concentrations together in the same way you get:

$$[Pb^{2+}][Cl^-]^2 = 0.050 \times (0.10)^2$$
$$= 5.0 \times 10^{-4}\,\text{mol}^3\,\text{dm}^{-9}$$

> ➤ **Hint:** If you get confused about which number is bigger than the other if they are expressed in scientific notation, use your calculator to divide one by the other. In this case, 5.0×10^{-4} divided by 1.6×10^{-5} gives 31.25. So 5.0×10^{-4} is definitely the bigger number!
>
> If the answer turned out to be less than 1, then the first number is smaller than the second.

This answer is bigger than the solubility product. This is not allowed! You will therefore get a precipitate in order to reduce the ion concentrations in solution until $[Pb^{2+}][Cl^-]^2 = 1.6 \times 10^{-5}\,\text{mol}^3\,\text{dm}^{-9}$.

Example 11

Will a precipitate of calcium hydroxide form if $5.0\,cm^3$ of $0.050\,mol\,dm^{-3}$ sodium hydroxide solution, NaOH, is added to $5.0\,cm^3$ of $0.050\,mol\,dm^{-3}$ calcium chloride solution, $CaCl_2$? $K_{sp}(Ca(OH)_2) = 5.5 \times 10^{-6}\,mol^3\,dm^{-9}$ at 298 K.

Again, mixing dilutes both solutions by a factor of 2. Before any reaction takes place, the important ion concentrations are:

$$[Ca^{2+}] = 0.025\,mol\,dm^{-3} \qquad [OH^-] = 0.025\,mol\,dm^{-3}$$

The solubility product expression for calcium hydroxide is given by:

$$K_{sp} = [Ca^{2+}][OH^-]^2 = 5.5 \times 10^{-6}\,mol^3\,dm^{-9}$$

If you multiply our ion concentrations together in the same way you get:

$$[Ca^{2+}][OH^-]^2 = 0.025 \times (0.025)^2$$
$$= 1.6 \times 10^{-5}\,mol^3\,dm^{-9}$$

Again, this number is greater than the solubility product, and this is not allowed. Calcium ions and hydroxide ions will precipitate out as calcium hydroxide until the ion concentrations are sufficiently reduced.

Example 12

Will a precipitate of calcium hydroxide form if $5.0\,cm^3$ of ammonia solution containing OH^- ions with a concentration of $2.0 \times 10^{-3}\,mol\,dm^{-3}$ is added to $5.0\,cm^3$ of $0.050\,mol\,dm^{-3}$ calcium chloride solution, $CaCl_2$?

$K_{sp}(Ca(OH)_2) = 5.5 \times 10^{-6}\,mol^3\,dm^{-9}$ at 298 K.

This is very similar to the last problem – except in the conclusion. Remembering the dilution factor, the important ion concentrations are:

$$[Ca^{2+}] = 0.025\,mol\,dm^{-3} \qquad [OH^-] = 1.0 \times 10^{-3}\,mol\,dm^{-3}$$

The solubility product expression for calcium hydroxide is given by:

$$K_{sp} = [Ca^{2+}][OH^-]^2 = 5.5 \times 10^{-6}\,mol^3\,dm^{-9}$$

If you multiply our ion concentrations together in the same way you get:

$$[Ca^{2+}][OH^-]^2 = 0.025 \times (1.0 \times 10^{-3})^2$$
$$= 2.5 \times 10^{-8}\,mol^3\,dm^{-9}$$

This time the actual product $[Ca^{2+}][OH^-]^2$ is smaller than the solubility product. This **is** allowable. It simply means that you have not reached equilibrium conditions. The solution is not saturated with calcium hydroxide, so no precipitate will form.

Problem • 9

Ammonia is a weak base which reacts with water to produce hydroxide ions. A $1.0\,mol\,dm^{-3}$ solution of ammonia has $[OH^-] = 4.2 \times 10^{-3}\,mol\,dm^{-3}$. $10\,cm^3$ of this ammonia solution was added in turn to $10\,cm^3$ of $0.10\,mol\,dm^{-3}$ solutions of magnesium nitrate, calcium nitrate, strontium nitrate and barium nitrate (all the nitrates have formula $X(NO_3)_2$). The experiments were then repeated with $10\,cm^3$ samples of a $1.0\,mol\,dm^{-3}$ solution of sodium hydroxide, where $[OH^-] = 1.0\,mol\,dm^{-3}$. In which cases will a precipitate be formed?

Solubility products (in $mol^3\,dm^{-9}$): $Mg(OH)_2$ 1.1×10^{-11}
$Ca(OH)_2$ 5.5×10^{-6}
$Sr(OH)_2$ 3.2×10^{-4}
$Ba(OH)_2$ 5.0×10^{-3}

Partition coefficients

Suppose you had a substance X which was soluble in both ether and water, and you shook a mixture of both solvents up with some X in a separating funnel. Suppose also that X is more soluble in ether than it is in water.

When you stop shaking the mixture, the two solvents will separate out because they are **immiscible**. The ether will float on top of the water because it is less dense than water. A dynamic equilibrium is set up with X molecules crossing the boundary between the ether and the water. At equilibrium, equal numbers will be crossing in both directions (see Figure 9.1).

X (in solution in water) ⇌ X (in solution in ether)

As in any other dynamic equilibrium, we can write an equilibrium constant expression:

$$K_c = \frac{[\text{X in ether}]}{[\text{X in water}]}$$

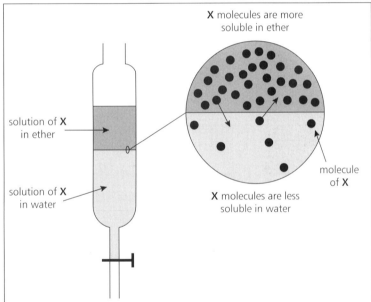

Figure 9.1 Diagram representing dynamic equilibrium of X in solution between ether and water

This equilibrium constant is called the **partition coefficient** or **distribution coefficient**, and is constant at a particular temperature. Changing the solvents or changing X will, of course, change the value of the partition coefficient.

The effect of this is that the ratio of the concentrations of X in the two solvents will be constant (at a particular temperature), however much X you take, and whatever volumes of solvents you use. As long as you work out the concentrations, their ratio will always be the same. There are two limitations to this:

■ The solutions should be reasonably dilute.

■ X must be chemically identical in both solvents. For example, it must not react with either solvent, and it must not ionise or associate.

229

Simple calculations involving partition coefficients

Partition coefficients are ratios

Because a partition coefficient measures the ratio of the concentrations in the two solvents, it is often useful to **write** it as a ratio. If you get into the habit of doing this, it makes life much easier if you have to do slightly more difficult sums.

For example, suppose you were given the partition coefficient of X between ether and water as:

$$\frac{[\text{X in ether}]}{[\text{X in water}]} = 49$$

It is helpful to think of it (and even write it) as:

$$\frac{[\text{X in ether}]}{[\text{X in water}]} = \frac{49}{1}$$

Apart from anything else, this solves a problem which sometimes occurs in questions, where it may say something like "The partition coefficient of Y between benzene and water is 36." How do you know which concentration goes on top of the expression?

If you think of the partition coefficient as a ratio, then the statement reads "The partition coefficient of Y between benzene and water is 36:1." In other words [Y in benzene]:[Y in water] is 36:1.

$$\frac{[\text{Y in benzene}]}{[\text{Y in water}]} = \frac{36}{1}$$

Concentration units do not matter

Because a partition coefficient is a simple ratio between two concentrations, it doesn't matter in the least what units these concentrations are measured in – **provided they are both the same**.

For example, you could measure concentration in any of the following units: $mol\,dm^{-3}$, $g\,dm^{-3}$, or even $g\,cm^{-3}$.

The last unit ($g\,cm^{-3}$) is one of the most commonly used in these calculations. You will frequently be working with some mass of solute in a volume of, say, $50\,cm^3$ of solvent. It is much easier to convert this into $g\,cm^{-3}$ by dividing by 50, than to work out a concentration in $g\,dm^{-3}$.

This is really important:

> *You can work in whatever concentration units are most convenient to you, as long as you use the same units for both solvents.*

Example 13

A solution of P in water was shaken with some benzene, and the concentrations of P in both solvents were measured. The concentration of P in water was $0.00100\,mol\,dm^{-3}$ and its concentration in benzene was found to be $0.0200\,mol\,dm^{-3}$. Calculate the partition coefficient for P between benzene and water.

Note that the implication is that you are finding the ratio of concentration in benzene to concentration in water as "something":1. That means that the benzene concentration goes on top of the expression.

➤ Would it matter if you wrote the concentrations upside-down? Not really! As long as you made it clear what ratio you were finding, you would still have a completely valid answer.

$$K_c = \frac{[\text{P in benzene}]}{[\text{P in water}]}$$

$$= \frac{0.0200}{0.00100}$$

$$= 20.0 \left(= \frac{20.0}{1} \text{ if you like} \right)$$

Example 14

Example 13 was insultingly trivial. This one needs a shade more effort.

2.00 g of R was shaken with a mixture of 100 cm³ of hexane and 50.0 cm³ of water. At equilibrium, the water layer was found to contain 0.400 g of R. Calculate the partition coefficient of R between hexane and water.

All you need to do is to find the concentrations in each solvent. This is an example where it is convenient to measure concentrations in g cm^{-3}.

The water contains 0.400 g in 50.0 cm³.

➤ Technically you **cannot use the square bracket notation**. [X] means the concentration of X in mol dm^{-3}, and should not be used for any other units. This is why we have used the more long-winded expression "concentration of R in water", etc.

$$\text{Concentration of R in water} = \frac{0.400}{50.0}$$

$$= 0.00800 \, \text{g cm}^{-3}$$

The hexane contains $(2.00 - 0.400)$ g in 100 cm³.

$$\text{Concentration of R in hexane} = \frac{2.00 - 0.400}{100}$$

$$= 0.0160 \, \text{g cm}^{-3}$$

$$K_c = \frac{\text{concentration of R in hexane}}{\text{concentration of R in water}}$$

$$= \frac{0.0160}{0.00800}$$

$$= 2.00$$

Example 15

This example shows how you might measure a partition coefficient experimentally. It finds the partition coefficient for iodine between tetrachloromethane and water. The concentration of iodine in both layers is found by titrating it with standard sodium thiosulphate solution, $Na_2S_2O_3$.

➤ You might need to do some revision on titration calculations before you read this example.

A solution of iodine in tetrachloromethane, CCl_4, was shaken with water until equilibrium was established, and then the two layers were allowed to separate out. A 25.0 cm³ sample of the lower organic layer was titrated with $0.100 \, \text{mol dm}^{-3}$ sodium thiosulphate solution until the colour of the iodine was removed. 21.4 cm³ of sodium thiosulphate solution was required.

25.0 cm³ of the aqueous layer was titrated with $1.00 \times 10^{-3} \, \text{mol dm}^{-3}$ sodium thiosulphate solution. In this case, 25.0 cm³ of the sodium thiosulphate solution was needed to remove the colour of the iodine.

Calculate the partition coefficient of iodine between tetrachloromethane and water.

$$I_2 + 2Na_2S_2O_3 \rightarrow 2NaI + Na_2S_4O_6$$

First find the concentration of the iodine in the CCl_4 layer:

$$\text{Number of moles of } Na_2S_2O_3 = \frac{21.4}{1000} \times 0.100$$

$$= 2.14 \times 10^{-3}$$

The equation shows that there will only be half that number of moles of I_2.

$$\text{Number of moles of } I_2 = 1.07 \times 10^{-3} \text{ (in } 25.0\,cm^3 \text{ of solution)}$$

$$[I_2 \text{ in } CCl_4] = 1.07 \times 10^{-3} \times \frac{1000}{25.0}$$

$$= 0.0428\,mol\,dm^{-3}$$

Then repeat this for the water layer:

$$\text{Number of moles of } Na_2S_2O_3 = \frac{25.0}{1000} \times 1.00 \times 10^{-3}$$

$$= 2.50 \times 10^{-5}$$

The equation shows that there will only be half that number of moles of I_2.

$$\text{Number of moles of } I_2 = 1.25 \times 10^{-5} \text{ (in } 25.0\,cm^3 \text{ of solution)}$$

$$[I_2 \text{ in } CCl_4] = 1.25 \times 10^{-5} \times \frac{1000}{25.0}$$

$$= 5.00 \times 10^{-4}\,mol\,dm^{-3}$$

Now slot these concentrations into the partition coefficient expression:

$$K_c = \frac{[I_2 \text{ in } CCl_4]}{[I_2 \text{ in water}]}$$

$$= \frac{0.0428}{5.00 \times 10^{-4}}$$

$$= 85.6$$

Problem • 10

A solution of 1.0 g of X in 100 cm^3 of water was shaken with 25 cm^3 of ethoxyethane (ether) until equilibrium had been established. The two layers were separated and the ethoxyethane layer was found to contain 0.80 g of X. Calculate the partition coefficient of X between ethoxyethane and water.

Problem • 11

Some dilute aqueous ammonia solution was shaken with trichloromethane, $CHCl_3$, and the layers allowed to separate. 25.0 cm^3 of the aqueous layer was titrated with 1.00 $mol\,dm^{-3}$ hydrochloric acid. 26.0 cm^3 of the acid was needed to neutralise the ammonia. A 10.0 cm^3 sample of the organic layer needed 8.40 cm^3 of 0.0500 $mol\,dm^{-3}$ hydrochloric acid for neutralisation:

$$NH_3 + HCl \rightarrow NH_4Cl$$

Calculate (a) the concentration of ammonia in the aqueous layer, (b) the concentration of ammonia in the organic layer, and (c) the partition coefficient of ammonia between water and trichloromethane.

Solvent extraction

During laboratory preparations of organic substances, the organic substance is sometimes dissolved in water together with a number of impurities. Solvent extraction is a way of separating the substance from the water and impurities.

The impure mixture is shaken with an organic solvent in which only the substance that you want dissolves. Ether (ethoxyethane) is frequently used. The solution of your substance in ether forms a layer on top of the water and can be removed using a separating funnel. The ether has a very low boiling point and is easily distilled off, leaving the substance that you want behind in the flask.

> **Warning!** It is easy to describe this, but experimentally it is **extremely dangerous**. Ether is a powerful anaesthetic, and is very very flammable. Considerable precautions have to be taken during an ether extraction.

Calculations involving solvent extraction

These are cases where the maths is made much easier if you think of the partition coefficient as a ratio. All the examples which follow use the same substance P which has a partition coefficient between ether and water given by:

$$\frac{\text{concentration of P in ether}}{\text{concentration of P in water}} = \frac{10}{1}$$

During an organic preparation, 10.0 g of P was produced, and this ended up dissolved in 100 cm^3 of water. The problems revolve around the best way of extracting as much as possible using 20.0 cm^3 of ether.

Example 16

In this example, the whole 20.0 cm^3 of ether was shaken with the solution of P. How much P was removed from the water?

$$\frac{\text{concentration of P in ether}}{\text{concentration of P in water}} = \frac{10}{1}$$

$$\frac{\text{mass of P in ether/volume of ether}}{\text{mass of P in water/volume of water}} = \frac{10}{1}$$

To divide by a fraction, you turn it upside-down and then multiply:

$$\frac{\text{mass of P in ether}}{\text{volume of ether}} \times \frac{\text{volume of water}}{\text{mass of P in water}} = \frac{10}{1}$$

Now you can substitute the volumes into this:

$$\frac{\text{mass of P in ether}}{20} \times \frac{100}{\text{mass of P in water}} = \frac{10}{1}$$

Re-arranging this:

$$\frac{\text{mass of P in ether}}{\text{mass of P in water}} = \frac{200}{100}$$
$$= \frac{2}{1}$$

> **If you aren't happy about** this, you can do some algebra instead. If the mass transferred is "m", then $(10 - m)$ is left in the water.
> $$\frac{\text{mass of P in ether}}{\text{mass of P in water}} = \frac{200}{100}$$
> $$\frac{m}{(10 - m)} = 2$$
> $$m = 2(10 - m)$$
> $$3m = 20$$
> $$m = 6.67\,\text{g}$$
> It does not matter much which way you do this particular question, but the algebra route is going to get much more tedious in the next two examples!

The simple way forward now is to think about what this ratio means. For every 3 parts by mass of P, 2 parts will transfer to the ether, and 1 will be left in the water. In other words, 2/3 of the P will be extracted by the ether. Since we started with 10.0 g of P, 6.67 g will be extracted.

Example 17

It turns out to be more efficient to use the ether in several small lots rather than all at once. In this example, 10.0 cm³ of the ether is shaken with all the aqueous solution, and the ether layer is separated and kept on one side. Then the other 10.0 cm³ of fresh ether is shaken with the aqueous solution. This is separated and the two ether layers combined before distillation. How much P is extracted this time?

For each extraction:

$$\frac{\text{concentration of P in ether}}{\text{concentration of P in water}} = \frac{10}{1}$$

$$\frac{\text{mass of P in ether/volume of ether}}{\text{mass of P in water/volume of water}} = \frac{10}{1}$$

$$\frac{\text{mass of P in ether}}{\text{volume of ether}} \times \frac{\text{volume of water}}{\text{mass of P in water}} = \frac{10}{1}$$

$$\frac{\text{mass of P in ether}}{10} \times \frac{100}{\text{mass of P in water}} = \frac{10}{1}$$

$$\frac{\text{mass of P in ether}}{\text{mass of P in water}} = \frac{100}{100}$$

$$= \frac{1}{1}$$

> ➤ You could do this using the alternative method as above, except that it involves two separate bits of algebra corresponding to each extraction. If you are happier doing it that way, there's no problem as long as you have the time. Just check to make sure you get the same answer.

Each time you use 10 cm³ of ether, P divides itself evenly between the ether and the water. Each extraction removes 1/2 of the P from the water.

After 1 extraction, 1/2 of the original P will be left in the water.

After 2 extractions, 1/4 of the original P will be left in the water – 3/4 will have been extracted, which is 7.50 g.

By using the ether in two portions rather than as a whole, 7.50 g rather than 6.67g will be removed from the water.

Example 18

Now suppose you repeated this using four lots of 5.00 cm³ of ether. How much would you extract this time?

For each extraction:

> ➤ The derivation of the first line is exactly the same as in the previous examples, and has been missed out to save space.

$$\frac{\text{mass of P in ether}}{\text{volume of ether}} \times \frac{\text{volume of water}}{\text{mass of P in water}} = \frac{10}{1}$$

$$\frac{\text{mass of P in ether}}{5} \times \frac{100}{\text{mass of P in water}} = \frac{10}{1}$$

$$\frac{\text{mass of P in ether}}{\text{mass of P in water}} = \frac{50}{100}$$

$$= \frac{1}{2}$$

For every 3 parts by mass of P, 1 part ends up in the ether, and 2 parts remain in the water. This time each extraction removes 1/3 of the total mass of P, leaving 2/3 in the water.

Work out the amount **remaining in the water** after each extraction:

After the first 5 cm³   2/3 × 10 g of P remains in the water.

After the second 5 cm³   2/3 × 2/3 × 10 g of P remains in the water.

After the third 5 cm³   2/3 × 2/3 × 2/3 × 10 g of P remains in the water.

After the final 5 cm³   2/3 × 2/3 × 2/3 × 2/3 × 10 g of P remains in the
                                      water = 1.98 g

This time 8.02 g of P has been extracted.

> This would be very time consuming to work out algebraically.

Problem . 12

The partition coefficient of X between ether and water is 20.0:1. An aqueous solution contained 3.00 g of X in 200 cm³ of solution. Calculate the mass of X remaining in the water if the solution was shaken with

(a) 30.0 cm³ of ether,
(b) two separate portions of 15.0 cm³ of ether,
(c) three separate portions of 10.0 cm³ of ether.

Henry's Law

Henry's Law relates to the solubility of gases. In the usual examples, the solvent is more often than not water, but it does not have to be.

Oxygen, for example, is very sparingly soluble in water, and an equilibrium will be set up between the oxygen dissolved in the water and gaseous oxygen above the water:

oxygen (in solution in water) ⇌ gaseous oxygen

If you increase the pressure, the position of equilibrium will shift (according to Le Chatelier's Principle) so that the pressure reduces again. More of the oxygen gas will dissolve in the water.

> Although Henry's Law is based on an equilibrium, the numerical questions involving it never make use of this fact. You could perfectly well do calculations on Henry's Law without ever realising that it had anything to do with equilibria!

Defining Henry's Law

> If you are hazy about partial pressures, re-read page 166 in Chapter 7 before you go any further.

The mass of a gas dissolved in a given volume of solvent at a particular temperature is proportional to the partial pressure of the gas in contact with the solvent.

For example, if you have 1 dm³ of water at 298 K in contact with pure oxygen, if you double the pressure of the oxygen, you will double the mass of it which dissolves. If you reduce the pressure to a half, only half the mass of oxygen will dissolve – and so on.

There are restrictions to Henry's Law, much the same as with partition coefficients. The gas must not react with the solvent in any way, and must not ionise or associate. It would not apply to hydrogen chloride, for example, because this reacts with the water to produce ions:

$$HCl_{(g)} + H_2O_{(l)} \rightarrow H_3O^+{}_{(aq)} + Cl^-{}_{(aq)}$$

It does, however, apply to gases like oxygen or nitrogen which are in exactly the same molecular state whether they are gases or dissolved in water.

Absorption coefficients

Confusingly, Henry's Law talks about the **mass** of gas which dissolves, but calculations involving it nearly always work with **volumes** dissolved. This is not quite as odd as it sounds. As long as you are measuring the gas volumes under some standard conditions, if you double the volume of gas which dissolves, you have automatically doubled the mass dissolved. One measure of the solubility of a gas is its **absorption coefficient**.

> ➤ We are talking about pressures in atmospheres, because it sounds less worrying than using SI units. If you want to be fussy, 1 atmosphere translates to 101,325 Pa.

Suppose you had $1 dm^3$ of water at $293 K$ ($20 °C$) with some oxygen above it at a partial pressure of 1 atmosphere (1 atm). Some of that oxygen will dissolve. To find out how much oxygen had dissolved, you could boil the oxygen solution to expel the gas, and measure the volume of oxygen collected. Because the volume of a gas will vary depending on its temperature and pressure, we need to record its volume at some standard temperature and pressure, chosen as $273 K$ ($0 °C$) and 1 atmosphere – known as "stp".

The volume of oxygen collected from $1 dm^3$ of the solution at $293 K$ would be $0.031 dm^3$ (measured at stp). 0.031 is called the absorption coefficient of oxygen at $293 K$.

As temperature falls, gases become more soluble. At $273 K$ ($0 °C$), $1 dm^3$ of water will dissolve $0.049 dm^3$ of oxygen (again measured at stp) as long as the partial pressure of oxygen is still 1 atmosphere. 0.049 is called the absorption coefficient of oxygen at $273 K$.

Defining absorption coefficients

> ➤ Absorption coefficients are much more long winded to define than to use! It is very unlikely that you would ever be asked to **define** absorption coefficients rather than just use them – and that's easy.

> *The absorption coefficient of a gas is the volume of gas (measured at stp) which will dissolve in unit volume of the solvent at a given temperature, and under a partial pressure of the gas of 1 atmosphere (101 325 Pa).*

Note that absorption coefficients do not have units. The absorption coefficient of oxygen in water at $273 K$ is 0.049. That means that $1 dm^3$ of water will dissolve $0.049 dm^3$ of oxygen under the necessary conditions. Or it means that $1 cm^3$ will dissolve $0.049 cm^3$, or whatever other units you want to choose.

Calculations involving Henry's Law

Example 19

The absorption coefficient of hydrogen in water is 0.018 at $20 °C$. What volume of hydrogen (measured at stp) will dissolve in $1 dm^3$ of water at $20 °C$ if the partial pressure of hydrogen in contact with the water is 0.50 atm?

If the partial pressure was 1 atm, $1 dm^3$ of water would dissolve $0.018 dm^3$ of hydrogen (measured at stp). This is what the absorption coefficient means.

> ➤ **Hint:** If the pressure is halved the amount of hydrogen dissolved is also halved.

Using Henry's Law:

Volume dissolved (measured at stp) $= 0.50 \times 0.018 dm^3$
$$= 0.0090 dm^3 \text{ (or } 9.0 cm^3)$$

Example 20

The only difference this time is that the volume of water is less convenient.

The absorption coefficient of hydrogen sulphide, H_2S, in water at $0\,°C$ is 4.68. Calculate the volume of hydrogen sulphide (measured at stp) which will dissolve in $50\,cm^3$ of water if the partial pressure of the hydrogen sulphide is $0.90\,atm$.

1 volume of water dissolves 4.68 volumes of hydrogen sulphide if its partial pressure is 1 atm. At a pressure of $0.90\,atm$, 1 volume of water dissolves 0.90×4.68 volumes of $H_2S = 4.21$ volumes.

$50\,cm^3$ of water will therefore dissolve $4.21 \times 50\,cm^3 = 210\,cm^3$ of H_2S.

> ➤ No more than **2 significant figures**. The pressure and the volume of water are only given to this accuracy.

Example 21

Henry's Law applies just as well to mixtures of gases as to single gases. You treat each gas as if it were behaving independently of the others. The most commonly asked question relates to the solubility of air in water.

The absorption coefficient of oxygen in water at $20\,°C$ is 0.031. The absorption coefficient for nitrogen at the same temperature is 0.016. Assuming air consists of 20% oxygen and 80% nitrogen, calculate the volumes of the two gases which will dissolve in $1\,dm^3$ of water if the total pressure of the air is $1.0\,atm$.

If air is 20% oxygen, then the mole fraction of oxygen in the air is 20%, or 0.20.

The partial pressure of the oxygen is therefore $0.20 \times 1.0 = 0.20\,atm$.

By a similar argument, the partial pressure of nitrogen will be $0.80\,atm$.

Now use Henry's Law:

> ➤ **Remember:**
> Partial pressure =
> mole fraction × total pressure

If the partial pressure of **oxygen** was 1 atm, the volume dissolved would be $0.031\,dm^3$.

$$\text{At a partial pressure of } 0.20\,atm, \text{ volume dissolved} = 0.20 \times 0.031\,dm^3$$
$$= 0.0062\,dm^3$$

> ➤ In all these sums, whether we say so or not, the dissolved volumes are always measured at stp.

If the partial pressure of **nitrogen** was 1 atm, the volume dissolved would be $0.016\,dm^3$.

$$\text{At a partial pressure of } 0.80\,atm, \text{ volume dissolved} = 0.80 \times 0.016\,dm^3$$
$$= 0.0128\,dm^3$$

Example 22

The last example might well be phrased differently so that you are asked for the percentage composition of the air dissolved in the water.

Assuming air is 20% oxygen and 80% nitrogen, calculate the percentage composition of the gases dissolved in water at $0\,°C$ if the total air pressure is 1.1 atm. Absorption coefficients at $0\,°C$: oxygen 0.049; nitrogen 0.024.

$$\text{Partial pressure of oxygen } = 0.20 \times 1.1$$
$$= 0.22\,atm$$
$$\text{Partial pressure of nitrogen} = 0.80 \times 1.1$$
$$= 0.88\,atm$$

Since you are asked for a percentage composition rather than actual volumes dissolved, it does not matter how much water you choose to take. So choose $1\,dm^3$ to make life easier.

> Strictly speaking, we do not actually need the total pressure in order to do this sum. You would get the same answer irrespective of what the total pressure was. If you don't believe that, work the sum through again using "P" for the pressure. You will find that by the time you get to the end, the "P"s have cancelled out.

There are other ways of working this out, but you would have to think carefully about what you are doing. The way given here takes up a bit of space, but is comparatively effort-free.

If the partial pressure of **oxygen** was 1 atm, $0.049\,dm^3$ would dissolve.

$$\text{Volume of oxygen dissolved} = 0.22 \times 0.049$$
$$= 0.0108\,dm^3$$

If the partial pressure of **nitrogen** was 1 atm, $0.024\,dm^3$ would dissolve.

$$\text{Volume of nitrogen dissolved} = 0.88 \times 0.024$$
$$= 0.0211\,dm^3$$

$$\text{Total volume of dissolved gases} = 0.0108 + 0.0211$$
$$= 0.0319\,dm^3$$

$$\text{Percentage of oxygen} = \frac{0.0108}{0.0319} \times 100$$
$$= 34\%$$

$$\text{Percentage of nitrogen} = \frac{0.0211}{0.0319} \times 100$$
$$= 66\%$$

Problem • 13

The absorption coefficient of ethene, C_2H_4, in water at $0\,°C$ is 0.25. Calculate the volume of ethene (measured at stp) that will dissolve in $100\,cm^3$ of water if the partial pressure of the ethene is $2.0\,atm$.

Problem • 14

A mixture containing 50% by volume of both carbon monoxide and carbon dioxide was allowed to stand over $1.0\,dm^3$ of water at $0\,°C$. The total pressure of the mixture at equilibrium was found to be $0.80\,atm$. Calculate the volumes of carbon monoxide and carbon dioxide (measured at stp) which are dissolved in the water. The absorption coefficients at $0\,°C$ are: CO 0.035; CO_2 1.71.

Problem • 15

The atmosphere contains approximately 78% nitrogen, 21% oxygen and 0.93% argon. The absorption coefficients at $0\,°C$ are: N_2 0.024; O_2 0.049; Ar 0.056. If air at a total pressure of $0.97\,atm$ is left in contact with $1.0\,m^3$ of water at $0\,°C$, calculate

(a) the volume of each gas (measured at stp) dissolved in the water;
(b) the percentage of each gas in the mixture collected if the dissolved air is expelled from the water.

End of chapter check list

Can you do the following things?

■ Write expressions, with units, for the solubility products for simple ionic substances.

■ Calculate solubility products from solubilities and vice versa.

■ Perform simple calculations involving the "common ion effect".

■ Use solubility products to decide whether precipitates will form on mixing suitable solutions.

■ Understand what is meant by "partition coefficient", and calculate partition coefficients from concentration data (including finding concentrations using titration calculations if necessary).

■ Use partition coefficients in calculations involving solvent extraction.

■ State Henry's Law, and use it in simple calculations.

Revision problems

Numerical answers are provided for these problems, but no worked solutions.

Problem • 16

Calculate the solubility products of the following substances at 298 K from their given solubilities:

(a) $BaCrO_4$ (containing Ba^{2+} and CrO_4^{2-} ions): 2.2×10^{-5} mol dm^{-3}.
(b) $AgCl$: 1.9×10^{-3} g dm^{-3}.
(c) $Ca(OH)_2$: 0.011 mol dm^{-3}.
(d) Ag_3PO_4 (containing Ag^+ and PO_4^{3-} ions): 1.1×10^{-3} g dm^{-3}.

($O = 16$; $P = 31$; $Cl = 35.5$; $Ag = 108$)

Problem • 17

Calculate the solubilities of the following substances at 298 K from their given solubility products:

(a) $MgCO_3$: $K_{sp} = 1.0 \times 10^{-5}$ mol^2 dm^{-6}. (Answer in mol dm^{-3}.)
(b) CuS: $K_{sp} = 6.3 \times 10^{-36}$ mol^2 dm^{-6}. (Answer in g dm^{-3}.)
(c) $Ni(OH)_2$: $K_{sp} = 6.5 \times 10^{-18}$ mol^3 dm^{-9}. (Answer in mol dm^{-3}.)
(d) Ag_2S: $K_{sp} = 6.3 \times 10^{-51}$ mol^3 dm^{-9}. (Answer in g dm^{-3}.)

($S = 32$; $Cu = 63.5$; $Ag = 108$)

Problem • 18

Calculate the solubility in mol dm^{-3} of strontium sulphate, $SrSO_4$, in 0.10 mol dm^{-3} sulphuric acid at 298 K. $K_{sp}(SrSO_4) = 3.2 \times 10^{-7}$ mol^2 dm^{-6}.

Problem • 19

Calculate the solubility in mol dm^{-3} of iron(II) hydroxide, $Fe(OH)_2$, in 0.10 mol dm^{-3} sodium hydroxide solution, NaOH, at 298 K. $K_{sp}(Fe(OH)_2) = 7.9 \times 10^{-16}$ mol^3 dm^{-9}.

Problem • 20

Calculate the solubility in mol dm^{-3} of lead(II) chloride, $PbCl_2$, in 0.050 mol dm^{-3} lead(II) nitrate solution, $Pb(NO_3)_2$, at 298 K. $K_{sp}(PbCl_2) = 1.6 \times 10^{-5}$ mol^3 dm^{-9}.

Problem • 21

Will a precipitate be formed if 10 cm^3 of 0.0010 mol dm^{-3} silver nitrate solution, $AgNO_3$, is added to 10 cm^3 of 0.0010 mol dm^{-3} hydrochloric acid? The solubility product of silver chloride, $AgCl = 1.8 \times 10^{-10}$ mol^2 dm^{-6} at 298 K.

Problem • 22

Will a precipitate be formed if $1.0 \, cm^3$ of $0.0010 \, mol \, dm^{-3}$ sodium carbonate solution, Na_2CO_3, is added to $4.0 \, cm^3$ of $0.050 \, mol \, dm^{-3}$ magnesium sulphate solution, $MgSO_4$? $K_{sp}(MgCO_3) = 1.0 \times 10^{-5} \, mol^2 \, dm^{-6}$ at $298 \, K$. (Hint: Think carefully about the concentrations of the important ions after the dilution which occurs when the solutions are mixed.)

Problem • 23

A solution of $2.0 \, g$ of an organic compound, X, in $500 \, cm^3$ of water was shaken with $20 \, cm^3$ of benzene. The two layers were allowed to settle, and then separated. The aqueous layer was found to contain $0.50 \, g$ of X. Calculate the partition coefficient of X between benzene and water.

Problem • 24

A solution of an organic acid, HA, in water was shaken with ether, and the layers allowed to separate. A $10 \, cm^3$ sample of the ether layer was titrated with sodium hydroxide solution of concentration $0.10 \, mol \, dm^{-3}$ in the presence of the indicator phenolphthalein. $16 \, cm^3$ of sodium hydroxide solution was required to neutralise the acid. A $25 \, cm^3$ sample of the aqueous layer was titrated with the same sodium hydroxide solution. This time, $20 \, cm^3$ was needed.

$$NaOH + HA \rightarrow NaA + H_2O$$

(a) Calculate the concentrations of the acid in both the ether and the water.
(b) Calculate a value of the partition coefficient of the acid between ether and water.

Problem • 25

The partition coefficient of an organic compound C between hexane and water is 10.0. An aqueous solution of C contained $10.0 \, g$ of C dissolved in $100 \, cm^3$ of water. Calculate the mass of C remaining in the water if the solution was shaken with:

(a) $40.0 \, cm^3$ of hexane;
(b) four separate portions of $10.0 \, cm^3$ of hexane.

Problem • 26

The absorption coefficient for nitrogen in water is 0.024 at $0 \, °C$ and 0.011 at $50 \, °C$. Calculate the volume of nitrogen (measured at stp) which would dissolve in $100 \, cm^3$ of water at (a) $0 \, °C$, and (b) $50 \, °C$, under a partial pressure of nitrogen of $0.78 \, atm$.

Problem • 27

A gaseous mixture containing equal numbers of moles of carbon monoxide and carbon dioxide was left in contact with water at a combined pressure of $1.00 \, atm$ and a temperature of $273 \, K$. The water was then boiled to remove the dissolved gases. Calculate the percentage of carbon dioxide in the gases collected. The absorption coefficients at $0 \, °C$ are: CO 0.035; CO_2 1.71.

Problem • 28

Carbon dioxide was dissolved in water at $0 \, °C$ with a partial pressure of CO_2 of $1.1 \, atm$. $1.0 \, dm^3$ of this solution (still at $0 \, °C$) was then left open to the atmosphere containing 0.030% by volume of carbon dioxide. The total atmospheric pressure was $1.0 \, atm$. Calculate (a) the volume of carbon dioxide (measured at stp) that would have dissolved in $1 \, dm^3$ of the original solution, and (b) the volume of CO_2 remaining in $1 \, dm^3$ of the solution after exposure to the atmosphere. The absorption coefficient of CO_2 at $0 \, °C$ is 1.71.

10 Redox Equilibria

This chapter investigates the uses of **standard electrode potentials** – also called **standard redox potentials**. Before you start it would be a good idea to re-read pages 11 to 12 in Chapter 1 on "Redox reactions". Trying to understand redox equilibria without being totally confident about the use of terms like oxidation, reduction, oxidising agent and reducing agent is a waste of time. It is also important to take your time over the lengthy introductory part of this chapter before you start the problems. If you understand what is going on, the problems are mostly trivial. If you don't understand, the whole topic can be a nightmare.

Standard electrode potentials (standard redox potentials)

The standard electrode potential of a metal is a way of measuring how readily it gives away electrons to form positive ions in solution. For example, it is well known that magnesium is a fairly reactive metal. It has quite a strong tendency to give away electrons and form Mg^{2+} ions:

$$Mg_{(s)} \rightarrow Mg^{2+}_{(aq)} + 2e^-$$

On the other hand copper is much less reactive because it has a much lower tendency to release electrons and form copper(II) ions:

$$Cu_{(s)} \rightarrow Cu^{2+}_{(aq)} + 2e^-$$

Standard electrode potentials compare the tendency of a metal to form its ions with the tendency of hydrogen to form ions:

$$H_{2(g)} \rightarrow 2H^+_{(aq)} + 2e^-$$

> ➤ We will not define standard electrode potential yet. Some descriptions and explanations are needed first.

We are going to start by showing how standard electrode potentials are measured, and describing some conventions that are used.

Measuring the standard electrode potential for $Mg^{2+}_{(aq)}/Mg_{(s)}$

The standard hydrogen electrode

In Figure 10.1, the left-hand beaker and its contents are described as a standard hydrogen electrode. The hydrogen gas flows over a piece of platinum foil covered in a spongy layer of platinum. This serves two purposes. The platinum is an almost inert metal which provides electrical contact with the sulphuric acid. It also acts as a catalyst for the establishment of an important equilibrium between hydrogen gas and hydrogen ions in solution, which we will look at shortly.

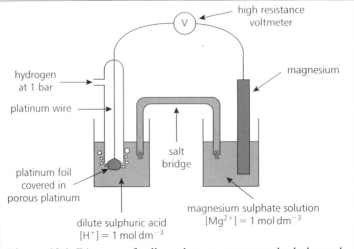

Figure 10.1 Diagram of cell used to measure standard electrode potential (temperature = 298 K)

The salt bridge

The salt bridge drawn here is a piece of glass tubing filled with a solution such as potassium nitrate solution. The ends are stoppered with bits of cotton wool, which prevents too much mixing of the solutions. Ions moving around in the potassium nitrate solution enable electrical contact to be made between the two beakers without introducing any more bits of metal into the system.

The solution in the salt bridge is chosen so that it does not react with the solution in either beaker. Potassium nitrate solution is a fairly safe choice.

Standard conditions

■ Gases are at a pressure of 1 bar (100 kPa).

■ The temperature is 298 K.

■ All ions present are at a concentration of $1 \, mol \, dm^{-3}$.

The high resistance voltmeter

There is a potential difference between the magnesium and the hydrogen electrode. You can picture the set-up as a little "battery" that is capable of generating a voltage. It is important that no current flows when you measure this voltage. If current does flow, the voltage measured is less than it would otherwise be. We are aiming to measure the maximum voltage possible, which is called the **electromotive force (emf)**.

In this case, the emf measured is 2.37 volts, with the magnesium the negative terminal of the "battery" and the hydrogen electrode the positive.

Two important conventions

The apparatus in Figure 10.1 is properly described as a **cell** – not a battery. A battery is a number of cells joined together. The two components of this cell (the hydrogen electrode and the magnesium in magnesium sulphate solution) are described as **half cells**.

> ➤ Older text books may well give the standard pressure as 1 atmosphere (101.325 kPa).

> ➤ All a "**potential difference**" means is that one part of the system (in this case the magnesium) has a much richer supply of electrons than another part. Given half a chance, the electrons would flow from where there is a lot of them to where they are more scarce – you would get an electric current. By using a high resistance voltmeter to measure emf, we are trying to prevent this flow from happening.

The first convention

If you had to draw a diagram every time you wanted to describe a cell, it would be extremely tedious. Instead we use the following convention for the cell diagram:

$$Pt[H_{2(g)}]|2H^+_{(aq)}\|Mg^{2+}_{(aq)}|Mg_{(s)}$$

The vertical line (|) represents a boundary between two phases – for example between the solution of magnesium ions and the solid magnesium.

The double vertical lines (‖) represent the salt bridge. You may also find a broken or dotted vertical line or lines used instead.

The square brackets around the hydrogen simply show the hydrogen flowing over the platinum electrode.

You would read the cell diagram above as: "Hydrogen flowing over a platinum electrode is in contact with a solution containing hydrogen ions. This is connected via a salt bridge to a solution containing magnesium ions in which is placed a piece of magnesium."

The second convention

You may remember that the voltage produced by the above cell is 2.37 volts, with the magnesium as the negative terminal. When you write down the emf of the cell, you write it including the **sign of the right hand electrode** as you have drawn or described the cell.

So in the above case:

$$Pt[H_{2(g)}]|2H^+_{(aq)}\|Mg^{2+}_{(aq)}|Mg_{(s)} \qquad E^\ominus_{cell} = -2.37\,volts$$

If you had written the cell diagram the other way round:

$$Mg_{(s)}|Mg^{2+}_{(aq)}\|2H^+_{(aq)}|Pt[H_{2(g)}] \qquad E^\ominus_{cell} = +2.37\,volts$$

> *The sign of the emf tells you the sign of the right hand electrode.*

Defining standard electrode potential

The emf measured when a metal in a solution of its ions is coupled to a hydrogen electrode is called the standard electrode potential for that metal/metal ion combination. The hydrogen electrode must be the left-hand electrode, and everything must be under standard conditions (all ion concentrations $1\,mol\,dm^{-3}$, a temperature of $298\,K$, gas pressures of $1\,bar$).

Standard electrode potential is given the symbol $E^\ominus$ (read as "E-nought" or "E-standard"). What we previously described as $E^\ominus_{cell}$ in the following case is, in fact, the standard electrode potential for Mg^{2+}/Mg.

$$Pt[H_{2(g)}]|2H^+_{(aq)}\|Mg^{2+}_{(aq)}|Mg_{(s)} \quad E^\ominus = -2.37\,volts$$

> ➤ You might find the first part of this cell convention written as
> $$Pt|H_{2(g)}|2H^+_{(aq)}$$
> or $\quad Pt|H_{2(g)}\|H^+_{(aq)}$
> or some such variant. They all mean the same thing!

> ➤ The "$\ominus$" sign shows that the emf is being measured under standard conditions. It is the same as its use in $\Delta H^\ominus$.

> ➤ Learn this.

> ➤ You might find standard electrode potentials referred to in a number of ways – for example, you might come across "the standard electrode potential for Mg/Mg^{2+}", where the magnesium and magnesium ions are written the other way round. It doesn't matter! However it is described, the $E^\ominus$ value always refers to the cell diagram on the right.

Two other standard electrode potentials

$$Pt[H_{2(g)}]|2H^+_{(aq)}||Zn^{2+}_{(aq)}|Zn_{(s)} \quad E^\ominus = -0.76 \text{ volts}$$

$$Pt[H_{2(g)}]|2H^+_{(aq)}||Cu^{2+}_{(aq)}|Cu_{(s)} \quad E^\ominus = +0.34 \text{ volts}$$

Notice that not only does the voltage change as you change the metal/metal ion combination, but the sign can change as well. In the copper case, the copper (the right hand electrode) is now the positive one.

Why is the $E^\ominus$ value for Mg²⁺/Mg negative (−2.37 volts)?

What's happening in the half cell containing the metal?

Think about what is happening in the beaker containing the magnesium and magnesium sulphate solution.

Magnesium has a high tendency to form ions. Some of the magnesium atoms in the piece of metal will lose electrons and break away into the solution as $Mg^{2+}_{(aq)}$:

$$Mg_{(s)} \rightarrow Mg^{2+}_{(aq)} + 2e^-$$

The electrons will be left behind on the piece of magnesium, giving it a negative charge. This will attract magnesium ions from the solution which may recombine with electrons to re-form magnesium atoms:

$$Mg^{2+}_{(aq)} + 2e^- \rightarrow Mg_{(s)}$$

The net effect is that an equilibrium is established:

$$Mg^{2+}_{(aq)} + 2e^- \rightleftharpoons Mg_{(s)}$$

Because the magnesium is a fairly reactive metal, the position of equilibrium will leave quite a lot of excess electrons in the piece of magnesium metal.

A third convention

> *When you write these equilibria, they are always written with the electrons on the left hand side. This is extremely important. If you always obey that convention, it makes much of the rest of this topic a lot easier.*

What's happening in the hydrogen electrode?

A similar equilibrium is established here:

$$2H^+_{(aq)} + 2e^- \rightleftharpoons H_{2(g)}$$

Hydrogen is much less reactive than magnesium, so this time the position of equilibrium isn't anything like as far to the left.

Why is the magnesium the negative terminal?

Figure 10.2 ignores everything except the two important pieces of metal, and shows the greater build-up of electrons on the magnesium. The magnesium is relatively more negative than the platinum, so if you tested the system with a voltmeter, the magnesium would prove to be the negative terminal of the cell, and the platinum the positive one.

> ➤ **Note!** You must get used to thinking about negative and positive in **relative** terms. In the case on the right, both pieces of metal are negatively charged in **absolute** terms because both have a build-up of electrons. The magnesium is relatively more negative. This leaves the platinum relatively less negative, or **relatively more positive** – which means exactly the same thing.

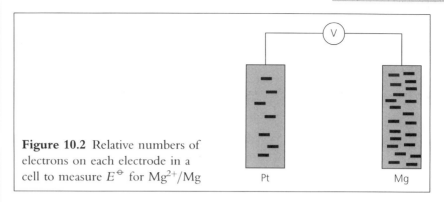

Figure 10.2 Relative numbers of electrons on each electrode in a cell to measure $E^\ominus$ for Mg^{2+}/Mg

Important conclusion

The $E^\ominus$ value measures the relative positions of the two equilibria:

$$Mg^{2+}_{(aq)} + 2e^- \rightleftharpoons Mg_{(s)}$$
$$2H^+_{(aq)} + 2e^- \rightleftharpoons H_{2(g)}$$

The $E^\ominus$ value is negative because the position of the magnesium equilibrium lies further to the left than the hydrogen equilibrium – it releases more electrons.

Exploring the $E^\ominus$ value for Zn^{2+}/Zn (-0.76 volts)

By the same logic, this compares the positions of the two equilibria:

$$Zn^{2+}_{(aq)} + 2e^- \rightleftharpoons Zn_{(s)}$$
$$2H^+_{(aq)} + 2e^- \rightleftharpoons H_{2(g)}$$

Zinc is not so reactive as magnesium, and so the position of the zinc equilibrium is not so far to the left. It still builds up more electrons on the zinc than the hydrogen leaves on the platinum, and so zinc is still the negative terminal. The potential difference is not so great as with magnesium, because there isn't so much difference between the numbers of electrons left on both pieces of metal (see Figure 10.3).

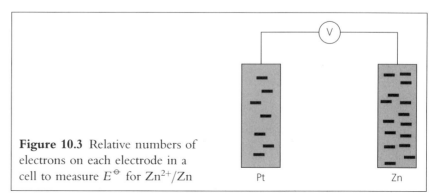

Figure 10.3 Relative numbers of electrons on each electrode in a cell to measure $E^\ominus$ for Zn^{2+}/Zn

Exploring the $E^{\ominus}$ value for Cu^{2+}/Cu ($+0.34$ volts)

$$Cu^{2+}_{(aq)} + 2e^- \rightleftharpoons Cu_{(s)}$$

$$2H^+_{(aq)} + 2e^- \rightleftharpoons H_{2(g)}$$

Copper is less reactive than hydrogen, and does not shed electrons so readily. This time the position of the copper equilibrium lies to the right of the hydrogen equilibrium. Since there will be more electrons on the platinum than on the copper, this time the platinum will be relatively more negative, and the copper relatively positive (see Figure 10.4).

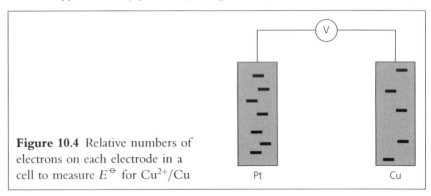

Figure 10.4 Relative numbers of electrons on each electrode in a cell to measure $E^{\ominus}$ for Cu^{2+}/Cu

The electrochemical series (ecs)

If you arrange the electrode potentials in order, putting the most negative ones at the top and ending with the most positive ones at the bottom, you get a list like this:

	$E^{\ominus}$/volts
$Li^+_{(aq)} + e^- \rightleftharpoons Li_{(s)}$	-3.03
$K^+_{(aq)} + e^- \rightleftharpoons K_{(s)}$	-2.92
$Ca^{2+}_{(aq)} + 2e^- \rightleftharpoons Ca_{(s)}$	-2.87
$Na^+_{(aq)} + e^- \rightleftharpoons Na_{(s)}$	-2.71
$Mg^{2+}_{(aq)} + 2e^- \rightleftharpoons Mg_{(s)}$	-2.37
$Al^{3+}_{(aq)} + 3e^- \rightleftharpoons Al_{(s)}$	-1.66
$Zn^{2+}_{(aq)} + 2e^- \rightleftharpoons Zn_{(s)}$	-0.76
$Fe^{2+}_{(aq)} + 2e^- \rightleftharpoons Fe_{(s)}$	-0.44
$Pb^{2+}_{(aq)} + 2e^- \rightleftharpoons Pb_{(s)}$	-0.13
$2H^+_{(aq)} + 2e^- \rightleftharpoons H_{2(g)}$	0.00
$Cu^{2+}_{(aq)} + 2e^- \rightleftharpoons Cu_{(s)}$	$+0.34$
$Ag^+_{(aq)} + e^- \rightleftharpoons Ag_{(s)}$	$+0.80$
$Au^{3+}_{(aq)} + 3e^- \rightleftharpoons Au_{(s)}$	$+1.50$

The ones at the top, with the most negative $E^{\ominus}$ values, are the ones whose equilibria lie furthest to the left – in other words which are best at forming their ions and releasing electrons. Those at the bottom are reluctant to form ions, with their positions of equilibrium lying most to the right.

A metal like sodium is very good at giving electrons away. Whatever else picks up those electrons is reduced. Sodium is a good reducing agent.

Gold (at the bottom of this particular list) is very reluctant to give away electrons. Gold is therefore a poor reducing agent.

On the other hand, $Au^{3+}_{(aq)}$ ions will be very good at picking up electrons to form gold metal. $Au^{3+}_{(aq)}$ will be a very good oxidising agent.

Important summary

A very negative $E^{\ominus}$ value shows that whatever is on the right hand side of the equilibrium releases electrons readily, and so is a good reducing agent.

A very positive $E^{\ominus}$ value shows that whatever is on the left hand side of the equilibrium gains electrons easily, and so is a good oxidising agent.

Adding other oxidising and reducing agents to the ecs

Since the electrochemical series is essentially about redox reactions, it would make sense to include reducing agents and oxidising agents other than metals and their ions – for example, oxidising agents like chlorine or acidified potassium dichromate(VI) or acidified potassium manganate(VII). There is no reason why this cannot be done. All of these have measurable $E^{\ominus}$ values. Because we are thinking about these changes as redox reactions, they are often called "redox potentials" rather than "electrode potentials".

To measure the electrode potential for the chlorine system, an electrode similar to a hydrogen electrode is used:

$$Cl_{2(g)} + 2e^- \rightleftharpoons 2Cl^-_{(aq)}$$

Chlorine gas is bubbled into a solution containing Cl^- ions using platinum in exactly same way as in the hydrogen case.

The measured $E^{\ominus}$ value is $+1.36$ volts, implying that the chlorine equilibrium lies well to the right of the hydrogen equilibrium, and that chlorine is a good oxidising agent – because it is good at picking up electrons.

In a conventional diagram, the chlorine electrode would be written as:

$$||Cl_{2(g)}, 2Cl^-_{(aq)}|Pt_{(s)}$$

or, if it were written as the left hand part of a cell, as:

$$Pt_{(s)}|2Cl^-_{(aq)}, Cl_{2(g)}||$$

The convention is that the species which loses electrons is always written next to the platinum electrode. In this case, it is the chloride ion.

In the acidified potassium manganate(VII) case, the equilibrium is:

$$MnO_4^-_{(aq)} + 8H^+_{(aq)} + 5e^- \rightleftharpoons Mn^{2+}_{(aq)} + 4H_2O_{(l)}$$

Remember: OIL RIG. Reduction is gain of electrons.

Note! These statements are potentially quite confusing to remember. It is much better if you can work them out. Remember that the $E^{\ominus}$ value gives you a guide to the position of equilibrium. The more negative the $E^{\ominus}$ value, the further the equilibrium lies to the left; the more positive, the further it lies to the right.

Notice that the electrons must be written on the left hand side. It does not matter what system you are talking about.

This is the same thing as saying that you write the species with the lowest oxidation state next to the electrode.

The half cell contains all the ions in the equilibrium in concentrations of $1 \, mol \, dm^{-3}$, with a piece of platinum dipping into the mixture. The conventional cell diagram looks like this:

$$||[MnO_4^-{}_{(aq)} + 8H^+{}_{(aq)}], [Mn^{2+}{}_{(aq)} + 4H_2O_{(l)}]|Pt_{(s)}$$

or, if it were the left hand part of a cell:

$$Pt_{(s)}|[Mn^{2+}{}_{(aq)} + 4H_2O_{(l)}], [MnO_4^-{}_{(aq)} + 8H^+{}_{(aq)}]||$$

> Notice the way things are kept tidy by wrapping brackets around them if there is more than one thing on each side of the equilibrium.

Once again, the side of the equilibrium which is losing electrons is written next to the platinum.

The measured $E^{\ominus}$ value is $+1.51$ volts, which means that the MnO_4^- ion is a strong oxidising agent. It is stronger than chlorine because the $E^{\ominus}$ value is even more positive and so the position of equilibrium lies further to the right – implying that MnO_4^- picks up electrons even better than Cl_2 does.

Calculations involving $E^{\ominus}$ values

Suppose you coupled two cells together like this:

$$Cu_{(s)}|Cu^{2+}{}_{(aq)}||2H^+{}_{(aq)}|[H_{2(g)}]Pt_{(s)} - Pt_{(s)}[H_{2(g)}]|2H^+{}_{(aq)}||Zn^{2+}{}_{(aq)}|Zn_{(s)}$$

The total emf could be worked out from the $E^{\ominus}$ values. The copper value is $+0.34$ volts, but this applies when the copper is the right hand electrode. The contribution of the left hand half of this system will therefore be -0.34 volts, because the platinum end is negative. The contribution of the other half will be its $E^{\ominus}$ value of -0.76 volts. That gives a total of -1.10 volts. The negative sign shows that the zinc end (the right hand end as we have written it) is negative.

Since the hydrogen electrode parts of the two cells are, as it were, back-to-back, their contributions simply cancel each other out, and you would get exactly the same voltage if you left them out,

i.e. $\quad Cu_{(s)}|Cu^{2+}{}_{(aq)}||Zn^{2+}{}_{(aq)}|Zn_{(s)}$

This means that we can calculate the value for $E^{\ominus}{}_{cell}$ for any combination of half cells from their $E^{\ominus}$ values. Notice what we have done. We have reversed the sign of the left hand $E^{\ominus}$ value, and added on the right hand one. This is the same as saying:

> *Write down the $E^{\ominus}$ value of the right hand electrode, and take away the $E^{\ominus}$ value of the left hand one.*

Example 1

Find the emf of the cell

$$Fe_{(s)}|Fe^{2+}{}_{(aq)}||Pb^{2+}{}_{(aq)}|Pb_{(s)}$$

The $E^{\ominus}$ values are: Fe^{2+}/Fe -0.44 volts; Pb^{2+}/Pb -0.13 volts

$E^{\ominus}{}_{cell}$ = right hand $E^{\ominus}$ value – left hand $E^{\ominus}$ value

$\qquad = -0.13 - (-0.44)$

$\qquad = +0.31$ volts

> Don't forget to write in the sign of the voltage, even if it's a "+" sign.

Notice that this automatically works out the sign of the right hand electrode. Lead is the positive electrode in this cell.

Example 2

Find the emf of the cell

$$Cu_{(s)}|Cu^{2+}{}_{(aq)}||Mg^{2+}{}_{(aq)}|Mg_{(s)}$$

The $E^{\ominus}$ values are: Cu^{2+}/Cu +0.34 volts; Mg^{2+}/Mg −2.37 volts

$$E^{\ominus}{}_{cell} = \text{right hand } E^{\ominus} \text{ value} - \text{left hand } E^{\ominus} \text{ value}$$
$$= -2.37 - (+0.34)$$
$$= -2.71 \text{ volts}$$

This shows magnesium to be the negative electrode.

Example 3

If you already know one of the $E^{\ominus}$ values, and can measure the cell emf, you can use it to find an $E^{\ominus}$ value for something else.

$$Ag_{(s)}|Ag^+{}_{(aq)}||Sn^{2+}{}_{(aq)}|Sn_{(s)} \qquad E^{\ominus}{}_{cell} = -0.94 \text{ volts}$$

If the $E^{\ominus}$ value for Ag^+/Ag is +0.80 volts, find $E^{\ominus}$ for Sn^{2+}/Sn.

Call the unknown $E^{\ominus}$ value "e".

$$E^{\ominus}{}_{cell} = \text{right hand } E^{\ominus} \text{ value} - \text{left hand } E^{\ominus} \text{ value}$$
$$-0.94 = e - (+0.80)$$
$$e = -0.14 \text{ volts}$$

Example 4

> **Notice** the way the Cr^{3+}/Cr^{2+} electrode system is written. It would consist of a piece of platinum dipped into a mixture of chromium(II) and chromium(III) ions – each of concentration 1 mol dm^{-3}. The Cr^{2+} ion loses an electron, and this is written next to the platinum according to the convention.

Given:

$$Pt_{(s)}|Cr^{2+}{}_{(aq)}, Cr^{3+}{}_{(aq)}||Cu^{2+}{}_{(aq)}|Cu_{(s)} \qquad E^{\ominus}{}_{cell} = +0.75 \text{ volts}$$
$$Cu^{2+}{}_{(aq)} + 2e^- \rightleftharpoons Cu_{(s)} \qquad E^{\ominus} = +0.34 \text{ volts}$$

Find $E^{\ominus}$ for $Cr^{3+}{}_{(aq)} + e^- \rightleftharpoons Cr^{2+}{}_{(aq)}$

Call the unknown $E^{\ominus}$ value "e".

$$E^{\ominus}{}_{cell} = \text{right hand } E^{\ominus} \text{ value} - \text{left hand } E^{\ominus} \text{ value}$$
$$+0.75 = +0.34 - e$$
$$e = -0.41 \text{ volts}$$

Problem • 1

Calculate the emfs of the following cells:

(a) $Al_{(s)}|Al^{3+}{}_{(aq)}||Cd^{2+}{}_{(aq)}|Cd_{(s)}$

(b) $Ag_{(s)}|Ag^+{}_{(aq)}||Cu^{2+}{}_{(aq)}|Cu_{(s)}$

(c) $Pt_{(s)}|Fe^{2+}{}_{(aq)}, Fe^{3+}{}_{(aq)}||Cl_{2(g)}, 2Cl^-{}_{(aq)}|Pt_{(s)}$

($E^{\ominus}$ values: $Al^{3+}/Al = -1.66$ volts; $Cd^{2+}/Cd = -0.40$ volts; $Ag^+/Ag = +0.80$ volts; $Cu^{2+}/Cu = +0.34$ volts; $Fe^{3+}/Fe^{2+} = +0.77$ volts; $Cl_2/2Cl^- = +1.36$ volts)

Problem • 2

Calculate the unknown $E^{\ominus}$ values from $E^{\ominus}{}_{cell}$ and the $E^{\ominus}$ given values below:

(a) Cr^{3+}/Cr if $E^{\ominus}{}_{cell} = -0.49$ volts for $Ni_{(s)}|Ni^{2+}{}_{(aq)}||Cr^{3+}{}_{(aq)}|Cr_{(s)}$

(b) V^{3+}/V^{2+} if $E^{\ominus}{}_{cell} = -2.11$ volts for $Pt_{(s)}|V^{2+}{}_{(aq)}, V^{3+}{}_{(aq)}||Mg^{2+}{}_{(aq)}|Mg_{(s)}$

(c) Mn^{2+}/Mn if $E^{\ominus}{}_{cell} = +0.79$ volts for $Mn_{(s)}|Mn^{2+}{}_{(aq)}||Cd^{2+}{}_{(aq)}|Cd_{(s)}$

($E^{\ominus}$ values: $Ni^{2+}/Ni = -0.25$ volts; $Mg^{2+}/Mg = -2.37$ volts; $Cd^{2+}/Cd = -0.40$ volts)

Using $E^{\ominus}$ values to predict the feasibility of redox reactions

Suppose you set up a cell so that electrons could flow from one electrode to the other, for example as in Figure 10.5.

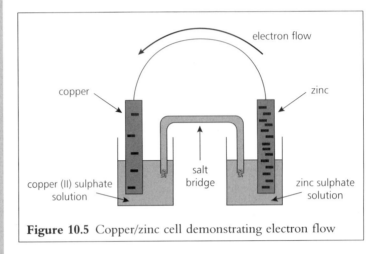

Figure 10.5 Copper/zinc cell demonstrating electron flow

Electrons will flow from where there are lots of them to where there are less. Now consider the two equilibria involved:

$$Zn^{2+}_{(aq)} + 2e^- \rightleftharpoons Zn_{(s)} \qquad E^{\ominus} = -0.76\,volts$$

$$Cu^{2+}_{(aq)} + 2e^- \rightleftharpoons Cu_{(s)} \qquad E^{\ominus} = +0.34\,volts$$

Because electrons are flowing, the equilibria are disturbed, and you can apply Le Chatelier's Principle.

The loss of electrons from the left hand side of the zinc equilibrium causes more zinc to ionise to replace them. The addition of electrons to the copper equilibrium causes that equilibrium to move to the right:

$$Zn^{2+}_{(aq)} + 2e^- \rightleftharpoons Zn_{(s)}$$

$$\downarrow$$

$$Cu^{2+}_{(aq)} + 2e^- \rightleftharpoons Cu_{(s)}$$

As long as electrons continue to flow, the zinc reaction becomes one way – moving from right to left. The zinc electrode dissolves to give zinc ions.

Similarly, the copper(II) ions will continue to pick up electrons and be deposited onto the electrode as metallic copper:

$$Zn_{(s)} \rightarrow Zn^{2+}_{(aq)} + 2e^-$$

$$Cu^{2+}_{(aq)} + 2e^- \rightarrow Cu_{(s)}$$

➤ If you are not happy about combining half-equations to give the overall equation for a reaction, read pages 12 to 14 in Chapter 1.

These two half equations can be combined to give an overall equation for the reaction taking place in the cell as a whole:

$$Zn_{(s)} + Cu^{2+}_{(aq)} \rightarrow Zn^{2+}_{(aq)} + Cu_{(s)}$$

Now this is **exactly** the same as would happen if you placed a piece of zinc into some copper(II) sulphate solution in a test-tube. The only difference now is that the zinc would give its electrons directly to the copper(II) ions, instead of them having to flow along a bit of wire first.

The net effect of all this is that we could take **any** redox reaction (one involving electron transfer) and consider it as if the two half reactions were taking place in two half cells and use $E^{\ominus}$ values to make predictions about whether the reaction was feasible or not. Some examples will make the process clear.

Example 5

➤ **Notice** that some text books and examiners give you $E^{\ominus}$ values with the equations written with arrows ($\rightarrow$) rather than equilibrium signs. This immediately confuses everything! $E^{\ominus}$ values refer to equilibria – so physically (or at least mentally) replace the offending arrows with $\rightleftharpoons$.

Will magnesium reduce copper(II) ions in solution to copper?

$$Mg^{2+}_{(aq)} + 2e^- \rightleftharpoons Mg_{(s)} \qquad E^{\ominus} = -2.37 \text{ volts}$$
$$Cu^{2+}_{(aq)} + 2e^- \rightleftharpoons Cu_{(s)} \qquad E^{\ominus} = +0.34 \text{ volts}$$

Think of it like this – the magnesium equilibrium has the more negative $E^{\ominus}$ value. Its equilibrium lies further to the left and therefore produces more electrons. These will pass to the copper equilibrium, and the two equilibria will tip as follows:

➤ The **bold** is to pick out the things we are starting from.

$$Mg^{2+}_{(aq)} + 2e^- \rightleftharpoons \mathbf{Mg_{(s)}} \qquad E^{\ominus} = -2.37 \text{ volts}$$
$$\downarrow$$
$$\mathbf{Cu^{2+}_{(aq)}} + 2e^- \rightleftharpoons Cu_{(s)} \qquad E^{\ominus} = +0.34 \text{ volts}$$

So will magnesium reduce copper(II) ions to copper? Yes, it will. The equilibria will tip in the directions shown to give the half equations:

$$Mg_{(s)} \rightarrow Mg^{2+}_{(aq)} + 2e^-$$
$$Cu^{2+}_{(aq)} + 2e^- \rightarrow Cu_{(s)}$$

These could be combined to give the overall equation:

$$Mg_{(s)} + Cu^{2+}_{(aq)} \rightarrow Mg^{2+}_{(aq)} + Cu_{(s)}$$

Example 5a

Another way of looking at the same problem

If the equilibria are allowed to tip in this way, it will always happen that the one with the more positive $E^{\ominus}$ value will move to the right and the one with the less positive $E^{\ominus}$ value to the left. You can use this to decide whether a reaction is possible by checking to see whether the half reaction you want to move to the right has the more positive $E^{\ominus}$ value.

➤ To find out whether "a" is more positive than "b", subtract "b" from "a" and see if you get a positive answer.

■ Write down the $E^{\ominus}$ value for the reaction you want to move to the right.

■ Subtract the $E^{\ominus}$ value of the reaction you want to move to the left.

■ If the answer is positive, these changes are possible. If the answer is negative, your reactions will not work.

> ➤ You may wonder what the point is of working out $E^{\ominus}_{cell}$. It is obvious that $+0.34$ is more positive than -2.37! You may find that your examiners phrase questions in such a way that you are forced to calculate $E^{\ominus}_{cell}$. It would be worth your while to research some recent exam papers to find out how your examiners approach this sort of problem, and then make sure that you can use the method they seem to prefer.

In this case, you want the copper equilibrium to move to the right. Has this got the more positive $E^{\ominus}$ value? $+0.34 - (-2.37) = +2.71$. Yes!

What you are doing in essence is working out $E^{\ominus}_{cell}$ for the cell where the right hand electrode is the equilibrium you want to move to the right.

Summary: Work out $E^{\ominus}_{cell}$ for the cell where the reaction you want to move to the right is the right hand electrode. If $E^{\ominus}_{cell}$ is positive, the reaction is possible. If it is negative, it won't work.

Example 6

Will copper reduce nickel(II) ions in solution to nickel?

$$Cu^{2+}_{(aq)} + 2e^- \rightleftharpoons Cu_{(s)} \qquad E^{\ominus} = +0.34 \text{ volts}$$

$$Ni^{2+}_{(aq)} + 2e^- \rightleftharpoons Ni_{(s)} \qquad E^{\ominus} = -0.25 \text{ volts}$$

Nickel has a more negative $E^{\ominus}$ value and so gives away electrons more readily than copper does. The two equilibria would tend to move as follows:

$$Cu^{2+}_{(aq)} + 2e^- \rightleftharpoons \mathbf{Cu_{(s)}} \qquad E^{\ominus} = +0.34 \text{ volts}$$

$$\mathbf{Ni^{2+}_{(aq)}} + 2e^- \rightleftharpoons Ni_{(s)} \qquad E^{\ominus} = -0.25 \text{ volts}$$

This time there is a problem. The equilibria would tend to move to give the things we are starting from. The Ni^{2+} ions can't turn into nickel because that would go against the equilibrium's preferred direction. Similarly copper cannot turn into Cu^{2+} ions.

So will copper reduce nickel(II) ions to nickel? No, it won't.

Example 6a

Another way of looking at the same problem

If copper is going to reduce nickel(II) ions to nickel, you want the nickel equilibrium to move to the right. Work out $E^{\ominus}_{cell}$ for the cell where the nickel equilibrium is the right hand electrode:

$$-0.25 - (+0.34) = -0.59 \text{ volts}$$

The negative answer implies that the reaction won't work.

Example 7

Will iron(III) ions oxidise iodide ions in solution to iodine?

$$Fe^{3+}_{(aq)} + e^- \rightleftharpoons Fe^{2+}_{(aq)} \qquad E^{\ominus} = +0.77 \text{ volts}$$

$$I_{2(aq)} + 2e^- \rightleftharpoons 2I^-_{(aq)} \qquad E^{\ominus} = +0.54 \text{ volts}$$

> In each case, you are simply looking at the relative positions of the two equilibria. If electrons are allowed to flow, the one which lies furthest to the left will tend to move leftwards. The one which lies furthest to the right will tend to move to the right if electrons are allowed to flow. If the substances that you start with can, as it were, "slide along the arrows" that you have drawn, there will be a reaction. If not, the reaction is not feasible.

> The iron half equation has to be multiplied by 2 to provide the two electrons that the iodine half equation needs. If you are not sure about that, then you really do need to refer back to Chapter 1.

The iodine equilibrium lies further to the left because it is less positive. It releases more electrons than the iron equilibrium, and the preferred movements are therefore:

$$Fe^{3+}_{(aq)} + e^- \rightleftharpoons Fe^{2+}_{(aq)} \qquad E^\ominus = +0.77 \text{ volts}$$

$$I_{2(aq)} + 2e^- \rightleftharpoons 2I^-_{(aq)} \qquad E^\ominus = +0.54 \text{ volts}$$

That movement is possible given what we are starting from, and so the reaction will work. The half equations are:

$$(Fe^{3+}_{(aq)} + e^- \rightarrow Fe^{2+}_{(aq)}) \times 2$$

$$2I^-_{(aq)} \rightarrow I_{2(aq)} + 2e^-$$

These combine to give:

$$2Fe^{3+}_{(aq)} + 2I^-_{(aq)} \rightarrow 2Fe^{2+}_{(aq)} + I_{2(aq)}$$

Example 7a

Another way of looking at the same problem

This time you want the iron equilibrium to move to the right. Work out $E^\ominus_{cell}$ for the cell where the iron system is the right hand electrode:

$$+0.77 - (+0.54) = +0.23 \text{ volts}$$

The positive answer shows that the reaction is feasible.

Example 8

Is this reaction feasible? $Pb_{(s)} + 2Cr^{3+}_{(aq)} \rightarrow Pb^{2+}_{(aq)} + 2Cr^{2+}_{(aq)}$

$$Cr^{3+}_{(aq)} + e^- \rightleftharpoons Cr^{2+}_{(aq)} \qquad E^\ominus = -0.41 \text{ volts}$$

$$Pb^{2+}_{(aq)} + 2e^- \rightleftharpoons Pb_{(s)} \qquad E^\ominus = -0.13 \text{ volts}$$

The chromium equilibrium lies further to the left:

> When you are investigating the $E^\ominus$ values, you take no account of the balance in the overall equation. In this case, the overall equation has $2Cr^{3+}$. You **must not** double the $E^\ominus$ value. $E^\ominus$ values are always used in their "raw" state.

$$Cr^{3+}_{(aq)} + e^- \rightleftharpoons Cr^{2+}_{(aq)} \qquad E^\ominus = -0.41 \text{ volts}$$

$$Pb^{2+}_{(aq)} + 2e^- \rightleftharpoons Pb_{(s)} \qquad E^\ominus = -0.13 \text{ volts}$$

Any reaction between Cr^{3+} ions and lead would need the equilibria to move against their preferred directions, and this is impossible. The reaction is not feasible.

Example 8a

Another way of looking at the same problem

The reaction you want to move to the right is the chromium one. Work out $E^{\ominus}_{cell}$ for the cell where the chromium system is the right hand electrode:

$$-0.41 - (-0.13) = -0.28 \, \text{volts}$$

The negative answer shows that the reaction is not feasible.

Example 9

Potassium manganate(VII) solution acidified with dilute sulphuric acid, and potassium dichromate(VI) solution acidified with dilute sulphuric acid are both oxidising agents. Are either, or both, strong enough to oxidise chloride ions to chlorine?

$$Cl_{2(g)} + 2e^- \rightleftharpoons 2Cl^-_{(aq)} \qquad\qquad\qquad\qquad\qquad E^{\ominus} = +1.36 \, \text{volts}$$

$$MnO_4{}^-_{(aq)} + 8H^+_{(aq)} + 5e^- \rightleftharpoons Mn^{2+}_{(aq)} + 4H_2O_{(l)} \qquad E^{\ominus} = +1.51 \, \text{volts}$$

$$Cr_2O_7{}^{2-}_{(aq)} + 14H^+_{(aq)} + 6e^- \rightleftharpoons 2Cr^{3+}_{(aq)} + 7H_2O_{(l)} \quad E^{\ominus} = +1.33 \, \text{volts}$$

If chloride ions are oxidised to chlorine, the chlorine equilibrium will have to release electrons and tip to the left. For the reaction to work, the chlorine $E^{\ominus}$ value must therefore be the more negative (or less positive) one.

+1.36 (the chlorine value) is less positive than +1.51, so the acidified potassium manganate(VII) is a strong enough oxidising agent to "persuade" the chloride ions to give up electrons.

Comparing the chlorine and chromium equilibria, +1.36 is **more positive** than +1.33. This is not what you need, and so acidified potassium dichromate(VI) will not oxidise chloride ions to chlorine.

A word of warning!

Potassium dichromate(VI) solution does in fact oxidise **concentrated** hydrochloric acid (containing both hydrogen ions and chloride ions as the equations demand) to chlorine.

If you use concentrated hydrochloric acid, the concentrations of the ions are about $10 \, \text{mol dm}^{-3}$ – not the $1 \, \text{mol dm}^{-3}$ that standard conditions demand. If you change the conditions the electrode potentials also change.

$$Cl_{2(g)} + 2e^- \rightleftharpoons 2Cl^-_{(aq)} \qquad E^{\ominus} = +1.36 \, \text{volts}$$

Increasing the Cl^- ion concentration moves the chlorine equilibrium to the left according to Le Chatelier. This means that the electrode potential value will become less positive, i.e. less than $+1.36$ volts.

$$Cr_2O_7{}^{2-}_{(aq)} + 14H^+_{(aq)} + 6e^- \rightleftharpoons 2Cr^{3+}_{(aq)} + 7H_2O_{(l)}$$
$$E^{\ominus} = +1.33 \, \text{volts}$$

Increasing the H^+ concentration will tip this equilibrium to the right, making the electrode potential more positive, i.e. more than $+1.33$ volts.

The electrode potentials do not have to change very much before their relative positiveness and negativeness reverses, and so a reaction becomes possible.

So be careful about applying $E^{\ominus}$ values under non-standard conditions – particularly if the values you are considering are numerically close together.

Example 10

Water can be oxidised to oxygen according to the equation

$$2H_2O_{(l)} \rightarrow O_{2(g)} + 4H^+_{(aq)} + 4e^-$$

Given the following $E^\ominus$ values, what can you use to oxidise water in this way?

$MnO_4^-_{(aq)} + 8H^+_{(aq)} + 5e^- \rightleftharpoons Mn^{2+}_{(aq)} + 4H_2O_{(l)}$	$E^\ominus = +1.51$ volts
$Cl_{2(g)} + 2e^- \rightleftharpoons 2Cl^-_{(aq)}$	$E^\ominus = +1.36$ volts
$Cr_2O_7^{2-}_{(aq)} + 14H^+_{(aq)} + 6e^- \rightleftharpoons 2Cr^{3+}_{(aq)} + 7H_2O_{(l)}$	$E^\ominus = +1.33$ volts
$O_{2(g)} + 4H^+_{(aq)} + 4e^- \rightleftharpoons 2H_2O_{(l)}$	$E^\ominus = +1.23$ volts
$Br_{2(l)} + 2e^- \rightleftharpoons 2Br^-_{(aq)}$	$E^\ominus = +1.07$ volts

In order to get oxygen from water, the water equilibrium has to move from right to left:

$$O_{2(g)} + 4H^+_{(aq)} + 4e^- \rightleftharpoons \mathbf{2H_2O_{(l)}} \quad E^\ominus = +1.23 \text{ volts}$$

To drive it this way, you would have to couple it with an equilibrium with a more positive $E^\ominus$ value. You could use any oxidising agent with an $E^\ominus$ value more positive than $+1.23$ volts.

You could therefore use MnO_4^-/H^+, Cl_2, or $Cr_2O_7^{2-}/H^+$, but not bromine.

Another word of warning!
We have just shown that dichromate(VI) ions – usually from potassium dichromate(VI) – can oxidise water to oxygen. In practice, potassium dichromate(VI) **never** oxidises water to oxygen!
The problem is that although the reaction is feasible according to the $E^\ominus$ values, a very high activation energy barrier prevents the reaction actually happening.

So be careful! Although, if the $E^\ominus$ values are right, a reaction may be possible, you cannot be sure that it will actually happen in the test tube. What you can say with certainty is that if the $E^\ominus$ values are wrong then it definitely will not happen (at least as long as you are working under standard conditions – see the previous warning note).

Problem • 3

Which of the following reactions are feasible?

(a) $3Co^{2+}_{(aq)} + 2Al_{(s)} \rightarrow 3Co_{(s)} + 2Al^{3+}_{(aq)}$

(b) $2Na^+_{(aq)} + Mg_{(s)} \rightarrow 2Na_{(s)} + Mg^{2+}_{(aq)}$

(c) $2Br^-_{(aq)} + Cl_{2(g)} \rightarrow Br_{2(l)} + 2Cl^-_{(aq)}$

(d) $2Fe^{2+}_{(aq)} + Cl_{2(g)} \rightarrow 2Fe^{3+}_{(aq)} + 2Cl^-_{(aq)}$

($E^\ominus$ values: $Al^{3+}/Al = -1.66$ volts; $Co^{2+}/Co = -0.28$ volts; $Na^+/Na = -2.71$ volts; $Mg^{2+}/Mg = -2.37$ volts; $Br_2/2Br^- = +1.07$ volts; $Cl_2/2Cl^- = +1.36$ volts; $Fe^{3+}/Fe^{2+} = +0.77$ volts)

Problem • 4

In each of the following examples, decide whether the reaction is feasible, and if it is, write the equation for the reaction.

(a) Using chlorine to oxidise sulphide ions to sulphur:

$$S_{(s)} + 2e^- \rightleftharpoons S^{2-}_{(aq)} \qquad E^{\ominus} = -0.48 \text{ volts}$$
$$Cl_{2(g)} + 2e^- \rightleftharpoons 2Cl^-_{(aq)} \qquad E^{\ominus} = +1.36 \text{ volts}$$

(b) Using iodate(V) ions to oxidise iodide ions to iodine:

$$2IO_3^-_{(aq)} + 12H^+_{(aq)} + 10e^- \rightleftharpoons I_{2(aq)} + 6H_2O_{(l)} \qquad E^{\ominus} = +1.19 \text{ volts}$$
$$I_{2(aq)} + 2e^- \rightleftharpoons 2I^-_{(aq)} \qquad E^{\ominus} = +0.54 \text{ volts}$$

(c) Using silver to reduce tin(IV) ions to tin(II) ions:

$$Ag^+_{(aq)} + e^- \rightleftharpoons Ag_{(s)} \qquad E^{\ominus} = +0.80 \text{ volts}$$
$$Sn^{4+}_{(aq)} + 2e^- \rightleftharpoons Sn^{2+}_{(aq)} \qquad E^{\ominus} = +0.15 \text{ volts}$$

(d) Using zinc to reduce chromium(III) ions to chromium(II) ions:

$$Zn^{2+}_{(aq)} + 2e^- \rightleftharpoons Zn_{(s)} \qquad E^{\ominus} = -0.76 \text{ volts}$$
$$Cr^{3+}_{(aq)} + e^- \rightleftharpoons Cr^{2+}_{(aq)} \qquad E^{\ominus} = -0.41 \text{ volts}$$

End of chapter checklist

Can you do the following things?

■ Understand what is meant by a standard electrode (redox) potential.

■ Understand the conventions used in cell diagrams.

■ Know that the sign of $E^{\ominus}_{cell}$ tells you the sign of the right hand electrode.

■ Know that cell equilibria are always written with the electrons on the left hand side.

■ Calculate $E^{\ominus}_{cell}$ from given $E^{\ominus}$ values.

■ Use $E^{\ominus}$ values to predict the feasibility of redox reactions.

Revision problems

Numerical answers are provided for these problems, but no worked solutions.

Use the $E^{\ominus}$ values after question 11 for questions 5 to 11.

Calculate the emfs of the following cells:

Problem • 5

(a) $Cu_{(s)}|Cu^{2+}_{(aq)}||Zn^{2+}_{(aq)}|Zn_{(s)}$

(b) $Pt_{(s)}|Cr^{2+}_{(aq)}, Cr^{3+}_{(aq)}||Fe^{3+}_{(aq)}, Fe^{2+}_{(aq)}|Pt_{(s)}$

(c) $Pt_{(s)}|V^{2+}_{(aq)}, V^{3+}_{(aq)}||Mg^{2+}_{(aq)}|Mg_{(s)}$

Problem • 6

Calculate the unknown $E^{\ominus}$ values from the given values of $E^{\ominus}_{cell}$:

(a) Al^{3+}/Al if $E^{\ominus}_{cell} = -0.71$ volts for $Al_{(s)}|Al^{3+}_{(aq)}||Mg^{2+}_{(aq)}|Mg_{(s)}$

(b) Ni^{2+}/Ni if $E^{\ominus}_{cell} = -1.05$ volts for $Ag_{(s)}|Ag^+_{(aq)}||Ni^{2+}_{(aq)}|Ni_{(s)}$

Problem • 7

Which of the following reactions are feasible?

(a) $Zn_{(s)} + 2V^{3+}_{(aq)} \rightarrow Zn^{2+}_{(aq)} + 2V^{2+}_{(aq)}$

(b) $Fe^{3+}_{(aq)} + Ag_{(s)} \rightarrow Fe^{2+}_{(aq)} + Ag^+_{(aq)}$

(c) $2Fe^{2+}_{(aq)} + I_{2(aq)} \rightarrow 2Fe^{3+}_{(aq)} + 2I^-_{(aq)}$

(d) $3Cu_{(s)} + 2NO_3^-_{(aq)} + 8H^+_{(aq)} \rightarrow 3Cu^{2+}_{(aq)} + 2NO_{(g)} + 4H_2O_{(l)}$

Problem • 8

From the list of $E^\ominus$ values after problem 11, give an oxidising agent which could be used to oxidise Mn^{2+} ions to MnO_4^- ions, and write an equation for the reaction.

Problem • 9

Will Cr^{2+} ions reduce V^{3+} ions to V^{2+} ions? If so write the equation for the change.

Problem • 10

Will nitric acid (containing $H^+_{(aq)}$ and $NO_3^-_{(aq)}$) oxidise Fe^{2+} ions to Fe^{3+} ions? If so write the equation for the change.

Problem • 11

Will acidified potassium dichromate(VI) solution oxidise SO_4^{2-} ions to $S_2O_8^{2-}$ ions? If so write the equation for the change.

$E^\ominus$ values:

$Mg^{2+}_{(aq)} + 2e^- \rightleftharpoons Mg_{(s)}$	$E^\ominus = -2.37$ volts
$Zn^{2+}_{(aq)} + 2e^- \rightleftharpoons Zn_{(s)}$	$E^\ominus = -0.76$ volts
$Cr^{3+}_{(aq)} + e^- \rightleftharpoons Cr^{2+}_{(aq)}$	$E^\ominus = -0.41$ volts
$V^{3+}_{(aq)} + e^- \rightleftharpoons V^{2+}_{(aq)}$	$E^\ominus = -0.26$ volts
$Cu^{2+}_{(aq)} + 2e^- \rightleftharpoons Cu_{(s)}$	$E^\ominus = +0.34$ volts
$I_{2(aq)} + 2e^- \rightleftharpoons 2I^-_{(aq)}$	$E^\ominus = +0.54$ volts
$Fe^{3+}_{(aq)} + e^- \rightleftharpoons Fe^{2+}_{(aq)}$	$E^\ominus = +0.77$ volts
$Ag^+_{(aq)} + e^- \rightleftharpoons Ag_{(s)}$	$E^\ominus = +0.80$ volts
$NO_3^-_{(aq)} + 4H^+_{(aq)} + 3e^- \rightleftharpoons NO_{(g)} + 2H_2O_{(l)}$	$E^\ominus = +0.96$ volts
$Cr_2O_7^{2-}_{(aq)} + 14H^+_{(aq)} + 6e^- \rightleftharpoons 2Cr^{3+}_{(aq)} + 7H_2O_{(l)}$	$E^\ominus = +1.33$ volts
$MnO_4^-_{(aq)} + 8H^+_{(aq)} + 5e^- \rightleftharpoons Mn^{2+}_{(aq)} + 4H_2O_{(l)}$	$E^\ominus = +1.51$ volts
$S_2O_8^{2-}_{(aq)} + 2e^- \rightleftharpoons 2SO_4^{2-}_{(aq)}$	$E^\ominus = +2.01$ volts

Problem • 12

Nitric acid (containing $H^+_{(aq)}$ and $NO_3^-_{(aq)}$) was added to a violet coloured solution containing $V^{2+}_{(aq)}$ ions. Use the following $E^\ominus$ values to predict what colour the solution will become. $V^{3+}_{(aq)}$ ions are green; $VO^{2+}_{(aq)}$ ions are blue; $VO_2^+_{(aq)}$ ions are yellow.

$V^{3+}_{(aq)} + e^- \rightleftharpoons V^{2+}_{(aq)}$	$E^\ominus = -0.26$ volts
$VO^{2+}_{(aq)} + 2H^+_{(aq)} + e^- \rightleftharpoons V^{3+}_{(aq)} + H_2O_{(l)}$	$E^\ominus = +0.34$ volts
$VO_2^+_{(aq)} + 2H^+_{(aq)} + e^- \rightleftharpoons VO^{2+}_{(aq)} + H_2O_{(l)}$	$E^\ominus = +1.00$ volts
$NO_3^-_{(aq)} + 4H^+_{(aq)} + 3e^- \rightleftharpoons NO_{(g)} + 2H_2O_{(l)}$	$E^\ominus = +0.96$ volts

Entropy and Free Energy

This chapter looks at how you can work out whether a particular reaction is feasible or not, and how that feasibility changes with temperature. There isn't any difficult maths involved.

It is especially important with this topic to know what sort of questions your examiners are going to ask. Different Examination Boards may put the emphasis in quite different places, and you will only know exactly which parts your examiners are going to ask about if you do some research on past papers.

Feasible and spontaneous reactions

Spontaneous reactions

If you drop some magnesium ribbon into a test tube of dilute sulphuric acid you get an immediate reaction with lots of fizzing as hydrogen is produced. It happens spontaneously:

$$Mg + H_2SO_4 \rightarrow MgSO_4 + H_2$$

Similarly, if you added some solid sodium hydrogencarbonate to a test tube of dilute hydrochloric acid, there is immediate fizzing as carbon dioxide is evolved – another spontaneous change:

$$NaHCO_3 + HCl \rightarrow NaCl + H_2O + CO_2$$

Or again, if you drop some salt into water, it dissolves in time without any intervention on your part – another spontaneous process.

However, if you have a diamond (made of pure carbon) it does not burn spontaneously in oxygen to form carbon dioxide – although it would if you heated it to get the reaction started. And if you were to drop a gold ring into some dilute hydrochloric acid, it would never react, however much you heated it or however long you waited.

There are two quite separate reasons why reactions might not happen.

■ The reaction might have a **large activation energy** which is preventing it from happening at the particular temperature you are using. The diamond which will not burn at room temperature is an example of this. The reaction is, however, **feasible** once that activation energy barrier is breached.
■ The reaction may **not be feasible** – in other words, something other than activation energy is stopping it from working. The gold and hydrochloric acid reaction is a good example of this kind.

Confusingly, in this area of work, the words "spontaneous" and "feasible" are often used interchangeably – so that the combustion of diamond at room temperature is said to be **spontaneous**. This so obviously defies common sense, that we shall use the word **feasible** from now on. A feasible (or spontaneous) reaction is one which could go of its own accord at a particular temperature if there wasn't an activation energy barrier in the way.

Why are some reactions feasible while others aren't?

It is very tempting to relate the feasibility of a reaction to whether it is exothermic or endothermic. It is common experience that things fall downhill – in other words, from a higher energy level to a lower one. It would be quite surprising to find something spontaneously falling uphill!

You might think that an endothermic change is not feasible, and cannot happen spontaneously. You might also think that an exothermic change is feasible and may happen spontaneously provided the activation energy barrier is not too high. Unfortunately, it's not quite as simple as that, and you would be wrong!

In the examples of reactions given on the previous page:

- The magnesium and sulphuric acid reaction is clearly **feasible**. It is **exothermic**; it has a **low activation energy**; it happens spontaneously.

- The diamond burning to form carbon dioxide is a strongly **exothermic** change. It is **feasible**, but has a **high activation energy** and so does not happen spontaneously.

- The reaction (or lack of it) between gold and hydrochloric acid is **endothermic** and turns out **not to be feasible**.

So far so good! **But**...

- The reaction between sodium hydrogencarbonate and hydrochloric acid is **endothermic** – and yet it happens spontaneously in the cold. Clearly, it is a **feasible** reaction.

- Most of the ionic solids which dissolve in water do so by an **endothermic** process, and salt is a typical example. Everyday experience says that dissolving salt in water is a **feasible** process.

So, although the enthalpy change (whether the reaction is exothermic or endothermic) does matter in deciding if a process is feasible or not, there is a second factor which also has to be considered. That second factor is the change in **entropy** during the reaction.

Entropy

What is entropy?

One of the problems with this topic is that the key terms are mathematically derived, and this can make it quite daunting. However it is possible to survive A level by simply taking entropy to be a measure of the amount of disorder in a particular substance.

A perfectly ordered crystalline substance at absolute zero has an entropy of zero. Liquids are more disordered than solids, and so have greater entropy. Gases are more disordered still, and so their entropy is greater still.

Entropy is given the symbol S. Standard entropy is given the symbol $S^{\ominus}$. "Standard" implies a temperature of 298 K and a pressure of 1 atmosphere.

Entropy is measured in units of $J K^{-1} mol^{-1}$. You may also come across $J mol^{-1} K^{-1}$. It means exactly the same thing.

➤ If you want to explore other values, you will find extensive tables of them in data books.

Some examples (all values in $J K^{-1} mol^{-1}$)

carbon (as diamond)	2.4
silicon	18.8
calcium oxide	39.7
calcium carbonate	92.9

All of these are highly ordered solids: their entropy is therefore low. You can see that as the solid gets more complicated, the entropy tends to increase.

water (solid – ice)	48 (approximate value)
water (liquid)	69.9
water (gas – steam)	189

➤ The liquid water value is lower than you might expect for a liquid. This is due to the order imposed by the hydrogen bonds in water.

This illustrates the greater entropy as you go from solid to liquid to gas, because of the greater disorder amongst the particles.

carbon monoxide	197.6
carbon dioxide	213.6

And, again, this illustrates the fact that as molecules get more complicated their entropy tends to increase.

Entropy changes during reactions, $\Delta S^{\ominus}_{system}$

The word "system" refers to the reaction taking place. Later on, you may also have to worry about entropy changes in the surroundings as well. These are referred to as $\Delta S^{\ominus}_{surroundings}$.

➤ **Check** past examination papers! If questions **never** include symbols like $\Delta S^{\ominus}_{system}$, $\Delta S^{\ominus}_{surroundings}$ and $\Delta S^{\ominus}_{total}$, then you can leave the word "system" out. Any reference in a question on such an examination paper to the entropy change $\Delta S^{\ominus}$ implies $\Delta S^{\ominus}_{system}$.

$$\Delta S^{\ominus}_{system} = \Sigma S^{\ominus}(\textbf{products}) - \Sigma S^{\ominus}(\textbf{reactants})$$

This rather worrying looking expression is actually trivial! The symbol "Σ" (sigma) means "the sum of". So, to find the entropy change of the system, you add up the entropies of all the products and take away the entropies of all the reactants. Put simply:

Change in entropy = what you end up with – what you started with

Example 1

➤ In this example, and subsequent examples in this section, "entropy change" implies entropy change of the system – i.e. of the reaction that is happening.

Calculate the entropy change during the reaction

$$CaCO_{3(s)} \rightarrow CaO_{(s)} + CO_{2(g)}$$

$S^{\ominus}(CaCO_{3(s)})$	$92.9 \, J K^{-1} \, mol^{-1}$
$S^{\ominus}(CaO_{(s)})$	$39.7 \, J K^{-1} \, mol^{-1}$
$S^{\ominus}(CO_{2(g)})$	$213.6 \, J K^{-1} \, mol^{-1}$

The entropy of the things you end up with $= 39.7 + 213.6 \, J K^{-1} \, mol^{-1}$

$$= 253.3 \, J K^{-1} \, mol^{-1}$$

The entropy of the things you started with $= 92.9 \, J K^{-1} \, mol^{-1}$

$$\Delta S^{\ominus}_{system} = 253.3 - 92.9 = +160.4 \, J K^{-1} \, mol^{-1}$$

➤ It is **essential** to quote the sign of the final entropy change. The + sign matters!

The entropy of the system has increased. Is this surprising? No. You start with a single substance and produce two new ones, one of which is a gas. The products are bound to be more disordered than the original calcium carbonate. Any reaction in which there is an increase in the number of gas molecules is likely to lead to an increase in entropy.

Example 2

Work out the entropy change during the reaction:

$$2NaHCO_{3(s)} \rightarrow Na_2CO_{3(s)} + CO_{2(g)} + H_2O_{(l)}$$

$S^{\ominus}(NaHCO_{3(s)})$	101.7 J K^{-1} mol^{-1}
$S^{\ominus}(Na_2CO_{3(s)})$	135.0 J K^{-1} mol^{-1}
$S^{\ominus}(CO_{2(g)})$	213.6 J K^{-1} mol^{-1}
$S^{\ominus}(H_2O_{(l)})$	69.9 J K^{-1} mol^{-1}

Entropy of the things you end up with $= 135.0 + 213.6 + 69.9$ J K^{-1} mol^{-1}
$$= 418.5 \text{ J K}^{-1} \text{ mol}^{-1}$$

➤ **Hint!** There are 2 moles of NaHCO$_3$, so the entropy value has to be multiplied by 2

Entropy of the things you started with $= 2 \times 101.7$ J K^{-1} mol^{-1}
$$= 203.4 \text{ J K}^{-1} \text{ mol}^{-1}$$

$$\Delta S^{\ominus}_{\text{system}} = 418.5 - 203.4 = +215.1 \text{ J K}^{-1} \text{ mol}^{-1}$$

Note that the mol^{-1} in the units refers to the equation as a whole, and not to one mole of NaHCO$_3$.

Once again the entropy of the system has increased, and once again you could have predicted it. A single solid has produced three different substances, including a gas and a liquid. Those are bound to be more disordered than the original solid.

Example 3

Calculate the entropy change for the reaction:

$$N_{2(g)} + 3H_{2(g)} \rightarrow 2NH_{3(g)}$$

$S^{\ominus}(N_{2(g)})$	191.6 J K^{-1} mol^{-1}
$S^{\ominus}(H_{2(g)})$	130.6 J K^{-1} mol^{-1}
$S^{\ominus}(NH_{3(g)})$	192.3 J K^{-1} mol^{-1}

Entropy of the things you end up with $= 2 \times 192.3$ J K^{-1} mol^{-1}
$$= 384.6 \text{ J K}^{-1} \text{ mol}^{-1}$$

Entropy of the things you started with $= 191.6 + (3 \times 130.6)$ J K^{-1} mol^{-1}
$$= 583.4 \text{ J K}^{-1} \text{ mol}^{-1}$$

➤ **Note!** You must not just take the smaller number away from the bigger one. In this case, you would get the sign wrong. You must use "what you end up with minus what you started with".

$$\Delta S^{\ominus}_{\text{system}} = 384.6 - 583.4 = -198.8 \text{ J K}^{-1} \text{ mol}^{-1}$$

This time the entropy has decreased. This was predictable. You are starting with 4 moles of assorted gases, and producing only 2 moles of a single gas. You are creating a more ordered system, and so the entropy drops.

Problem • 1

Without referring to any data source, predict whether the entropy of the system will increase or decrease in the following reactions:

(a) $2H_{2(g)} + O_{2(g)} \rightarrow 2H_2O_{(l)}$

(b) $CaCO_{3(s)} + 2HCl_{(aq)} \rightarrow CaCl_{2(aq)} + H_2O_{(l)} + CO_{2(g)}$

(c) $2Na_{(s)} + Cl_{2(g)} \rightarrow 2NaCl_{(s)}$

(d) $CaO_{(s)} + 2NH_4Cl_{(s)} \rightarrow CaCl_{2(s)} + 2NH_{3(g)} + H_2O_{(l)}$

Problem • 2

Calculate the entropy change of the system in the following reactions at 298 K. Standard entropies are given at the end of the question.

(a) $2KNO_{3(s)} \rightarrow 2KNO_{2(s)} + O_{2(g)}$

(b) $3Fe_{(s)} + 2O_{2(g)} \rightarrow Fe_3O_{4(s)}$

(c) $(NH_4)_2SO_{4(s)} + Ca(OH)_{2(s)} \rightarrow CaSO_{4(s)} + 2NH_{3(g)} + 2H_2O_{(l)}$

$S^{\ominus}$ (in $J\,K^{-1}\,mol^{-1}$): $KNO_{3(s)}$ 133.1; $KNO_{2(s)}$ 152.1; $O_{2(g)}$ 205.0; $Fe_{(s)}$ 27.3; $Fe_3O_{4(s)}$ 146.4; $(NH_4)_2SO_{4(s)}$ 220.1; $Ca(OH)_{2(s)}$ 83.4; $CaSO_{4(s)}$ 106.7; $NH_{3(g)}$ 192.3; $H_2O_{(l)}$ 69.9

Entropy changes and feasibility

➤ You may have noticed that the "standard" symbol, $\ominus$, has been left out of these equations. The reason is that we will be looking at different temperatures – other than the standard 298 K. Don't worry about this. If your exam question uses the standard symbol, you should use it. If it doesn't, you shouldn't either.

In all feasible or spontaneous reactions the **total** entropy has to increase:

> **For a reaction to be feasible, ΔS_{total} must be positive.**

Notice that we are talking about ΔS_{total} – **not** ΔS_{system}. To find the total entropy change you have to consider not only the system, but also the surroundings.

> $$\Delta S_{\text{total}} = \Delta S_{\text{surroundings}} + \Delta S_{\text{system}}$$

For example, during an exothermic reaction, the heat evolved is obviously transferred to the surroundings. This extra heat energy increases the disorder of the surroundings and therefore increases their entropy. In an endothermic reaction, the reverse happens, and the entropy of the surroundings decreases.

➤ The negative sign in front of ΔH is to give the overall expression a positive value if the reaction is exothermic. An exothermic reaction has a negative value for ΔH. The negative sign changes that to a positive one.

There is a simple relationship between the enthalpy change of a reaction, $\Delta H_{\text{reaction}}$, and the entropy change in the surroundings:

> $$\Delta S_{\text{surroundings}} = \frac{-\Delta H_{\text{reaction}}}{T}$$

The following examples show how the three statements in boxes above can be used to determine the feasibility of reactions.

Example 4

➤ You are quite likely to be asked in the question to calculate a value for $\Delta H_{\text{reaction}}$ from given enthalpy changes of formation. If you have forgotten how to do this, revise it from Chapter 5.

Is the decomposition of calcium carbonate feasible at (a) 300 K, (b) 1200 K?

$$CaCO_{3(s)} \rightarrow CaO_{(s)} + CO_{2(g)} \qquad \Delta H_{\text{reaction}} = +178\,kJ\,mol^{-1}$$

We have already calculated ΔS_{system} for this reaction as $+160.4\,J\,K^{-1}\,mol^{-1}$.

Before going any further, notice that the energy units do not match. Enthalpy changes of reaction are measured in kJ, entropies in J. Since we are aiming to calculate **entropy** changes, then all values in kilojoules must first be multiplied by 1000 to convert them to joules.

(a) At 300 K:

$$\Delta S_{surroundings} = \frac{-\Delta H_{reaction}}{T}$$

$$= \frac{-178\,000}{300}$$

$$= -593.3\,J\,K^{-1}\,mol^{-1}$$

$$\Delta S_{total} = \Delta S_{surroundings} + \Delta S_{system}$$

$$= -593.3 + 160.4\,J\,K^{-1}\,mol^{-1}$$

$$= -433\,J\,K^{-1}\,mol^{-1} \text{ (to 3 significant figures)}$$

Because the answer is negative, the reaction is not feasible at 300 K.

(b) At 1200 K:

$$\Delta S_{surroundings} = \frac{-\Delta H_{reaction}}{T}$$

$$= \frac{-178\,000}{1200}$$

$$= -148.3\,J\,K^{-1}\,mol^{-1}$$

$$\Delta S_{total} = \Delta S_{surroundings} + \Delta S_{system}$$

$$= -148.3 + 160.4\,J\,K^{-1}\,mol^{-1}$$

$$= +12.1\,J\,K^{-1}\,mol^{-1} \text{ (to 3 significant figures)}$$

Because the answer is positive, the reaction is feasible at 1200 K. This is entirely consistent with the common experience that you have to heat calcium carbonate continuously to high temperatures to persuade it to decompose.

Example 5 For the reaction:

$$CaO_{(s)} + 2NH_4Cl_{(s)} \rightarrow CaCl_{2(s)} + 2NH_{3(g)} + H_2O_{(l)}$$

(a) Calculate the enthalpy change for the reaction.

(b) Use this to calculate $\Delta S_{surroundings}$ at 293 K.

(c) Calculate ΔS_{system}.

(d) Is the reaction feasible at 293 K?

Compound	$\Delta H_{formation}$ (kJ mol^{-1})	Entropy, S ($J\,K^{-1}\,mol^{-1}$)
$CaO_{(s)}$	−635	39.7
$NH_4Cl_{(s)}$	−314	94.6
$CaCl_{2(s)}$	−796	104.6
$NH_{3(g)}$	−46.1	192.3
$H_2O_{(l)}$	−286	69.9

➤ **Note!** If you forget to convert kJ into J, you will get quite the opposite answer. This is the only real pitfall in these questions.

➤ You may not be aware of it, but we are making assumptions in these calculations. It is obvious from the formula we are using that the value of $\Delta S_{surroundings}$ changes with temperature. However, we are assuming that $\Delta H_{reaction}$ and ΔS_{system} are constant. They are worked out from standard values, and we are using them under non-standard conditions of temperature.

This is an assumption which is always made at A level, and is approximately true as long as the temperature does not change excessively. In example 4, the difference between the standard 298 K and the value of 1200 K in (b) is quite large, and so there is likely to be some error in the final answer.

Because that final answer is only slightly positive, it would be risky to assume that the reaction is definitely feasible at 1200 K – it would not take much error to make the answer negative.

(a)

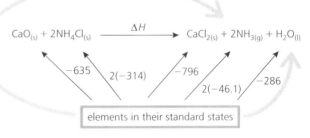

$$-635 + 2(-314) + \Delta H = -796 + 2(-46.1) - 286$$

$$\Delta H = +88.8\,\text{kJ}\,\text{mol}^{-1}$$

➤ **Don't forget** to convert kJ to J by multiplying by 1000. We are calculating an entropy change which always has the energy unit of joules.

(b) $\quad \Delta S_{\text{surroundings}} = \dfrac{-\Delta H_{\text{reaction}}}{T}$

$$= \dfrac{-88\,800}{293}$$

$$= -303\,\text{J}\,\text{K}^{-1}\,\text{mol}^{-1}$$

(c) Entropy of what you end up with $= 104.6 + 2(192.3) + 69.9\,\text{J}\,\text{K}^{-1}\,\text{mol}^{-1}$
$$= 559.1\,\text{J}\,\text{K}^{-1}\,\text{mol}^{-1}$$

Entropy of what you started with $= 39.7 + 2(94.6)\,\text{J}\,\text{K}^{-1}\,\text{mol}^{-1}$
$$= 228.9\,\text{J}\,\text{K}^{-1}\,\text{mol}^{-1}$$

$\Delta S_{\text{system}} = 559.1 - 228.9$
$$= +330.2\,\text{J}\,\text{K}^{-1}\,\text{mol}^{-1}$$

(d) $\Delta S_{\text{total}} = \Delta S_{\text{surroundings}} + \Delta S_{\text{system}}$
$$= -303 + 330.2\,\text{J}\,\text{K}^{-1}\,\text{mol}^{-1}$$
$$= +27.2\,\text{J}\,\text{K}^{-1}\,\text{mol}^{-1}$$

Because the answer is positive, the reaction is feasible at 293 K. Mixing solid calcium oxide and ammonium chloride at room temperature does in fact spontaneously produce ammonia. This reaction happens despite the fact that it is endothermic, because of the large increase in entropy of the system.

Problem . 3

For the reaction:

$$CaO_{(s)} + H_2O_{(l)} \rightarrow Ca(OH)_{2(s)} \qquad \Delta H_{\text{reaction}} = -65\,\text{kJ}\,\text{mol}^{-1}$$

(a) Calculate $\Delta S_{\text{surroundings}}$ at 298 K.

(b) Calculate ΔS_{system} given the following standard entropies (in $\text{J}\,\text{K}^{-1}\text{mol}^{-1}$): $CaO_{(s)}$ 39.7; $H_2O_{(l)}$ 69.9; $Ca(OH)_{2(s)}$ 83.4.

(c) Calculate ΔS_{total} and use it to predict whether this reaction is feasible at 298 K.

Problem . 4

For the reaction:

$$Cu_{(s)} + 2H_2O_{(l)} \rightarrow Cu(OH)_{2(s)} + H_{2(g)}$$

(a) Calculate $\Delta H_{reaction}$ given the following standard enthalpies of formation (in $kJ\,mol^{-1}$): $H_2O_{(l)}$ −286; $Cu(OH)_{2(s)}$ −450

(b) Calculate $\Delta S_{surroundings}$ at 373 K.

(c) Calculate ΔS_{system} given the following standard entropies (in $J\,K^{-1}\,mol^{-1}$): $Cu_{(s)}$ 33.2; $H_2O_{(l)}$ 69.9; $Cu(OH)_{2(s)}$ 75.0; $H_{2(g)}$ 130.6

(d) Calculate ΔS_{total} and use it to predict whether this reaction between copper and boiling water is feasible at 373 K.

Problem . 5

For the reaction:

$$C_2H_{4(g)} + H_{2(g)} \rightarrow C_2H_{6(g)}$$

(a) Calculate $\Delta H_{reaction}$ given the following standard enthalpies of combustion (in $kJ\,mol^{-1}$): $C_2H_{4(g)}$ −1411; $H_{2(g)}$ −286; $C_2H_{6(g)}$ −1560

(b) Calculate $\Delta S_{surroundings}$ at 273 K.

(c) Calculate ΔS_{system} given the following standard entropies (in $J\,K^{-1}\,mol^{-1}$): $C_2H_{4(g)}$ 219.5; $H_{2(g)}$ 130.6; $C_2H_{6(g)}$ 229.5

(d) Calculate ΔS_{total} and use it to predict whether the hydrogenation of ethene is feasible at 273 K.

Problem . 6

At high temperatures carbon reduces carbon dioxide to carbon monoxide:

$$C_{(s)} + CO_{2(g)} \rightarrow 2CO_{(g)} \qquad \Delta H_{reaction} = +173\,kJ\,mol^{-1}$$

If $\Delta S_{system} = +175.9\,J\,K^{-1}\,mol^{-1}$, work out whether the reaction is feasible at (a) 850 K, (b) 1050 K.

Free energy changes, ΔG

What is ΔG?

➤ It is quite likely that you won't actually need to know this derivation – just the result of it. Check your syllabus and past exam papers.

The calculations in the last section can be done in a slightly different way by reorganising the equation:

$$\Delta S_{total} = \Delta S_{surroundings} + \Delta S_{system}$$

➤ You often find this expression written as:

$$\Delta G = \Delta H - T\Delta S$$

If you use it in this form, remember that ΔS refers to the entropy change in the **system**. The reason that ΔG has to be negative for a feasible reaction comes from the way it is derived.
$\Delta G = -T\Delta S_{total}$. For a reaction to be feasible ΔS_{total} must be positive. $-T\Delta S_{total}$ will therefore be negative.

Substituting for $\Delta S_{surroundings}$ in terms of $\Delta H_{reaction}$ and T gives:

$$\Delta S_{total} = \frac{-\Delta H_{reaction}}{T} + \Delta S_{system}$$

Multiplying everything by $-T$ gives:

$$-T\Delta S_{total} = \Delta H_{reaction} - T\Delta S_{system}$$

The term on the left hand side, $-T\Delta S_{total}$, is called the **free energy change** for the reaction (more properly, the Gibbs free energy change), and is given the symbol ΔG:

$$\Delta G = \Delta H_{reaction} - T\Delta S_{system}$$

In order for a reaction to be feasible, ΔG must be negative.

Calculations using $\Delta G = \Delta H_{reaction} - T\Delta S_{system}$

Example 6

Show that the thermal decomposition of sodium carbonate is not feasible at 1200 K. At what temperature does it become feasible?

$$Na_2CO_{3(s)} \rightarrow Na_2O_{(s)} + CO_{2(g)} \quad \Delta H_{reaction} = +323 \text{ kJ mol}^{-1}$$

$$\Delta S_{system} = +153.7 \text{ JK}^{-1}\text{mol}^{-1}$$

ΔG has units of kJ mol^{-1}, exactly like ΔH. Since we are going to calculate ΔG, all our units must be consistent with this. In these calculations, you must remember to convert the ΔS units from joules to kilojoules by dividing by 1000. In this case, then, $\Delta S_{system} = +0.1537 \text{ kJ K}^{-1} \text{mol}^{-1}$.

$$\Delta G = \Delta H - T\Delta S$$

$$= 323 - (1200 \times 0.1537)$$

$$= +139 \text{ kJ mol}^{-1}$$

Because ΔG is positive at this temperature, the reaction is not feasible.

To find the temperature at which the reaction becomes feasible, we need to work out the temperature at which ΔG becomes less than 0. This means that $\Delta H - T\Delta S$ must be less than 0. Mathematically:

$$\Delta H - T\Delta S < 0$$

$$323 - 0.1537T < 0$$

$$323 < 0.1537T$$

$$2100 < T$$

Reversing this gives $T > 2100$ K

This means that ΔG will not become negative until the temperature reaches 2100 K, and so the reaction won't be feasible until then. In fact, we can't be that precise. We are making the assumption that ΔH and ΔS do not change with temperature, and although this is a reasonable approximation over small temperature differences, we are hardly talking about **small** temperature differences here!

> **Note!** This is potentially confusing. Last time we had this problem (when we were calculating $\Delta S_{surroundings}$), we converted ΔH from kJ to J. The secret is to think about the units of what you are working out, and convert other units to match them.

> For the rest of this chapter, we will use the simplified version of this expression. This is in line with the way it is most likely to be met in exams.

> You can use less than (<) and greater than (>) signs just like equals signs in solving equations. You can move things from one side to the other just as you would in any other equation. The last step here is the one which needs most care. Before we reversed the equation, we were left with the odd, but true, statement that 2100 K is less than T (the temperature we are trying to find). It is much more usual to say that T is greater than 2100 K.

Example 7

Two reactions which are involved in the extraction of iron in a blast furnace are:

A $Fe_2O_{3(s)} + 3CO_{(g)} \rightarrow 2Fe_{(s)} + 3CO_{2(g)}$ $\quad\quad \Delta H = -25.0 \text{ kJ mol}^{-1}$
$\quad\quad\quad \Delta S = +15.2 \text{ J K}^{-1} \text{mol}^{-1}$

B $Fe_2O_{3(s)} + 3C_{(s)} \rightarrow 2Fe_{(s)} + 3CO_{(g)}$ $\quad\quad \Delta H = +491 \text{ kJ mol}^{-1}$
$\quad\quad\quad \Delta S = +542.9 \text{ J K}^{-1} \text{mol}^{-1}$

Which reaction is the more feasible at (a) 800 K, (b) 1800 K?

We need to calculate ΔG for both reactions at both temperatures.

> You are given values of ΔH and ΔS_{system} in all these examples. In an exam, you could well be asked to work them out from other data – in the same way as in the last section.

> ➤ **Don't forget** to convert the entropy term into kJ by dividing by 1000.

(a) At 800 K:

A $\quad \Delta G = \Delta H - T\Delta S$
$= -25.0 - (800 \times 0.0152)$
$= -37.2\,\text{kJ}\,\text{mol}^{-1}$

B $\quad \Delta G = \Delta H - T\Delta S$
$= 491 - (800 \times 0.5429)$
$= +56.7\,\text{kJ}\,\text{mol}^{-1}$

At this temperature reaction A is feasible, but reaction B is not. Only reaction A has a negative value for ΔG.

(b) At 1800 K:

A $\quad \Delta G = \Delta H - T\Delta S$
$= -25.0 - (1800 \times 0.0152)$
$= -52.4\,\text{kJ}\,\text{mol}^{-1}$

B $\quad \Delta G = \Delta H - T\Delta S$
$= 491 - (1800 \times 0.5429)$
$= -486\,\text{kJ}\,\text{mol}^{-1}$

At this temperature, both reactions are feasible, but since ΔG is more negative for reaction B, that is the more feasible of the two reactions.

Predicting how the feasibility of a reaction changes with temperature

In this section we are going to look at how you can make predictions about how the feasibility of a reaction changes as you change the temperature **without** doing calculations. It depends on whether the enthalpy change is exothermic or endothermic, and whether there is an increase or decrease in the entropy of the system. It is important that you **understand** how to do this. Trying to learn the various combinations is potentially very confusing.

An endothermic reaction with a decrease in entropy

e.g. $\quad 6C_{(s)} + 3H_{2(g)} \rightarrow C_6H_{6(l)} \qquad \Delta H = +49\,\text{kJ}\,\text{mol}^{-1}$

You can tell from the equation that there is likely to be a decrease in entropy of the system. In particular, the conversion of 3 moles of gas into 1 mole of liquid will lead to a considerable fall in disorder. ΔS for this reaction is negative.

$\Delta G = \Delta H - T\Delta S$

What can you say about the value of ΔG, and what is the effect on this value of increasing temperature?

Think about the equation in two parts: "ΔH", and "$-T\Delta S$". Think about the sign of both of those.

> ➤ **Hint:** T is always a positive number if you are using the kelvin scale. "$T\Delta S$" will be negative, because you are multiplying a positive number by a negative one. Therefore "$-T\Delta S$" will be positive.

■ ΔH is positive.

■ ΔS is negative, and therefore "$-T\Delta S$" is positive.

■ Whatever the value of T, ΔG must be positive, because you are adding two positive numbers together.

■ The reaction is never feasible at any temperature.

An exothermic reaction with an increase in entropy

e.g. $2C_{(s)} + O_{2(g)} \rightarrow 2CO_{(g)}$ $\Delta H = -221 \, \text{kJ mol}^{-1}$

The entropy change will be positive because you are generating more moles of gas than you started with. The carbon is so highly ordered that its entropy is negligible.

$$\Delta G = \Delta H - T\Delta S$$

- ΔH is negative.

- ΔS is positive, and therefore "$-T\Delta S$" is negative. "$-T\Delta S$" becomes even more negative as T increases.

- ΔG is negative whatever the temperature (because you are adding two negative numbers), but gets more negative at higher temperatures.

- The reaction is always feasible, but becomes even more feasible as the temperature increases.

An endothermic reaction with an increase in entropy

e.g. $CaCO_{3(s)} \rightarrow CaO_{(s)} + CO_{2(g)}$ $\Delta H = +178 \, \text{kJ mol}^{-1}$

There is an increase in entropy because of the formation of the gas.

$$\Delta G = \Delta H - T\Delta S$$

- ΔH is positive.

- Because ΔS is positive (an increase in entropy), "$-T\Delta S$" is negative.

- At low temperatures, the "$-T\Delta S$" term probably will not be negative enough to compensate for the positive ΔH, and so ΔG will be positive. The reaction is not feasible.

- As T increases, the "$-T\Delta S$" term becomes more negative, and will eventually cancel out the positive ΔH. At that point the reaction will become feasible.

- The reaction is not feasible at low temperatures, but will become feasible at higher ones.

An exothermic reaction with a decrease in entropy

e.g. $2Mg_{(s)} + O_{2(g)} \rightarrow 2MgO_{(s)}$ $\Delta H = -1203 \, \text{kJ mol}^{-1}$

The entropy has decreased because of the loss of a mole of gas.

$$\Delta G = \Delta H - T\Delta S$$

- ΔH is negative.

- ΔS is negative, and therefore "$-T\Delta S$" is positive, and becomes increasingly positive as the temperature increases.

- Because of the very high negative value of ΔH, ΔG will be negative at ordinary temperatures, and so the reaction will be feasible.

- At very high temperatures, the positive value of "$-T\Delta S$" will eventually cancel out the negative value of ΔH. ΔG will then become positive, and so the reaction will cease to be feasible.

➤ You could try estimating the temperature at which the reaction stops being feasible using the sort of calculations carried out earlier in this chapter.

$\Delta S_{system} = -433.2 \, \text{J K}^{-1} \text{mol}^{-1}$.

You should find that the reaction stops being feasible at 2777 K (although, for reasons we have looked at previously, you must not take that figure too seriously – there will be errors due to changes in ΔH and ΔS over this large temperature increase).

Graphing changes in ΔG with temperature

We have taken both ΔH and ΔS as constants, because they do not change significantly with temperature (at least over small temperature ranges).

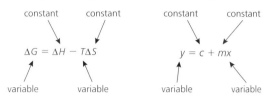

The equation on the right is the equation for a straight line graph. If you compare the two, you will see that "ΔG" corresponds to "y", and "T" corresponds to "x".

The constant "c" is "ΔH". The constant "m" – which is the slope of the graph – corresponds to "$-\Delta S$".

For a reaction with an increase in entropy

"ΔS" is positive and so "$-\Delta S$" is negative. The graph has a negative slope, which means that ΔG decreases as T increases (see Figure 11.1).

> ➤ The ΔG scale does not necessarily start from 0. It might range from, say, $+50$ at the top to -100 at the bottom. It might go from -100 at the top to -400 at the bottom. It might be $+100$ at the top to $+50$ at the bottom. It doesn't matter – as long as you always run from more positive (or less negative) at the top to less positive (or more negative) at the bottom.

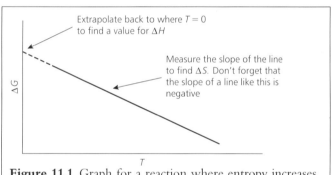

Figure 11.1 Graph for a reaction where entropy increases

Suppose the slope of the line was measured as $-0.4\,\mathrm{kJ\,mol^{-1}\,K^{-1}}$. This means that $-\Delta S = -0.4\,\mathrm{kJ\,mol^{-1}\,K^{-1}}$, and so $\Delta S = +0.4\,\mathrm{kJ\,mol^{-1}\,K^{-1}}$. Because entropy changes are normally measured in joules, this would normally be quoted as $+400\,\mathrm{J\,mol^{-1}\,K^{-1}}$ (or $\mathrm{J\,K^{-1}\,mol^{-1}}$).

For a reaction with a decrease in entropy

"ΔS" is negative and so "$-\Delta S$" is positive. The graph has a positive slope, which means that ΔG increases as T increases (see Figure 11.2).

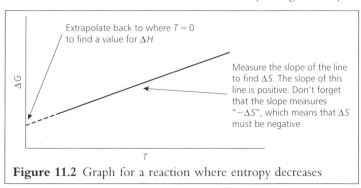

Figure 11.2 Graph for a reaction where entropy decreases

269

Example 8

When lead(II) nitrate is heated it decomposes according to the equation:

$$2Pb(NO_3)_{2(s)} \rightarrow 2PbO_{(s)} + 4NO_{2(g)} + O_{2(g)}$$

Plot the following values of ΔG against T, and use the graph to find $\Delta H_{\text{reaction}}$ and ΔS_{system}. At what temperature does the reaction become feasible?

> ➤ **Do this!** Don't just read the answer. It would be much better if you didn't read any further until you have attempted the question.

T (K)	300	600	900	1200
ΔG (kJ mol^{-1})	+339	+76	−187	−450

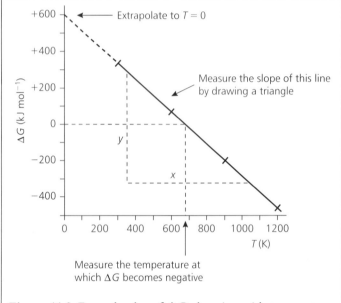

Figure 11.3 Example plot of ΔG changing with temperature

$$\Delta G = \Delta H - T\Delta S$$

When $T = 0$, $\Delta G = \Delta H$. Extrapolating the line back to $T = 0$ gives you a value for ΔH. You should get $+600 \text{ kJ mol}^{-1}$.

The slope of the line is found by measuring y and x. The slope is negative because ΔG is falling as T increases. The slope is therefore $-y/x$. You should get a value for the slope of $-0.875 \text{ kJ mol}^{-1} \text{K}^{-1}$ (Figure 11.3).

The slope of the line from the equation ($\Delta G = \Delta H - T\Delta S$) is $-\Delta S$. If $-\Delta S$ is $-0.875 \text{ kJ mol}^{-1} \text{K}^{-1}$, then ΔS is $+0.875 \text{ kJ mol}^{-1} \text{K}^{-1}$. You can leave the value like that or convert the energy unit into J by multiplying by 1000.

When you get your answer you should check that the sign is sensible. The most likely thing to get wrong is the sign of the slope. Is a positive value for entropy change reasonable given the original equation? Yes – the products are obviously far more disordered than the reactants.

To find the temperature at which the reaction becomes feasible, you need to find the temperature at which ΔG becomes less than 0. You should get an answer of 690 K.

A special case where $\Delta G = 0$

For reversible physical changes taking place at a constant temperature, $\Delta G = 0$. The obvious changes of this kind are melting and boiling.

$$\Delta G = \Delta H - T\Delta S_{system}$$

If $\quad \Delta G = 0 \qquad \Delta H = T\Delta S_{system}$

$$\Delta S_{system} = \frac{\Delta H}{T}$$

> ➤ **Note!** If your syllabus expects you to be able to calculate $\Delta S_{surroundings}$, be very careful not to confuse this equation with the very similar $\Delta S_{surroundings} = -\Delta H/T$.

Example 9

Calculating the entropy change when ice melts

The enthalpy change of melting of ice is $+6.0\,\text{kJ mol}^{-1}$. Calculate the entropy change of the system on melting 1 mole of ice at its melting point of 273 K.

$$\Delta S_{system} = \frac{\Delta H}{T}$$

$$= \frac{+6000}{273}$$

$$= +22\,\text{J K}^{-1}\,\text{mol}^{-1}$$

> ➤ ΔS is normally calculated in joules – hence ΔS is slotted in as 6000 and not 6.0.

Example 10

Calculating the entropy change when water boils

The enthalpy change of vaporisation of water is $+41\,\text{kJ mol}^{-1}$. Calculate the entropy change of the system on boiling 1 mole of water at its boiling point of 373 K.

$$\Delta S_{system} = \frac{\Delta H}{T}$$

$$= \frac{+41\,000}{373}$$

$$= +110\,\text{J K}^{-1}\,\text{mol}^{-1}$$

Problem • 7

Note: In all these calculations, ΔS refers to ΔS_{system}.

Calculate ΔG for the reaction between triiron tetroxide and hydrogen at 500 K. Is the reaction feasible at this temperature?

$$Fe_3O_{4(s)} + 4H_{2(g)} \rightarrow 3Fe_{(s)} + 4H_2O_{(g)} \qquad \Delta H = -144\,\text{kJ mol}^{-1}$$
$$\Delta S = +226.9\,\text{J K}^{-1}\,\text{mol}^{-1}$$

Problem • 8

Zinc is manufactured by heating zinc oxide with carbon. Calculate ΔG at (a) 1000 K and (b) 1500 K, and decide whether the reaction is feasible at these temperatures.
(c) At what temperature does the reaction become feasible?

$$ZnO_{(s)} + C_{(s)} \rightarrow Zn_{(s)} + CO_{(g)} \qquad \Delta H = +237\,\text{kJ mol}^{-1}$$
$$\Delta S = +189.9\,\text{J K}^{-1}\,\text{mol}^{-1}$$

Problem • 9

Calculate ΔG for the reaction between magnesium and steam at 373 K.

$$Mg_{(s)} + H_2O_{(g)} \rightarrow MgO_{(s)} + H_{2(g)}$$

	$Mg_{(s)}$	$H_2O_{(g)}$	$MgO_{(s)}$	$H_{2(g)}$
$\Delta H^{\ominus}_{formation}$ (kJ mol^{-1})	0	-242	-602	0
$S^{\ominus}$ (J K^{-1} mol^{-1})	32.7	188.7	26.9	130.6

Problem • 10

Hydrogen is manufactured by heating methane with steam in the presence of a nickel catalyst at a temperature of about 1200 K. By calculating ΔG, confirm that the reaction is feasible at this temperature. What is the minimum temperature required for the reaction to be feasible?

$$CH_{4(g)} + H_2O_{(g)} \rightarrow CO_{(g)} + 3H_{2(g)}$$

	$CH_{4(g)}$	$H_2O_{(g)}$	$CO_{(g)}$	$H_{2(g)}$
$\Delta H^{\ominus}_{formation}$ (kJ mol^{-1})	-75	-242	-111	0
$S^{\ominus}$ (J K^{-1} mol^{-1})	186.2	188.7	197.6	130.6

Problem • 11

Reactions may be

  A feasible at all temperatures
  B not feasible at any temperature
  C not feasible at low temperatures, but feasible at high ones
  D feasible at low temperatures, but not feasible at high ones

In each of the following cases, say whether A, B, C or D applies. Briefly explain your reasoning.

(a) $X_{(s)} \rightarrow Y_{(s)} + Z_{(g)}$ $\Delta H = +250$ kJ mol^{-1}
(b) $2X_{(g)} + Y_{(g)} \rightarrow 2Z_{(g)}$ $\Delta H = -100$ kJ mol^{-1}
(c) $X_{(l)} \rightarrow Y_{(l)} + Z_{(g)}$ $\Delta H = -200$ kJ mol^{-1}
(d) $2X_{(s)} + 2Y_{(g)} \quad Z_{(g)}$ $\Delta H = +50$ kJ mol^{-1}

Problem • 12

When heated, ammonium nitrate decomposes according to the equation:

$$NH_4NO_{3(s)} \rightarrow N_2O_{(g)} + 2H_2O_{(g)}$$

Plot the following values of ΔG against temperature, T, and use your graph to find the enthalpy change for the reaction and ΔS_{system}.

T (K)	300	500	700	900
ΔG (kJ mol^{-1})	-170	-259	-348	-437

Problem • 13

Sulphur dioxide reacts with oxygen in the presence of a vanadium(V) oxide catalyst to produce sulphur trioxide:

$$2SO_{2(g)} + O_{2(g)} \rightarrow 2SO_{3(g)}$$

Plot the following values of ΔG against temperature, T, and use your graph to find the enthalpy change for the reaction and ΔS_{system}.

T (K)	400	600	800	1000
ΔG (kJ mol^{-1})	-120	-82	-45	-7

Problem . 14	The enthalpy change of vaporisation of liquid cyclohexane is $+30 \, \text{kJ mol}^{-1}$. Cyclohexane boils at 81 °C. Calculate the entropy change of the system when 1 mole of cyclohexane is vaporised at its boiling point.

End of chapter checklist

> You may not need to do all these things. Check your syllabus and past exam papers.

Can you do the following things?

■ Understand what is meant by a feasible (or spontaneous) reaction.

■ Calculate a value for ΔS_{system} from a given equation and values of $S^{\ominus}$ for the substances involved.

■ In simple cases, predict whether ΔS_{system} is positive or negative by looking at the equation for the reaction.

■ Calculate $\Delta S_{\text{surroundings}}$ using the expression $\Delta S_{\text{surroundings}} = -\Delta H/T$.

■ Calculate ΔS_{total} and understand that this must be positive for the reaction to be feasible.

■ Use the expression $\Delta G = \Delta H - T\Delta S_{\text{system}}$ to calculate ΔG, and understand that ΔG must be negative for the reaction to be feasible.

■ Use the expression $\Delta G = \Delta H - T\Delta S_{\text{system}}$ to calculate the temperature at which a reaction becomes feasible.

■ Make predictions about the changes in feasibility with temperature for particular reactions given the sign of the enthalpy change, and of ΔS_{system}.

■ Use graphs of ΔG against T to find ΔH and ΔS_{system}.

■ Calculate entropy changes during changes of state.

Revision problems

Numerical answers are provided for these problems, but no worked solutions.

Problem . 15	Predict whether the entropy of the system will increase or decrease in the following reactions: (a) $2H_2O_{2(l)} \rightarrow 2H_2O_{(l)} + O_{2(g)}$ (b) $2Na_{(s)} + O_{2(g)} \rightarrow Na_2O_{2(s)}$ (c) $2Al_{(s)} + 3Cl_{2(g)} \rightarrow 2AlCl_{3(s)}$ (d) $2KClO_{3(s)} \rightarrow 2KCl_{(s)} + 3O_{2(g)}$

Problem • 16

Calculate ΔS_{system} for the reactions in question 15 given the following standard entropies (in $J K^{-1} mol^{-1}$): $H_2O_{2(l)}$ 109.6; $H_2O_{(l)}$ 69.9; $O_{2(g)}$ 205; $Na_{(s)}$ 51.2; $Na_2O_{2(s)}$ 95.0; $Al_{(s)}$ 28.3; $Cl_{2(g)}$ 165; $AlCl_{3(s)}$ 110.7; $KClO_{3(s)}$ 143.1; $KCl_{(s)}$ 82.6

Problem • 17

Predict the feasibility of each of the following reactions at the stated temperature by calculating (i) $\Delta S_{surroundings}$ and (ii) ΔS_{total}.

(a) $2A_{(s)} + B_{(g)} \rightarrow C_{(g)}$ at 350 K. $\Delta H = +49.5 \, kJ \, mol^{-1}$;
   $\Delta S_{system} = -17.6 \, J K^{-1} mol^{-1}$.

(b) $2D_{(s)} \rightarrow 2E_{(s)} + F_{(g)}$ at 900 K. $\Delta H = +141 \, kJ \, mol^{-1}$;
   $\Delta S_{system} = +230 \, J K^{-1} mol^{-1}$.

Problem • 18

Benzene can be hydrogenated to make cyclohexane:

$$C_6H_{6(l)} + 3H_{2(g)} \rightarrow C_6H_{12(l)}$$

(a) The enthalpy changes of combustion (in $kJ \, mol^{-1}$) are: $C_6H_{6(l)}$ −3276; $H_{2(g)}$ −286; $C_6H_{12(l)}$ −3920. Calculate the enthalpy change for the hydrogenation of benzene.

(b) Calculate $\Delta S_{surroundings}$ if the reaction occurs at 330 K.

(c) Calculate ΔS_{system} from the standard entropy values (in $J K^{-1} mol^{-1}$): $C_6H_{6(l)}$ 173; $H_{2(g)}$ 130.6; $C_6H_{12(l)}$ 204.4

(d) Calculate ΔS_{total} and comment on the feasibility of the reaction at 330 K.

Problem • 19

This question is about the possible reduction of zinc oxide by carbon monoxide at 1000 K.

$$ZnO_{(s)} + CO_{(g)} \rightarrow Zn_{(s)} + CO_{2(g)}$$

	$ZnO_{(s)}$	$CO_{(g)}$	$Zn_{(s)}$	$CO_{2(g)}$
$\Delta H^{\ominus}_{formation}$ (kJ mol^{-1})	−348	−111	0	−394
$S^{\ominus}$ (J K^{-1} mol^{-1})	43.6	197.6	41.6	213.6

(a) Calculate the enthalpy change for the reaction.

(b) Calculate ΔS_{system}.

(c) Calculate $\Delta S_{surroundings}$ at 1000 K.

(d) Calculate ΔS_{total} and comment on the feasibility of the reaction at 1000 K.

Problem • 20

On heating, silver(I) oxide decomposes into silver and oxygen:

$$2Ag_2O_{(s)} \rightarrow 4Ag_{(s)} + O_{2(g)} \qquad \Delta H = +62.0 \, kJ \, mol^{-1}$$
$$\Delta S_{system} = +132.8 \, J K^{-1} mol^{-1}$$

(a) Calculate the free energy change, ΔG, for this reaction at (i) 400 K, (ii) 600 K, and comment on the feasibility of the reaction at these temperatures.

(b) What is the minimum temperature you would have to use to decompose silver(I) oxide?

Problem • 21

Magnesium carbonate and barium carbonate both decompose on heating according to the equation:

$$XCO_{3(s)} \rightarrow XO_{(s)} + CO_{2(g)}$$

(a) Calculate ΔH and ΔS_{system} for both reactions, and use these values to calculate ΔG at 900 K for both reactions. Which (if either) of the carbonates will decompose on heating to 900 K?
(b) Calculate the minimum temperature needed to decompose each carbonate.

	$MgCO_{3(s)}$	$MgO_{(s)}$	$CO_{2(g)}$	$BaCO_{3(s)}$	$BaO_{(s)}$
$\Delta H^{\ominus}_{formation}$ (kJ mol^{-1})	-1096	-602	-394	-1216	-554
$S^{\ominus}$ (J K^{-1} mol^{-1})	65.7	26.9	213.6	112.1	70.4

Problem • 22

Reactions may be

   A feasible at all temperatures
   B not feasible at any temperature
   C not feasible at low temperatures, but feasible at high ones
   D feasible at low temperatures, but not feasible at high ones

In each of the following cases, say whether A, B, C or D applies:

(a) An exothermic reaction with an increase in entropy.
(b) An exothermic reaction with a decrease in entropy.
(c) An endothermic reaction with an increase in entropy.
(d) An endothermic reaction with a decrease in entropy.

Problem • 23

When heated strongly, copper(II) sulphate decomposes according to the equation:

$$CuSO_{4(s)} \rightarrow CuO_{(s)} + SO_{3(g)}$$

Plot the following values of ΔG against temperature, T, and use your graph to find (a) the enthalpy change for the reaction, (b) ΔS_{system}, and (c) the minimum temperature needed for the decomposition to become feasible.

T (K)	400	800	1200	1600
ΔG (kJ mol^{-1})	$+145$	$+71$	-4	-78

Problem • 24

Mercury melts at 234 K with an enthalpy change of melting of $+2.3$ kJ mol^{-1}. It boils at 630 K with an enthalpy change of vaporisation of $+59$ kJ mol^{-1}. Calculate the entropy change of the system (per mole of mercury) on (a) melting, (b) boiling.

Answers to Problems

Chapter 1

1. PbO, NaBr, $MgSO_4$, $ZnCl_2$, K_2CO_3, $(NH_4)_2S$, $Ca(NO_3)_2$, $Fe(OH)_3$, $FeSO_4$, $CuCO_3$, $Al_2(SO_4)_3$, $Ca(OH)_2$, $CoCl_2$, CaO, $AgNO_3$, FeF_3, NH_4NO_3, RbI, Na_2SO_4, Cr_2O_3

2.
(a) $Ca + 2H_2O \rightarrow Ca(OH)_2 + H_2$

(b) $2Al + Cr_2O_3 \rightarrow Al_2O_3 + 2Cr$

(c) $Fe_2O_3 + 3CO \rightarrow 2Fe + 3CO_2$

(d) $CH_4 + 2O_2 \rightarrow CO_2 + 2H_2O$

(e) $2C_8H_{18} + 25O_2 \rightarrow 16CO_2 + 18H_2O$

(f) $2NaHCO_3 + H_2SO_4 \rightarrow Na_2SO_4 + 2CO_2 + 2H_2O$

3.
(a) $Na_2CO_3 + 2HCl \rightarrow 2NaCl + CO_2 + H_2O$

(b) $2NaOH + H_2SO_4 \rightarrow Na_2SO_4 + 2H_2O$

(c) $2Na + 2H_2O \rightarrow 2NaOH + H_2$

(d) $2Na + Cl_2 \rightarrow 2NaCl$

(e) $Fe_2O_3 + 6HNO_3 \rightarrow 2Fe(NO_3)_3 + 3H_2O$

4.
(a) $Ag^+_{(aq)} + Br^-_{(aq)} \rightarrow AgBr_{(s)}$

(b) $Ca^{2+}_{(aq)} + CO_3^{2-}_{(aq)} \rightarrow CaCO_{3(s)}$

(c) $Mg^{2+}_{(aq)} + 2OH^-_{(aq)} \rightarrow Mg(OH)_{2(s)}$

5.
(a) $Fe_{(s)} + Cu^{2+}_{(aq)} \rightarrow Fe^{2+}_{(aq)} + Cu_{(s)}$

(b) $Ca^{2+}_{(aq)} + 2OH^-_{(aq)} \rightarrow Ca(OH)_{2(s)}$

(c) $H^+_{(aq)} + OH^-_{(aq)} \rightarrow H_2O_{(l)}$

(d) $CO_3^{2-}_{(s)} + 2H^+_{(aq)} \rightarrow CO_{2(g)} + H_2O_{(l)}$

6.
(a) $H_2O_2 \rightarrow O_2 + 2H^+ + 2e^-$

(b) $SO_3^{2-} + H_2O \rightarrow SO_4^{2-} + 2H^+ + 2e^-$

(c) $CH_3CH_2OH + H_2O \rightarrow CH_3COOH + 4H^+ + 4e^-$

(d) $Cr_2O_7^{2-} + 14H^+ + 6e^- \rightarrow 2Cr^{3+} + 7H_2O$

7. Multiply equation (c) by 3, and equation (d) by 2. In this way you transfer 12 electrons. If you transferred 24 electrons, your final equation can be simplified by dividing by 2. The addition leaves you with water molecules and hydrogen ions on both sides of the equation. The version below has had the spare ones cancelled out:

$3CH_3CH_2OH + 2Cr_2O_7^{2-} + 16H^+ \rightarrow 3CH_3COOH + 4Cr^{3+} + 11H_2O$

8.
(a) $-3, +4, +5, +3, -2$ (b) $-2, +4, +4, +6$

(c) $+5, +3, +4, +5$ (d) $+2, +2, +3$

26. Urea; 46.7%

27. (a) 331 g (b) 68.8 g (c) 68.64 g

28. (a) 0.2 (b) 17900 (c) 5×10^{-4} (0.0005)

29. (a) 1.8×10^{24} (b) 2.5×10^{27} (c) 6.4×10^{26}

30. $1.7 \times 10^{12} \text{ m}^3$

31. (a) KNO_2 (b) $Na_2S_2O_3$ (c) C_2H_5Br

32. C_4H_{10}

33. (a) 0.333 tonnes (b) 0.533 tonnes

34. 9.98 g

35. (a) 0.02 mol (b) 0.01 mol (c) 203 g (d) 24

36. 84%

37. 80.2%

Chapter 3

1. $2H_{2(g)} + O_{2(g)} \rightarrow 2H_2O_{(l)}$

You need half as many molecules of oxygen as you do of hydrogen, and so you need half the volume.

Volume of oxygen needed $= 250 \text{ cm}^3$

Volume of air needed $= 5 \times 250 \text{ cm}^3$ (to allow for the fact that air is only 1/5 oxygen)

$= 1250 \text{ cm}^3$

2. $2C_4H_{10(g)} + 13O_{2(g)} \rightarrow 8CO_{2(g)} + 10H_2O_{(l)}$

You get 4 times as many carbon dioxide molecules formed as you had butane to start with, and so you will also get 4 times the volume.

Volume of carbon dioxide $= 4 \times 1 \text{ dm}^3 = 4 \text{ dm}^3$

3. The volumes are in the ratio of $1C_xH_y : 6O_2 : 4CO_2$, and so the numbers of molecules of these must be in that same ratio:

$C_xH_y + 6O_2 \rightarrow 4CO_2 + \text{some } H_2O$

Balancing the carbons gives you $x = 4$.
Balancing the oxygens shows that there must be $4H_2O$, and so $y = 8$.
Hydrocarbon is C_4H_8 (butene)

4. $10 \, cm^3$ of C_xH_y were used.

$50 \, cm^3$ of oxygen was used up. (You start with $90 \, cm^3$; the gas left over at the end is the excess oxygen ($40 \, cm^3$).)

$30 \, cm^3$ of CO_2 are formed. (The volume contraction with sodium hydroxide solution is caused by the CO_2 reacting.)

The volumes are in the ratio $1C_xH_y : 5O_2 : 3CO_2$, and so the numbers of molecules of these must be in that same ratio:

$$C_xH_y + 5O_2 \rightarrow 3CO_2 + \text{some } H_2O$$

Balancing the carbons gives you $x = 3$.

Balancing the oxygens shows that there must be $4H_2O$, and so $y = 8$.

Hydrocarbon is C_3H_8 (propane)

5. (a) $24\,000 \, cm^3$ of chlorine would weigh $71 \, g$ (1 mol Cl_2)

$200 \, cm^3$ of chlorine would weigh $\dfrac{200}{24\,000} \times 71 \, g = 0.592 \, g$

(b) $24 \, dm^3$ of argon weighs $40 \, g$ (1 mol Ar)

$1 \, dm^3$ of argon weighs $\dfrac{40}{24} \, g = 1.67 \, g$

The density is therefore $1.67 \, g \, dm^{-3}$.

(c) $32 \, g$ of oxygen (1 mol O_2) occupies $24 \, dm^3$

$0.16 \, g$ oxygen occupies $\dfrac{0.16}{32} \times 24 \, dm^3 = 0.12 \, dm^3$ (or $120 \, cm^3$)

(d) $1.42 \, g \, dm^{-3}$ means that $1 \, dm^3$ weighs $1.42 \, g$

$24 \, dm^3$ (the volume of 1 mole) weighs $24 \times 1.42 \, g = 34.1 \, g$

6. $1.25 \, g$ of nitrogen occupies a volume of $1 \, dm^3$. (That's what a density of $1.25 \, g \, dm^{-3}$ means.)

$28 \, g$ of nitrogen (1 mol N_2) occupies a volume of $\dfrac{28}{1.25} \times 1 \, dm^3 = 22.4 \, dm^3$

7. $MnO_2 + 4HCl \rightarrow MnCl_2 + Cl_2 + 2H_2O$

1 mol MnO_2 gives 1 mol Cl_2

$87 \, g \, MnO_2$ gives $24 \, dm^3 \, Cl_2$ at rtp

$2 \, g \, MnO_2$ gives $\dfrac{2}{87} \times 24 \, dm^3 = 0.552 \, dm^3$ (or $552 \, cm^3$)

8. $2KNO_3 \rightarrow 2KNO_2 + O_2$

2 mol KNO_3 gives 1 mol O_2

$2 \times 101 \, g \, KNO_3$ gives $24 \, dm^3 \, O_2$ at rtp

$202 \, g \, KNO_3$ gives $24 \, dm^3 \, O_2$ at rtp

$1 \, dm^3$ of oxygen would be given by $\dfrac{1}{24} \times 202 \, g \, KNO_3 = 8.42 \, g$

9. $pV = nRT$

$$pV = \dfrac{\text{mass (g)}}{\text{mass of 1 mole (g)}} \times RT$$

$$V = \dfrac{\text{mass (g)}}{\text{mass of 1 mole (g)}} \times \dfrac{RT}{P}$$

$$= \dfrac{0.100}{2} \times \dfrac{8.31 \times 293}{100\,000} \, m^3 = 1.22 \times 10^{-3} \, m^3 \qquad (1.22 \, dm^3)$$

10. Rearranging the second equation from Q9:

$$\text{Mass (g)} = \frac{pV}{RT} \times \text{mass of 1 mole (g)}$$

$$= \frac{98\,900 \times 200 \times 10^{-6}}{8.31 \times 290} \times 28 = 0.230\,\text{g}$$

11. Again rearranging the second equation from Q9:

$$\text{Mass of 1 mole (g)} = \text{mass (g)} \times \frac{RT}{pV}$$

$$= 1.25 \times \frac{8.31 \times 290}{102\,000 \times 923 \times 10^{-6}} = 32.0\,\text{g}$$

Therefore, RFM = 32.0

12. (a) $3.5\,\text{dm}^3$ (b) $2\,\text{dm}^3$

13. (a) $6.25\,\text{m}^3$ (b) $1\,\text{m}^3$ of NO; $1.5\,\text{m}^3$ of steam; $5\,\text{m}^3$ of nitrogen (from the air)

14. C_3H_6

15. C_4H_{10}

16. (a) $1.83\,\text{g}\,\text{dm}^{-3}$ (b) $0.0658\,\text{dm}^3$ ($65.8\,\text{cm}^3$)

(c) $0.160\,\text{g}$ (d) $64.0\,\text{g}$ (e) $71.0\,\text{g}$

17. $240\,\text{cm}^3$

18. $41\,700\,\text{g}$ ($41.7\,\text{kg}$)

19. (a) 0.02 (b) $138\,\text{g}$ (c) 39

20. (a) $0.204\,\text{g}$ (b) $8.61 \times 10^{-3}\,\text{m}^3$ ($8.61\,\text{dm}^3$)

(c) $141\,000\,\text{Pa}$ (d) $854\,\text{K}$ (e) 46.1

21. (a) $40\,000$ moles (b) 372 moles, 2.24×10^{26} molecules

22. $4.76 \times 10^{-4}\,\text{m}^3$ ($0.476\,\text{dm}^3$ or $476\,\text{cm}^3$)

23. (a) $0.0136\,\text{mol}$ (b) $1.36\,\text{g}$ (c) 90.7%

24. (a) 10.8 (b) $117.3\,\text{g}$ (c) 3

Chapter 4

1. 1 mol H_2SO_4 weighs $98\,\text{g}$.
$4.90\,\text{g}$ H_2SO_4 is $4.90/98\,\text{mol} = 0.0500\,\text{mol}$
Concentration is $0.0500\,\text{mol}\,\text{dm}^{-3}$.

2. 1 mol KOH weighs $56\,\text{g}$.
$0.200\,\text{mol}$ KOH weighs $0.200 \times 56\,\text{g} = 11.2\,\text{g}$
Concentration is $11.2\,\text{g}\,\text{dm}^{-3}$.

3. 1 mol Na_2O_3 weighs 106 g.

$0.100 \text{ mol dm}^{-3}$ would need $0.100 \times 106 \text{ g} = 10.6 \text{ g } Na_2CO_3$ dissolved in 1 dm^3 (1000 cm^3)

If you only had 100 cm^3 (a tenth as much), you would only need 1.06 g.

4. Number of moles of copper(II) sulphate solution $= \dfrac{20.0}{1000} \times 0.400$

$$= 0.00800 \text{ mol}$$

$CuSO_4 + 2NaOH \rightarrow Cu(OH)_2 + Na_2SO_4$

$Cu(OH)_2 \rightarrow CuO + H_2O$

1 mol $CuSO_4$ gives 1 mol $Cu(OH)_2$ which in turn gives 1 mol CuO

1 mol $CuSO_4$ gives 80 g CuO (1 mol)

$0.00800 \text{ mol } CuSO_4$ gives $0.00800 \times 80 \text{ g CuO} = 0.640 \text{ g CuO}$

> **Hint:** If you need to take the last step in this problem more slowly, use one of the formula methods. For example

Volume in $dm^3 = \dfrac{\text{moles}}{\text{concentration}}$

$= \dfrac{0.0250}{2.00}$

$= 0.0125$

This is 12.5 cm^3 – as before.

---

5. Start from what you know everything about.

Number of moles of sodium carbonate $= \dfrac{25.0}{1000} \times 0.500 = 0.0125$

$Na_2CO_3 + 2HCl \rightarrow 2NaCl + CO_2 + H_2O$

You need twice as many moles of HCl as of sodium carbonate.

Number of moles of HCl needed $= 2 \times 0.0125 = 0.0250 \text{ mol}$

Concentration of HCl is 2.00 mol dm^{-3}, i.e. 2.00 mol in every 1 dm^3 (1000 cm^3)

You therefore need $\dfrac{0.0250}{2.00} \times 1000 \text{ cm}^3 = 12.5 \text{ cm}^3$ of HCl

6. Calculate the numbers of moles of everything.

Number of moles of $NaHCO_3 = \dfrac{25.0}{1000} \times 0.100 = 2.50 \times 10^{-3}$

Number of moles of $H_2SO_4 = \dfrac{12.5}{1000} \times 0.100 = 1.25 \times 10^{-3}$

Number of moles of $CO_2 = \dfrac{60.0}{24\,000} = 2.50 \times 10^{-3}$

Number of moles of $Na_2SO_4 = \dfrac{0.178}{142} = 1.25 \times 10^{-3}$ (where 142 is the RFM)

> **Hint:** $24\,000 \text{ cm}^3$ of CO_2 at rtp contains 1 mol CO_2.

1 cm^3 contains $1/24\,000$ mol.

60 cm^3 contains $60/24\,000$ mol.

So, looking at the ratios:

2 mol $NaHCO_3$ react with 1 mol H_2SO_4 to give 2 mol CO_2 and 1 mol Na_2SO_4

The equation: $2NaHCO_3 + H_2SO_4 \rightarrow 2CO_2 + Na_2SO_4 + ?$

This is as far as you can go with the data. Now you need to check the balancing. You are missing 4 hydrogens and 2 oxygens – i.e. $2H_2O$. The final equation is:

$2NaHCO_3 + H_2SO_4 \rightarrow 2CO_2 + Na_2SO_4 + 2H_2O$

7. Number of moles of $Na_2CO_3 = \dfrac{25.0}{1000} \times 0.200 = 0.00500$

From the equation, 1 mol Na_2CO_3 reacts with 2 mol HCl.

Number of moles of HCl $= 2 \times 0.00500 = 0.0100$ (in 20.0 cm^3 of solution)

Concentration of HCl $= \dfrac{1000}{20.0} \times 0.0100 = 0.500 \text{ mol dm}^{-3}$

1 mol HCl weighs 36.5 g

Therefore concentration of HCl $= 0.500 \times 36.5 \text{ g dm}^{-3} = 18.3 \text{ g dm}^{-3}$

8. 25.0 cm³ of unknown $Sr(OH)_2 \equiv 32.8\,cm^3$ of 0.100 mol dm⁻³ HCl

Number of moles of $HCl = \dfrac{32.8}{1000} \times 0.100 = 3.28 \times 10^{-3}$

From the equation, you only need half as many moles of $Sr(OH)_2$ as HCl.

Number of moles of $Sr(OH)_2 = 0.5 \times 3.28 \times 10^{-3} = 1.64 \times 10^{-3}$ (in 25.0 cm³ of solution)

Concentration of $Sr(OH)_2 = \dfrac{1000}{25.0} \times 1.64 \times 10^{-3} = 0.0656$ mol dm⁻³

1 mol $Sr(OH)_2$ weighs 122 g.

Concentration of $Sr(OH)_2 = 0.0656 \times 122\,g\,dm^{-3} = 8.00\,g\,dm^{-3}$

9. 1 mol NaOH weighs 40 g.

1.00 g in 250 cm³ $\equiv$ 4.00 g dm⁻³ = 0.100 mol dm⁻³

Number of moles of $NaOH = \dfrac{25.0}{1000} \times 0.100 = 2.50 \times 10^{-3}$

From the equation, you only need half as much sulphuric acid as sodium hydroxide.

Number of moles of $H_2SO_4 = 0.5 \times 2.50 \times 10^{-3}$

$= 1.25 \times 10^{-3}$ (in 23.5 cm³ of solution)

Concentration of $H_2SO_4 = \dfrac{1000}{23.5} \times 1.25 \times 10^{-3} = 0.0532$ mol dm⁻³

But the original acid was 10 times more concentrated than this, i.e. 0.532 mol dm⁻³

10. Number of moles of $Na_2S_2O_3 = \dfrac{18.8}{1000} \times 0.100 = 1.88 \times 10^{-3}$

From the equation, you only need half as much iodine as sodium thiosulphate.

Number of moles of $I_2 = 0.5 \times 1.88 \times 10^{-3}$

$= 9.4 \times 10^{-4}$ (in 25.0 cm³ of solution)

Concentration of $I_2 = \dfrac{1000}{25.0} \times 9.4 \times 10^{-4} = 0.0376$ mol dm⁻³

> **Care!** It's I_2, not I.

1 mol I_2 weighs 254 g.

Concentration of $I_2 = 0.0376 \times 254\,g\,dm^{-3} = 9.55\,g\,dm^{-3}$

11. Number of moles of $MnO_4^-{}_{(aq)}$ = no of moles of $KMnO_4$ because each $KMnO_4$ contains 1 MnO_4^- ion.

Number of moles of $MnO_4^-{}_{(aq)} = \dfrac{28.1}{1000} \times 0.0200 = 5.62 \times 10^{-4}$

The equation shows that you need more hydrogen peroxide than MnO_4^- ions. Specifically, you need 2.5 times as much (5/2 times as much).

Number of moles of $H_2O_2 = 2.5 \times 5.62 \times 10^{-4}$

$= 1.405 \times 10^{-3}$ (in 25.0 cm³ of solution)

Concentration of $H_2O_2 = \dfrac{1000}{25.0} \times 1.405 \times 10^{-3} = 0.0562$ mol dm⁻³

12. Number of moles of $KMnO_4 = \dfrac{24.0}{1000} \times 0.0200 = 4.80 \times 10^{-4}$

The equation shows that you need 5/2 times as much K_2SO_3 as $KMnO_4$.

Number of moles of $K_2SO_3 = \dfrac{5}{2} \times 4.80 \times 10^{-4}$

$$= 1.20 \times 10^{-3} \text{ (in } 25.0 \text{ cm}^3 \text{ of solution)}$$

Total moles of K_2SO_3 in 250 cm^3 = $10 \times 1.20 \times 10^{-3} = 0.0120$
1 mol K_2SO_3 weighs 158 g.
Mass of K_2SO_3 in 250 cm^3 = 0.0120×158 g = 1.896 g

Percentage purity $= \dfrac{1.896}{2.00} \times 100 = 94.8\%$

13. Number of moles NaOH $= \dfrac{18.0}{1000} \times 0.200 = 3.60 \times 10^{-3}$

The equation shows that you need half as much H_2SO_4 as NaOH.
Number of moles of $H_2SO_4 = 1.80 \times 10^{-3}$ (in 25.0 cm^3 of solution)
Number of moles of H_2SO_4 in 250 cm^3 = $10 \times 1.80 \times 10^{-3} = 0.0180$
i.e. 0.0180 moles of H_2SO_4 was left after reaction with the zinc.

Number of moles of H_2SO_4 originally $= \dfrac{50.0}{1000} \times 0.500 = 0.0250$

Number of moles of H_2SO_4 used by Zn = $0.0250 - 0.0180 = 0.0070$
The equation shows that 1 mole of H_2SO_4 reacts with 1 mole of Zn.
Number of moles of Zn = 0.0070
Mass of zinc = 0.0070×65 g = 0.455 g

Percentage purity $= \dfrac{0.455}{0.462} \times 100 = 98.5\%$

14. Number of moles of $NaHCO_3$ in titration $= \dfrac{40.0}{1000} \times 0.100 = 4.00 \times 10^{-3}$

The equation shows that 1 mole $NaHCO_3$ reacts with 1 mole HCl.
Number of moles HCl = 4.00×10^{-3} (in 25.0 cm^3 of diluted solution)
Number of moles HCl left over in mixture = $10 \times 4.00 \times 10^{-3} = 0.0400$

Number of moles of HCl originally $= \dfrac{100}{1000} \times 1.00 = 0.100$

Number of moles of HCl used up = $0.100 - 0.0400 = 0.060$

The equation shows that HCl and NaOH react 1:1.
Number of moles of NaOH in original mixture $= 0.060$

15. A1 $Na_2CO_3 + HCl \rightarrow NaCl + NaHCO_3$
This reaction needs 12.7 cm^3 of HCl

A2 $NaHCO_3 + HCl \rightarrow NaCl + CO_2 + H_2O$

B $NaHCO_3 + HCl \rightarrow NaCl + CO_2 + H_2O$
The two sodium hydrogencarbonate reactions need 20.9 cm^3 of HCl

If reaction A1 needs 12.7 cm^3, then so does reaction A2. That means that the sodium hydrogencarbonate originally in the solution (reaction B) needs $(20.9 - 12.7)$ cm^3 = 8.2 cm^3.

Finding the concentration of the sodium carbonate:

Number of moles of HCl $= \dfrac{12.7}{1000} \times 0.250 = 3.175 \times 10^{-3}$ mol

Equation A1 shows the reaction is 1:1 for this first stage.
Number of moles of $Na_2CO_3 = 3.175 \times 10^{-3}$ (in $25.0\,cm^3$)

Concentration of $Na_2CO_3 = 3.175 \times 10^{-3} \times \dfrac{1000}{25.0} = 0.127\,mol\,dm^{-3}$

Finding the concentration of the sodium hydrogencarbonate:

Number of moles of HCl $= \dfrac{8.2}{1000} \times 0.250 = 2.05 \times 10^{-3}$ mol

Equation B shows the reaction is 1:1.
Number of moles of $NaHCO_3 = 2.05 \times 10^{-3}$ (in $25.0\,cm^3$)

Concentration of $NaHCO_3 \quad = 2.05 \times 10^{-3} \times \dfrac{1000}{25.0} = 0.082\,mol\,dm^{-3}$

16. A $NaOH + HCl \rightarrow NaCl + H_2O$

B1 $Na_2CO_3 + HCl \rightarrow NaCl + NaHCO_3$

B2 $NaHCO_3 + HCl \rightarrow NaCl + CO_2 + H_2O$

Reactions A and B1 are picked up by the phenolphthalein. Reaction B2 needs an extra $(50.0 - 46.9\,cm^3) = 3.1\,cm^3$ acid. Reaction B1 needs the same amount as reaction B2 because it is the first half of the overall reaction between sodium carbonate and HCl.

(a) Finding the concentration of the sodium carbonate:

Number of moles of HCl $= \dfrac{3.1}{1000} \times 0.100 = 3.1 \times 10^{-4}$ mol

Equation B1 shows the reaction is 1:1 for this first stage.
Number of moles of $Na_2CO_3 = 3.1 \times 10^{-4}$ (in $25.0\,cm^3$)

Concentration of $Na_2CO_3 = 3.1 \times 10^{-4} \times \dfrac{1000}{25.0} = 0.0124\,mol\,dm^{-3}$

(b) The total volume of the solution made up was $1.00\,dm^3$, and so 0.0124 mol of Na_2CO_3 was produced. The equation shows that 1 mol CO_2 gives 1 mol Na_2CO_3.

Number of moles of CO_2 present in $1.0\,m^3$ of air $= 0.0124$

(c) Volume of $CO_2 = 0.0124 \times 0.024\,m^3 = 2.976 \times 10^{-4}\,m^3$

Percentage of $CO_2 = \dfrac{2.976 \times 10^{-4}}{1.0} \times 100 = 0.030\%$ (to 2 significant figures)

17. (a) $0.0738\,mol\,dm^{-3}$

(b) $3.16\,g\,dm^{-3}$

(c) $0.180\,mol\,dm^{-3}$

(d) $3.58\,g$

18. (a) $0.600 \, dm^3$ (b) $2.50 \, g$

19. $14.9 \, cm^3$

20. $1.2 \, dm^3$ (no more than 2 significant figures acceptable)

21. $31.8 \, g \, dm^{-3}$

22. (a) YCl_2 (b) $Y + 2HCl \rightarrow YCl_2 + H_2$

23. (a) $0.179 \, mol \, dm^{-3}$ (b) $0.0444 \, mol \, dm^{-3}$ (c) $0.394 \, mol \, dm^{-3}$

24. $1.11 \, g \, dm^{-3}$

25. (a) $0.0206 \, mol \, dm^{-3}$ (b) $0.115 \, mol \, dm^{-3}$

26. $1.05 \, mol \, dm^{-3}$

27. 91.7%

28. (a) $0.0250 \, mol$ (b) 4.00×10^{-3} (0.00400) mol
(c) $0.0210 \, mol$ (d) $44.9 \, g \, dm^{-3}$

29. (a) $0.0250 \, mol$ (b) $0.0205 \, mol$
(c) $0.00225 \, mol$ (d) 0.466 tonnes

30. (a) $0.00100 \, mol$ (b) Cl^- $0.355 \, g$; M^{n+} $0.855 \, g$ (c) MCl

31. Na_2CO_3 $0.0500 \, mol \, dm^{-3}$; $NaHCO_3$ $0.0800 \, mol \, dm^{-3}$

32. Na_2CO_3 $4.24 \, g \, dm^{-3}$; $NaOH$ $4.80 \, g \, dm^{-3}$

Chapter 5

1. (a) $29.7 \, ^\circ C$ (The temperature is falling by a steady $0.2 \, ^\circ C$ per minute.)

(b) Temperature increase of sodium hydroxide solution $= 29.7 - 20.5 \, ^\circ C$
$$= 9.2 \, ^\circ C$$
Temperature increase of acid $= 29.7 - 20.8 \, ^\circ C$
$$= 8.9 \, ^\circ C$$
Heat evolved = mass × specific heat × temperature rise
Total heat evolved $= (50 \times 4.18 \times 9.2) + (25 \times 4.18 \times 8.9) \, J$
$$= 2850 \, J \text{ (or } 2.85 \, kJ)$$

➤ If you were talking about the heat change during the reaction, you would have to quote this as $-57\,kJ\,mol^{-1}$ to show that the heat was evolved.

(c) Number of moles of water produced = number of moles of NaOH at start (see equation)

Number of moles of NaOH $= \dfrac{50}{1000} \times 1 = 0.05$

2.85 kJ are evolved when 0.05 moles of water are formed.

Heat evolved per mole of water $= \dfrac{2.85}{0.05}\,kJ\,mol^{-1} = 57\,kJ\,mol^{-1}$

2. (a) Temperature increase $= 24.9 - 19.7°C$
$$= 5.2°C$$

Heat evolved $= 5.2 \times 1.15\,kJ$
$$= 5.98\,kJ\ (6.0\,kJ\ \text{to 2 significant figures})$$

(b) Mass of hexane burnt $= 45.63 - 45.50\,g$
$$= 0.13\,g$$

1 mole of hexane weighs 86 g.

If 0.13 g evolves 5.98 kJ, then 86 g evolves

➤ See the side note above.

$5.98 \times \dfrac{86}{0.13}\,kJ\,mol^{-1} = 4000\,kJ\,mol^{-1}\ (\text{to 2 significant figures})$

3. (a) $C_{(s)} + O_{2(g)} \rightarrow CO_{2(g)}$

(b) $CH_{4(g)} + 2O_{2(g)} \rightarrow CO_{2(g)} + 2H_2O_{(l)}$

(c) $C_2H_5OH_{(l)} + 3O_{2(g)} \rightarrow 2CO_{2(g)} + 3H_2O_{(l)}$

(d) $C_8H_{18(l)} + 12\frac{1}{2}O_{2(g)} \rightarrow 8CO_{2(g)} + 9H_2O_{(l)}$

4. (a) $Na_{(s)} + \frac{1}{2}I_{2(s)} \rightarrow NaI_{(s)}$

(b) $H_{2(g)} + \frac{1}{2}O_{2(g)} \rightarrow H_2O_{(l)}$

(c) $2C_{(s)} + 3H_{2(g)} + \frac{1}{2}O_{2(g)} \rightarrow C_2H_5OH_{(l)}$

(d) $Ca_{(s)} + C_{(s)} + 1\frac{1}{2}O_{2(g)} \rightarrow CaCO_{3(s)}$

(e) $Na_{(s)} + \frac{1}{2}Cl_{2(g)} + 1\frac{1}{2}O_{2(g)} \rightarrow NaClO_{3(s)}$

5.

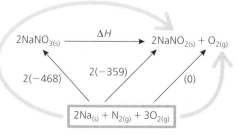

$\Delta H + 2(-468) = 2(-359)$

Giving: $\Delta H = +218\,kJ\,mol^{-1}$

6.

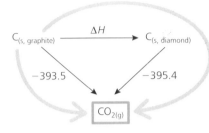

$\Delta H - 395.4 = -393.5$

Giving: $\Delta H = +1.9\,\text{kJ mol}^{-1}$

7.

> ➤ People sometimes worry about the oxygen in a question like this – there isn't an arrow attaching it to anything else. In any cycle involving combustion, we don't bother to include the oxygens coming from the air – they will automatically balance. In this case, because of the oxygen present already in the equation, we simply need a correspondingly smaller amount from the air. The oxygens in the equation are part of those ending up in CO_2 and H_2O.

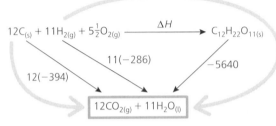

$\Delta H - 5640 = 12(-394) + 11(-286)$

Giving: $\Delta H = -2234\,\text{kJ mol}^{-1}$

8.

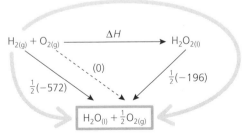

$\Delta H + 4(-178) = 2(-824) + 8(-297)$

Giving: $\Delta H = -3312\,\text{kJ mol}^{-1}$

9.

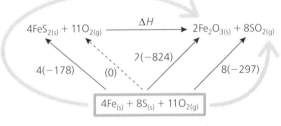

$\Delta H + \frac{1}{2}(-196) = \frac{1}{2}(-572)$

Giving: $\Delta H = -188\,\text{kJ mol}^{-1}$

10.

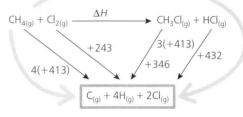

$\Delta H + 3(+413) + 346 + 432 = 4(+413) + 243$

Giving: $\Delta H = -122 \, \text{kJ mol}^{-1}$

11.

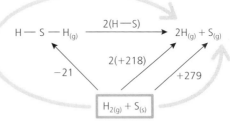

$2(\text{H--S}) - 21 = 2(+218) + 279$

Giving: $(\text{H--S}) = +368 \, \text{kJ mol}^{-1}$

12.

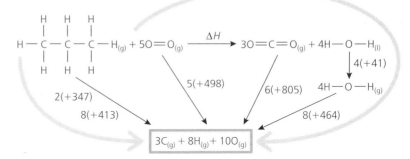

$\Delta H + 6(+805) + 4(+41) + 8(+464) = 2(+347) + 8(+413) + 5(+498)$

Giving: $\Delta H = -2218 \, \text{kJ mol}^{-1}$

13.

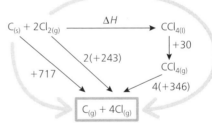

$\Delta H + 30 + 4(+346) = +717 + 2(+243)$

Giving $\Delta H = -211 \, \text{kJ mol}^{-1}$

14.

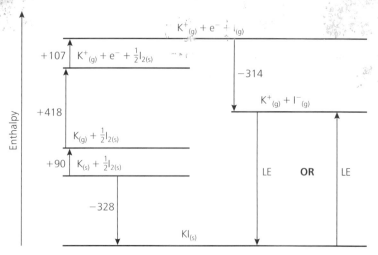

If you define LE as the exothermic change when the solid is formed from the gaseous ions:

$+90 + 418 + 107 - 314 + LE = -328$

Giving: $\qquad LE = -629\,kJ\,mol^{-1}$

If you define LE as the endothermic change when gaseous ions are formed from the solid:

$+90 + 418 + 107 - 314 = -328 + LE$

Giving: $\qquad LE = +629\,kJ\,mol^{-1}$

15.

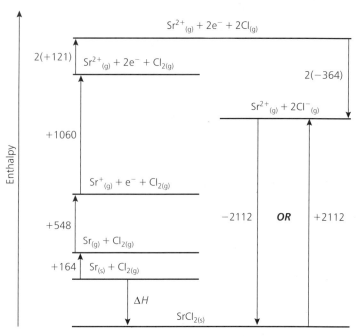

If you define LE as the exothermic change when the solid is formed from the gaseous ions:

$$\Delta H = +164 + 548 + 1060 + 2(+121) + 2(-364) - 2112$$

Giving $\Delta H = -826\,kJ\,mol^{-1}$

if you define LE as the endothermic change when gaseous ions are formed from the solid:

$\Delta H + 2112 = +164 + 548 + 1060 + 2(+121) + 2(-364)$

Giving: $\Delta H = -826 \text{ kJ mol}^{-1}$

16.

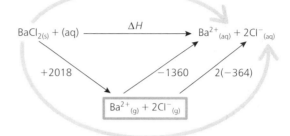

$\Delta H = +2018 - 1360 + 2(-364)$

Giving: $\Delta H = -70 \text{ kJ mol}^{-1}$

17. (a) 32.0 °C   (b) 5390 J (5.39 kJ)

(c) -54 kJ mol^{-1} (2 significant figures)

18. (a) 1.21 kJ °C^{-1} (b) $-1800 \text{ kJ mol}^{-1}$ (2 sig figs)

19. -205 kJ mol^{-1}

20. (a) $+224 \text{ kJ mol}^{-1}$ (b) $+323 \text{ kJ mol}^{-1}$

21. -279 kJ mol^{-1}

22. $-1302 \text{ kJ mol}^{-1}$

23. (a) $-534.6 \text{ kJ mol}^{-1}$ (b) $1.67 \times 10^7 \text{ kJ}$

24. $-90.5 \text{ kJ mol}^{-1}$

25. HF -542 kJ mol^{-1}; HCl -185 kJ mol^{-1}

26. -307 kJ mol^{-1}

27. (a) $+327 \text{ kJ mol}^{-1}$ (b) $+323 \text{ kJ mol}^{-1}$

28. $-281.6 \text{ kJ mol}^{-1}$

29. (a) -349 kJ mol^{-1} (b) -860 kJ mol^{-1}

30. -3 kJ mol^{-1}

Chapter 6

1. Second order with respect to A. Tripling the concentration of A between experiments 2 and 3 causes the rate to go up 9 times ($9 = 3^2$).

   Zero order with respect to B. Changing the concentration of B between experiments 1 and 2 has no effect on the rate.

   Rate $= k[A]^2$

   $$k = \frac{\text{rate}}{[A]^2} = \frac{1.0 \times 10^{-5}}{(0.010)^2} = 0.10\,\text{mol}^{-1}\,\text{dm}^3\,\text{s}^{-1}$$

   (See example 2 on pages 130 to 131 if you have problems with the units.)

2. (a) D: first order. Tripling the concentration between experiments 1 and 4 triples the rate.

   E: zero order. Halving the concentration between experiments 1 and 3 has no effect on rate.

   F: first order. Doubling the concentration between experiments 1 and 2 doubles the rate.

   Rate $= k[D][F]$

   $$k = \frac{\text{rate}}{[D][F]} = \frac{4.40 \times 10^{-6}}{0.10 \times 0.20} = 2.2 \times 10^{-4}\,\text{mol}^{-1}\,\text{dm}^3\,\text{s}^{-1}$$

   (See example 2 on pages 130 to 131 if you have problems with the units.)

   (b) (i) $8.80 \times 10^{-6}\,\text{mol}\,\text{dm}^{-3}\,\text{s}^{-1}$. Compare experiments 1 and 5. The change in the concentration of E will not affect the rate. The concentration of D has doubled and so the rate doubles as well. (Alternatively you could feed the concentration values into the rate equation now that you have worked out the rate constant, k.)

   (ii) $0.40\,\text{mol}\,\text{dm}^{-3}$. Compare experiments 1 and 6. The concentration of F has halved and that would halve the rate to $2.20 \times 10^{-6}\,\text{mol}\,\text{dm}^{-3}\,\text{s}^{-1}$. To increase the rate to the desired value, the concentration of D would have to increase 4 times. (Alternatively – saving some thought, but using more maths – slot the known numbers from experiment 6 into the rate equation and solve it for [D].)

3. R: zero order. Changing the concentration between experiments 1 and 2 does not change the rate.

   S: first order. You can ignore the concentrations of R since they have no effect. Multiplying the concentration of S four times (experiments 1 and 3 or experiments 2 and 3) increases the rate four times.

   Rate $= k[S]$

   $$k = \frac{\text{rate}}{[S]} = \frac{1.6 \times 10^{-7}}{0.10} = 1.6 \times 10^{-6}\,\text{s}^{-1}$$

   (See the side box on page 138 if you have problems with the units.)

4. L: second order. Doubling the concentration between experiments 1 and 2 increases the rate four times.

M: zero order. Changing the concentration of M between experiments 2 and 3 has no effect on rate.

N: first order. Doubling its concentration between experiments 3 and 4 doubles the rate.

Rate = $k[L]^2[N]$

$$k = \frac{\text{rate}}{[L]^2[N]} = \frac{9.60 \times 10^{-5}}{(0.10)^2 \times 0.10} = 0.096\,\text{mol}^{-2}\,\text{dm}^6\,\text{s}^{-1}$$

(See pages 129 to 130 if you have problems with the units.)

5. (a) rate = $k[X]^2 = 1.44 \times 10^4 \times (0.200)^2 = 5.76 \times 10^{-6}\,\text{mol}\,\text{dm}^{-3}\,\text{s}^{-1}$

(b) $[X]^2 = \dfrac{\text{rate}}{k} = \dfrac{1.20 \times 10^{-5}}{1.44 \times 10^{-4}} = 0.08333$

$[X] = \sqrt{0.08333} = 0.289\,\text{mol}\,\text{dm}^{-3}$

6. Your graph should be a straight line through the origin (0,0) with a slope of 0.055. Because it is a straight line, the rate is proportional to the concentration of X – in other words, it is first order with respect to X. Because rate = $k[X]$, the slope gives you the rate constant, which is $0.055\,\text{s}^{-1}$. (See the side box on page 138 if you have problems with the units.)

7. Plotting rate against [Y] gives a curve, but a plot of rate against $[Y]^2$ gives a straight line through the origin (0,0). This graph shows that the rate is proportional to $[Y]^2$ – in other words the reaction is second order with respect to Y. Because rate = $k[Y]^2$, the slope gives you the rate constant, which is $1.20 \times 10^{-4}\,\text{mol}^{-1}\,\text{dm}^3\,\text{s}^{-1}$. (See example 2 on pages 130 to 131 if you have problems with the units.)

Incidentally, it would save you time if you didn't plot the unnecessary graph of rate against [Y]. Look at the figures before you start – it is fairly obvious that the rate **is not** proportional to [Y]. Look, for example, at the rates corresponding to concentrations of 0.200 and 0.445. The concentration has slightly more than doubled, but the rate has gone up much more than that.

8. Your graph will be a straight line starting at 1.00 and sloping down as time increases. The concentration is falling at a steady rate throughout. Because this rate is constant even though the concentration is falling, the reaction is zero order. Rate = k. The rate of the reaction is given by the slope of the line, and the rate constant has the same value. $k = 0.0075\,\text{mol}\,\text{dm}^{-3}\,\text{s}^{-1}$. The units are the units of rate.

9. The graph will be a curve, with a constant half life showing that it is first order. The half life is 500 seconds. (To be precise, the half life is 499 seconds, but your graph will not produce that degree of accuracy.)

10. (a)

Time (mins)	0	5	10	15	20
%	100	50	25	12.5	6.25

After 20 minutes, 6.25% remains.

(b) The concentration falls to a quarter (25%) in two half lives (see table in part (a) for example). If 36 minutes is two half lives, one half life is 18 minutes.

(c)

Time (mins)	0	8	16	24	32	40	48
Concentration $(mol\,dm^{-3})$		0.64	0.32	0.16	0.08	0.04	0.02	0.01

It takes 48 minutes for the concentration to fall to $0.01\,mol\,dm^{-3}$.

(d)

Time (mins)	0	5	10	15	20	25	30
[A] $(mol\,dm^{-3})$	1.00	?	?	0.50	?	?	0.25
[B] $(mol\,dm^{-3})$	2.00	?	1.00	?	0.50	?	0.25

You can see that the two concentrations become equal after 30 minutes. (The question marks are for concentrations that you can't work out from half lives. You can only work out the concentration easily if you have a whole number of half lives – one half life, two half lives, etc.)

11. Reorganise the table so that you have values of $1/T$ and $\ln k$. The values of k quoted in the table have been multiplied by 10^3. Don't forget to multiply them by 10^{-3} (or divide by 10^3) before you find $\ln k$. In the table below, the $1/T$ values have been multiplied by 10^3 to make them easier to plot.

$1/T \times 10^3$	3.448	3.226	3.030	2.857
$\ln k$	−6.90	−5.29	−3.88	−2.63

You should get a straight line with a slope of −7220 K (theoretical value). The slope is equal to $-E_A/R$.

$-E_A/R = -7220$

$E_A = 7220 \times 8.31 = 60{,}000\,J\,mol^{-1}$ $(60\,kJ\,mol^{-1})$

12. K first order; L first order; Rate $= k[K][L]$

$k = 5.5 \times 10^{-3}\,mol^{-1}\,dm^3\,s^{-1}$

13. (a) A zero order; B second order; C first order; Rate $= k[B]^2[C]$

$k = 2.10 \times 10^{-3}\,mol^{-2}\,dm^6\,s^{-1}$

(b) $3.28 \times 10^{-5}\,mol\,dm^{-3}\,s^{-1}$

14. (a) Rate $= k[G][F]$

(b) $1.4 \times 10^{-4}\,mol\,dm^{-3}\,s^{-1}$

(c) $0.50\,mol\,dm^{-3}$

15. $a = 0.20$; $b = 5.0 \times 10^{-4}$; $c = 0.30$

16. Reaction U: first order; $k = 2.0 \times 10^{-3}\,s^{-1}$. (Graph of rate against [U] gives a straight line; slope gives k.)

Reaction V: zero order; $k = 0.016\,mol\,dm^{-3}\,s^{-1}$. (Rate is independent of concentration. Rate $= k$.)

Reaction W: second order; $k = 1.0 \times 10^{-4}\,mol^{-1}\,dm^3\,s^{-1}$. (Graph of rate against $[W]^2$ gives a straight line; slope gives k.)

Reaction X: first order; $k = 4.5 \times 10^{-3}\,s^{-1}$. (Graph of rate against [X] gives a straight line; slope gives k.)

17. Graph of concentration against time has a constant half life $= 240$ seconds.

18. (a) 8 minutes   (b) $0.025\,mol\,dm^{-3}$

19. $83\,kJ\,mol^{-1}$

Chapter 7

1. (a) $K_c = \dfrac{[SO_3]^2}{[SO_2]^2[O_2]}\,mol^{-1}\,dm^3$ (b) $K_c = \dfrac{[NO_2]^2}{[N_2O_4]}\,mol\,dm^{-3}$

(c) $K_c = \dfrac{[H_2][I_2]}{[HI]^2}$ (no units)   (d) $K_c = \dfrac{[N_2][H_2]^3}{[NH_3]^2}\,mol^2\,dm^{-6}$

2. $K_c = \dfrac{[N]}{[M]^2} = \dfrac{0.872}{(0.141)^2} = 43.9\,mol^{-1}\,dm^3$

3. (a)

	X	⇌	Y	+	Z
Start (moles)	1.00		0		0
Equilibrium (moles)	1.00 − 0.200		0.200		0.200
Equilibrium concentration (mol dm⁻³)	0.800/25.0 = 0.0320		0.200/25.0 = 8.00 × 10⁻³		0.200/25.0 = 8.00 × 10⁻³

> **Hint**: It is easy to mis-read $25.0\,dm^3$ in the question as $25.0\,cm^3$, because this is such a familiar value. Read questions carefully!

$$K_c = \frac{[Y][Z]}{[X]}$$

$$= \frac{(8.00 \times 10^{-3})(8.00 \times 10^{-3})}{0.0320} = 2.00 \times 10^{-3}\,mol\,dm^{-3}$$

(b) K_c increases with temperature. Therefore more Y and Z are formed at the higher temperature. Therefore the forward reaction is endothermic. According to Le Chatelier, the system "tries" to reduce the higher temperature by favouring the reaction which absorbs heat.

4.

	A	+	B	⇌	C	+	D
Start (moles)	2.00		1.00		0		0
Equilibrium (moles)	2.00 − 0.600 = 1.400		0.400		0.600		0.600
Equilibrium concentration (mol dm⁻³)	1.400/V		0.400/V		0.600/V		0.600/V

> **Hint**: If there is 0.400 mole of B left, 1.00 − 0.400 mole has been used up = 0.600 mole. This means that 0.600 mole of A will be used up as well, and 0.600 mole of C and D will be formed.

$$K_c = \frac{[C][D]}{[A][B]}$$

$$= \frac{(0.600/V)(0.600/V)}{(1.400/V)(0.400/V)} = \frac{0.600 \times 0.600}{1.400 \times 0.400} = 0.643 \text{ (no units)}$$

5.

> **Hint**: For each mole of I_2 formed, 2 moles of HI are used up.

	2HI	$\rightleftharpoons$	H_2	+	I_2
Start (moles)	1.00		0		0
Equilibrium (moles)	$1.00 - (2 \times 0.114)$		0.114		0.114
	$= 0.772$				
Equilibrium concentration (mol dm^{-3})	$0.772/20.0$ $= 0.0386$		$0.114/20.0$ $= 5.70 \times 10^{-3}$		$0.114/20.0$ $= 5.70 \times 10^{-3}$

$$K_c = \frac{[H_2][I_2]}{[HI]^2}$$

$$= \frac{(5.70 \times 10^{-3})(5.70 \times 10^{-3})}{(0.0386)^2} = 0.0218 \text{ (no units)}$$

6.

> **Hint**: If there is 0.257 mole of ethanoic acid left, $1.00 - 0.257$ mole has been used up $= 0.743$ mole.
>
> In the case of the water, the 0.743 mole formed is added to the 1.00 mole there to start with.

	$CH_3COOH_{(l)}$	+	$C_2H_5OH_{(l)}$	$\rightleftharpoons$	$CH_3COOC_2H_{5(l)}$	+	$H_2O_{(l)}$
Start (moles)	1.00		2.00		0		1.00
Equilibrium (moles)	0.257		$2.00 - 0.743$ $= 1.257$		0.743		1.743
Equilibrium concentrations (mol dm^{-3})	$0.257/V$		$1.257/V$		$0.743/V$		$1.743/V$

$$K_c = \frac{[CH_3COOC_2H_5][H_2O]}{[CH_3COOH][C_2H_5OH]}$$

$$= \frac{(0.743/V)(1.743/V)}{(0.257/V)(1.257/V)} = \frac{0.743 \times 1.743}{0.257 \times 1.257} = 4.01 \text{ (no units)}$$

7. Moles of $CH_3COOC_2H_5$ at start $= 44.0/88 = 0.500$ mol

Moles of water at start $= 36.0/18 = 2.00$ mol

Moles of NaOH used in titration $= \frac{29.5}{1000} \times 1.00 = 0.0295$

Because the neutralisation reaction is 1:1, number of moles of CH_3COOH in 25.0 cm$^3 = 0.0295$

Therefore number of moles of CH_3COOH in 250 cm$^3 = 0.295$ mol

	$CH_3COOC_2H_{5(l)}$	+	$H_2O_{(l)}$	$\rightleftharpoons$	$CH_3COOH_{(l)}$	+	$C_2H_5OH_{(l)}$
Start (moles)	0.500		2.00		0		0
Equilibrium (moles)	$0.500 - 0.295$ $= 0.205$		$2.00 - 0.295$ $= 1.705$		0.295		0.295
Equilibrium concentrations (mol dm^{-3})	$0.205/V$		$1.705/V$		$0.295/V$		$0.295/V$

$$K_c = \frac{[CH_3COOH][C_2H_5OH]}{[CH_3COOC_2H_5][H_2O]}$$

$$= \frac{(0.295/V)(0.295/V)}{(0.205/V)(1.705/V)} = \frac{0.295 \times 0.295}{0.205 \times 1.705} = 0.249 \text{ (no units)}$$

8.

➤ **Hint**: Let the number of moles of A at equilibrium be "a". (2.0 − a) moles of A will have converted into B.

	A	⇌	B
Start (moles)	2.0		0
Equilibrium (moles)	a		2.0 − a
Equilibrium concentrations (mol dm^{-3})	a/V		(2.0 − a)/V

$$K_c = \frac{[B]}{[A]}$$

$$39 = \frac{(2.0 - a)/V}{a/V} = \frac{2.0 - a}{a}$$

$$39a = 2.0 - a$$
$$40a = 2.0$$
$$a = 0.050 \, mol$$

9.

➤ **Hint**: Let the percentage converted be "p" and start with 100 moles. You could also start with 1 mole, work out the **fraction** converted and then multiply by 100 at the end.

	S	⇌	T
Start (moles)	100		0
Equilibrium (moles)	100 − p		p
Equilibrium concentrations (mol dm^{-3})	(100 − p)/V		p/V

$$K_c = \frac{[T]}{[S]}$$

$$24 = \frac{p/V}{(100 - p)/V} = \frac{p}{(100 - p)}$$

$$2400 - 24p = p$$
$$25p = 2400$$
$$p = 96\%$$

10. (a)

	CH$_3$COOC$_2$H$_{5(l)}$	+	H$_2$O$_{(l)}$	⇌	CH$_3$COOH$_{(l)}$	+	C$_2$H$_5$OH$_{(l)}$
Start (moles)	1		w		0		0
Equilibrium (moles)	1 − f		w − f		f		f
Equilibrium concentrations (mol dm^{-3})	(1 − f)/V		(w − f)/V		f/V		f/V

$$K_c = \frac{[CH_3COOH][C_2H_5OH]}{[CH_3COOC_2H_5][H_2O]}$$

$$0.25 = \frac{(f/V)(f/V)}{[(1-f)/V][(w-f)/V]} = \frac{f^2}{(1-f)(w-f)}$$

(b) If w = 1:

$$\frac{f^2}{(1-f)(1-f)} = 0.25$$

Since the left hand side is a perfect square, you can take the square root of both sides:

$$\frac{f}{(1-f)} = \pm 0.5$$

Solving this gives f = 0.33 or f = −1. Since the negative answer is impossible, f = 0.33.

If w = 10:

$$\frac{f^2}{(1-f)(10-f)} = 0.25$$

$$\frac{f^2}{(10 - 11f + f^2)} = 0.25$$

$$f^2 = 2.5 - 2.75f + 0.25f^2$$

$$0.75f^2 + 2.75f - 2.5 = 0$$

➤ If you have forgotten the equation, see page 164.

Solving this by the standard equation, gives f = 0.75 (the negative root is impossible).

11. $K_p = \dfrac{P_{PCl_3} \times P_{Cl_2}}{P_{PCl_5}} = \dfrac{80 \times 80}{40} = 160\,kPa$

12. $P_{NO_2} = 101 - 72.0 = 29.0\,kPa$

$K_p = \dfrac{P_{NO_2}^2}{P_{N_2O_4}} = \dfrac{(29.0)^2}{72.0} = 11.7\,kPa$

13. If $\qquad\qquad P_{HI} = 0.786$

$\qquad\qquad P_{H_2} + P_{I_2} = 1.00 - 0.786 = 0.214\,atm$

But $\qquad\qquad P_{H_2} = P_{I_2}$

So each of them $= 0.107\,atm$

$K_p = \dfrac{P_{H_2} \times P_{I_2}}{P_{HI}^2} = \dfrac{0.107 \times 0.107}{(0.786)^2} = 0.0185$ (no units)

> **Remember:** The total pressure is the sum of the partial pressures.

The partial pressures of hydrogen and iodine are identical because you are producing equal numbers of moles of them. Equal numbers of moles in the same container at the same temperature implies equal pressures.

14.

	$CO_{(g)}$	$+$	$H_2O_{(g)}$	$\rightleftharpoons$	$CO_{2(g)}$	$+$	$H_{2(g)}$
Start (moles)	1.00		1.00		0		0
Equilibrium (moles)	1.00 − 0.740		1.00 − 0.740		0.740		0.740
	= 0.260		= 0.260				

The total number of moles $= 0.260 + 0.260 + 0.740 + 0.740 = 2.00$

	$CO_{(g)}$	$+$	$H_2O_{(g)}$	$\rightleftharpoons$	$CO_{2(g)}$	$+$	$H_{2(g)}$
Mole fractions	0.130		0.130		0.370		0.370
Partial pressures (atm)	0.130 × 1.50 = 0.195		0.130 × 1.50 = 0.195		0.370 × 1.50 = 0.555		0.370 × 1.50 = 0.555

> **Remember:** Mole fraction is number of moles divided by total number of moles.
>
> Partial pressure is mole fraction × total pressure.

$K_p = \dfrac{P_{CO_2} \times P_{H_2}}{P_{CO} \times P_{H_2O}} = \dfrac{0.555 \times 0.555}{0.195 \times 0.195} = 8.10$ (no units)

15. 640 g of SO_2 is 10.0 mol; 256 g of O_2 is 8.00 mol; 792 g of SO_3 is 9.90 mol.

	$2SO_{2(g)}$	$+$	$O_{2(g)}$	$\rightleftharpoons$	$2SO_{3(g)}$
Start (moles)	10.0		8.00		0
Equilibrium (moles)	10.0 − 9.90		8.00 − (9.90/2)		9.90
	= 0.10		= 3.05		

The total number of moles $= 0.10 + 3.05 + 9.90$
$\qquad\qquad\qquad\qquad\qquad = 13.05$

	$2SO_{2(g)}$	$+$	$O_{2(g)}$	$\rightleftharpoons$	$2SO_{3(g)}$
Mole fractions	0.10/13.05 = 7.663×10^{-3}		3.05/13.05 = 0.2337		9.90/13.05 = 0.7586
Partial pressures (atm)	0.01073		0.3272		1.062

> **Hint:** Multiply the mole fractions by the total pressure (1.40 atm) to get the partial pressures.

$K_p = \dfrac{P_{SO_3}^2}{P_{SO_2}^2 \times P_{O_2}} = \dfrac{(1.062)^2}{(0.01073)^2 \times 0.3272} = 29\,900\,atm^{-1}$

16. If the partial pressure of $H_2 = p$, then the partial pressure of $I_2 = p$ as well.

$$K_p = \frac{P_{H_2} \times P_{I_2}}{P^2_{HI}}$$

$$0.0185 = \frac{p \times p}{(1.32)^2}$$

$$p^2 = 0.0185 \times (1.32)^2$$

$$p = 0.180$$

Partial pressures of hydrogen and iodine are both 0.180 atm.

Total pressure $= 1.32 + 0.180 + 0.180 = 1.68\,\text{atm}$

17. (a)

	$2SO_{2(g)}$	$+$	$O_{2(g)}$	$\rightleftharpoons$	$2SO_{3(g)}$
Start (moles)	2.00		1.00		0
Equilibrium (moles)	1.00		0.50		1.00

(b) The total number of moles $= 2.50$

	$2SO_{2(g)}$	$+$	$O_{2(g)}$	$\rightleftharpoons$	$2SO_{3(g)}$
Mole fractions	1.00/2.50		0.50/2.50		1.00/2.50
	$= 0.400$		$= 0.200$		$= 0.400$
Partial pressures (atm)	$0.400P$		$0.200P$		$0.400P$

(c) $$K_p = \frac{P^2_{SO_3}}{P^2_{SO_2} \times P_{O_2}}$$

$$0.130 = \frac{(0.400P)^2}{(0.400P)^2 \times 0.200P}$$

$$P = \frac{1}{0.200 \times 0.130} = 38.5\,\text{atm}$$

18. (a)

	$N_2O_{4(g)}$	$\rightleftharpoons$	$2NO_{2(g)}$
Start (moles)	100		0
Equilibrium (moles)	80.0		$2 \times 20.0 = 40.0$

> **Hint:** It would make your answer more accurate if you realised that 80.0/120 is 2/3, and that 40.0/120 is 1/3, and then used these fractions rather than converting to decimals.

(b) Total moles $= 120$

	$N_2O_{4(g)}$	$\rightleftharpoons$	$2NO_{2(g)}$
Mole fractions	80.0/120		40.0/120
	$= 0.6667$		$= 0.3333$
Partial pressures (atm)	$0.6667P$		$0.3333P$

(c) $$K_p = \frac{P^2_{NO_2}}{P_{N_2O_4}}$$

$$0.115 = \frac{(0.3333P)^2}{0.6667P}$$

$$P = \frac{0.115 \times 0.6667}{(0.3333)^2} = 0.690\,\text{atm}$$

(d) $P_{N_2O_4} = 0.6667 \times 0.690\,\text{atm} = 0.460\,\text{atm}$

$P_{NO_2} = 0.3333 \times 0.690\,\text{atm} = 0.230\,\text{atm}$

19. (a) The partial pressures of chlorine and PCl_3 will both be "p" because they are produced 1:1.

The partial pressure of PCl_5 will be the total pressure minus the other partial pressures $= 400 - 2p$

(b)
$$K_p = \frac{P_{PCl_3} \times P_{Cl_2}}{P_{PCl_5}}$$

$$160 = \frac{p \times p}{(400 - 2p)}$$

$$160(400 - 2p) = p^2$$

$$p^2 + 320p - 64\,000 = 0$$

$$p = \frac{-320 \pm \sqrt{320^2 + (4 \times 64\,000)}}{2}$$

$$= 139 \text{ kPa (the negative root is impossible)}$$

(c) The partial pressures are:

Cl_2: 139 kPa
PCl_3: 139 kPa
PCl_5: $400 - (2 \times 139) = 122$ kPa

20.

	$C_{(s)}$	$+$	$CO_{2(g)}$	$\rightleftharpoons$	$2CO_{(g)}$
Mole fractions			0.217		0.783
Partial pressures (atm)			0.217×5.00 $= 1.085$		0.783×5.00 $= 3.915$

$$K_p = \frac{P_{CO}^2}{P_{CO_2}} = \frac{(3.915)^2}{1.085} = 14.1 \text{ atm}$$

21.

	$Sn_{(s)}$	$+$	$Pb^{2+}_{(aq)}$	$\rightleftharpoons$	$Pb_{(s)}$	$+$	$Sn^{2+}_{(aq)}$
Start concentration (mol dm^{-3})			1.0				0
Equilibrium concentration (mol dm^{-3})			$1.0 - f$				f

$$K_c = \frac{[Sn^{2+}]}{[Pb^{2+}]}$$

$$2.2 = \frac{f}{(1.0 - f)}$$

$$2.2(1.0 - f) = f$$

$$3.2f = 2.2$$

$$f = 0.69$$

22.

	H_2O	H_2	CO
Mole fractions	0.50	0.25	0.25
Partial pressures (atm)	$0.50P$	$0.25P$	$0.25P$

$$K_p = \frac{P_{H_2} \times P_{CO}}{P_{H_2O}}$$

$$3.7 = \frac{(0.25P) \times (0.25P)}{0.50P}$$

$$P = \frac{3.7 \times 0.50}{0.25 \times 0.25} = 30 \text{ atm (no more than 2 significant figures)}$$

23. (a) $K_c = \dfrac{[HI]^2}{[H_2][I_2]} = 53.8$ (no units)

(b) $K_p = \dfrac{P_{HI}^2}{P_{H_2} \times P_{I_2}} = 53.8$ (no units)

24. (a) 0.600 mol N_2O_4; 0.800 mol NO_2

(b) $K_c = \dfrac{[NO_2]^2}{[N_2O_4]} = 0.135\,\text{mol dm}^{-3}$

(c) N_2O_4 222 kPa; NO_2 295 kPa

(d) $K_p = \dfrac{P_{NO_2}^2}{P_{N_2O_4}} = 392$ kPa

25. (a) N_2 18.7%; H_2 56.1%

(b) N_2 18.7 atm; H_2 56.1 atm; NH_3 25.2 atm

(c) $K_p = \dfrac{P_{NH_3}^2}{P_{N_2} \times P_{H_2}^3} = 1.92 \times 10^{-4}\,\text{atm}^{-2}$

26. (a) 0.0400 mol PCl_5; 0.160 mol PCl_3; 0.160 mol Cl_2

(b) $K_c = \dfrac{[PCl_3][Cl_2]}{[PCl_5]} = 0.0408\,\text{mol dm}^{-3}$

(c) PCl_5 10 kPa; PCl_3 40 kPa; Cl_2 40 kPa

(d) $K_p = \dfrac{P_{PCl_3} \times P_{Cl_2}}{P_{PCl_5}} = 160$ kPa

27. 4.0 (no units)

28. (a) Both partial pressures are 741 kPa.

(b) $K_p = \dfrac{P_{H_2} \times P_{CO}}{P_{H_2O}} = 1730$ kPa

29. Both partial pressures are 0.330 atm.

30. Partial pressure of $NO_2 = 0.240$ atm. Total pressure $= 0.740$ atm.

31. $[Pb^{2+}] = 0.47\,\text{mol dm}^{-3}$; $[Sn^{2+}] = 1.03\,\text{mol dm}^{-3}$

32. (a) Partial pressures: PCl_5 0.0526P; PCl_3 0.474P; Cl_2 0.474P

(b) $K_p = \dfrac{P_{PCl_3} \times P_{Cl_2}}{P_{PCl_5}}$

$P = 37.5$ kPa

(c) Partial pressures: PCl_5 1.97 kPa; PCl_3 17.8 kPa; Cl_2 17.8 kPa

33. 9.6 atm

Chapter 8

1. (a) 2.00   (b) 1.60   (c) 3.52   (d) 7.00   (e) 9.12

2. (a) 3.80×10^{-4} (b) 0.0631   (c) 2.24×10^{-6}
   (d) 3.98×10^{-9} (e) 1.00×10^{-13}

3. (a) 3.00   (b) $7.08 \times 10^{-5}\,\text{mol dm}^{-3}$ (c) 2.57   (d) $5.01 \times 10^{-11}\,\text{mol dm}^{-3}$

4. (a) $[H^+] = 0.0300\,\text{mol dm}^{-3}$; $pH = -\log_{10}[H^+] = 1.52$
   (b) $[H^+] = 2 \times 0.00500 = 0.0100\,\text{mol dm}^{-3}$; $pH = -\log_{10}[H^+] = 2.00$
   (c) $[H^+] = 0.120\,\text{mol dm}^{-3}$; $pH = -\log_{10}[H^+] = 0.92$

5. (a) $[H^+] = 0.20\,\text{mol dm}^{-3}$; $[HCl] = 0.20\,\text{mol dm}^{-3}$
   (b) $[H^+] = 0.032\,\text{mol dm}^{-3}$; $[H_2SO_4] = 0.016\,\text{mol dm}^{-3}$
   (c) $[H^+] = 0.010\,\text{mol dm}^{-3}$; $[HNO_3] = 0.010\,\text{mol dm}^{-3}$

> ➤ Answers to 2 significant figures only.

6. (a) $K_w = [H^+][OH^-]$
$[OH^-] = [H^+]$ because the water is pure
$K_w = [H^+]^2$
$[H^+]^2 = 4.52 \times 10^{-15}$
$[H^+] = 6.72 \times 10^{-8}$
$pH = -\log_{10}[H^+] = 7.17$

(b) Repeating (a) with the different value of K_w gives $pH = 6.63$.

7. (a) $[OH^-] = 0.250$
$[H^+][OH^-] = 1.00 \times 10^{-14}$
$[H^+] \times 0.250 = 1.00 \times 10^{-14}$
$$[H^+] = \frac{1.00 \times 10^{-14}}{0.250} = 4.00 \times 10^{-14}\,\text{mol dm}^{-3}$$
$pH = -\log_{10}[H^+] = 13.4$

(b) Each $Ba(OH)_2$ gives $2OH^-$.
$[OH^-] = 2 \times 0.100$
$[H^+][OH^-] = 1.00 \times 10^{-14}$
$[H^+] \times 0.200 = 1.00 \times 10^{-14}$
$$[H^+] = \frac{1.00 \times 10^{-14}}{0.200} = 5.00 \times 10^{-14}\,\text{mol dm}^{-3}$$
$pH = -\log_{10}[H^+] = 13.3$

(c) $[OH^-] = 0.00500$
$[H^+][OH^-] = 1.00 \times 10^{-14}$
$[H^+] \times 0.00500 = 1.00 \times 10^{-14}$
$$[H^+] = \frac{1.00 \times 10^{-14}}{0.00500} = 2.00 \times 10^{-12}\,\text{mol dm}^{-3}$$
$pH = -\log_{10}[H^+] = 11.7$

8. (a) "Unlog" pH to find $[H^+]$.

$$[H^+] = 6.310 \times 10^{-14}$$
$$[H^+][OH^-] = 1.00 \times 10^{-14}$$
$$6.310 \times 10^{-14} \times [OH^-] = 1.00 \times 10^{14}$$

$$[OH^-] = \frac{1.00 \times 10^{-14}}{6.310 \times 10^{-14}} = 0.158 \, mol \, dm^{-3}$$

Therefore, $[NaOH] = 0.158 \, mol \, dm^{-3}$

(b) "Unlog" pH to find $[H^+]$.

$$[H^+] = 5.012 \times 10^{-12}$$
$$[H^+][OH^+] = 1.00 \times 10^{-14}$$
$$5.012 \times 10^{-12} \times [OH^-] = 1.00 \times 10^{-14}$$

$$[OH^-] = \frac{1.00 \times 10^{-14}}{5.012 \times 10^{-12}} = 2.00 \times 10^{-3} \, mol \, dm^{-3}$$

$$[Sr(OH)_2] = \tfrac{1}{2} \times 2.00 \times 10^{-3} = 1.00 \times 10^{-3} \, mol \, dm^{-3}$$

(Each $Sr(OH)_2$ gives $2OH^-$.)

9. (a)

$$\text{Moles of } H^+ = \frac{30.0}{1000} \times 1.00 = 0.0300$$

$$\text{Moles of } OH^- = \frac{25.0}{1000} \times 1.00 = 0.0250$$

$$\text{Moles of excess } H^+ = 0.0300 - 0.0250 = 0.0050$$

$$[H^+] = \frac{1000}{55.0} \times 0.0050 = 0.09091 \, mol \, dm^{-3}$$

$$pH = 1.04$$

> **Hint:** The total volume of the solution is $55 \, cm^3$.

(b)

$$\text{Moles of } H^+ = \frac{15.0}{1000} \times 1.00 = 0.0150$$

$$\text{Moles of } OH^- = \frac{25.0}{1000} \times 1.00 = 0.0250$$

$$\text{Moles of excess } OH^- = 0.0250 - 0.0150 = 0.0100$$

$$[OH^-] = \frac{1000}{40.0} \times 0.0100 = 0.250 \, mol \, dm^{-3}$$

$$[H^+][OH^-] = 1.00 \times 10^{-14}$$
$$[H^+] \times 0.250 = 1.00 \times 10^{-14}$$

$$[H^+] = \frac{1.00 \times 10^{-14}}{0.250} = 4.00 \times 10^{-14} \, mol \, dm^{-3}$$

$$pH = 13.4$$

(c)

$$\text{Moles of } H^+ = \frac{40.0}{1000} \times 0.100 = 4.00 \times 10^{-3}$$

$$\text{Moles of } OH^- = \frac{25.0}{1000} \times 0.200 = 5.00 \times 10^{-3}$$

$$\text{Moles of excess } OH^- = 1.00 \times 10^{-3}$$

$$[OH^-] = \frac{1000}{65.0} \times 1.00 \times 10^{-3} = 0.01538 \, mol \, dm^{-3}$$

$$[H^+][OH^-] = 1.00 \times 10^{-14}$$

$$[H^+] \times 0.01538 = 1.00 \times 10^{-14}$$

$$[H^+] = \frac{1.00 \times 10^{-14}}{0.01538} = 6.50 \times 10^{-13} \text{ mol dm}^{-3}$$

$$pH = 12.2$$

> Each mole of sulphuric acid gives 2 moles of H^+.

(d)

$$\text{Moles of } H^+ = 2 \times \frac{25.0}{1000} \times 0.0500 = 2.50 \times 10^{-3}$$

$$\text{Moles of } OH^- = \frac{10.0}{1000} \times 0.100 = 1.00 \times 10^{-3}$$

$$\text{Moles of excess } H^+ = 1.50 \times 10^{-3}$$

$$[H^+] = \frac{1000}{35.0} \times 1.50 \times 10^{-3} = 0.04286 \text{ mol dm}^{-3}$$

$$pH = 1.37$$

(e)

$$\text{Moles of } H^+ = \frac{20.0}{1000} \times 0.100 = 2.00 \times 10^{-3}$$

$$\text{Moles of } OH^- = 2 \times \frac{25.0}{1000} \times 0.0500 = 2.50 \times 10^{-3}$$

> Each mole of barium hydroxide gives 2 moles of OH^-.

$$\text{Moles of excess } OH^- = 0.50 \times 10^{-3}$$

$$[OH^-] = \frac{1000}{45.0} \times 0.50 \times 10^{-3} = 0.01111 \text{ mol dm}^{-3}$$

$$[H^+][OH^-] = 1.00 \times 10^{-14}$$

$$[H^+] \times 0.01111 = 1.00 \times 10^{-14}$$

$$[H^+] = \frac{1.00 \times 10^{-14}}{0.01111} = 9.00 \times 10^{-13} \text{ mol dm}^{-3}$$

$$pH = 12.0$$

10. pH at $0 \text{ cm}^3 = 14$; pH at $25 \text{ cm}^3 = 7$. The pHs from 5 to 24.9 are calculated in exactly the same way as Q9(b). The pHs from 25.1 to 40 are calculated in exactly the same way as Q9(a). If you don't get an absolutely smooth version of the typical strong acid–strong base pH curve, you have made a careless error.

11. (a) $K_a = \dfrac{[H^+][CN^-]}{[HCN]} \text{ mol dm}^{-3}$

(b) $K_a = \dfrac{[H^+][NO_2^-]}{[HNO_2]} \text{ mol dm}^{-3}$

(c) $K_a = \dfrac{[CH_2ClCOO^-][H^+]}{[CH_2ClCOOH]} \text{ mol dm}^{-3}$

12. (a) 3.91 (b) 4.43 (c) 2.25

13. (a) $1.05 \times 10^{-3} \text{ mol dm}^{-3}$

(b) $2.88 \times 10^{-6} \text{ mol dm}^{-3}$

(c) $2.40 \times 10^{-5} \text{ mol dm}^{-3}$

14. **(a)**

$$HOCl_{(aq)} \rightleftharpoons H^+_{(aq)} + OCl^-_{(aq)}$$

Start concentration (mol dm^{-3}): 0.0200   0   0

Equilibrium concentration (mol dm^{-3}): $0.0200 - [H^+] \approx 0.0200$ $[H^+]$ $[H^+]$

$$K_a = \frac{[H^+][OCl^-]}{[HOCl]}$$

$$3.72 \times 10^{-8} = \frac{[H^+]^2}{0.0200}$$

$$[H^+]^2 = 0.0200 \times 3.72 \times 10^{-8}$$

$$[H^+] = \sqrt{0.0200 \times 3.72 \times 10^{-8}} = 2.728 \times 10^{-5} \, \text{mol dm}^{-3}$$

$$pH = 4.56$$

(b)

$$HNO_{2(aq)} \rightleftharpoons H^+_{(aq)} + NO_2^-_{(aq)}$$

Start concentration (mol dm^{-3}): 0.0500   0   0

Equilibrium concentration (mol dm^{-3}): $0.0500 - [H^+] \approx 0.0500$ $[H^+]$ $[H^+]$

$$K_a = \frac{[H^+][NO_2^-]}{[HNO_2]}$$

$$4.57 \times 10^{-4} = \frac{[H^+]^2}{0.0500}$$

$$[H^+]^2 = 0.0500 \times 4.57 \times 10^{-4}$$

$$[H^+] = \sqrt{0.0500 \times 4.57 \times 10^{-4}} = 4.780 \times 10^{-3} \, \text{mol dm}^{-3}$$

$$pH = 2.32$$

(c)

$$CH_2ICOOH_{(aq)} \rightleftharpoons CH_2ICOO^-_{(aq)} + H^+_{(aq)}$$

Start concentration (mol dm^{-3}): 1.00   0   0

Equilibrium concentration (mol dm^{-3}): $1.00 - [H^+] \approx 1.00$ $[H^+]$ $[H^+]$

$$K_a = \frac{[CH_2ICOO^-][H^+]}{[CH_2ICOOH]}$$

$$6.76 \times 10^{-4} = \frac{[H^+]^2}{1.00}$$

$$[H^+]^2 = 1.00 \times 6.76 \times 10^{-4}$$

$$[H^+] = \sqrt{1.00 \times 6.76 \times 10^{-4}} = 0.0260 \, \text{mol dm}^{-3}$$

$$pH = 1.59$$

(d) "Unlogging" pK_a gives $K_a = 1.35 \times 10^{-5} \, \text{mol dm}^{-3}$.

$$C_2H_5COOH_{(aq)} \rightleftharpoons C_2H_5COO^-_{(aq)} + H^+_{(aq)}$$

Start concentration (mol dm^{-3}): 0.100   0   0

Equilibrium concentration (mol dm^{-3}): $0.100 - [H^+] \approx 0.100$ $[H^+]$ $[H^+]$

$$K_a = \frac{[C_2H_5COO^-][H^+]}{[C_2H_5COOH]}$$

$$1.35 \times 10^{-5} = \frac{[H^+]^2}{0.100}$$

$$[H^+]^2 = 0.100 \times 1.35 \times 10^{-5}$$

$$[H^+] = \sqrt{0.100 \times 1.35 \times 10^{-5}} = 1.162 \times 10^{-3} \, mol \, dm^{-3}$$

$$pH = 2.93$$

(e) "Unlogging" pK_a gives $K_a = 3.98 \times 10^{-10} \, mol \, dm^{-3}$.

	$HCN_{(aq)}$	$\rightleftharpoons$	$H^+{}_{(aq)}$	$+$	$CN^-{}_{(aq)}$
Start concentration (mol dm^{-3})	0.250		0		0
Equilibrium concentration (mol dm^{-3})	$0.250 - [H^+]$ ≈ 0.250		$[H^+]$		$[H^+]$

$$K_a = \frac{[H^+][CN^-]}{[HCN]}$$

$$3.98 \times 10^{-10} = \frac{[H^+]^2}{0.250}$$

$$[H^+]^2 = 0.250 \times 3.98 \times 10^{-10}$$

$$[H^+] = \sqrt{0.250 \times 3.98 \times 10^{-10}} = 9.975 \times 10^{-6} \, mol \, dm^{-3}$$

$$pH = 5.00$$

15. (a) If the pH is 4.50, then $[H^+] = 3.16 \times 10^{-5} \, mol \, dm^{-3}$

	$HX_{(aq)}$	$\rightleftharpoons$	$H^+{}_{(aq)}$	$+$	$X^-{}_{(aq)}$
Start concentration (mol dm^{-3})	0.0400		0		0
Equilibrium concentration (mol dm^{-3})	$0.0400-$ 3.16×10^{-5} $= 0.03997$		3.16×10^{-5}		3.16×10^{-5}

> It would be perfectly sensible in this instance to make the approximation that $0.0400 - 3.16 \times 10^{-5}$ ≈ 0.0400. To 3 significant figures this is true.

$$K_a = \frac{[H^+][X^-]}{[HX]} = \frac{(3.16 \times 10^{-5})^2}{0.03997} = 2.498 \times 10^{-8} \, mol \, dm^{-3}$$

$$pK_a = -\log_{10} K_a = 7.60$$

(b) If the pH is 3.25, then $[H^+] = 5.26 \times 10^{-4} \, mol \, dm^{-3}$

	$HY_{(aq)}$	$\rightleftharpoons$	$H^+{}_{(aq)}$	$+$	$Y^-{}_{(aq)}$
Start concentration (mol dm^{-3})	0.125		0		0
Equilibrium concentration (mol dm^{-3})	$0.125-$ 5.62×10^{-4} $= 0.1244$		5.62×10^{-4}		5.62×10^{-4}

$$K_a = \frac{[H^+][Y^-]}{[HY]} = \frac{(5.62 \times 10^{-4})^2}{0.1244} = 2.539 \times 10^{-6} \, mol \, dm^{-3}$$

$$pK_a = -\log_{10} K_a = 5.60$$

(c) If the pH is 5.70, then $[H^+] = 2.00 \times 10^{-6} \, \text{mol dm}^{-3}$

	$HZ_{(aq)}$	$\rightleftharpoons$	$H^+_{(aq)}$	$+$	$Z^-_{(aq)}$
Start concentration (mol dm^{-3})	0.885		0		0
Equilibrium concentration (mol dm^{-3})	0.885 -2.00×10^{-6} $= 0.885$		2.00×10^{-6}		2.00×10^{-6}

$$K_a = \frac{[H^+][Z^-]}{[HZ]} = \frac{(2.00 \times 10^{-6})^2}{0.885} = 4.520 \times 10^{-12} \, \text{mol dm}^{-3}$$

$$pK_a = -\log_{10} K_a = 11.3$$

16. The steep bit of the curve (which gives you the end-point) occurs at 25 cm³. Half way through the titration is therefore 12.5 cm³. The pH half way through is equal to pK_a. If your graph is accurate, you should get a value close to 4.76. (This is the value the results were calculated on.)

17. (a) "Unlogging" pK_a gives $K_a = 1.74 \times 10^{-5} \, \text{mol dm}^{-3}$

(b) $$K_a = \frac{[CH_3COO^-][H^+]}{[CH_3COOH]}$$

$$[H^+] = \frac{K_a \times [CH_3COOH]}{[CH_3COO^-]} = \frac{1.74 \times 10^{-5} \times [CH_3COOH]}{[CH_3COO^-]}$$

(c) $$K_w = [H^+][OH^-] = 1.00 \times 10^{-14}$$

$$[OH^-] = \frac{1.00 \times 10^{-14}}{[H^+]}$$

(d) $$[CH_3COOH] = [OH^-] = \frac{1.00 \times 10^{-14}}{[H^+]}$$

(e) $0.200 \, \text{mol dm}^{-3}$. The ethanoate ion is such a weak base that its equilibrium concentration is approximately the same as its original concentration.

(f) $$[H^+] = \frac{1.74 \times 10^{-5} \times [CH_3COOH]}{[CH_3COO^-]} = \frac{1.74 \times 10^{-5}}{0.200} \times \frac{1.00 \times 10^{-14}}{[H^+]}$$

$$[H^+]^2 = \frac{1.74 \times 10^{-5} \times 1.00 \times 10^{-14}}{0.200} = 8.70 \times 10^{-19}$$

$$[H^+] = 9.327 \times 10^{-10} \, \text{mol dm}^{-3}$$

$$pH = 9.03$$

(g) $pH = 7 + \frac{1}{2} \times 4.76 + \frac{1}{2}\log_{10} 0.200 = 9.03$

18. (a) (i) "Unlogging" pK_a gives $K_a = 1.45 \times 10^{-11}$ mol dm^{-3}

$$C_3H_7NH_3^+{}_{(aq)} \rightleftharpoons C_3H_7NH_{2(aq)} + H^+{}_{(aq)}$$

$$K_a = \frac{[C_3H_7NH_2][H^+]}{[C_3H_7NH_3^+]} = 1.45 \times 10^{-11}$$

$$[H^+] = \frac{1.45 \times 10^{-11} \times [C_3H_7NH_3^+]}{[C_3H_7NH_2]}$$

$$[C_3H_7NH_3^+] = [OH^-] = \frac{1.00 \times 10^{-14}}{[H^+]}$$

$[C_3H_7NH_2] = 0.0500$ to a reasonable approximation

$$[H^+] = \frac{1.45 \times 10^{-11}}{0.0500} \times \frac{1.00 \times 10^{-14}}{[H^+]}$$

$$[H^+]^2 = \frac{1.45 \times 10^{-11} \times 1.00 \times 10^{-14}}{0.0500} = 2.90 \times 10^{-24}$$

$$[H^+] = 1.703 \times 10^{-12} \text{ mol dm}^{-3}$$

$$pH = 11.8$$

(a) (ii) $pH = 7 + \frac{1}{2}pK_a + \frac{1}{2}\log_{10} c = 7 + \frac{1}{2} \times 10.84 + \frac{1}{2}\log_{10} 0.0500 = 11.8$

(b) (i) "Unlogging" pK_a gives $K_a = 2.40 \times 10^{-5}$ mol dm^{-3}

$$C_6H_5NH_3^+{}_{(aq)} \rightleftharpoons C_6H_5NH_{2(aq)} + H^+{}_{(aq)}$$

$$K_a = \frac{[C_6H_5NH_2][H^+]}{[C_6H_5NH_3^+]} = 2.40 \times 10^{-5}$$

$$[H^+] = \frac{2.40 \times 10^{-5} \times [C_6H_5NH_3^+]}{[C_6H_5NH_2]}$$

$$[C_6H_5NH_3^+] = [OH^-] = \frac{1.00 \times 10^{-14}}{[H^+]}$$

$[C_6H_5NH_2] = 0.00500$ to a reasonable approximation

$$[H^+] = \frac{2.40 \times 10^{-5}}{0.00500} \times \frac{1.00 \times 10^{-14}}{[H^+]}$$

$$[H^+]^2 = \frac{2.40 \times 10^{-5} \times 1.00 \times 10^{-14}}{0.00500}$$

$$= 4.80 \times 10^{-17}$$

$$[H^+] = 6.928 \times 10^{-9} \text{ mol dm}^{-3}$$

$$pH = 8.16$$

(b) (ii) $pH = 7 + \frac{1}{2}pK_a + \frac{1}{2}\log_{10} c = 7 + \frac{1}{2} \times 4.62 + \frac{1}{2}\log_{10} 0.00500 = 8.16$

19. Equilibrium concentrations are:

$[C_2H_5COOH] = 0.500$ mol dm^{-3}; $[C_2H_5COO^-] = 1.00$ mol dm^{-3}.

$$K_a = \frac{[C_2H_5COO^-][H^+]}{[C_2H_5COOH]}$$

$$1.35 \times 10^{-5} = \frac{1.00 \times [H^+]}{0.500}$$

$$[H^+] = \frac{1.35 \times 10^{-5} \times 0.500}{1.00} = 6.75 \times 10^{-6} \text{ mol dm}^{-3}$$

$$pH = 5.17$$

20. RFM ethanoic acid $= 60$; RFM sodium ethanoate $= 82$.

Moles ethanoic acid in $100\,cm^3 = 12.0/60 = 0.200$

Moles sodium ethanoate in $100\,cm^3 = 4.10/82 = 0.0500$

$[CH_3COOH] = 2.00\,mol\,dm^{-3}$; $[CH_3COONa] = 0.500\,mol\,dm^{-3}$.

$$K_a = \frac{[CH_3COO^-][H^+]}{[CH_3COOH]}$$

$$1.74 \times 10^{-5} = \frac{0.500 \times [H^+]}{2.00}$$

$$[H^+] = \frac{1.74 \times 10^{-5} \times 2.00}{0.500} = 6.96 \times 10^{-5}\,mol\,dm^{-3}$$

$$pH = 4.16$$

21. The methanoic acid has been diluted from 20 to $100\,cm^3$ – by a factor of 5. The new concentration is therefore $0.100/5 = 0.0200\,mol\,dm^{-3}$.

➤ If you prefer to do this differently, see page 209.

The sodium methanoate has been diluted from 80 to $100\ cm^3$. Its concentration is now 4/5 of the original $= 0.0400\,mol\,dm^{-3}$.

$$K_a = \frac{[HCOO^-][H^+]}{[HCOOH]}$$

$$1.78 \times 10^{-4} = \frac{0.0400 \times [H^+]}{0.0200}$$

$$[H^+] = \frac{1.78 \times 10^{-4} \times 0.0200}{0.0400} = 8.90 \times 10^{-5}\,mol\,dm^{-3}$$

$$pH = 4.05$$

22. (a) "Unlogging" pK_a gives $K_a = 1.51 \times 10^{-5}\,mol\,dm^{-3}$

$$K_a = \frac{[H^+][A^-]}{[HA]}$$

$$1.51 \times 10^{-5} = \frac{[H^+] \times 0.300}{0.500}$$

$$[H^+] = \frac{1.51 \times 10^{-5} \times 0.500}{0.300} = 2.517 \times 10^{-5}\,mol\,dm^{-3}$$

$$pH = 4.60$$

(b) Moles of H^+ added $= \dfrac{2.00}{1000} \times 5.00 = 0.0100$

This uses up 0.0100 mol of A^- ions and produces an extra 0.0100 mol of HA.

$[A^-] = 0.290\,mol\,dm^{-3}$; $[HA] = 0.510\,mol\,dm^{-3}$.

$$K_a = \frac{[H^+][A^-]}{[HA]}$$

$$1.51 \times 10^{-5} = \frac{[H^+] \times 0.290}{0.510}$$

$$[H^+] = \frac{1.51 \times 10^{-5} \times 0.510}{0.290} = 2.656 \times 10^{-5}\,mol\,dm^{-3}$$

$$pH = 4.58$$

(c) Moles of OH^- added $= \dfrac{2.00}{1000} \times 5.00 = 0.0100$

This uses up 0.0100 mol of HA and produces an extra 0.0100 mol of A^- ions.

$[HA] = 0.490 \, mol \, dm^{-3}$; $[A^-] = 0.310 \, mol \, dm^{-3}$

$$K_a = \frac{[H^+][A^-]}{[HA]}$$

$$1.51 \times 10^{-5} = \frac{[H^+] \times 0.310}{0.490}$$

$$[H^+] = \frac{1.51 \times 10^{-5} \times 0.490}{0.310} = 2.387 \times 10^{-5} \, mol \, dm^{-3}$$

$$pH = 4.62$$

23. "Unlogging" the pH gives $[H^+] = 3.16 \times 10^{-4} \, mol \, dm^{-3}$

$$K_a = \frac{[HCOO^-][H^+]}{[HCOOH]}$$

$$1.78 \times 10^{-4} = \frac{[HCOO^-] \times 3.16 \times 10^{-4}}{[HCOOH]}$$

$$\frac{[HCOO^-]}{[HCOOH]} = \frac{1.78 \times 10^{-4}}{3.16 \times 10^{-4}} = \frac{0.563}{1}$$

Since both solutions have the same concentration, they can be mixed in this ratio by volume.

24. (a) "Unlogging" pK_a gives $K_a = 2.29 \times 10^{-11} \, mol \, dm^{-3}$
On mixing, each solution is diluted by a factor of 2.

$[B] = 0.500 \, mol \, dm^{-3}$; $[BH^+] = [BH^+Cl^-] = 0.500 \, mol \, dm^{-3}$

$$K_a = \frac{[B][H^+]}{[BH^+]} = 2.29 \times 10^{-11}$$

$$[H^+] = \frac{2.29 \times 10^{-11} \times [BH^+]}{[B]} = \frac{2.29 \times 10^{-11} \times 0.500}{0.500} = 2.29 \times 10^{-11}$$

$$pH = 10.6$$

(b) (i) Moles of H^+ added $= \dfrac{4.00}{1000} \times 5.00 = 0.0200$

This uses up 0.0200 mol of B and produces an extra 0.0200 mol of BH^+.

$[B] = 0.480 \, mol \, dm^{-3}$; $[BH^+] = 0.520 \, mol \, dm^{-3}$

$$K_a = \frac{[B][H^+]}{[BH^+]} = 2.29 \times 10^{-11}$$

$$[H^+] = \frac{2.29 \times 10^{-11} \times [BH^+]}{[B]} = \frac{2.29 \times 10^{-11} \times 0.520}{0.480} = 2.481 \times 10^{-11}$$

$$pH = 10.6$$

> ➤ The solution originally contained 0.500 mol dm^{-3} of each component, because the solutions were diluted by a factor of 2 on mixing.

(b) (ii) Moles of OH^- added $= \dfrac{4.00}{1000} \times 5.00 = 0.0200$

This uses up $0.0200\,mol$ of BH^+ and produces an extra $0.0200\,mol$ of B.

$[BH^+] = 0.480\,mol\,dm^{-3}$; $[B] = 0.520\,mol\,dm^{-3}$.

$$K_a = \frac{[B][H^+]}{[BH^+]} = 2.29 \times 10^{-11}$$

$$[H^+] = \frac{2.29 \times 10^{-11} \times [BH^+]}{[B]} = \frac{2.29 \times 10^{-11} \times 0.480}{0.520} = 2.114 \times 10^{-11}$$

$$pH = 10.7$$

(c) "Unlogging" the pH gives $[H^+] = 3.16 \times 10^{-11}\,mol\,dm^{-3}$.

$$K_a = \frac{[B][H^+]}{[BH^+]} = 2.29 \times 10^{-11}$$

$$\frac{[B]}{[BH^+]} = \frac{2.29 \times 10^{-11}}{[H^+]} = \frac{2.29 \times 10^{-11}}{3.16 \times 10^{-11}} = \frac{0.725}{1}$$

Because the concentrations of the two solutions are the same, they can be mixed in this ratio by volume.

25. (a) (i) 2.59 (ii) 0.07 (iii) 11.1

(b) (i) $0.0123\,mol\,dm^{-3}$ (ii) $3.98 \times 10^{-7}\,mol\,dm^{-3}$
(iii) $5.01 \times 10^{-15}\,mol\,dm^{-3}$

26. (a) 0.30 (b) 1.40

27. (a) $0.0631\,mol\,dm^{-3}$ (b) $0.50\,mol\,dm^{-3}$ (c) $0.5\,mol\,dm^{-3}$

28. 7.08

29. (a) 13 (b) 12.3

30. (a) $2.00\,mol\,dm^{-3}$ (b) $5.00 \times 10^{-4}\,mol\,dm^{-3}$

31. (a) 0.70 (b) 13.8 (c) 7.00

32. (a) 3.23 (b) 3.41 (c) 1.58

33. 4.63

34. (a) Assuming you haven't made any approximations, $pK_a = 3.23$ (b) 9.30

35. 5.00

36. 4.0

37. (a) 11.6 (b) 12.1 (c) 10.3

38. 9.38

39. (a) 4.86   (b) 4.23   (c) 8.95   (d) 10.6

40. (a) 4.76   (b) 4.75   (c) 4.77

41. (a) Mix sodium ethanoate and ethanoic acid solutions in the ratio 0.550:1.

(b) Mix ammonium chloride and ammonia solutions in the ratio 0.562:1.

Chapter 9

1. $AgBr_{(s)} \rightleftharpoons Ag^+_{(aq)} + Br^-_{(aq)}$

Each mole of silver bromide that dissolves gives 1 mole of each ion in solution.

$[Ag^+_{(aq)}] = 8.8 \times 10^{-7}$ mol dm^{-3}

$[Br^-_{(aq)}] = 8.8 \times 10^{-7}$ mol dm^{-3}

$K_{sp} = [Ag^+][Br^-] = (8.8 \times 10^{-7})^2 = 7.7 \times 10^{-13}$ mol^2 dm^{-6}

2. RFM of $MgCO_3 = 84$

Solubility $= 0.27/84$ mol dm$^{-3} = 3.21 \times 10^{-3}$ mol dm^{-3}

$MgCO_{3(s)} \rightleftharpoons Mg^{2+}_{(aq)} + CO_3^{2-}_{(aq)}$

Each mole of magnesium carbonate that dissolves gives 1 mole of each ion in solution.

$[Mg^{2+}_{(aq)}] = 3.21 \times 10^{-3}$ mol dm^{-3}

$[CO_3^{2-}_{(aq)}] = 3.21 \times 10^{-3}$ mol dm^{-3}

$K_{sp} = [Mg^{2+}][CO_3^{2-}] = (3.21 \times 10^{-3})^2 = 1.0 \times 10^{-5}$ mol^2 dm^{-6}

3. $Al(OH)_{3(s)} \rightleftharpoons Al^{3+}_{(aq)} + 3OH^-_{(aq)}$

Each mole of aluminium hydroxide which dissolves gives 1 mole of $Al^{3+}_{(aq)}$ and 3 moles of $OH^-_{(aq)}$ in solution.

$[Al^{3+}_{(aq)}] = 2.5 \times 10^{-9}$ mol dm^{-3}

$[OH^-_{(aq)}] = 3 \times 2.5 \times 10^{-9} = 7.5 \times 10^{-9}$ mol dm^{-3}

$K_{sp} = [Al^{3+}][OH^-]^3 = 2.5 \times 10^{-9} \times (7.5 \times 10^{-9})^3 = 1.1 \times 10^{-33}$ mol^4 dm^{-12}

4. RFM of $PbI_2 = 461$

Solubility $= 0.29/461$ mol dm$^{-3} = 6.29 \times 10^{-4}$ mol dm^{-3}

$PbI_{2(s)} \rightleftharpoons Pb^{2+}_{(aq)} + 2I^-_{(aq)}$

Each mole of lead(II) iodide which dissolves gives 1 mole of $Pb^{2+}_{(aq)}$ and 2 moles of $I^-_{(aq)}$ in solution.

$[Pb^{2+}_{(aq)}] = 6.29 \times 10^{-4}$ mol dm^{-3}

$[I^-] = 2 \times 6.29 \times 10^{-4} = 1.258 \times 10^{-3}$ mol dm^{-3}

$K_{sp} = [Pb^{2+}][I^-]^2$

$= 6.29 \times 10^{-4} \times (1.258 \times 10^{-3})^2$

$= 1.0 \times 10^{-9}$ mol^3 dm^{-9}

➤ Your calculator will give you an answer of 9.95 (etc.) $\times 10^{-10}$. This rounds to 1.0×10^{-9} to 2 significant figures.

5. $Ag_2SO_{4(s)} \rightleftharpoons 2Ag^+_{(aq)} + SO_4^{2-}_{(aq)}$

Each mole of silver(I) sulphate which dissolves gives 2 moles of $Ag^+_{(aq)}$ and 1 mole of $SO_4^{2-}_{(aq)}$.

$[Ag^+_{(aq)}] = 2 \times 0.016 = 0.032 \, mol \, dm^{-3}$

$[SO_4^{2-}_{(aq)}] = 0.016 \, mol \, dm^{-3}$

$K_{sp} = [Ag^+]^2[SO_4^{2-}]$

$= (0.032)^2 \times 0.016$

$= 1.6 \times 10^{-5} \, mol^3 \, dm^{-9}$

6. (a) $BaCO_{3(s)} \rightleftharpoons Ba^{2+}_{(aq)} + CO_3^{2-}_{(aq)}$

> ➤ Your answer should only be quoted to 2 **significant figures** because this is the accuracy of the solubility product. However, if you carry on with the calculation using this 2 sig fig result you could introduce rounding errors into your final answer. The easiest way is to quote your first answer to 2 sig figs, but use the number which is still on your calculator to complete the calculation.

(i) Let the solubility of barium carbonate be "s" $mol \, dm^{-3}$.

Each mole of barium carbonate that dissolves gives 1 mole of each ion in solution.

$[Ba^{2+}_{(aq)}] = s \, mol \, dm^{-3}$

$[CO_3^{2-}_{(aq)}] = s \, mol \, dm^{-3}$

$K_{sp} = [Ba^{2+}][CO_3^{2-}]$

$5.1 \times 10^{-9} = s^2$

$s = 7.1(4) \times 10^{-5} \, mol \, dm^{-3}$

(ii) 1 mole of $BaCO_3$ weighs 197 g.

Solubility $= 7.14 \times 10^{-5} \times 197 \, g \, dm^{-3} = 0.014 \, g \, dm^{-3}$

(b) $Ca(OH)_{2(s)} \rightleftharpoons Ca^{2+}_{(aq)} + 2OH^-_{(aq)}$

(i) Let the solubility of calcium hydroxide be "s" $mol \, dm^{-3}$.

Each mole of calcium hydroxide that dissolves gives 1 mole of $Ca^{2+}_{(aq)}$ and 2 moles of $OH^-_{(aq)}$ in solution.

$[Ca^{2+}_{(aq)}] = s \, mol \, dm^{-3}$

$[OH^-_{(aq)}] = 2s \, mol \, dm^{-3}$

$K_{sp} = [Ca^{2+}][OH^-]^2$

$5.5 \times 10^{-6} = s \times (2s)^2$

$4s^3 = 5.5 \times 10^{-6}$

$s = 0.011(1) \, mol \, dm^{-3}$

(ii) 1 mole of $Ca(OH)_2$ weighs 74 g.

Solubility $= 0.0111 \times 74 \, g \, dm^{-3} = 0.82 \, g \, dm^{-3}$

(c) $Al(OH)_{3(s)} \rightleftharpoons Al^{3+}_{(aq)} + 3OH^-_{(aq)}$

(i) Let the solubility of aluminium hydroxide be "s" $mol \, dm^{-3}$.

Each mole of aluminium hydroxide that dissolves gives 1 mole of $Al^{3+}_{(aq)}$ and 3 moles of $OH^-_{(aq)}$ in solution.

$[Al^{3+}_{(aq)}] = s \, mol \, dm^{-3}$

$[OH^-_{(aq)}] = 3s \, mol \, dm^{-3}$

$$K_{sp} = [Al^{3+}][OH^-]^3$$
$$1.0 \times 10^{-33} = s \times (3s)^3$$
$$27s^4 = 1.0 \times 10^{-33}$$
$$s = 2.5 \times 10^{-9} \, mol \, dm^{-3} \, (2.47 \times 10^{-9} \, mol \, dm^{-3})$$

(ii)   1 mole of $Al(OH)_3$ weighs 78 g.

Solubility $= 2.47 \times 10^{-9} \times 78 \, g \, dm^{-3} = 1.9 \times 10^{-7} \, g \, dm^{-3}$

(d) $Sb_2S_{3(s)} \rightleftharpoons 2Sb^{3+}_{(aq)} + 3S^{2-}_{(aq)}$

(i)   Let the solubility of antimony(III) sulphide be "s" $mol \, dm^{-3}$.
Each mole of antimony(III) sulphide that dissolves gives 2 moles of $Sb^{3+}_{(aq)}$ and 3 moles of $S^{2-}_{(aq)}$ in solution.

$$[Sb^{3+}_{(aq)}] = 2s \, mol \, dm^{-3}$$
$$[S^{2-}_{(aq)}] = 3s \, mol \, dm^{-3}$$
$$K_{sp} = [Sb^{3+}]^2[S^{2-}]^3$$
$$1.7 \times 10^{-93} = (2s)^2 \times (3s)^3$$
$$4s^2 \times 27s^3 = 1.7 \times 10^{-93}$$
$$108s^5 = 1.7 \times 10^{-93}$$
$$s = 1.1 \times 10^{-19} \, mol \, dm^{-3} \, (1.09 \times 10^{-19} \, mol \, dm^{-3})$$

(ii)   1 mole of Sb_2S_3 weighs 340 g.
Solubility $= 1.09 \times 10^{-19} \times 340 \, g \, dm^{-3} = 3.7 \times 10^{-17} \, g \, dm^{-3}$

7.   Let the solubility of lead(II) sulphate be "s" $mol \, dm^{-3}$.

Each mole of lead(II) sulphate produces 1 mole of $Pb^{2+}_{(aq)}$ ions in solution.

$[Pb^{2+}_{(aq)}] \quad = s \, mol \, dm^{-3}$

Virtually all the sulphate ions will be coming from the sodium sulphate solution.

$[SO_4^{2-}_{(aq)}] \quad = 0.10 \, mol \, dm^{-3}$

$$K_{sp} = [Pb^{2+}][SO_4^{2-}]$$
$$1.6 \times 10^{-8} = s \times 0.10$$
$$s = 1.6 \times 10^{-7} \, mol \, dm^{-3}$$

8. $Ag_2SO_{4(s)} \rightleftharpoons 2Ag^+_{(aq)} + SO_4^{2-}_{(aq)}$

Let the solubility of silver(I) sulphate be "s" $mol \, dm^{-3}$.

Each mole of silver(I) sulphate which dissolves gives 2 moles of $Ag^+_{(aq)}$ and 1 mole of $SO_4^{2-}_{(aq)}$.

(a) $[Ag^+_{(aq)}] = 2s \, mol \, dm^{-3}$

$[SO_4^{2-}_{(aq)}] = s \, mol \, dm^{-3}$

$$K_{sp} = [Ag^+]^2[SO_4^{2-}]$$
$$1.6 \times 10^{-5} = (2s)^2 \times s$$
$$4s^3 = 1.6 \times 10^{-5}$$
$$s = 0.016 \, mol \, dm^{-3}$$

(b) Virtually all the silver ions will be coming from the silver(I) nitrate solution.

$[Ag^+_{(aq)}] = 0.10 \, mol \, dm^{-3}$

The concentration of the sulphate ions will be the same as the dissolved silver(I) sulphate.

$[SO_4^{2-}{}_{(aq)}] = s \, mol \, dm^{-3}$

$$K_{sp} = [Ag^+]^2[SO_4^{2-}]$$

$$1.6 \times 10^{-5} = (0.10)^2 \times s$$

$$s = 1.6 \times 10^{-3} \, mol \, dm^{-3}$$

(c) As in part (a) the silver ion concentration will be twice that of the dissolved silver(I) sulphate.

$[Ag^+_{(aq)}] = 2s \, mol \, dm^{-3}$

Virtually all the sulphate ions will be coming from the sulphuric acid.

$[SO_4^{2-}{}_{(aq)}] = 0.50 \, mol \, dm^{-3}$

$$K_{sp} = [Ag^+]^2[SO_4^{2-}]$$

$$1.6 \times 10^{-5} = (2s)^2 \times 0.50$$

$$4s^2 \times 0.50 = 1.6 \times 10^{-5}$$

$$s = 2.8 \times 10^{-3} \, mol \, dm^{-3}$$

9. In every case, you need to consider the solubility of $X(OH)_2$:

$$X(OH)_{2(s)} \rightleftharpoons X^{2+}{}_{(aq)} + 2OH^-{}_{(aq)}$$

$$K_{sp} = [X^{2+}][OH^-]^2$$

With ammonia solution, $[OH^-{}_{(aq)}] = 2.1 \times 10^{-3} \, mol \, dm^{-3}$, because the original ammonia is diluted by a factor of 2 when the two solutions are mixed.

$[X^{2+}{}_{(aq)}]$ is also half of what it was originally for the same reason.

$[X^{2+}{}_{(aq)}] = 0.050 \, mol \, dm^{-3}$

Multiplying these ion concentrations together in the same way as the solubility product expression gives:

$$0.050 \times (2.1 \times 10^{-3})^2 = 2.2 \times 10^{-7} \, mol^3 \, dm^{-9}$$

If this number is bigger than the solubility product you will get a precipitate as the excess ions are removed from solution. If this number is smaller than the solubility product, equilibrium has not been reached and so no precipitate will form. Comparing the numbers given, only magnesium hydroxide will form a precipitate.

With sodium hydroxide solution, $[OH^-{}_{(aq)}] = 0.50 \, mol \, dm^{-3}$, because the original solution is diluted by a factor of 2 when the two solutions are mixed. Once again, $[X^{2+}{}_{(aq)}] = 0.050 \, mol \, dm^{-3}$

Multiplying these ion concentrations together in the same way as the solubility product expression gives:

$$0.050 \times (0.50)^2 = 0.0125 \, mol^3 \, dm^{-9}$$

This number is bigger than all the solubility product values, and so you will get a precipitate in each case.

10. The ethoxyethane contains 0.80 g of X in 25 cm³:

$$\text{concentration of X in ethoxyethane} = \frac{0.80}{25} = 0.032\,\text{g cm}^{-3}$$

The water contains $(1.0 - 0.80)\,\text{g}$ in 100 cm³:

$$\text{concentration of X in water} = \frac{0.20}{100} = 0.0020\,\text{g cm}^{-3}$$

$$K_c = \frac{\text{concentration of X in ethoxyethane}}{\text{concentration of X in water}} = \frac{0.032}{0.0020} = 16$$

11. (a) Aqueous layer:

$$\text{Number of moles of HCl} = \frac{26.0}{1000} \times 1.00$$

$$= 0.0260$$

The equation shows that the ammonia and HCl react 1:1.

Number of moles of $NH_3 = 0.0260$ (in 25.0 cm³)

$$[NH_3] = \frac{1000}{25.0} \times 0.0260$$

$$= 1.04\,\text{mol dm}^{-3}$$

(b) CHCl₃ layer:

$$\text{Number of moles of HCl} = \frac{8.40}{1000} \times 0.0500 = 4.20 \times 10^{-4}$$

The equation shows that the ammonia and HCl react 1:1.
Number of moles of $NH_3 = 4.20 \times 10^{-4}$ (in 10.0 cm³)

$$[NH_3] = \frac{1000}{10.0} \times 4.20 \times 10^{-4} = 0.0420\,\text{mol dm}^{-3}$$

(c) The partition coefficient:

$$K_c = \frac{[NH_3\text{ in }H_2O]}{[NH_3\text{ in }CHCl_3]} = \frac{1.04}{0.0420} = 24.8$$

12.
$$\frac{\text{concentration of X in ether}}{\text{concentration of X in water}} = \frac{20.0}{1}$$

$$\frac{\text{mass of X in ether/volume of ether}}{\text{mass of X in water/volume of water}} = \frac{20.0}{1}$$

$$\frac{\text{mass of X in ether}}{\text{volume of ether}} \times \frac{\text{volume of water}}{\text{mass of X in water}} = \frac{20.0}{1}$$

(a) Substituting volumes:

$$\frac{\text{mass of X in ether}}{30.0} \times \frac{200}{\text{mass of X in water}} = \frac{20.0}{1}$$

$$\frac{\text{mass of X in ether}}{\text{mass of X in water}} = \frac{600}{200} = \frac{3}{1}$$

Of every 4 parts of X, 1 part remains in the water and 3 parts transfer to the ether.

Mass remaining in the water $= 1/4 \times 3.00\,\text{g} = 0.75\,\text{g}$

(b) Substituting volumes for one extraction:

$$\frac{\text{mass of X in ether}}{.50} \times \frac{200}{\text{mass of X in water}} = \frac{20.0}{1}$$

$$\frac{\text{mass of X in ether}}{\text{mass of X in water}} = \frac{300}{200} = \frac{3}{2}$$

For every 5 parts of X, 2 parts remain in the water after each extraction.

Mass remaining after 1 extraction $= 2/5 \times 3.00\,\text{g}$

Mass remaining after 2 extractions $= 2/5 \times 2/5 \times 3.00\,\text{g} = 0.48\,\text{g}$

(c) Substituting volumes for one extraction:

$$\frac{\text{mass of X in ether}}{10.0} \times \frac{200}{\text{mass of X in water}} = \frac{20.0}{1}$$

$$\frac{\text{mass of X in ether}}{\text{mass of X in water}} = \frac{200}{200} = \frac{1}{1}$$

This time, half of X remains in the water after each extraction.

Mass remaining after 1 extraction $= 1/2 \times 3.00\,\text{g}$

Mass remaining after 2 extractions $= 1/2 \times 1/2 \times 3.00\,\text{g}$

Mass remaining after 3 extractions $= 1/2 \times 1/2 \times 1/2 \times 3.00\,\text{g} = 0.375\,\text{g}$

13. 1 volume of water dissolves 0.25 volumes of ethene if the partial pressure of ethene is 1 atm. At a pressure of 2.0 atm, 1 volume of water will dissolve 2.0×0.25 volumes of ethene $= 0.50$ volumes

$100\,\text{cm}^3$ of water will dissolve $0.50 \times 100\,\text{cm}^3$ of ethene $= 50\,\text{cm}^3$.

14. Mole fractions of both CO and CO_2 are 0.50.

Partial pressures of both $= 0.50 \times 0.80\,\text{atm} = 0.40\,\text{atm}$.

If the partial pressure of CO was 1 atm, $1\,\text{dm}^3$ of water would dissolve $0.035\,\text{dm}^3$ of CO.

At the lower partial pressure of 0.40 atm, it will dissolve $0.40 \times 0.035\,\text{dm}^3 = 0.014\,\text{dm}^3$.

If the partial pressure of CO_2 was 1 atm, $1\,\text{dm}^3$ of water would dissolve $1.71\,\text{dm}^3$ of CO_2.

> Only 2 significant figures.

At the lower partial pressure of 0.40 atm, it will dissolve $0.40 \times 1.71\,\text{dm}^3 = 0.68\,\text{dm}^3$.

15. (a) Mole fractions: N_2: 0.78 O_2: 0.21   Ar: 0.0093

Partial pressures: N_2: 0.78×0.97 O_2: 0.21×0.97 Ar: 0.0093×0.97
$= 0.757\,\text{atm}$ $= 0.204\,\text{atm}$ $= 9.02 \times 10^{-3}\,\text{atm}$

Volumes dissolved in $1.0\,\text{m}^3$:

N_2: $0.757 \times 0.024 = 0.018\,\text{m}^3$ ($0.0182\,\text{m}^3$ for use in part (b))
O_2: $0.204 \times 0.049 = 0.010\,\text{m}^3$ ($0.0100\,\text{m}^3$ for use in part (b))
Ar: $9.02 \times 10^{-3} \times 0.056 = 5.1 \times 10^{-4}\,\text{m}^3$ ($5.05 \times 10^{-4}\,\text{m}^3$ for use in part (b))

(b) Total volume of dissolved gases $= 0.0182 + 0.0100 + 5.05 \times 10^{-4} \, m^3$

$$= 0.0287 \, m^3$$

% $N_2 = 0.0182/0.0287 \times 100 = 63\%$

% $O_2 = 0.0100/0.0287 \times 100 = 35\%$

% $Ar = (5.05 \times 10^{-4})/0.0287 \times 100 = 1.8\%$

16. (a) $4.8 \times 10^{-10} \, mol^2 \, dm^{-6}$ (b) $1.8 \times 10^{-10} \, mol^2 \, dm^{-6}$

(c) $5.3 \times 10^{-6} \, mol^3 \, dm^{-9}$ (d) $1.3 \times 10^{-21} \, mol^4 \, dm^{-12}$

17. (a) $3.2 \times 10^{-3} \, mol \, dm^{-3}$ (b) $2.4 \times 10^{-16} \, g \, dm^{-3}$

(c) $1.2 \times 10^{-6} \, mol \, dm^{-3}$ (d) $2.9 \times 10^{-15} \, g \, dm^{-3}$

18. $3.2 \times 10^{-6} \, mol \, dm^{-3}$

19. $7.9 \times 10^{-14} \, mol \, dm^{-3}$

20. $8.9 \times 10^{-3} \, mol \, dm^{-3}$

21. Yes. $[Ag^+][Cl^-]$ on mixing is 2.5×10^{-7}, which is greater than the solubility product.

22. No. $[Mg^{2+}][CO_3^{2-}]$ on mixing is 8×10^{-6}, which is less than the solubility product.

23. 75

24. (a) In ether, $[HA] = 0.16 \, mol \, dm^{-3}$; in water, $[HA] = 0.080 \, mol \, dm^{-3}$ (b) 2.0

25. (a) $2.00 \, g$ (b) $0.625 \, g$

26. (a) $1.9 \, cm^3$ (b) $0.86 \, cm^3$

27. 98%

28. (a) $1.9 \, dm^3$ (b) $5.1 \times 10^{-4} \, dm^3$

Chapter 10

1. In each of these questions,

$E^{\ominus}_{cell} = E^{\ominus}$ of right hand electrode $- E^{\ominus}$ of left hand electrode

(a) $E^{\ominus}_{cell} = -0.40 - (-1.66) = +1.26 \, volts$

(b) $E^{\ominus}_{cell} = +0.34 - (+0.80) = -0.46 \, volts$

(c) $E^{\ominus}_{cell} = +1.36 - (+0.77) = +0.59 \, volts$

2. In each of these questions,

$E^{\ominus}_{cell} = E^{\ominus}$ of right hand electrode $- E^{\ominus}$ of left hand electrode

(a) $-0.49 = e - (-0.25)$ $e = -0.74$ volts

(b) $-2.11 = -2.37 - e$ $e = -0.26$ volts

(c) $+0.79 = -0.40 - e$ $e = -1.19$ volts

3. (a) The two equilibria involved are:

$$Co^{2+}_{(aq)} + 2e^- \rightleftharpoons Co_{(s)} \qquad E^{\ominus} = -0.28 \text{ volts}$$
$$Al^{3+}_{(aq)} + 3e^- \rightleftharpoons Al_{(s)} \qquad E^{\ominus} = -1.66 \text{ volts}$$

Either the more negative equilibrium will move to the left; the more positive (less negative) to the right. Since you are starting from Al and Co^{2+}, those movements are possible and so the reaction is feasible.

Or calculate $E^{\ominus}_{cell}$ for the cell with the equilibrium you want to move to the right as the right hand electrode. You want the cobalt equilibrium to move right:

$$E^{\ominus}_{cell} = -0.28 - (-1.66) \text{ volts} = +1.38 \text{ volts}$$

A positive answer shows the reaction is feasible.

(b) The two equilibria involved are:

$$Na^+_{(aq)} + e^- \rightleftharpoons Na_{(s)} \qquad E^{\ominus} = -2.71 \text{ volts}$$
$$Mg^{2+}_{(aq)} + 2e^- \rightleftharpoons Mg_{(s)} \qquad E^{\ominus} = -2.37 \text{ volts}$$

Either the more negative equilibrium will move to the left; the more positive (less negative) to the right. Since you are starting from Na^+ and Mg, no movements are possible and so the reaction is not feasible.

Or calculate $E^{\ominus}_{cell}$ for the cell with the equilibrium you want to move to the right as the right hand electrode. You want the sodium equilibrium to move right:

$$E^{\ominus}_{cell} = -2.71 - (-2.37) \text{ volts} = -0.34 \text{ volts}$$

A negative answer shows the reaction is not feasible.

(c) The two equilibria involved are:

$$Br_{2(l)} + 2e^- \rightleftharpoons 2Br^-_{(aq)} \qquad E^{\ominus} = +1.07 \text{ volts}$$
$$Cl_{2(g)} + 2e^- \rightleftharpoons 2Cl^-_{(aq)} \qquad E^{\ominus} = +1.36 \text{ volts}$$

Either the more negative (less positive) equilibrium will move to the left; the more positive to the right. Since you are starting from Br^- and Cl_2, movement is possible and so the reaction is feasible.

Or calculate $E^{\ominus}_{cell}$ for the cell with the equilibrium you want to move to the right as the right hand electrode. You want the chlorine equilibrium to move right:

$$E^{\ominus}_{cell} = +1.36 - (+1.07) \text{ volts} = +0.29 \text{ volts}$$

A positive answer shows the reaction is feasible.

(d) The two equilibria involved are:

$$Fe^{3+}_{(aq)} + e^- \rightleftharpoons Fe^{2+}_{(aq)} \qquad E^{\ominus} = +0.77 \text{ volts}$$
$$Cl_{2(g)} + 2e^- \rightleftharpoons 2Cl^-_{(aq)} \qquad E^{\ominus} = +1.36 \text{ volts}$$

Either: the more negative (less positive) equilibrium will move to the left; the more positive to the right. Since you are starting from Fe^{2+} and Cl_2, movement is possible and so the reaction is feasible.

Or calculate $E^{\ominus}_{cell}$ for the cell with the equilibrium you want to move to the right as the right hand electrode. You want the chlorine equilibrium to move right:

$$E^{\ominus}_{cell} = +1.36 - (+0.77) \text{ volts} = +0.59 \text{ volts}$$

A positive answer shows the reaction is feasible.

4. Work out the feasibility using either of the methods above.

   (a) Feasible. (The more positive equilibrium moves to the right, the negative one to the left, which is what you need to happen.)

   $$S^{2-}_{(aq)} \rightarrow S_{(s)} + 2e^-$$
   $$Cl_{2(g)} + 2e^- \rightarrow 2Cl^-_{(aq)}$$

   Combining:

   $$S^{2-}_{(aq)} + Cl_{2(g)} \rightarrow S_{(s)} + 2Cl^-_{(aq)}$$

   (b) Feasible. (The more positive equilibrium moves to the right, the less positive (more negative) one to the left, which is what you need to happen.)

   $$2IO_3^-{}_{(aq)} + 12H^+{}_{(aq)} + 10e^- \rightarrow I_{2(aq)} + 6H_2O_{(l)}$$
   $$5 \times (2I^-{}_{(aq)} \rightarrow I_{2(aq)} + 2e^-)$$

   Combining:

   $$2IO_3^-{}_{(aq)} + 12H^+{}_{(aq)} + 10I^-{}_{(aq)} \rightarrow 6I_{2(aq)} + 6H_2O_{(l)}$$

   (Note that this should ideally be divided by 2 to simplify it.)

   (c) Not feasible. (You want the silver equilibrium to move to the left, which needs it to have the more negative $E^{\ominus}$ value.)

   (d) Feasible. (The zinc equilibrium is more negative and so will move to the left, while the chromium equilibrium moves right – which is what you want.)

   $$Zn_{(s)} \rightarrow Zn^{2+}_{(aq)} + 2e^-$$
   $$2 \times (Cr^{3+}_{(aq)} + e^- \rightarrow Cr^{2+}_{(aq)})$$

   Combining:

   $$Zn_{(s)} + 2Cr^{3+}_{(aq)} \rightarrow Zn^{2+}_{(aq)} + 2Cr^{2+}_{(aq)}$$

5. (a) -1.10 volts   (b) $+1.18$ volts   (c) -2.11 volts

6. (a) -1.66 volts   (b) -0.25 volts

7. (a) feasible   (b) not feasible   (c) not feasible   (d) feasible

8. $S_2O_8^{2-}{}_{(aq)}$
   $$2Mn^{2+}_{(aq)} + 8H_2O_{(l)} + 5S_2O_8^{2-}{}_{(aq)} \rightarrow 2MnO_4^-{}_{(aq)} + 16H^+{}_{(aq)} + 10SO_4^{2-}{}_{(aq)}$$

9. Yes: $Cr^{2+}_{(aq)} + V^{3+}_{(aq)} \rightarrow Cr^{3+}_{(aq)} + V^{2+}_{(aq)}$

10. Yes: $3Fe^{2+}_{(aq)} + NO_3^-{}_{(aq)} + 4H^+_{(aq)} \rightarrow 3Fe^{3+}_{(aq)} + NO_{(g)} + 2H_2O_{(l)}$

11. No

12. Blue

Chapter 11

1. (a) Decrease. (System becomes less disordered as 3 moles of assorted gases form 2 moles of liquid.)

(b) Increase. (Increase in disorder mainly due to gas being produced.)

(c) Decrease. (Less disorder mainly due to loss of gas.)

(d) Increase. (Increase in disorder mainly due to gas and liquid being produced from solids.)

2. (a) Entropy of products $= (2 \times 152.1) + 205.0$ $= 509.2 \, J\,K^{-1}\,mol^{-1}$

Entropy of reactants $= (2 \times 133.1)$ $= 266.2 \, J\,K^{-1}\,mol^{-1}$

Entropy change $= 509.2 - 266.2$ $= +243 \, J\,K^{-1}\,mol^{-1}$

(b) Entropy of products $= 146.4 \, J\,K^{-1}\,mol^{-1}$

Entropy of reactants $= (3 \times 27.3) + (2 \times 205.0)$ $= 491.9 \, J\,K^{-1}\,mol^{-1}$

Entropy change $= 146.4 - 491.9$ $= -345.5 \, J\,K^{-1}\,mol^{-1}$

(c) Entropy of products $= 106.7 + (2 \times 192.3) + (2 \times 69.9) = 631.1 \, J\,K^{-1}\,mol^{-1}$

Entropy of reactants $= 220.1 + 83.4$ $= 303.5 \, J\,K^{-1}\,mol^{-1}$

Entropy change $= 631.1 - 303.5$ $= +327.6 \, J\,K^{-1}\,mol^{-1}$

3. (a) $\Delta S_{surroundings} = \dfrac{-\Delta H}{T} = \dfrac{-(-65\,000)}{298} = +218.1 \, J\,K^{-1}\,mol^{-1}$

(b) Entropy of products $= 83.4 \, J\,K^{-1}\,mol^{-1}$

Entropy of reactants $= 39.7 + 69.9 = 109.6 \, J\,K^{-1}\,mol^{-1}$

$\Delta S_{system} = 83.4 - 109.6 = -26.2 \, J\,K^{-1}\,mol^{-1}$

(c) $\Delta S_{total} = \Delta S_{surroundings} + \Delta S_{system} = +218.1 - 26.2 = +191.9 \, J\,K^{-1}\,mol^{-1}$

A positive ΔS_{total} shows the reaction is feasible.

4. (a)

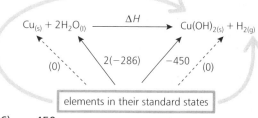

$\Delta H + 2(-286) = -450$

$\Delta H = +122 \, kJ\,mol^{-1}$

(b) $\Delta S_{surroundings} = \dfrac{-\Delta H}{T} = \dfrac{-122\,000}{373} = -327.1\,J\,K^{-1}\,mol^{-1}$

(c) Entropy of products $= 75.0 + 130.6 = 205.6\,J\,K^{-1}\,mol^{-1}$

Entropy of reactants $= 33.2 + (2 \times 69.9) = 173.0\,J\,K^{-1}\,mol^{-1}$

$\Delta S_{system} = 205.6 - 173.0 = +32.6\,J\,K^{-1}\,mol^{-1}$

(d) $\Delta S_{total} = \Delta S_{surroundings} + \Delta S_{system} = -327.1 + 32.6 = -294.5\,J\,K^{-1}\,mol^{-1}$

A negative ΔS_{total} shows the reaction is not feasible.

5. (a)

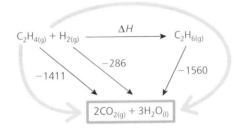

$\Delta H - 1560 = -1411 - 286$

$\Delta H = -137\,kJ\,mol^{-1}$

(b) $\Delta S_{surroundings} = \dfrac{-\Delta H}{T} = \dfrac{-(-137\,000)}{273} = +501.8\,J\,K^{-1}\,mol^{-1}$

(c) Entropy of products $= 229.5\,J\,K^{-1}\,mol^{-1}$

Entropy of reactants $= 219.5 + 130.6 = 350.1\,J\,K^{-1}\,mol^{-1}$

$\Delta S_{system} = 229.5 - 350.1 = -120.6\,J\,K^{-1}\,mol^{-1}$

(d) $\Delta S_{total} = \Delta S_{surroundings} + \Delta S_{system} = +501.8 - 120.6 = +381.2\,J\,K^{-1}\,mol^{-1}$

A positive ΔS_{total} shows the reaction is feasible.

6. (a) $\Delta S_{surroundings} = \dfrac{-\Delta H}{T} = \dfrac{-173\,000}{850} = -203.5\,J\,K^{-1}\,mol^{-1}$.

$\Delta S_{total} = \Delta S_{surroundings} + \Delta S_{system} = -203.5 + 175.9 = -27.6\,J\,K^{-1}\,mol^{-1}$

A negative ΔS_{total} shows the reaction is not feasible.

(b) $\Delta S_{surroundings} = \dfrac{-\Delta H}{T} = \dfrac{-173\,000}{1050} = -164.8\,J\,K^{-1}\,mol^{-1}$.

$\Delta S_{total} = \Delta S_{surroundings} + \Delta S_{system} = -164.8 + 175.9 = +11.1\,J\,K^{-1}\,mol^{-1}$

A positive ΔS_{total} shows the reaction is feasible.

7. $\Delta G = \Delta H - T\Delta S$

$= -144 - (500 \times 0.2269)$ (Remember to convert ΔS into $kJ\,K^{-1}\,mol^{-1}$)

$= -257\,kJ\,mol^{-1}$

A negative ΔG shows the reaction is feasible.

8. (a) $\Delta G = \Delta H - T\Delta S = +237 - (1000 \times 0.1899) = +47.1\,kJ\,mol^{-1}$

A positive ΔG shows the reaction is not feasible.

(b) $\Delta G = \Delta H - T\Delta S = +237 - (1500 \times 0.1899) = -47.9 \, kJ \, mol^{-1}$

A negative ΔG shows the reaction is feasible.

(c) To be feasible, $\Delta G < 0$

Therefore, $\Delta H - T\Delta S < 0$

$$237 - 0.1899T < 0$$

$$237 < 0.1899T$$

$$T > 1250 \, K$$

> **If** $237 < 0.1899T$
>
> $237/0.1899 < T$
>
> $1250 < T$
>
> which is the same as saying
>
> $T > 1250$

9.

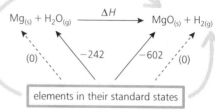

$\Delta H - 242 = -602 \, kJ \, mol^{-1}$

$\Delta H = -360 \, kJ \, mol^{-1}$

Entropy of products $= 26.9 + 130.6 \ = 157.5 \, J \, K^{-1} \, mol^{-1}$

Entropy of reactants $= 32.7 + 188.7 \ = 221.4 \, J \, K^{-1} \, mol^{-1}$

$\Delta S_{system} \qquad\qquad = 157.5 - 221.4 = -63.9 \, J \, K^{-1} \, mol^{-1}$

$\Delta G = \Delta H - T\Delta S$

$\quad = -360 - 373 \times (-0.0639)$ (Remember to convert ΔS into $kJ \, K^{-1} \, mol^{-1}$)

$\quad = -336 \, kJ \, mol^{-1}$

10.

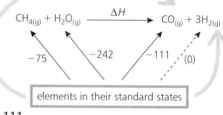

$\Delta H - 75 - 242 = -111$

$\Delta H = +206 \, kJ \, mol^{-1}$

Entropy of products $= 197.6 + (3 \times 130.6) = 589.4 \, J \, K^{-1} \, mol^{-1}$

Entropy of reactants $= 186.2 + 188.7 \qquad = 374.9 \, J \, K^{-1} \, mol^{-1}$

$\Delta S_{system} \qquad\qquad = 589.4 - 374.9 \qquad = +214.5 \, J \, K^{-1} \, mol^{-1}$

$\Delta G = \Delta H - T\Delta S$

$\quad = +206 - (1200 \times 0.2145)$ (Remember to convert ΔS into $kJ \, K^{-1} \, mol^{-1}$)

$\quad = -51.4 \, kJ \, mol^{-1}$

The negative value shows the reaction is feasible.

To be feasible, $\Delta G < 0$

Therefore, $\Delta H - T\Delta S < 0$

$$206 - 0.2145T < 0$$

$$206 < 0.2145T$$

$$T > 960 \, K$$

> ➤ See the help box above if you have problems.

11. (a) ΔS is positive (mainly because of gas prod ed). $-T\Delta S$ is therefore negative. At low temperatures, ΔG is positive because of the positive ΔH. At higher temperatures the negative $-T\Delta S$ eventually outweighs ΔH, and so $\Delta H - T\Delta S$ becomes negative: **C**.

    (b) ΔS is negative (3 moles of gas going to 2). $-T\Delta S$ is therefore positive. At low temperatures, ΔG is negative because of the negative ΔH. At higher temperatures the positive $-T\Delta S$ eventually outweighs ΔH, and so $\Delta H - T\Delta S$ becomes positive: **D**.

    (c) ΔS is positive (mainly because of gas produced). $-T\Delta S$ is therefore negative. ΔH is also negative. $\Delta H - T\Delta S$ will be negative at all temperatures: **A**.

    (d) ΔS is negative (products are much more ordered). $-T\Delta S$ is therefore positive. ΔH is also positive. $\Delta H - T\Delta S$ will be positive at all temperatures: **B**.

12.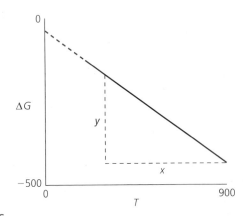

$\Delta G = \Delta H - T\Delta S$

When $T = 0$, $\Delta G = \Delta H$. Extrapolating the line to $T = 0$ gives $\Delta H = -36\,\text{kJ mol}^{-1}$.

Slope of line $= -\Delta S$. Measure the slope as $-y/x$. It is a negative slope because ΔG decreases with temperature.

Slope $= -0.446\,\text{kJ mol}^{-1}\,\text{K}^{-1}$

$-\Delta S = -0.446\,\text{kJ mol}^{-1}\,\text{K}^{-1}$

$\Delta S = +0.446\,\text{kJ mol}^{-1}\,\text{K}^{-1}$ (or $+446\,\text{J K}^{-1}\,\text{mol}^{-1}$)

13.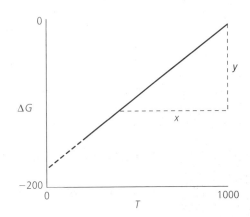

$$\Delta G = \Delta H - T\Delta S$$

When $T = 0$, $\Delta G = \Delta H$. Extrapolating the line to $T = 0$ gives $\Delta H = -196\,\text{kJ}\,\text{mol}^{-1}$.

Slope of line $= -\Delta S$. Measure the slope as y/x. It is a positive slope because ΔG increases with temperature.

Slope $= +0.189\,\text{kJ}\,\text{mol}^{-1}\,\text{K}^{-1}$

$-\Delta S = +0.189\,\text{kJ}\,\text{mol}^{-1}\,\text{K}^{-1}$

$\Delta S = -0.189\,\text{kJ}\,\text{mol}^{-1}\,\text{K}^{-1}$ (or $-189\,\text{J}\,\text{K}^{-1}\,\text{mol}^{-1}$)

> **Don't forget** to convert °C to K, and kJ to J.

14. $\Delta S_{\text{system}} = \dfrac{\Delta H}{T} = \dfrac{+30\,000}{354} = +84.7\,\text{J}\,\text{K}^{-1}\,\text{mol}^{-1}$

15. (a) Increase   (b) decrease

(c) decrease   (d) increase

16. (a) $+125.6\,\text{J}\,\text{K}^{-1}\,\text{mol}^{-1}$ (b) $-212.4\,\text{J}\,\text{K}^{-1}\,\text{mol}^{-1}$

(c) $-330.2\,\text{J}\,\text{K}^{-1}\,\text{mol}^{-1}$ (d) $+494\,\text{J}\,\text{K}^{-1}\,\text{mol}^{-1}$

17. (a) (i) $-141\,\text{J}\,\text{K}^{-1}\,\text{mol}^{-1}$ (ii) $-159\,\text{J}\,\text{K}^{-1}\,\text{mol}^{-1}$, therefore not feasible.

(b) (i) $-157\,\text{J}\,\text{K}^{-1}\,\text{mol}^{-1}$ (ii) $+73\,\text{J}\,\text{K}^{-1}\,\text{mol}^{-1}$, therefore feasible.

18. (a) $-214\,\text{kJ}\,\text{mol}^{-1}$ (b) $+648\,\text{J}\,\text{K}^{-1}\,\text{mol}^{-1}$ (c) $-360.4\,\text{J}\,\text{K}^{-1}\,\text{mol}^{-1}$

(d) $+287.6\,\text{J}\,\text{K}^{-1}\,\text{mol}^{-1}$, therefore feasible.

19. (a) $+65\,\text{kJ}\,\text{mol}^{-1}$ (b) $+14\,\text{J}\,\text{K}^{-1}\,\text{mol}^{-1}$ (c) $-65\,\text{J}\,\text{K}^{-1}\,\text{mol}^{-1}$

(d) $-51\,\text{J}\,\text{K}^{-1}\,\text{mol}^{-1}$, therefore not feasible.

20. (a) (i) $+8.88\,\text{kJ}\,\text{mol}^{-1}$, therefore not feasible
(ii) $-17.7\,\text{kJ}\,\text{mol}^{-1}$, therefore feasible

(b) $467\,\text{K}$

21. (a) $MgCO_3$: $\Delta H = +100\,\text{kJ}\,\text{mol}^{-1}$; $\Delta S = +174.8\,\text{J}\,\text{K}^{-1}\,\text{mol}^{-1}$;
$\Delta G = -57.3\,\text{kJ}\,\text{mol}^{-1}$
$BaCO_3$: $\Delta H = +268\,\text{kJ}\,\text{mol}^{-1}$; $\Delta S = +171.9\,\text{J}\,\text{K}^{-1}\,\text{mol}^{-1}$;
$\Delta G = +113\,\text{kJ}\,\text{mol}^{-1}$

Only $MgCO_3$ decomposes at 900 K.

(b) $MgCO_3$ 572 K; $BaCO_3$ 1560 K

22. (a) A   (b) D   (c) C   (d) B

23. (a) $+220\,\text{kJ}\,\text{mol}^{-1}$ (b) $+187\,\text{J}\,\text{K}^{-1}\,\text{mol}^{-1}$ (c) 1180 K

24. (a) $+9.8\,\text{J}\,\text{K}^{-1}\,\text{mol}^{-1}$ (b) $+94\,\text{J}\,\text{K}^{-1}\,\text{mol}^{-1}$

INDEX